A History of the
Division of Psychoanalysis
of the
American Psychological Association

A History of the Division of Psychoanalysis of the American Psychological Association

Edited by

Robert C. Lane
Nova Southeastern University

Murray Meisels
Ann Arbor, MI

Routledge
Taylor & Francis Group

LONDON AND NEW YORK

First published 1994 by Lawrence Erlbaum Associates, Inc.

Published 2020 by Routledge
2 Park Square, Milton Park, Abingdon, Oxon OX14 4RN
52 Vanderbilt Avenue, New York, NY 10017

Routledge is an imprint of the Taylor & Francis Group, an informa business

Copyright © 1994 Taylor & Francis.

Logo design by Robert C. Lane, 1979.

The chapters in this book constitute history as seen by their authors at the time the material was assembled. The individual chapters do not necessarily reflect the point of view of the editors, the Division of Psychoanalysis, or the American Psychological Association.

Library of Congress Cataloging-in-Publication Data

A History of the Division of Psychoanalysis of the American
    Psychological Association / edited by Robert C. Lane, Murray
    Meisels.
        p.   cm.
    Includes bibliographical references and index.
    ISBN 0-8058-1323-3
    1. American Psychological Association.   Division of
Psychoanalysis—History. I. Lane, Robert C. II. Meisels, Murray.
BF11.A68 1994
    150.19′5′06073—dc20   93-35654
                                                                    CIP

ISBN 13: 978-0-8058-1323-4 (pbk)

Contents

Acronyms

The following acronyms are used in this book:

ABPP, American Board of Professional Psychology
ABPsaP, American Board of Psychoanalysis in Psychology
APA, American Psychological Association
APsaA, American Psychoanalytic Association
GAPPP, Group for the Advancement of Psychotherapy and Psychoanalysis in Psychology
IPA, International Psychoanalytic Association.

About the Contributors

Mark Adair, Ph.D., is a psychoanalyst who lives and practices in Vermont. He is the current president of the Vermont chapter.

Robert M. Aguado, Ph.D., is the founding President of the Southern California Chapter, a member of Section I, a faculty member of the Psychoanalytic Department at the California Graduate Institute, and a certified analyst. He practices psychoanalysis in Beverly Hills, California.

Ricardo Ainslie, Ph.D., is Associate Professor at the University of Texas, and in private practice in Austin. He is past President and one of the current chapter representatives to the Section of Local Chapters.

Marvin L. Aronson, Ph.D., is Director of the Group Therapy Department and a Training Analyst and Supervisor at the Postgraduate Center for Mental Health, New York City. He is currently President of Section VII, Psychoanalysis and Groups.

James W. Barron, Ph.D., is a member of the faculties of the Massachusetts Institute for Psychoanalysis and the Psychoanalytic Institute of New England, East. He is Editor of the Division Newsletter, President-Elect of Division 39, and in private practice in Boston.

Don J. Brix, Ph.D., a charter member of Division 39, practices individual and group psychotherapy in Dallas. He is Associate Clinical Professor, Division of Psychology, University of Texas Southwestern Medical School.

Leopold Caligor, Ph.D., is currently President of the Division. He is a Training and Supervising analyst at the William Alanson White Institute, a Clinical Professor at the Adelphi University Postdoctoral Program in Psychotherapy and Psychoanalysis, and in private practice in New York City.

Joanne E. Callan, Ph.D., is the Executive Director of APA's Education Directorate. She is on leave from faculty appointments as Professor at CSPP-San Diego and Clinical Associate Professor in the Department of Psychiatry at the University of California, San Diego. She was in charge of Continuing Education for the Division from 1986 to 1991.

Bertram J. Cohler, Ph.D., is William Rainey Harper Professor of the Social Sciences at the University of Chicago and Editor of the Division journal, *Psychoanalytic Psychology*. He is one of the founders of the Chicago chapter and its allied institute, and is in private practice in Chicago.

Harold Cook, Ph.D., is Professor, Department of Clinical Psychology, Teachers College, Columbia University, and President of the Psychoanalytic Research Society, Section VI of Division 39.

Harold B. Davis, Ph.D., is a Supervisor in the NYU Postdoctoral Program and at the Institute for Contemporary Psychotherapy. He chairs the Division's Award Committee, and is in private practice in New York City.

Helen Desmond, Ph.D., is a psychologist in private practice, a graduate and member of the Los Angeles Psychoanalytic Society and Institute, a clinical instructor at the University of Southern California/Los Angeles County Hospital, and Co-Chair of the GAPPP enforcement commission.

David L. Downing, Psy.D., is Assistant Director of Clinical Training at the Illinois School of Professional Psychology in Chicago. He is President of the Chicago Open Chapter and Editor of its Newsletter. He is a candidate in psychoanalysis at the Center for Psychoanalytic Study, and in private practice.

Patricia Freiberg, Ph.D., is a clinical psychologist in private practice in Bethesda, Maryland. She is a faculty member and supervisor at the Washington School of Psychiatry. For the past 10 years, she has held a number of offices on the Board of WPSP.

Stephen R. Friedlander, Ph.D., is in private practice in Knoxville, Tennessee. He is a founder of the Appalachian Psychoanalytic Society.

John D. Gartner, Ph.D., is one of the founders and current president of the Baltimore Society for Psychoanalytic Studies. He is Clinical Assistant Professor of Psychology at Johns Hopkins University and in private practice in Baltimore and Columbia, Maryland.

Stanley I. Gochman, Ph.D., is an Adjunct Professor at American University and on the Washington, D.C., Commission on Community Mental Health Services. He co-chaired the Division's Committee on Social Issues and Public Policy for a decade, and practices in Washington, D.C.

Franklin H. Goldberg, Ph.D., is a supervisor at the NYU Postdoctoral Program in Psychoanalysis and Psychotherapy, and Faculty and Supervisor at the Manhattan Institute for Psychoanalysis. He is also President of Section V.

Lorraine H. Goldberg, Ph.D., has served for 10 years in the Chicago Association for Psychoanalytic Psychology and is now President-Elect. She is a member of the Board and Director of Administration at the Chicago Center for Psychoanalysis. She has long been established in private practice in Chicago.

Helen K. Golden, Ph.D., is faculty and Supervisor, Einstein Postgraduate Psychotherapy Training Program and faculty at the Westchester Center for the Study of Psychoanalysis and Psychotherapy. She is in private practice in Larchmont, NY.

Nancy R. Goodman, Ph.D., is in private practice in Bethesda, Maryland. A graduate and member of the New York Freudian Society, she is presently on the faculty of the Washington School of Psychiatry, and has been on the Board of WPSP.

Marvin Hyman, Ph.D., is a practicing psychoanalyst in West Bloomfield, Michigan, past President of the Michigan Society for Psychoanalytic Psychology, and Distinguished Service Award winner of Division 39.

Rochelle G. K. Kainer, Ph.D., was a founding member of the local chapters movement in Washington, D.C., and in the Division. She is on the teaching and supervising faculty of the Washington School of Psychiatry and the faculty of WSPP, and in private practice in Washington, D.C.

Bertram P. Karon, Ph.D., was president, Division of Psychoanalysis, 1990–1991. He is Professor of Clinical Psychology, Michigan State University, and President-Elect, Michigan Psychoanalytic Council.

Susan Kavaler-Adler, Ph.D., is founding Director of the Object Relations Institute, on the faculty of the Psychoanalytic Institute of Postgraduate Center, and faculty and supervisor for the National Institute for the Psychotherapies.

Oliver J. B. Kerner, Ph.D., has been active in the Division since its inception, including positions as Chair of the Committee on Local Chapters and member of the Board of Directors. He is currently President-Elect of Section I and in private practice in Chicago.

Michael P. Kowitt, Ph.D., is Director of Psychology at the Institute of Pennsylvania Hospital. He is on the faculties of the Philadelphia Association for Psychoanalysis and the University of Pennsylvania School of Medicine. His private practice is in psychoanalysis and psychoanalytic psychotherapy.

Robert C. Lane, Ph.D., was a founding father, Vice-President pro-tem, and President of the Division, 1981–1982. He has also been President of Sections I and IV. He is Director, Post Doctoral Institute of Psychoanalysis and Psychotherapy, and Psychoanalytic Scholar in Residence, Nova University; Clinical Professor of Psychology, Postdoctoral Programs, Adelphi University; and Director Emeritus, Long Island Division, New York Center for Psychoanalytic Training. He is a Distinguished Service Award winner of Division 39, a member of many committees, as well as Historian and Chair of the Bylaws Committee.

Ernest S. Lawrence, Ph.D., has been President of the Division of Psychoanalysis, as well as of Section I. He is currently Director of Training, Los Angeles Institute and Society for Psychoanalytic Studies.

Frederic J. Levine, Ph.D., is Adjunct Professor, Institute for Graduate Clinical Psychology, Widener University. He is on the faculty of the Institute of the Philadelphia Association for Psychoanalysis and the Department of Psychiatry, University of Pennsylvania School of Medicine. He is a member of the New York Freudian Society.

Paul Lippmann, Ph.D., is on the faculties of the William Alanson White Institute and NYU Postdoctoral Program in Psychoanalysis, and in private practice in both Stockbridge and New York City. He is one of the founders and a former President of the Western Massachusetts and Albany Association for Psychoanalytic Psychology.

Dorita Marina, Ph.D., born in Cuba, and presently living in Miami, Florida, is trying to initiate the bilingual/bicultural community to psychoanalysis.

Stanton Marlan, Ph.D., is in private practice in Pittsburgh and Director of the C. G. Jung Institute Analyst Training Program of Pittsburgh. He is past President of the Pittsburgh Association for the Theory and Practice of Psychoanalysis, and was the first President of Section V.

Robert J. Marshall, Ph.D., is a faculty member of the Postdoctoral Psychotherapy Program, Adelphi University, and the Center for Modern Psychoanalytic Studies in New York City. He is in private practice in New York City.

Dale Mendell, Ph.D., is faculty and Senior Supervisor, Postgraduate Center for Mental Health, New York City; and Senior Supervisor and Training Analyst, Training Institute for Mental Health, New York City.

Murray Meisels, Ph.D., is a former President of the Division and Co-Editor of the book on the Clark Conference. Currently, he is past President of the Michigan Psychoanalytic Council, and in private practice in Ann Arbor.

Stephen J. Miller, Ph.D., is President of the Oklahoma Society for Psychoanalytic Studies, and in private practice in Oklahoma City. He is a candidate in clinical psychoanalysis at the Colorado Society for Psychoanalytic Psychology.

David M. Moss III, Th.D., Ph.D., is an Episcopal priest and President of the Georgia Association for Psychoanalytic Psychology. His private practice of psychotherapy is in the Buckhead area of Atlanta. He is a member of the Division's Publications Committee.

John D. Munn, Ph.D., is connected with the Psychoanalytic Section of the Ontario Psychological Association, the Ontario Center for Short Term Dynamic Psychotherapy and the Ontario Institute for Contemporary Psychoanalysis. He is presently in private practice.

Maureen Murphy, Ph.D., is a former President of the Northern California Society for Psychoanalytic Psychology, of Section IV, and of the Psychoanalytic Institute of Northern California. She is one of those creative Division members who has launched an institute in order to be trained, and is in private practice in San Francisco.

Ruth Ochroch, Ph.D., is Secretary of the Division and a Professor of Psychology at NYU.

Jerry W. O'Dell, Ph.D., is Professor of Psychology at Eastern Michigan University.

Erwin R. Parson, Ph.D., is Chief Project Investigator of the U.S.-Vietnam Full Circle Project, and was Co-Chair of the Division's Committee on Social Issues and Public Policy for a decade.

Lynn H. Pierson, Ph.D., is a founding member of the Cincinnati Society for Psychoanalytic Psychology and past President of the Cincinnati Academy of Professional Psychology. He is in private practice in Montgomery, Ohio.

Stuart A. Pizer, Ph.D., is a clinical supervisor at the Cambridge Hospital. He is on the board and faculty at the Massachusetts Institute for Psychoanalysis, and member of the Executive Committee of the Massachusetts Association for Psychoanalytic Psychology.

Terry Pulver, Ph. D., is President of the Pittsburgh Association for the Theory and Practice of Psychoanalysis, and is in private practice in Pittsburgh.

Irving Raifman, Ph.D., is in private practice on a part-time basis, dividing his time between Chevy Chase, Maryland and Boca Raton, Florida. He is a former President and Treasurer of the Potomac Psychoanalytic Society, and former historian for Division 39.

Elizabeth J. Roll, Ph.D., is in private practice in Albuquerque, where she supervises and teaches psychoanalytic psychotherapy at the University of New Mexico Medical School.

Stanley Rosner, Ph.D., is in private practice in Fairfield and Stamford, Connecticut. He was the founder of the Connecticut Society for Psychoanalytic Psychology, and its first President.

Arnold Z. Schneider, Ph.D., was a Plaintiff in the GAPPP lawsuit. He is currently in private practice in the Clearwater-Tampa Bay area and continues his lawsuit activities as Co-Director of the GAPPP Commission on Settlement Enforcement.

Donald Shapiro, Ph.D., is on the faculty of the Union Graduate School. From 1985–1990 he was Chairman of the Professional Issues Committee of Section V.

Ester R. Shapiro, Ph.D., is Assistant Professor of Psychology, University of Massachusetts, and Co-Editor of the Division's book on The Clark Conference.

Ava L. Siegler, Ph.D., is the Director of the Institute for Child, Adolescent & Family Studies, member of ABPsaP, and the founding President of Section II.

Helen W. Silverman, Ph.D., is Supervisor at Long Island University, past President of the Psychoanalytic Society of the NYU Postdoctoral Program, and a member of the Board of The League School for emotionally disturbed children.

Norma P. Simon, Ph.D., a private practitioner in New York City, is also the Director of Training for the New Hope Guild and a Supervisor at the NYU Postdoctoral Program in Psychoanalysis.

Jonathan H. Slavin, Ph.D., is past President of the Division of Psychoanalysis and President and Chair of the Board of Directors of the Massachusetts Institute for Psychoanalysis. He is a former President of the Massachusetts Association for Psychoanalysis.

Charles Spezzano, Ph.D., is the founder of the Colorado Society for Psychology and Psychoanalysis and the Colorado Center for Psychoanalytic Studies. He is Chair of the Division's Publication Committee, and practices psychoanalysis in San Francisco, where he is also a faculty member and supervisor at the Psychoanalytic Institute of Northern California. He is the author of *What To Do Between Birth and Death: The Art of Growing Up*, published by Morrow (hardcover) and Avon (paperback), and *Affect in Psychoanalysis: A Clinical Synthesis*, published by The Analytic Press.

Gale Swan, Ph.D., is in private practice in West Bloomfield, Michigan and supervises doctoral candidates at the University of Detroit.

Joan P. Trachtman, Ph.D., is supervisor at the NYU Postdoctoral Institute, The Institute for Contemporary Psychotherapy, and The Manhattan Institute for Psychoanalysis, all in New York City. She is also in private practice. She is a former President of Section V.

Antonio R. Virsida, Ph.D., is faculty and Supervisor at the Nova University Postdoctoral Program. He is a former Secretary and President of the Southeast Florida Association for Psychoanalytic Psychology and in private practice in Boca Raton.

Muriel Weckstein, M.A., is a former President of the Massachusetts Association for Psychoanalytic Psychology and a Board member at the Massachusetts Institute for Psychoanalysis. She is a clinical fellow and supervisor at Massachusetts General Hospital, and is also in private practice.

Hilda J. Weissman, Ph.D., is in practice in the Washington, D.C. area and is a former President of the Potomac Psychoanalytic Society.

Harriet Kimble Wrye, Ph.D., is President, Training and Supervising Analyst, Los Angeles Institute and Society for Psychoanalytic Studies, and a former President of Section III.

Foreword

Leopold Caligor
President, Division of Psychoanalysis,
American Psychological Association

In 1909, G. Stanley Hall, the founder of APA, invited Sigmund Freud, Sandor Ferenczi, Carl Jung, and Ernest Jones to Clark University to present their understanding of psychoanalysis. Although their presentations were enthusiastically received by many, the discrepancy with the then-mainline American psychological thought was too great and the two fields remained separate.

The formation of the Division of Psychoanalysis in 1979, 70 years later, had as a major goal a rapprochement between psychoanalysis and psychology. Analytically trained psychologists and those seeking training have responded with enthusiasm to the formation of the Division, which now numbers over 3,500 members in 13 short years.

This volume records the history of the Division and the seminal contributions of its founding members. It describes the dynamic tensions that have existed over the years between differing clinical and theoretical concepts of psychoanalysis leading to creative dialogue.

The Division is proud of its seven Sections, which are described in detail: Psychologist-Psychoanalyst Practitioners; Childhood and Adolescence; Women and Psychoanalysis; Local Chapters; Psychologist-Psychoanalysts' Forum; Psychoanalytic Research Society; and Psychoanalysis and Groups. The Division's 26 local chapters are also described.

The Division's publications are recognized by psychoanalysts, scholars, and psychologists for their outstanding contributions. These include the newsletter, *The Psychologist-Psychoanalyst*; the journal, *Psychoanalytic-Psychology*; and *Psychoanalytic Abstracts*.

The unfolding of the historic GAPPP lawsuit that has expanded opportunities for psychoanalytic training and practice to Division members is reviewed in detail.

An account is provided of the Division 39 APA conferences, which have stimulated clinical and theoretical dialogue between divergent viewpoints. The excitement, enthusiasm, and creativity have been most gratifying.

Most importantly, the artificial gap that has existed between psychoanalysis and psychology has been forever closed by the formation of the Division of Psychoanalysis of the APA.

Acknowledgments*

We want to thank the APA for establishing the Division in 1979, and to congratulate the APA on its centennial year (1992). This book is dedicated to all those who have contributed to the development of the Division: the founding fathers; the Steering Committee; all the presidents, particularly Gordon F. Derner and Helen Block Lewis who did not live to see the centennial year and the tremendous growth and success of the Division to which they contributed their energies; and to all 26 local chapters and seven sections, as well as the membership in the Division. We thank Charles Spezzano for his superb editing and assistance, and for extending himself so ably in his role as Chair of the Publications Committee. Finally, special gratitude goes to our wives, Jean Betty Lane and Brenda Meisels for their extreme patience and tolerance while their husbands spent hours planning, organizing, assembling, and editing material for this book. We feel that the book, started more than 3 years ago, turned out to be a more than satisfactory endeavor. Hopefully, the membership will view it as a resource to be referred to again and again.

---

*Since the completion of this book, Reuben Fine, the principle organizer and President pro tem of the Division, passed away. We express our deepest gratitude to him for his vision and providing us with both a home and an identity.

I

Overview

The American Psychological Association's Division of Psychoanalysis was founded in 1979 and has become, in 13 years, the largest psychoanalytic organization in the United States, with 3,433 members (as of May 1992). Although there had always been great interest in psychoanalysis among psychologists, it was only the advent of the Division that organized psychologists and gave them a framework to form their own community. Part I contains two chapters that present overviews of the Division's development, and two chapters that summarize the results of membership surveys, surveys that tell us who we are, what we do, and what we value.

1

The First Five Years

Robert C. Lane

A number of psychologists met at the 1968 APA convention and formed Psychologists Interested in the Study of Psychoanalysis (PISP). PISP met simultaneously with the annual APA convention, but was not part of the APA.

The psychoanalytic movement within the APA was spearheaded in 1978 by Reuben Fine, assisted by Robert C. Lane, George D. Goldman, and the late Samuel Kutash. Fine sent a letter to members of Divisions 12 (Clinical) and 29 (Psychotherapy) to determine interest in forming a division of psychoanalysis within the APA. More than 850 respondents reacted favorably to the proposal.

A petition to establish the new division, and bylaws, were submitted to the APA Board of Directors. They were turned over to the APA Council for its meeting in January 1979. Then the petition was distributed to all divisions for action at the APA Council meeting in New York City in the summer of 1979.

When the proposal for a Division of Psychoanalysis was submitted to the Council, there were voices raised in opposition. Some said there were already too many divisions. Others feared setting a precedent for the formation of still more specialty groups. Still others wished to establish psychoanalysis as a specialty group within Division 29 (Psychotherapy). Finally, some feminists viewed certain aspects of psychoanalysis as inimical to the interests of women. Because of these objections, voting was postponed until the next day of the Council meeting.

During an interim strategy meeting held on September 1, 1979, a slate of officers was elected to serve until the next official APA election in the event of division acceptance by APA Council. The elected officers were:

President (pro-tem): Reuben Fine
Vice-President (pro-tem): Robert C. Lane
Secretary-Treasurer (pro-tem): George D. Goldman

Note was taken of the fact that, by this time, more than 1,000 APA members had expressed interest in joining a new Division of Psychoanalysis. Debate continued at the next Council meeting. When the vote was finally taken, more than the necessary two thirds of the Council voted aye, and Division 39 was born.

A meeting of the officers pro-tem was held in October 1979. A letter was sent to a number of people representing different geographic areas and analytic groups, inviting them to become members of the new Division Steering Committee. Forty-six members accepted the invitation. An appeal was also made to members for their support in the apportionment ballot for Division representation on APA Council. We attained two Council seats.

The Steering Committee held its first meeting on November 17, 1979. In attendance were 25 of the Committee's 46 members. The meeting took place at the New York Center for Psychoanalytic Training, the first Central Office of the Division.

There have been four central offices for the Division. From 1978 to 1980, the New York Center for Psychoanalytic Training; from 1980 to 1983, Adelphi University's Postdoctoral Center in Garden City, New York; from the Fall of 1983 to 1991, the Postgraduate Center for Mental Health (with Board meetings held since 1980 at the William Alanson White Institute); from 1991, The Administrators in Phoenix, Arizona.

The Division of Psychoanalysis voted to hold a minimum of four meetings a year. One of the meetings of the Board of Directors is held at the Annual Mid-Winter Meeting, the venue of which at first was at resort locations, and then shifted to major cities with New York City every third year. Another Board meeting is held at the APA annual meeting, along with an open meeting for the entire membership. The fourth Board meeting is held in the fall of each year.

There have been 14 presidents: Reuben Fine, Gordon F. Derner, Robert C. Lane, George D. Goldman, Ernest S. Lawrence, Helen Block Lewis, Nathan Stockhamer, Fred Pine, Murray Meisels, Zanvil Liff, Ruth Jean Eisenbud, Bertram Karon, Jonathan Slavin, and Leopold Caligor. James Barron is the president-elect.

Reuben Fine, our first president, said that "We should not think of ourselves as 'lay analysts,' but as analysts pure and simple." Fine wanted psychoanalysis to be assimilated into all of psychology. The primary thrust of Fine's administration (1979–1980) was to achieve for America's psychologist-psychoanalysts equal status to America's psychiatrist-psychoanalysts. He outlined the following:

1. Forming an APA division of those APA members interested in the study of psychoanalysis; a national organization similar to APsaA.

2. Forming a group within the Division of practicing psychoanalysts whose credentials were the equivalent of the IPA requirements.
3. Polling this group to see how many members wanted IPA affiliation, and then petitioning the IPA for membership.
4. Meeting with IPA officials and dealing directly with them rather than through APsaA.

Fine's first goal was attained with the formation of the Division of Psychoanalysis in September 1979. His second goal was reached in several stages. A qualifications committee of more experienced analysts was appointed, with Ernest Lawrence as Chairperson, and proposed standards that later became the membership requirements for Section I, the Section of Psychologist-Psychoanalyst Practitioners. These standards were accepted by the Board of the Division in 1981 (many years later they were changed). Reuben Fine viewed Section I as a step toward the goal of American psychologist-psychoanalysts becoming a component society of the IPA. In 1982, after the section was formed, he polled the 82 original members of Section I. Sixty-three percent agreed to petition the IPA. Letters were exchanged between Fine and Adam Limentani, President of the IPA. A committee of three, Reuben Fine, Gertrude Blanck, and Robert C. Lane, met with the IPA's Adam Limentani, Moses Laufer, and Irene Auletta, IPA Secretary, in 1983. The Division was told that APsaA was the sole arm of the IPA in America, and any group seeking society status would have to go through them. Fine wrote to the APA suggesting legal action. He informed the Board of the Division that an antitrust suit would have to be instituted against the APsaA, to investigate whether the APsaA constituted a monopoly, in violation of antitrust laws.

In the June 1980 Newsletter (Vol. I, No. 2), Murray Meisels and Marvin Hyman wrote, "A Proposal for Accrediting Psychologist-Psychoanalysts." They proposed that the Division itself accredit qualified psychologists as psychoanalysts. Once qualified psychoanalysts could be identified, an organization could then be formed. This in turn could lead to the development of local societies and the accreditation of institutes. They proposed a "Section of Psychoanalysts" (what became Section I) empowered to issue certificates of competency and publish a list of qualified members. This Section could certify local institutes, be responsible for the establishment of standards of training, and foster the growth of local societies.

This proposal was responded to by Bertram Cohler and Oliver Kerner in an article entitled, *Regarding the Meisels-Hyman Proposal on Credentialling* that appeared in the December 1980 issue of the Newsletter (Vol. II, No. 1). They pointed out that the proposal polarized the Division, and would create an elite subgroup and a two-tiered organization. They felt the proposal was exclusionary, arbitrary, offered rigid requirements, and demonstrated a very narrow approach to training. The argument was made moot when the APA ruled that divisions cannot accredit.

The first annual APA convention in which the Division participated occurred in Montreal in 1980 with Robert C. Lane, Vice-President of the Division, Program Chair. We received 18 hours of convention time.

We sent Gordon Derner to Washington, DC, as an official representative to the Health, Education and Welfare (HEW) meeting on certification of psychoanalysts. The Division's official position was to oppose the setting up of any one organization, medical or nonmedical, as a certifying body for all of psychoanalysis.

In the first APA election in which Division 39 participated, Reuben Fine (President pro-tem and founding president) ran against Gordon F. Derner for president, and Robert C. Lane (Vice-President pro-tem) ran against Martin Mayman for President-Elect. Reuben Fine was defeated and Robert Lane elected. Gordon Derner became the second and Lane the third president of the Division.

Although Reuben Fine pressed for high standards of training, specifying hours for the training and control analysis, Derner felt there should be initial grandfathering of active practicing psychoanalysts for a period of time based on education and experience. He believed the doctorate in clinical psychology, personal experience as a patient in intensive psychotherapy with a qualified therapist no less than twice weekly for a minimum of a year, the completion of two successful courses of patient treatment, a course of study of 3 to 5 years duration in an institute setting, and peer review for the display of evidence of clinical and psychoanalytic competence should be sufficient. For him, the number of sessions per week was less important than the quality of the experience. The polarization already seen in the Meisels/Hyman-Cohler/Kerner controversy received further impetus as the Qualification Committee's recommendations differed significantly from the Derner standards.

Gordon Derner also was interested in the development of local chapters, and appointed Jeffrey Binder Chair of the Local Chapter's Committee. Derner also appointed Sydney Smith Chair of the Publications Committee with the charge to develop a plan for a journal.

Derner was concerned with the place of psychoanalysis in America's doctoral programs, and with the development of the Champus Peer Review Manual for Psychoanalysis. The first Mid-Winter Meeting was held February 3 to 8, 1981 in Ixtapa - Zihuatenejo, Mexico.

As third president, Lane concentrated on the development of a strong committee structure, and attempted to fill positions with members residing in different areas of the country. He appointed Murray Bilmes and Philburn Ratoosh, both of California, Co-Chairs of the Membership Committee. When the Board of Directors voted to separate the office of secretary-treasurer, he appointed Ernest Lawrence of California, Treasurer of the Division.

Lane also established new committees that evolved into Sections II and III. These were the Committee on Child and Adolescent Psychoanalysis, and the Committee on Women and Psychoanalysis. A third Committee on Group Psychoanalysis also eventually became a section. Lane appointed an Awards Committee with Sidney Blatt as Chairperson, and the Division successfully sponsored Roy Schafer for the Distinguished Professional Contribution to Knowledge Award.

Lane strengthened the Committee on Local Chapters, and held the first conference of the Division on Local Chapters in Chicago with Oliver Kerner as host. The Chicago, Michigan, Washington DC, Cleveland, and New York chapters were present at this conference. Oliver Kerner was elected Chairperson of the Local Chapters Committee and Murray Meisels was appointed to write a column for the Newsletter entitled, *The Local Scene*. Lane established contact with ABPP to obtain diplomate status for psychoanalysts.

Lane also was coeditor with Marvin Daniels of the Newsletter and Co-Chair of the Publications Committee during Fine's administration. When Daniels resigned, Lane recommended Edward Penzer and Irving Solomon as Newsletter coeditors. He appointed Helen Block Lewis editor of a proposed journal, and she promptly secured a publisher and launched the journal. He invited Susan Knapp, then on the APA Publication Board, to address the Board of Directors on the possibility of the Division publishing a psychoanalytic abstract. This effort resulted in a new *Psyc SCAN* devoted to psychoanalysis.

During Lane's administration, the Division applied to the APA for continuing education approval. The proposal, written by Martin Mayman, was approved. During the summer of Lane's administration, CE courses were planned with Rudolph Ekstein, Frank Lachman, Herbert Schlessinger, and Robert Stolorow. During Lane's administration the Board approved the first Section, the Section of Psychologist-Psychoanalyst Practitioners, at the Rio Mar meeting.

The administration of the fourth president, George D. Goldman was characterized by struggle and controversy, despite his stated goals of greater communication with members and harmonious expansion of membership. Much of the conflict flowed from the establishment of a section (I) with specific membership criteria that excluded some members who thought of themselves as analysts. These criteria were: A PhD or its equivalent in clinical psychology; 2 years of supervised experience including the internship; membership in the APA and state licensure; 4 years of study at an institute or its equivalent; a minimum of 300 hours of analysis at a minimum of three times weekly; 200 hours of supervision with a minimum of two supervisors, patients being seen a minimum of three times weekly; and a curriculum that includes theory, technique, case seminars, electives, and a case presentation.

Although Section I had been established according to APA rules and regulations and the Executive Director of the APA had affirmed that a Section could establish standards for admission higher than those of the Division, NYU's community of 380 psychologists, argued that the methods used to establish Section I were, "ill-advised, hasty, and in dubious accord with precedent, rules and regulations, and governance procedures of the APA."

George Goldman sent a letter to Leopold Caligor, President of Section I, on February 28, 1983, expressing his concern that the conflict over Section I could split the Division. He also stated that he had referred the problem to the Professional Affairs Committee for study and advisement. He suggested that the mailing of applications by Section I be slowed down until the Board of Directors heard the report of the Professional Affairs Committee as he did not wish to inflame the situation further.

Kenneth Isaacs circulated a letter stating that Section I was the result of a long and careful process attempting to connect qualified Division members with the world community of psychoanalysts. Its founding, he argued, had not been "ill-advised" and "hasty." He believed that the Division had no right to control, direct, or nullify the Section, unless there was a bylaw violation.

The Board received a letter from Sabert Basescu, Chair of the Policy and Planning Committee of the Interpersonal / Humanistic (I/H) track of the NYU Postdoctorate Training Program, dated March 17, 1983. The members of that committee questioned the specific criteria for Section I membership, claiming that it constituted credentialling and represented a sidestepping of APA policy that stressed diversity and various models of training. The letter also questioned whether Division 39 was the appropriate body to establish credentialling criteria and offered several recommendations including: Continual discussion on accreditation with broad constituent participation, recognizing practitioner training outside of accredited programs and channeling the problem to appropriate APA bodies.

The report of the Professional Affairs Committee, known as the Cohler Report, recommended that Section I continue as an interest group, not concerned with credentialling or standards, that membership be open to all who express interest, that all funds collected be returned, and that the Division Board find a mechanism, independent of itself and the APA, to set standards. Quality of training as well as quantitative measures were recommended. The Committee also felt that if the ABPP approved the Diplomate in Psychoanalysis, Section I should be dissolved. The Cohler report was tabled, and never presented to the Board of Division 39. Goldman called an open meeting of the Board on April 23, 1983 with all reports and letters on the agenda.

The last statement concerning the controversy was the Meisels' report issued in May 1983, *A Proposed Solution to the Controversy Surrounding Section I.* This report outlined several possible solutions, but was never discussed.

The second preoccupation of the Goldman administration concerned the decision of ABPP on March 4, 1983, to offer the Diplomate to clinical neuropsychologists and psychoanalysts. Anna Antonovsky proposed a Liaison Committee to ABPP, comprised of nine members: the Chairperson of the Qualifications Committee (Stockhamer), the Chairperson of the Education and Training Committee (Mayman), four representatives from Section I (Antonovsky, Caligor, Isaacs, and Kaplan), and three representatives appointed by the President

(Cohler, Kalinkowitz, and Lane). This committee of nine members was accepted by the Board of Division 39.

Another important development was Murray Meisels and Oliver Kerner, Co-Chairpersons of the Committee on Psychoanalytic Education (COPE), submitting a proposal for a "National Program in Psychoanalytic Education." Meisels and Kerner, in consultation with Martin Mayman proposed five models of training: the local or institute model, the postdoctoral model, the colony model, the regional model, and the national model. Although this program was never implemented, it was to influence the activity of local chapters.

The fifth president was Ernest S. Lawrence. The most significant event of his administration was the preparation of an antitrust suit against the APsaA, the New York Psychoanalytic Institute, the Columbia University Center for Psychoanalytic Training and Research, and the IPA, by GAPPP. This suit was a follow-up to the work that Reuben Fine had initiated several years earlier. The suit was immediately supported by Division 39, the Association for the Advancement of Psychology (AAP), Divisions 29 and 42, and the APA in general. Division 39, added a $10 assessment onto the dues to have money for the suit, and this, added to the $5 Journal assessment during Goldman's administration, raised the dues to $40. The antitrust suit brought about by GAPPP dealt with patterns of discrimination against psychologists, hindrances both formal and coercive to psychologists in their psychoanalytic training efforts, and interferences with training by non-APsaA institutions as well as psychologists in the international area.

Another major concern during Lawrence's administration was insurance. The institution of Champus and Peer Review in the early 1980s brought a barrage of insurance forms to fill out and psychologists became more and more concerned with confidentiality. The insurance companies were demanding accountability, peer review was being mandated by the states, insurance companies were claiming the right to regulate how they wanted to spend their money, and the APA was involved in contracts with insurance companies. On the other hand, there was the issue of privacy and confidentiality, the disruption of the patient–therapist relationship, the validity of the peer review process itself, the choice of reviewer who need not be a true peer, financial issues, the sentinel effect that might discourage claims, professional issues, harassment and intimidation, and discrimination against analysis due to the frequency of visits and duration of treatment. Changes were necessary through legal and legislative measures, in the Peer Review concept, and in the APA's participation. The Special Provider Advisory Group (SPAG) was set up "to provide advice and commentary on the present and future operations of APA's Peer Review Program from the provider's viewpoint." This group recommended an almost complete overhaul of the system. Another group set up was the Subcommittee on Professional Services Review (SOPSR). Ernest Lawrence was active in both these groups, as was our insurance chair, Rogers Wright.

Other important items during Lawrence's administration included the establishment of the Foundation for Psychoanalytic Education and Research. The goal of this foundation incorporated in Chicago was to receive donations, grants, gifts, and services, and noncash contributions with the purpose of distributing funds for educational and research purposes. The settlement of the antitrust suit raised the question of what to do with the monies received and who should handle it? A very successful conference on Nationwide Training in Psychoanalysis was held at the William Alanson White Institute on December 1 and 2, 1984.

Other events were the publication of Volume I of the Journal of Psychoanalytic Psychology, approval for publication of *Psyc-SCAN : Psychoanalysis*, acceptance of the membership category of Associate and Student Affiliate with dues of 25% of the $40 dues at that time, and the acceptance of Section II (Child and Adolescent Psychoanalysis) and Section III (Women and Psychoanalysis) by the Board. A sad note was the death of Gordon F. Derner, the second president of the Division.

Summary

It is very clear that many of the Division's problems apparent during Reuben Fine's administration were still present after Ernest Lawrence's administration, 5 years later. These included controversy over accreditation and the formation of Section I, and agreement on criteria for the ABPsaP examination. Growth in membership in the Division more that doubled by 1984 with membership from rural areas increasing considerably. The success of both annual and mid-winter meetings was apparent from the beginning of the Division. The growth across the country of local chapters, the beginning of the institute movement, the development of new sections, our journal, newsletter and *Psyc-SCAN*, all attest to our success as a Division.

REFERENCES

Cohler, B. J., & Kerner, O. J. B. (1980, December). Regarding the Meisels and Hyman proposal on credentialing. *Newsletter, Division 39, APA* (Vol. II, No. 1, pp. 11–13).

Meisels, M. & Hyman, M. (1980, June). A proposal for accrediting psychoanalyst psychologists. *Newsletter, Division 39, APA* (Vol. I, No. 2, pp. 3–9).

A History of the Division of Psychoanalysis

Murray Meisels

Reuben Fine launched the Division of Psychoanalysis in 1979 by a selective mailing to members of APA, whose Council approved the petition at the 1979 annual meeting. Why did it take so long for one of the earliest psychologies to organize itself within APA? Ten years earlier, at an APA annual meeting, psychologist-psychoanalysts called a meeting to organize a division, but I've heard that some participants worried that psychologists would form training institutes if there were a psychoanalytic division—apparently, the idea of psychologists training themselves was not regarded as desirable—and the result of that 1968 convening was a compromise-formation called Psychologists Interested in the Study of Psychoanalysis (the acronym is PISP), a research group. The 1968 anxiety that psychologists would form training institutes were there a psychoanalytic division was prophetic, because this is precisely what happened once the Division of Psychoanalysis was established a decade later.

Once formed, the main political fight that emerged within the Division reflected a New York City antagonism. Approximately 55% of the Division membership came from New York area institutes, institutes that apparently rarely interacted with one another but who had representatives sitting together at Divisional Board meetings. In their training policies some of these institutes insisted that all control cases and training analyses be conducted at a frequency of four times per week, some had set the minimum at three times per week, and others at two. Within the Division, the line was drawn between two and three.

As events unfolded, it was the three to four times/week group that organized itself first. It largely filled the membership of the 1980 Qualifications Committee and then formed itself as the Division's first section, the Section of Psychologist-Psychoanalyst Practitioners (Section I). Section I, formed in 1982, maintained the necessity of at least thrice weekly meetings as a definition of analysis, not quite the four or five weekly frequencies advocated by IPA and APsaA, but enough to antagonize Division members who had graduated from institutes in which analyses were, at least sometimes, conducted twice a week. These members organized themselves more slowly, forming the Psychologist-Psychoanalyst Forum (Section V) in 1986.

The organization of local chapters was also slowed down by the concern of each New York group that new institutes might form along either side of the now infamous 3/2 dividing line. The Section of Local Chapters (Section IV) was formed in 1985.

The interval after the emergence of Section I and before the emergence of Sections IV and V is a most colorful history, filled with intense political and emotional strife, parochialism, and some painful, even horrid, Board meetings. The political strife was between Section I and (what became) Section V, and Board meetings were characterized by periodic eruptions of political infighting as now one issue, now another, was perceived as a battleground on which the issue of standards was fought. Some of the battlegrounds entailed meaningful content, such as battles over the composition of the ABPP committee or about whether the Division should sponsor the Clark Conference, but other battles were quite distant from the issue, such as the battle over who is the proper Section I representative, or whether section membership should be included in the Division's Membership Directory. Our Division became known in APA as a hotbed of cantankerous controversy. At this point, I should like to sketch the three positions.

The Section I Position. Although the Division was founded as, and remains, an interest group that is open to any APA member, within months of its founding efforts were underway to attempt to credential psychologist-psychoanalysts. Within a year, Meisels and Hyman wrote a proposal to that effect, a symposium on the subject was held at the 1980 APA meeting in Montreal, and a Qualifications Committee was appointed. By 1982, the Division board had approved the recommendations of the Qualifications Committee, so that *the thrice-weekly standard was, from 1982 to 1990, the Division's definition of analysis.* Section I then used the Division's standards as a membership requirement: This requirement, that only psychologists who met the Division's standards for qualification in psychoanalysis could join Section I, led to the widespread perception—widespread even in the leadership of Section I—that Section I was engaging in unofficial credentialling. However, in my view, Section I had acted strictly within APA and Division rules.

The Section I position, broadly, was: The field of psychoanalysis has defined standards of practice which entail a high frequency of contact; to play a role in the international psychoanalytic community it is necessary for the Division to maintain these standards; and that, compared to the IPA's four-times-per-week criterion, the thrice-weekly standard was already a compromise, so that any effort to further reduce frequency requirements—or to impose a concept such as equivalency—must be resisted. These were fiercely held convictions. These convictions, interestingly, did not have an ideological cast: Section I admitted psychologists of all theoretical stripes, and also admitted psychologists who were not trained in institutes, that is, colleagues who had engaged in self-directed training. It was the frequency/intensity dimension that Section I fiercely defended, not a particular theory.

The Section V Position. It was apparently the Division's official establishment of Section I that galvanized the (future) Section V people into organization and action. Before 1982, they had played a minor role, and the major Division initiatives had derived from Section I (these were the agreement on standards for qualification, the establishment of the Division's first section, and the possibility of ABPP credentialling). Now, however, New Yorkers whose institutes accepted some twice-weekly treatments became concerned that graduates of their institutes would not be admitted to Section I, and they were joined by some non-New Yorkers who also demanded grandparenting or equivalency of training. Section I was unwilling to do this.

In 1982–1983, the result was internecine warfare. The future Section V people were demanding a hearing, or calling for the decertification of Section I, and Section I felt under severe attack, and devoted enormous energy to the struggle. The Division Board, itself, was obsessed with this conflict, a conflict that was the fundamental agenda item of several Board meetings; and the issue was indeed the focus of conflict at Board meetings, and derivatives of the conflict attached themselves to numerous tangential issues, and the two ideologies fought each other again and again. There was much unhappiness. Some, including this writer, had fears that the Division might split.

The Local Chapters. This intense emotional issue of standards, which preoccupied the Division Board and the Section I Board for years, was almost irrelevant to non-New Yorkers. As a Michiganian who championed local-chapter formation, I distinctly and vividly recall many meetings of the Division Board and the Section I Board at which I broached the topic of encouraging local chapter development, only to find that the issue quickly turned back again to the fight about standards. The New York parochialism, which focused such intense emotion on the issue of standards, led to placing the rest of the country on hold.

The focal emotional issue for psychologists outside of greater New York City was the lack of training opportunities because of the successful exclusionary policy of APsaA. Except for the many institutes in New York City and the one in Los Angeles, psychoanalytically minded psychologists in the remainder of the

United States were virtually unable to train in psychoanalysis unless the local institute of APsaA gave them permission (in which case they had to undergo the odious waiver procedure). It has long seemed to me that the central success of U.S. psychiatrist-psychoanalysts was in establishing a national organization, the APsaA, and that the fundamental difficulty for psychologists was the lack of a central organization. Whereas we psychoanalysts like to explain phenomena at the psychological level, and even to reduce complex sociological phenomena to psychodynamics, I am here arguing the reverse, that is, that this particular difficulty of psychologists is best understood at the sociological level, as due to the absence of a national organization. Once Division 39 came into existence, once psychologists had their national organization, they immediately began to form local societies, exactly as had been feared in 1968.

The Shift From Standards To Local Chapters. Before 1979, APsaA was the major national psychoanalytic organization, with a network of local units throughout the country, and psychologists had neither a national organization nor a network: There were areas of the country where psychoanalytically minded psychologists had, literally, never seen a psychologist who was a psychoanalyst. Once the Division was launched, a network of local chapters began to emerge. Starting in 1981, the Committee on Local Chapters was chaired by an innovative Chicagoan, Oliver J. B. Kerner, who pressed the issue that the Division initiate training programs throughout the country. Eventually, he and I offered a concrete proposal that the Division establish a national program to train psychologists in the hinterlands—a proposal that never did materialize—and we also recommended that the Division establish a Foundation for Psychoanalytic Education and Research. The Foundation did materialize, but to date has garnered money only with great difficulty, and not in amounts large enough to impact on local training programs.

By late 1984, the Division's major agenda had shifted from standards to local training issues. There were two developments here. First, by 1984 Bryant Welch, Nathan Stockhamer, and Ernest Lawrence had organized a group to sue APsaA for restraint of trade, and indeed suit was filed on March 1, 1985. The purpose of the suit was to force local institutes of APsaA to admit psychologists and the IPA to admit our institutes, with the specific intent being to help psychologists throughout the United States. The lawsuit, with its expenses and purposes—and its focus on non-New Yorkers—would become a primary Division agenda item for many years.

The second development in 1984 was that Helen Block Lewis assumed the presidency of the Division. Helen Block Lewis, a stalwart of the less traditional viewpoint, had long since grasped and strongly supported the importance of local chapter development. Upon assuming the presidency she appointed me chair of the newly created National Program Committee—in line with the idea of developing a national program—and she and I called for a Nationwide Conference on Psychoanalytic Training, which was in fact held in New York City on December 1–2, 1984. And what a wonderful conference that was! The local chapter network had been developing apace, and confreres came from Boston, Washington, DC, Los Angeles, San Francisco, Chicago, Cleveland, Michigan, Philadelphia, Phoenix, Miami, Tampa, New Haven, New York, and Denver. All the delegates were fascinated to hear about the other local chapters and groups in various phases of development.

The participants issued a call for further conferences and further dialogue about matters such as local organizational development and training issues. A series of meetings were suggested including a major conference on psychoanalytic training. This idea suited the local chapters who were experimenting with new educational forms. Helen Block Lewis secured grant funding from the Exxon Foundation, $25,000 to be used first for a preconference and then for a major conference on psychoanalytic training. The preconference, the second convening of local chapters, was partially supported by the Exxon Foundation and met in Ann Arbor, Michigan, on June 21–23, 1985. Eventually a major training conference was held at Clark University in October, 1986. A petition was submitted to form a Section of Local Chapters (Section IV) in October, 1985.

Section I was still dominant in 1984 and Section V not yet organized. These antagonists took opposite sides in reference to the emerging local chapters, with the future Section V people strongly supporting local chapters and the Section I people in opposition—not in opposition to local chapters, just in opposition to the developments that were unfolding. These developments were not traditional developments. Perhaps the most peculiar aspect of this political scene was that the local groups, as far as standards were concerned, were strongly identified with the values of Section I. Hence, they could easily have become the allies of Section I—indeed, had Section I been so inclined (which it decidedly was not!), it could have organized the local chapter movement in 1983, rather than the Division doing so a year later.

The reason that local chapters were most closely identified with Section I values seems clear enough. Psychologists in places like Michigan, Chicago, Denver, Dallas, Washington, DC, and Boston were essentially aware of only one model of psychoanalysis, that of the local institute of APsaA, and generally accepted the traditional standards of APsaA. Often these psychologists hung around the fringes of the local medical society, and were analyzed, supervised (psychotherapy, of course), and taught by members of APsaA. In Michigan, for example, a 1981 survey of the fledgling Michigan Society for Psychoanalytic Psychology found that the theoretical focus of those non-New Yorkers was mainstream American Freudianism, so that those psychologists were natural allies of Section I, as far as standards were concerned.

On the other hand, the founders of local chapters were strong-willed individualists. They had defied the local authority of APsaA, had courageously launched new organizations, and were well-aware that any training activities in their areas would require innovative educational forms. It was *this* that Section I apparently opposed. At the time, Section I people largely controlled the Division's Education and Training Committee and argued that it should set standards and requirements for local training groups, that is, that training should be under the control of properly-qualified senior analysts. Already, at the December 1984, Nationwide Conference—the first conference—conflict between the local chapters and the Educational and Training Committee had emerged. Local leaders were outraged at the idea that, having finally achieved local autonomy for psychologists, they would be asked to surrender that autonomy to a new central authority—even to the central authority of their own Division.

Section I leaders were generally opposed to the events that were unfolding. They were either opposed to, or were fighting rearguard actions against, such developments as the National Program Committee; the December 1984, New York Nationwide Conference on Psychoanalytic Training; the June 1985, Ann Arbor Conference; the necessity for the formation of the Section of Local Chapters; and the Clark Conference on Psychoanalytic education.[1] Section I, which in its first years had launched the initiatives that had provided the Division's agenda, had misread the major currents that were developing, and had lost the initiative.

RECENT HISTORY

In retrospect, it might be said that the Division is constituted of diverse constituencies, much like the APA itself, and that the history of the Division is characterized by the emergence of these constituencies (the other four sections, which were much less controversial, were Childhood and Adolescence [II], Women and Psychoanalysis [III], Psychoanalytic Research Society [VI], and Psychoanalysis and Groups [VII]). The intense, emotional, colorful conflict of the 1980–1986 period may be understood as a playing out of some of the major antithetical paradigms that characterize the field of psychoanalysis, prior to the time that the Division developed the organizational solution of establishing new sections to accommodate emerging constituencies. Since 1986, conflict has greatly subsided. In general, there was more eros than thanatos, and all constituencies seemed to agree that, to paraphrase, ''If we don't hang together, we may hang separately.''

In 1990, under the leadership of its Division president, Ruth-Jean Eisenbud, in recognition of the diversity that exists in psychoanalysis and of the different

---

[1]For example, the Clark Conference would not have taken place had not Helen Block Lewis secured the $25,000 grant from Exxon Corporation; even with the grant, there was an acrimonious debate at a Division Board meeting, and on a first ballot the board voted against holding the conference. The pleadings, the outrage, and, the ardor of several local chapter leaders then turned the tide. There was a call for a revote, and the Clark Conference was approved by a narrow margin.

constituencies in the Division—and with an acceptance of the idea that all constituencies have a place within the Division—the Board revised its definition of psychoanalysis. The problematic issue of frequency as a standard, that is, the thrice-weekly frequency requirement, was set aside and psychoanalysis was defined without reference to controversial numbers. The tripartite model was retained and defined as requiring, "a substantial personal analysis," "intensive supervision" of "two patients, each carried two years in psychoanalysis," and didactic work that is "the equivalent of 12 courses in a traditional two-semester program." These requirements were considered as parts of broad training programs, and illustrations of 11 training programs were presented to provide concreteness to the terms *substantial, intensive,* and *12 courses.*

The problems of standards, nonetheless, continues to haunt the Division of Psychoanalysis, and will surely be revisited in the future. Most immediately, the committee that the Division charged in 1983 to develop a Diplomate in psychoanalysis has been frozen into inaction by this issue. There is as yet no Diplomate in psychoanalysis in large part because the Section I and Section V people have not yet by-passed the three-times-a-week frequency controversy. Similarly, efforts to establish a Federation of Psychoanalytic Training Programs has been plagued by the standards issue, namely, who should or should not be permitted membership in such an organization. The issues of standards, of frequency, and of definition, are thorny, intractable, and persistent.

DISCUSSION

This history can be retold from the point of view of two common fantasies.

Fantasy 1: There is a Higher Justice. One persistent theme in human history, and in the Division, is a complaint about being mistreated and misunderstood, accompanied by an appeal that some higher authority might rectify the situation. For example, I have heard a number of psychiatrist-psychoanalysts bemoan their mistreatment by legislatures, and they await the age when justice will prevail and the legislatures will declare that psychoanalysis—indeed, psychotherapy—is the province of medicine. So, too, have I heard numbers of Freudians who are aggrieved because so many non-Freudians label themselves psychoanalysts. These individuals await the day of justice, when their rivals will see the light, and leave the term *psychoanalysis* to its proper Freudian home. And psychologists and social workers—and others—who had so long felt betrayed and abused by APsaA and IPA, who had felt the sting of discrimination, longed for the day that APsaA, and IPA would realize that they had committed horrible injustices, would rue the errors of their ways, and would finally admit psychologists and social workers (and others) as peers.

In point of fact, it appears unlikely that legislatures will decide that "talk-therapy" is the province of medicine; or that Kleinians would forsake the designation of psychoanalyst; or that APsaA or IPA would voluntarily have changed their policies. In raw reality, there is evidence of just how unlikely it was that APsaA or IPA would ever have "seen the light," would ever have "recognized the errors of their ways," would ever have made reparation for their discriminatory actions. That evidence comes from the 1985 lawsuit that psychologists filed against APsaA and IPA, particularly from depositions of leaders of APsaA. I have read five of six of these depositions, and what emerged is that the psychiatrist-psychoanalysts who comprise the leadership of APsaA were very much identified with the field of psychiatry; that many had little contact with the social sciences; and that their attention was focused on the internal workings of their organization, and on psychiatry and medicine. One of the very striking features of these depositions was the callousness of these leaders toward the plight of psychologists. Psychologists had experienced years of frustration, years of disappointment and dashed hopes, and entire psychoanalytic careers had gone undeveloped, and had been mourned. Yet, the attitude toward this among leaders of APsaA—even leaders who favored training for psychologists— was bland indifference. No one expressed regret, or compassion, or seemed to feel a need to make repair. So much for the fantasy that "they" would realize an error.

In terms of the history of the Division of Psychoanalysis, the fantasy that there is a higher justice seemed to inform every development. Section I certainly felt entitled to define psychoanalysis in its traditional form, and considered that all who disagreed should "see the light," realize that they were not doing psychoanalysis, and redefine their activities. The future Section V people were looking to Section I for justice, hoping that Section I would be reasonable and hold an objective discourse about psychoanalytic process, more or less as non-psychiatrists had hoped APsaA would listen and understand. And, the response of Section I to the Section V people was very similar to the response of APsaA to psychologists and social workers: namely, indifference. And, the local chapters felt unjustly treated by a Division that barely supported or approved of their actions, a Division that was preoccupied with other issues.

There appears to be a psychoanalytic conclusion to be drawn from these observations. I am reminded here that Erich Fromm once wrote that the search for justice is universal because we all experienced injustices as children. Children are relatively helpless, and it it striking to me that one of the characteristics of the fantasy of a higher justice entails a theme of helplessness: There is a complainer who is unable to do for him or herself, so someone else must "realize" something. In the history of the Division, the frustration of the search for justice led to the eventual recognition that a higher justice would never materialize—APsaA would never admit psychologists, so psychologists must form their own organization, their own practitioner section, or launch a lawsuit; and those in Section V realized that Section I would never listen, would never provide justice, and thus set up their own section; and local chapters recognized the need for a power base within the Division, so another section was born. In summary, the plea for a higher justice is a statement of helplessness, and the proper reply is empowerment. It is the empowerment of psychologists through their sense of injustice; that, and the victory in the lawsuit.

Fantasy 2: The Striving For Perfection. This is a second ubiquitous theme in both human and psychoanalytic history. Glover wrote of the myth of the perfectly analyzed analyst, someone who does everything just right, who has resolved his or her transferences, has no countertransferences, and is seemingly not affected by past realities or even by present realities. This analyst is able to correctly use analytic technique, and the transferences become focussed, and are resolved properly, by interpretation. It is hard to know just who such an analyst might be, and there is much analytic mythology here. Certainly, I have heard it said, a young analyst could not be such an analyst, for young analysts lack seasoning and experience. Certainly, someone who has been thrice divorced, or drives a sports car, or is a Jungian, could not be such an analyst. Even graduation from an institute is no guarantee. So the number of *real analysts*, by which is meant perfectly analyzed analysts, becomes fewer and fewer. There then issues another problem, because there is no guarantee that an adjudged perfectly analyzed analyst—say, a married 55-year-old training analyst, a graduate of a first-rate institute who also has an excellent reputation—will not start living with a former patient in another year, or change theoretical orientation.

The Catholic Church has solved its version of the myth by not decreeing perfection—sainthood—until 100 years after the person dies. That way, the person cannot change, and all who knew what that person was really like are dead.

The Kleinians have it that idealizations serve as defenses against envy, and it is extremely apt and useful to think of perfection fantasies in terms of an underlying envy. The ideal of sainthood or of a perfectly analyzed analyst in itself provokes envy. Statements by IPA or APsaA about their special worthwhileness constitute provocations of envy, and the fear that one is not good enough intensifies the search for perfection.

One of the curious ways that the fantasy of the perfectly analyzed analyst gets manifested is in reference to the training analysis. The psychoanalytic literature contains a number of articles about the training analysis that generally bemoan its lack of effectiveness and attribute that lack to the fact the training analysts report to the institute. The reporting is then vilified as the cause of the poor quality of training analysis. The viewpoint is widespread. The facts, however, are quite different: First, because the two extant studies of how candidates view their training analysis showed that the overwhelming majority found it to be effective, and second, because most institutes no longer allow reporting. In my judgment, the reason that the training analysis is viewed as a failure is because many candidates pursue second analyses. (In fact, data indicate that two thirds of a group of analysts had multiple treatments; see chapter 3.) The bad reputation of the training analysis, and of reporting, are distractions from the far more penetrating issue of why multiple analyses are so commonplace among psychoanalysts. Indeed, the reason may be because multiple treatments are more effective than treatment by just one analyst, rather than because analysis is not effective. In any event, these data temper the fantasy of perfection.

In reference to Division 39, it seems that the fantasy of the perfectly analyzed analyst was intensely manifested in Section I. Indeed, I well recall an address by a Section I leader that argued that one learns the analyzing function by internalizing the analyzing functions of one's analyst, which meant, for that writer, that one's analyst's capacities prescribe the limits of one's own capacities, a variation on a lineage myth. This argument provokes envy of the "my father can beat up your father" variety. Also, this argument virtually means that no one thinks for themselves, that no one learns from experience. In my opinion, the fantasy of the perfectly analyzed analyst and envy of the IPA held such sway over the Section I leadership that it had difficulty coping with the changing agenda of the Division, much as the same fantasy, in APsaA, caused it grave difficulties in coping with the changing composition of mental health professionals in the United States.

For its part, Section V had its own definition of perfection, one that seemed to contain the vision that a perfect analyst was someone who was capable of altering technique to fit the circumstances of the patient. The ability to consider alternate perspectives and ideas and approaches was idealized, and the Section I position was discredited as rigid, autocratic, and arbitrary. As seen by some in Section V, Section I was devalued as the antithesis of the humanistic and the humane, and breadth and tolerance were regarded as the criteria of perfection.

CONCLUSION

In 1979, the decades of psychologists with no national organization were over; the nature of the organization that psychologists would develop was still in the future. As of 1991, the Division has experienced considerable growth and differentiation, and the fantasies and the intense psychoanalytic commitments discussed in this chapter, may be understood as the processes whereby growth has occurred.

3

The 1980 Membership Survey
of the Division of Psychoanalysis

Murray Meisels
Jerry W. O'Dell

This chapter reviews 1980 survey returns from 327 members (25%). Readers satisfied with a quick overview may find the following results sufficient: More than 54% of the Division members lived in the New York City area, 69% of the members were male and 31% female, and the vast majority were in private practice. About 51% of Division members were graduates of psychoanalytic institutes, and only 13% had *not* had some postdoctoral psychoanalytic training. Eighty-four percent of Division members had been psychoanalyzed, 83% had been supervised on psychoanalytic cases, 25% were doing training analyses, and 43% supervised analytic candidates. More than 76% were practicing psychoanalysis in their clinical work.

The decision to undertake the survey was made at the March 23, 1980 meeting of the Steering Committee of the Division of Psychoanalysis. The goal was to learn about ourselves, our psychoanalytic histories, and our attitudes toward Division functions. A Membership Survey was enclosed with the June 1980, edition of the Division's *Newsletter*. A copy of this Membership Survey is presented in Table 3.24 (see pp. 34–35). The data presented are based on 327 Membership Survey protocols, the total number of protocols received as of August 4, 1980. At that moment the Division had 1,311 members.

Geographical Location

Fifty-four percent of our members lived in the New York City area: 344 members lived in Manhattan, and 344 members lived in greater New York–New Jersey. There were 133 California members (11%). Most of the remainder lived in Illinois, Massachusetts, Michigan, Pennsylvania, Maryland–Washington, DC, Florida, Connecticut, Ohio, Texas, Virginia, Tennessee, North Carolina, and Georgia.

Many more psychologists were interested in psychoanalysis than had joined our Division. In Michigan, for example, 19 psychologists joined the Division between April 7, 1980 and July 31, 1980. This growth spurt from 41 to 60 Division members in 4 months was influenced by the formation of the Michigan Society for Psychoanalytic Psychology, the first psychoanalytic association for psychologists in Michigan. It was expected that, as more such psychoanalytic societies formed throughout the country, more psychologists would join Division 39.

The availability of these demographic data permitted comparison between the population of the Division and the sample that returned Survey forms. Inspection of Table 3.1 indicates that the incidence of survey respondents closely followed the pattern of Division membership. It appeared that, in reference to geographical distribution, the survey respondents were representative of the Divisional membership.

Age, Sex, and Educational Degree

We were 69% male, and 31% female. This was almost exactly the proportion found among graduates of psychoanalytic institutes, which was 70% and 30%. Our median age was 47 ($M = 47.3$, $SD = 10.6$), with 84% of us in our 30s, 40s, and 50s. More than 91% have the PhD as their highest degree. (See Tables 3.2 and 3.3.)

TABLE 3.1
A Comparison of Geographical Location for Division Members
and Survey Respondents

State	% Division Members	% Survey Respondents
New York	48.4	52.6
New Jersey	5.4	6.1
New York & New Jersey	53.8	58.7
California	10.6	5.8
Illinois	3.8	4.3
Massachusetts	3.4	2.8
Michigan	3.3	5.2
Pennsylvania	2.9	2.8
Maryland–Washington, D.C.	2.9	4.0
Florida	1.7	0.9
Connecticut	1.6	1.5
Other	16.0	14.0

TABLE 3.2
Age of Division 39 Members

	Number	Percent
Under 30	2	0.6
30–40	98	30.0
40–50	87	26.6
50–60	93	28.4
60–70	39	11.9
Over 70	5	1.5
Missing data	3	0.9

Work Settings

Table 3.4 presents data on our work situations. The vast majority of us (89%) were involved in private practice, which was the principle or sole position of about three out of five Division members. A college or university affiliation was the second most frequent work setting, and there were significant numbers of us involved in inpatient hospital or outpatient clinic work.

Psychoanalytic Training

Table 3.5 presents the results of self-reports of incidence of postdoctoral psychoanalytic training among Division 39 members. It was remarkable that about 51% of Division 39 members reported graduating from psychoanalytic training institutes. This occurred despite the efforts of medically dominated psychoanalytic associations to deprive psychologists of psychoanalytic educations. An ad-

TABLE 3.3
Sex and Education of Division 39 Members

	Number	Percent
Sex		
Male	227	69
Female	100	31
Education		
PhD	299	91
EdD	14	4
MA	6	2
Other	5	2
No data	3	1
Total	327	100

TABLE 3.4
Work Settings of Division 39 Members

Type	Primary		Secondary		Other		Total	
	No.	%	No.	%	No.	%	No.	%
Private practice	199	61	82	25	11	3	292	89
College or univ.	62	19	55	17	12	4	129	40
Inpatient hospital	35	11	25	7	6	2	66	20
Outpatient clinic	24	7	33	10	4	1	61	19
Other	6	2	33	10	28	9	67	20
None reported	1	<1	99	30	266	81		

ditional 13% were currently candidates at institutes, indicating the availability of training opportunities for (mostly New York City area) members of our Division. About one fifth of us (22%) were trained outside of institutes, and only a small fraction (13%) reported having had no postdoctoral psychoanalytic training. It was reasonable to conclude that there were 650 institute-trained psychoanalysts in our Division, and probably more than that in the country.

The attitude of the medically dominated psychoanalytic societies had not prevented significant numbers of psychologists from becoming practicing psychoanalysts. By implication, our attitudes will not prevent other groups from achieving the same goal.

Table 3.6 presents data on the psychoanalytic societies and institutes that Division 39 members have graduated from or were affiliated with. The overwhelming dominance of New York City area training facilities was evident. Yet, it was clear that we have been trained in many places, and from diverse theoretical orientations. Table 3.7 presents data on the number of us affiliated with local psychoanalytic societies, and indicates that 53% of us were so affiliated. Table 3.8 indicates that most of us who affiliated with any psychoanalytic society affiliated with just one. Table 3.9 cites the frequency and importance of psychoanalytic areas to Division 39 members.

TABLE 3.5
Postdoctoral Psychoanalytic Training of Division 39 Members

	Number	Percent
Graduate of an institute	165	51
In training at an institute	43	13
Training outside of an institute	73	22
No specific psychoanalytic training	44	13
Missing data	2	1

TABLE 3.6
Institutes and Societies of Division 39 Members

Graduate	Candidate	Member or Affiliate	Name
31	12	23	New York University Postdoctoral Program
27	1	31	National Psychological Association for Psychoanalysis (NPAP)
25	5	26	William Alanson White
23	3	9	Postgraduate Center for Mental Health
15	6	23	Adelphi
2			Alfred Adler (N.Y.)
2	1	1	Chicago Institute for Psychoanalysis
2			Institute for the Study of Psychotherapy (N.J.)
2	3		Inter-Regional Association of Jungian Analysts
2		7	New York Center for Psychoanalytic Training (NYCPT)
2	2	12	New York Freudian Society
2	2		Washington Square (N.Y.)
1			(Reported at 22 institutes throughout the country.)
	1		(Reported at 5 institutes throughout the country.)
		1	(Reported at 20 institutes throughout the country.)
2	2		Topeka Psychoanalytic Institute

TABLE 3.7
Affiliation of Division 39 Members with Psychoanalytic Societies

	Number	Percent
Affiliated	172	53
Unaffiliated	151	46
No answer	4	1

TABLE 3.8
Number of Psychoanalytic Societies that Division 39 Members Affiliate With

	Number	Percent
None/No answer	157	48
One	128	39
Two	27	8
Three	12	4
Four or more	3	1

TABLE 3.9
Areas of Psychoanalysis Important to Members of Division 39

Number	Concept
122	Transference, Countertransference
63	Development, any reference to
60	Object Relations
53	Clinical Technique, except transference, therapeutic alliance, or Psychoanalytic therapy
44	Metapsychology, theory, philosophy
42	Ego-Psychology
36	Specific clinical issue, e.g., affect, identity
32	Borderlines, psychotics
31	Defense, Resistance
31	Dreams
27	Applied Psychoanalysis
26	Psychoanalytic psychotherapy, Brief psychotherapy
25	Theory of therapy; Action of therapy
23	Psychopathology (other than borderlines, psychotics and narcissistic), Diagnosis
22	Specific theoretician, other than Freud, Sullivan or Kohut
20	Sullivan, Interpersonal
19	Freud, Freudian theory
14	Group analysis
13	Self, Kohut
13	Psychoanalytic training, Supervision
12	Child analysis
12	Nonpsychoanalytic technique
12	Nonpsychoanalytic theory
11	Narcissism, Narcissistic characters
8	Unconscious
8	Character analysis
7	Drive theory
6	Therapeutic alliance
6	Creativity
5	Research
3	Oedipus Complex
173	No answer

Responses to the Question: What Three Topics in Psychoanalysis Are Most Important to You?

Transference/countertransference, the very heart of our work, was by far the most frequently mentioned issue. The next three issues, in order of frequency were development, object relations, and technique. Oedipus barely made the list and castration anxiety was rarely if ever mentioned.

Other inferences from the survey include the following:

1. There was more interest in borderlines and psychotics than in narcissistic characters. It appears that Kohutian views were not widely influential.
2. We were far more interested in object relations theory than drive theory. The British school has had strong impact on American psychoanalytic psychologists.
3. We were not very interested in research.
4. Defense and resistance were once a hallmark of psychoanalysis, and Freud defined psychoanalysis as a technique that deals with transference and resistance.

We continue to be intensely involved with the idea of transference (and countertransference), but this was not so for the idea of resistance. It was possible that those clinical phenomena that were formerly viewed as resistances or defenses might now be viewed as transferences, or a developmental issue, or repetitions of object relations, or technical or treatment problems.

Responses to the Question: Which One Psychoanalytic View Was Most Compatible With Your Own?

The first view mentioned was the only one counted (e.g., "Freudian with object relations" was scored under "Freudian," not under "Object relations"). The results are presented in Table 3.10, and are noteworthy for the dominance of Freudian, ego-psychological, interpersonal, and object-relations viewpoints.

TABLE 3.10
Theoretical Orientation of Members of the Division of Psychoanalysis

Number	Percent	
100	31	Freudian
35	11	Ego-Psychology
33	10	Sullivanian, Interpersonal
27	8	Object Relations
15	5	Neo-Freudian
14	4	Eclectic
8	2	Spotnitz, Modern
6	2	Kohut
5	2	Kernberg
4	1	Jung
4	1	Adler
3	1	Erikson
3	1	Mahler
3	1	Greenson
32	10	Other
35	11	No data

There were few adherents of such significant figures as Melanie Klein, Jung, or Alfred Adler. We adhered to well-established views rather than to recent theories (such as Kohut, Spotnitz, etc.).

Apparently, "Freudian" does not imply interest in drive theory or Oedipal problems, but does imply interest in transference and countertransference, in development, in object relations, in treatment, and in theory.

Personal Analysis and Personal Therapy

The data here were surprising: *84% of us had been analyzed!* And, an additional 13% had had psychotherapy but no psychoanalysis, leaving only 11 out of 327 respondents, a bare 3%, who had not experienced personal treatment. These data are presented in Table 3.11.

For Tables 3.12 and 3.13, which report on the number of personal treatment hours and number of personal therapists, the respondents have been separated into three groups: Analysis Only, Analysis Plus Therapy, and Therapy Only. Inspection of Table 3.12 indicates that we were a well-analyzed group. The median number of analytic hours reported in the Analysis Only group was in the 800s, whereas the number of analytic hours in the Analysis Plus Therapy group, the median of the combined total of treatment hours was in the 700s. For the Therapy Only group the median number of hours was in the 200s.

These results might have some bearing on accreditation criteria. Specifically, the National Association for the Accreditation of Psychoanalysts, NAAP, specified that a minimum number of 300 hours of personal analysis was needed in order to be certified as a psychoanalyst. Based on the results of this Survey, it appears that only the smallest fraction of professionals who have been in analysis have had fewer than 300 treatment hours, making it a virtual certainty that almost any analyzed professional would meet that criterion. Perhaps there was ample rationale for using such a criterion. Nevertheless, the majority of profes-

TABLE 3.11
Personal Analysis and Personal Therapy of Division 39 Members

Personal Experience	Number	Percent
Have been analyzed	274	84
No analysis	53	16
Have been in therapy	119	36
No therapy	208	64
Analysis but not therapy	197	60
Both analysis and therapy	77	24
Therapy but not analysis	42	13
Either therapy or analysis	316	97
Neither therapy nor analysis	11	3

TABLE 3.12
Personal Treatment Hours Completed by Division 39 Members

| Hours | Analysis Only | Analysis Plus Therapy | | | Therapy Only | Total |
		Analysis	Therapy	Sum		
<100		1	17		9	9
100s	2	5	17	2	8	12
200s	5		13	2	4	11
300s	14	14	8	4	3	21
400s	11	13	5	6	1	18
500s	16	10	4	7	10	33
600s	22	5	5	13		35
700s	15	7		3	1	19
800s	12	4		7	1	20
900s	11	4	1	5		16
1000s	21			9		30
1100s	2			3	1	6
1200s	7	1				7
1300s	3					3
1400s	7					7
1500 or more	29	7		8	2	39
No data	20	5	6	7	2	

sional psychologists obtain far more than 300 hours—the overall median was in the 700-hour range—suggesting that many of us 'need' far more than 300 hours. In summary, the data obtained here may have bearing on discussions of certification, although it was obvious that what was normative was not necessarily prescriptive.

Table 3.13 presents data on the number of analyses and therapies undergone by Division 39 members. Multiple therapies were the rule here: Approximately 68% of those reporting treatment have had more than one treatment experience. The actual number was probably less than 68%, because some in-

TABLE 3.13
Number of Personal Analysts and Personal Therapists

| Number Treatments | Analysis Only | Analysis Plus Therapy | | | Therapy Only | Total |
		Analysis	Therapy	Sum		
1	86	52	47		13	99
2	68	19	20	33	12	113
3	27	3	4	24	10	61
4 or more	6	1	4	17	5	28
No data	10	2	2	3	2	

TABLE 3.14
Number of Cases Seen Under Supervision by Division 39 Members

	Number	Percent		Number	Percent
No cases	17	17	7 cases	4	1
1 case	4	1	8 cases	13	4
2 cases	32	10	9 cases	6	2
3 cases	37	11	10 cases	26	8
4 cases	48	15	11–15 cases	18	6
5 cases	25	8	More than 16	24	7
6 cases	21	6			

dividuals may have had the same therapist in both therapy and analysis. Of the Analysis Only group, 54% had more than one analyst, 68% of the Therapy Only group had more than one Therapist, and at least 55% but perhaps as many as 100% of the Analysis Plus Therapy group saw more than one therapist/analyst.

Experience as Supervisee

As with personal analyses, 83% of us had been supervised on psychoanalytic cases (Tables 3.14 and 3.15). The median number of cases was five and the median number of supervisory hours was between 200 and 250.

We were, as a group, well educated, well analyzed, and well supervised.

Psychoanalytic Training Activities

There were significant numbers of us who were actively involved in the training of psychoanalysts. These findings were summarized in Table 3.16: 111 (34%) of us were involved in training in an institute, 28 (9%) train outside of an institute, 80 (25%) do training analyses, 143 (43%) supervise, 135 (41%) teach and 52 (16%) do other training activities. Among training analysts, most were analyzing one (n = 9) , two (n = 26), or three (n = 12) analysands, with 24 training

TABLE 3.15
Total Number of Hours of Supervision Received by Division 39 Members

Hours	Number	Percent	Hours	Number	Percent
None	57	17	250–299	25	8
<50	7	2	300–399	31	9
50–99	17	5	400–499	20	6
100–149	31	9	500–599	22	7
150–199	27	8	>600	16	5
200–249	57	17			

TABLE 3.16
Psychoanalytic Training Activities of Division 39 Members

Number	Percent	Activity
111	34	Train in an institute
28	9	Train outside of an institute
80	25	Do training analyses
142	43	Supervise
135	41	Teach in an institute
52	16	Other analytic training activity

analysts working with four or more candidates. Among supervising analysts, the number of reported supervisees were: one—11, two—30, three—21, four—20, five—14, six—11, and seven or more—30.

Psychoanalyzing

Tables 3.17, 3.18, and 3.19 report the incidence of psychoanalyzing being done by Division 39 members. Fully 76% of us do psychoanalysis and the majority have between two and eight analysands who were seen between 7 and 21 hours per week. We were certainly actively involved in doing psychoanalysis.

A *Journal of Psychoanalytic Psychology*?

Tables 3.20 and 3.21 indicate that 66% of the Division membership favor the idea of establishing a new journal.

The Accreditation Issue

Tables 3.20 and 3.21 present the results of the survey of attitudes toward accrediting individuals in psychoanalysis, accrediting psychoanalytic institutes, and establishing a Section of Psychoanalysts in the Division to do the accrediting. These were forced choice items: Table 3.20 presents the breakdown by category and Table 3.21 dichotomizes favorable versus unfavorable categories. The results

TABLE 3.17
Psychoanalytic Treatment Activity of Division 39 Members

	Number	Percent
Do analysis	247	76
Do not do analysis	74	23
Do not treat	3	1

TABLE 3.18
Number of Analysands Currently Treated by Division 39 Members

	Number	Percent		Number	Percent
1 case	5	2	7 cases	11	3
2 cases	28	9	8 cases	18	6
3 cases	27	8	9 cases	3	1
4 cases	24	7	10 cases	26	8
5 cases	25	8	11–15 cases	19	6
6 cases	17	5	16 or more	21	6

TABLE 3.19
Number of Analytic Treatment Hours per Week
Currently Delivered by Division 39 Members

Hours	Number	Percent	Hours	Number	Percent
1–3	12	4	19–21	23	7
4–6	23	7	22–24	7	2
7–9	18	5	25–34	36	11
10–12	32	10	More than 35	29	9
13–15	31	10			
16–18	14	4			

TABLE 3.20
Attitudes of Division 39 Members Toward Accreditation
and Establishing a New Journal

Should the Division	Yes No.	Yes %	Probably Yes No.	Probably Yes %	Probably No No.	Probably No %	No No.	No %	Other No.	Other %
Certify institutes?	114	35	130	40	34	10	39	12	10	3
Certify individuals?	114	35	122	37	44	14	41	13	6	2
Set up a section of psychoanalysts?	88	27	129	39	37	11	55	17	18	6
Establish a journal?	115	35	101	31	67	20	37	11	7	2

TABLE 3.21
Summary of Division 39 Attitudes Toward Certification and a Journal

Should the Division	Favorable Number	Favorable Percent	Unfavorable Number	Unfavorable Percent	Other Number	Other Percent
Certify institutes?	244	75	73	22	10	3
Certify individuals?	236	72	85	26	6	2
Set up a section of psychoanalysts?	217	66	92	28	18	6
Establish a journal?	216	66	104	32	7	2

TABLE 3.22
Attitudes of Members Toward Various Possible Division 39 Activities

Should the Division	Favorable		Unfavorable		Other	
	Number	Percent	Number	Percent	Number	Percent
Have a newsletter?	253	77	74	23		
Take a position on national licensing	230	70	96	30	1	<1
Take a position on state licensing	206	63	120	37	1	<1
Have a speaker program	188	58	135	41	4	1
Grant continuing education credits	178	54	148	45	1	<1
Hold a midwinter Convention	171	52	153	47	3	1

were that the vast majority, more than 70% of us favored the credentialling of individuals and institutes, and nearly as many, 66%, favor the Section of Psychoanalysts proposed in the Meisels–Hyman accreditation proposal. This was perhaps not surprising in light of the fact that 61% of us were primarily of solely employed in private practice.

Division Activities

Table 3.22 presents those activities in which Division members were interested. It was apparent that the membership favors an active Division pursuing diverse goals, from accreditation to a journal, to a newsletter, to speakers, continuing education, and a midwinter convention.

Dues

Table 3.23 presents member preferences for dues, given that $25 would be allocated toward a new journal. As such, the median member would like a $50 dues assessment, with 32% favoring $75 or more.

TABLE 3.23
Member Attitudes Toward Amount of Annual Dues with $25 Allocated to a Journal

Prefer	Number	Percent	Prefer	Number	Percent
$ 35	91	28	$125	6	2
$ 50	91	28	$150	7	1
$ 75	41	12	More than $150	12	4
$100	38	12	Other	41	12

TABLE 3.24
The 1980 Membership Survey of the Division of Psychoanalysis

1. What are your major work settings (e.g., hospital, clinic, private practice, university, etc.)?
   Primary setting _____
   Secondary setting _____
   Other _____
2. Your age _____ 3. Sex _____ 4. Highest Degree_____
5. What state or province do you live in? _____
6. What kind of postdoctoral psychoanalytic training have you had?
   Graduate of an institute _____ If yes, which? _____
   In training at an institute _____ If yes, which? _____
   Training outside of the context of an institute _____
   No specific psychoanalytic training _____
7. What three areas of psychoanalytic theory and/or technique are most important to you?
   1. _____
   2. _____
   3. _____
8. Which one psychoanalytic view is most compatible with your views:
   _____
9. Do you affiliate with any particular psychoanalytic societies?
   Yes _____ No _____ If yes, which? _____
10. Have you had a personal analysis or personal therapy?
    Analysis: Yes _____ No _____
              If yes, how many hours? _____ How many analysts? _____
    Therapy: Yes _____ No _____
              If yes, how many hours? _____ How many therapists? _____
11. If you have been supervised on analytic cases, how many cases? _____
    How many hours of supervision? _____
12. If you are involved in the training of psychoanalysts,
    is it in an institute? _____ Not in an institute? _____
    Do you do training analyses? _____ If yes, how many candidates? _____
    Do you supervise? _____ If yes, how many supervisees? _____
    Do you teach? _____
    Other (please specify) _____
13. Do you do psychoanalysis in your work:
    Yes _____ No _____ Do not do clinical work _____
    If yes, how many analytic patients? _____
    If yes, how many analytic hours per week? _____
14. Are you in favor of the Division of Psychoanalysis certifying qualified psychologists as
    competent in psychoanalysis?
    Yes _____ Probably yes _____ Probably no _____ No _____
15. Are you in favor of the Division of Psychoanalysis formalizing training standards and ac-
    crediting local institutes for training psychologists in psychoanalysis?
    Yes _____ Probably yes _____ Probably no _____ No _____
16. The Division is considering the publication of a new journal, 'The Journal of Psychoanalyt-
    ic Psychology.' Would you be willing to have your Division dues increased by $25.00 in
    order to support the journal?
    Yes _____ Probably yes _____ Probably no _____ No _____

(Continued)

34

TABLE 3.24
(Continued)

17. Check those divisional activities that you favor:
    ____ Publish a new psychoanalytic journal
    ____ Publish a newsletter
    ____ Certify continuing education credits
    ____ Take a position on national licensing issues
    ____ Take a position on state licensing issues
    ____ Hold a midwinter convention. Which month is best for you? _____
    ____ Establish a program for speakers and workshops to be presented all over the country
18. If our Division is to be an important organization of psychoanalysts it needs money. In fact, some of the activities proposed above may require large sums if they are to be effectively pursued. How much are you willing to pay in annual dues, assuming $25.00 of the amount is used for the 'Journal?'
    $35.00 _____ $50.00 _____ $75.00 _____ $100.00 _____ $125.00 _____
    $150.00 _____ More than $150.00 _____
19. Are you in favor of our Division forming a section of psychoanalysts that would accredit individuals and institutes?
    Yes _____ Probably yes _____ No _____ Probably no _____
20. Name (optional) _____
Comments: _____
_____

Comments on Accreditation

There was room on the questionnaire for brief comments by respondents, and about 40% of the respondents did comment. About 60% of the comments referred to the certification issue, and a fair number of these comments were stridently anticredentialling. Some people appear to equate accrediting with capricious, self-serving, power-hungry, narcissistic, self-aggrandizing, grandiose, immoral, and antipsychoanalytic activity, and three respondents vowed to resign forthwith were the Division to credential. The feelings here were intense, indicating the sensitivity of this issue. Although there was some danger of arbitrariness, it was we psychologists who would determine the criteria for accreditation, and we could change any policy that we collectively did not like. Other comments on accreditation preferred that the Division accredit institutes, and that institutes accredit individuals. Or, that individuals be grandparented rather than given an ABPP-type evaluation. There was much heat emanating from this issue, and also some light.

The 1987 Survey of Psychoanalytic Training and Practice

Franklin H. Goldberg
Don Shapiro
Joan P. Trachtman

This chapter is divided into four parts: (a) demographics and training, (b) findings regarding current practice, (c) theoretical orientation, and (d) respondent views of the essential standards for training in psychoanalysis. We received about 600 responses. For different questions the actual N was sometimes less because all respondents did not answer every item.

DEMOGRAPHICS AND TRAINING

The membership of Division 39 in the spring of 1987 was 2,294. We received 593 scoreable replies, representing 26% of the membership (see Table 4.1), slightly higher than average for surveys of this type and the same as Meisels and O'Dell obtained in 1980.

Age and Gender

Breakdown by age revealed several interesting findings, among which was the fact that 21 of our respondents were 70 or older, the oldest being 85 and still practicing. Comparing our sample to the Division 39 data from 1988 in which the median age was 51.3 (vs. 45.8 for the 1987 survey) we found that more of the younger psychologists (below age 45) responded (47% to 37%). Otherwise, there are fairly close age parallels between 1988 Division 39 data and the 1987 survey data (see Table 4.1).

TABLE 4.1
Age and Sex of Division 39 Members (1988) and Survey Respondents
(1980 and 1987)

Age	Survey (1980)		Division 39 (1988)		Survey (1987)	
	N	%	N	%	N	%
30	2	0.6	2	0.1	0	0.3
30–39	98	30.0	302	14.9	138	23.8
40–49	87	26.6	814	40.2	219	37.5
50–59	93	29.4	408	20.1	114	19.7
60–69	39	11.9	365	18.0	75	14.7
70	5	1.5	138	6.8	21	4.0
Total	324	100	2025	100	579	100
Sex						
Male	227	69	1229	52.4	336	57.0
Female	100	31	1063	47.6	253	43.0
Total	327	100	2292	100	589	100

There has been a shift in age upward from 1980 to the present (see Table 4.1): 25% of the membership is now 60 or older compared to 13% in 1980.

With respect to gender, proportionately more males than females responded (57% to 43%). According to the latest figures (1988), our membership is 52% male and 47% female. In 1980, there was a 69% to 31% male–female distribution (see Table 4.1).

Experience

About 50% of the respondents to our questionnaire have been practicing as psychoanalysts for more than 10 years. About 75% have been practicing more than 5 years. Twenty percent (155) do not consider themselves to be psychoanalysts, but identified themselves as psychotherapists or as psychoanalytically oriented psychotherapists. These tend to be younger psychologists (36% below age 40 compared to about 24% of the total survey population) and are somewhat more likely to be women (51%) versus 43% in our total population.

Graduate Training

Forty-seven percent of respondents received their graduate training in New York state. The other states with a large representation (4% to 7% of the total population) were California, Massachusetts, Michigan, Illinois, and Pennsylvania (see Table 4.2). Comparing the 1980 with the 1987 survey data as to the area in which members live, there seems to be a small shift away from the New York area (57% to 51%) toward New England, the mountain states, and the Illinois–Michigan–Ohio region.

TABLE 4.2
Geographical Location of Graduate and Postgraduate Training
1987 Survey

Geographical Location	Postgraduate		Graduate	
	N	%	N	%
New York	304	68	268	47
California	35	8	39	7
Massachusetts	17	4	38	7
Michigan	10	2	33	6
Illinois	14	3	29	5
Pennsylvania	14	3	20	4
Florida	2	0	14	2
New Jersey	3	1	13	2
Ohio	2	0	12	2
Tennessee	0	0	10	2
Maryland	1	0	10	2
D.C.	5	1	1	0
Connecticut	6	1	11	2
Colorado	6	1	7	1
Kansas	7	2	2	0
Washington	9	2	10	2
Other	16	4	53	9

The vast majority of psychologist-psychoanalysts received PhD degrees (see Table 4.3). Most graduate degrees (about 75%) were in clinical psychology, followed by counseling and school psychology (see Table 4.3).

Geographic Area

Half of the Division 39 members reside in the New York–New Jersey–Pennsylvania area. Three quarters received their postdoctoral training in the mid-Atlantic region (see Table 4.2). The other main training sites were California, Illinois, Michigan, and Massachusetts (see Table 4.2).

Psychoanalytic Training

Of the 50 postgraduate psychoanalytic training institutes reported, 15 are located in the New York area. Respondents listed 78 facilities where they received training in psychoanalysis and we grouped these into three categories: (a) institutes, regardless of orientation, which had "psychoanalytic" in their titles, or that we knew offered psychoanalytic training (see Table 4.4); (b) hospital programs, offering psychoanalytic training; and (c) other programs, which includes family and group therapy institutes, university sponsored mini-programs, and

TABLE 4.3
Graduate Training—Type of Degree and Major Field
(1988 Division 39 Membership and 1980 and 1987 Survey)

Type of Degree	Survey (1980)	Division 39 (1988)	Survey (1987)
PhD	91%	89.1%	94.0%
EdD	4	4.7	3.7
PsyD	0	2.8	2.3
MA	2	3.5	0
Other	3	0.0	0.0
Major Field			
Clinical psychology	No data	72.6%	73.0%
Counseling psychology	No data	9.5	10.6
Education/School psychology	No data	9.9	9.8
Developmental psychology	No data	3.5	3.2
Experimental psychology	No data	2.0	1.3
Social psychology	No data	2.5	2.1

TABLE 4.4
Graduates of Postgraduate Psychoanalytic Training Institutes
(1980 and 1987 Surveys)

	Survey '80		Survey '87	
Institute	N	%	N	%
*NYU Postdoctoral Program	31	22.6	84	19
*NPAP	27	19.7	28	6
*WA White	25	18.2	45	10
*Post Graduate Center for MH	23	16.8	42	9
*Adelphi	15	10.9	33	7
*Alfred Adler	2	1.5	2	0
Chicago Institute for PA	2	1.5	5	1
Institute for Study of PT	2	1.5	1	0
Jungian Analysts	2	1.5	5	1
*NY Center for PA Training	2	1.5	8	2
*Freudian Society	2	1.5	6	1
*Washington Square Institute	2	1.5	3	1
Topeka PA Institute	2	1.5	3	1
*Karen Horney Institute	0	0	11	2
Boston Psychoanalytic Institute	0	0	8	2
Colorado Center for PT and PA	0	0	6	1
*IPTAR	0	0	7	2
Los Angeles Institute for PA Studies	0	0	7	2
Menninger	0	0	6	1
*Westchester Center for PA	0	0	12	3
*Institute for Contemporary PT	0	0	8	2
Other	0	0	32	27

*New York area institutes

mental health and psychotherapy training institutes. Among the 78 facilities there were 50 analytic institutes, 10 hospital programs, and 18 others. The NYU Post-doctoral Program, where 84 of the respondents (19% of the sample) received their analytic training (representing about one quarter of those who have graduated this program) produced the largest number of analysts. Second was the William Alanson White Institute with 45 graduates (10%), and close behind was the Post Graduate Center for Mental Health with 42 graduates (9%). Fourth was the Adelphi University program with 33 graduates (7%). Twenty-eight of the respondents were NPAP graduates (6%). The Karen Horney Institute and the Westchester Center for Psychoanalysis were next in number trained. All of these training programs are in the New York area. These seven (out of 78 programs) trained 53% of the respondents who are practicing as psychoanalysts.

About 75% of the respondents (448) graduated from postdoctoral training programs. In 1980, 51% were graduates of postgraduate psychoanalytic training programs, 35% were in training and 13% had no specific training. In the 1987 survey, 7 of 8 respondents were graduates of, or in training at, an analytic institute. In 1980 there were 9 training institutes in New York (now 15), and 24 others throughout the country (now at least 35).

Personal Analysis

Ninety-five percent of the 1987 respondents had been in analysis for 3 or more years, with 29% having been in analysis for more than 8 years (see Table 4.5).

With respect to frequency, analysis varied from one to six times a week. To summarize; 18% of the respondents reported being in analysis once or twice a week, 41% three times a week, and 41% four or five times a week.

Multiple Analyses

Another issue that was addressed by the 1980 survey, but was not included in the current study, is multiple analyses. Meisels and O'Dell found that 68% of respondents had been in treatment more than once. The authors noted that two out of three of their respondents had at least two analyses and that there was a one in three chance that the analysand would seek yet a third treatment. It is clear from the 1987 survey responses that many respondents had more than one analyst and we speculate that multiple analyses (including being in analyses with analysts of differing theoretical persuasions) is the rule.

Supervision

In the 1987 survey, the median number of years of postdoctoral supervision was 4.9; 56% of respondents spend more than 5 years in supervision, some up to 20 years. The mode was 4 years (see Table 4.5). The modes and medians

TABLE 4.5
Length of Time Reported in Analysis/Therapy and in Supervision
(1980 and 1987 Surveys)

Length of Time	% in Analysis/Therapy		% in Supervision	
	1980 Survey	1987 Survey	1980 Survey	1987 Survey
0–299 hrs	11	—	—	—
0–2 yrs	—	5	—	12
0–100 hrs	—	—	9.5	10.1
300–599 hrs	25	—	—	—
3–4 yrs	—	17	—	32
101–200 hrs	—	—	23.0	20.1
600–899 hrs	26	—	—	—
5–6 yrs	—	28	—	30
201–300 hrs	—	—	32.4	27.0
900–1,199 hrs	18	—	—	—
7–8 yrs	—	21	—	14
301–400 hrs	—	—	12.3	17.9
1,200–1,499 hrs	6	—	—	—
9–10 yrs	—	13	—	8
401–500 hrs	—	—	7.9	10.8
1,500+ hrs	14	—	—	—
11+ yrs	—	16	—	4
501+ hrs	—	—	15.4	7.3

were 200 hours or 4 years and 250 hours or 5 years, respectively. In comparison, the 1980 median was 200–250 hours. The 1987 psychologist-psychoanalyst respondents may have accumulated more supervisory hours than reported by their 1980 counterparts. With respect to numbers of supervisors we only have data from the 1987 survey where the average is four.

CURRENT PRACTICE

In 1980, 76% of the respondents indicated that they did analysis, 23% did not (presumably doing therapy), and 1% did not treat patients. The distinction between being an analyst and being a therapist in the 1987 study generally was in accord with the 1980 ratio, with about 80% identifying themselves as analysts and 20% as therapists.

Clinical Practices

According to the 1987 survey, the mean number of patients seen weekly was 18.1. One quarter of the respondents see 10 or fewer patients, and one quarter see 20 or more (see Table 4.6). More than 94% of psychologist-psychoanalyst

TABLE 4.6
Number of Patients Seen by Respondents (1987)

Individual Treatment Number of Patients	Number/Cumulative % of Respondents
1–5	7/7
6–10	17/24
11–15	26/50
16–20	18/68
21–25	14/82
26–30	9/91
31–35	4/95
36–40	2/97
41–45	1/98
46–50 +	2/100
Mean—17.1	Median—15.2

respondents see some patients once or twice a week, almost 60% see patients three times a week and about one third (32%) of the respondents see patients four or more times a week (see Table 4.7).

Of our average caseload of 18 patients, 9 (50%) are seen once a week, 4 are seen twice a week, about 2 patients are seen three times a week, and 3 patients are seen four or more times a week. Of those psychologists seeing patients three times a week, about 70% see only one or two at this frequency. Of those psychologists seeing patients five or more times a week, more than half (22) see only one such patient, although 25% (10) see five patients five or more times a week.

Other Modalities

One third of the respondents work with groups. Forty-five percent work with families. Two thirds work with couples.

TABLE 4.7
Frequency Per Week Individual Patients Are Seen

Frequency per Week	Mean	Median	No Respondents	% Respondents
1X	10.6	8.8	503	94.2
2X	4.6	4.2	506	94.8
3X	2.9	2.1	317	59.4
4X	2.3	1.7	131	24.5
5X or more	2.7	1.4	41	7.7

Supervision

There has been a marked increase in the percentage of respondents who supervise (43% in 1980 to 57% in 1987) and those who teach (41% in 1980 and
48% in 1987).

THEORETICAL ORIENTATION

There were 14 theoretical orientations with about half of the respondents listing only one. The three largest categories were Freudian (34%), Interpersonal
(17%), and Object Relations (16%), together totaling two thirds (67%) of the
responses (not respondents), of which there were 846 (many respondents listed multiple orientations; see Table 4.8).

The 1980 survey also noted multiple theoretical listings and, using the first
orientation mentioned for each respondent, the authors found that Freudian accounted for 34%, Interpersonal for 11%, and Object Relations for 9% (see Table 4.8). The 1987 data also show about one third of the responses (34%) to
be Freudian but there was an increase in the frequency of both Object Relations and Interpersonal perspectives. There has been a decrease in the listing
of ego psychology and neo-Freudian orientations and an increase in those listing Modern Freudian, self-psychology, and eclectic (see Table 4.8), almost one
of five respondents indicating eclectic as a, or the core orientation.

In an issue devoted to articles about the relationship between personality
and theoretical orientation, Steiner (1978), who conducted a survey of 30 therapists in Essex County, New Jersey, remarked that the primary influence underlying selection of theoretical orientation was one's therapist. Secondary
influences were course work and practical experience, and supervisors had the
least influence. Cummings and Lucchese (1979) concluded, "emergence of an
orientation, albeit a complex process, is one given to the whims of fate." As
Herron (1979) suggested when we embark upon our psychoanalytic careers we
at first search for the truth, and afterwards for the truest truth, then, after a
number of years and by dint of accumulated experience and wisdom, it occurs
to us that there are many truths—so we choose the truth which suits us best.

Almost half (46%) of the respondents regarded their postdoctoral analytic
training institutes as Freudian in orientation. About 16% regarded their institutes as interpersonal and 8% of the respondents each considered their institutes to be either object relational or eclectic. The respective percentages for
one's own analysis were 43% Freudian, 19% Interpersonal, 11% Object Relations, and 10% Modern Freudian. For supervisors, figures were 40% Freudians, 18% Interpersonal, and 14% Object Relations.

Almost half the female respondents (49%) indicated Object Relations as their
theoretical orientation, a finding that certainly should have implications for future

TABLE 4.8
Theoretical Orientation: Comparison of 1980 and 1987 Surveys

Orientation	1980 N	1980 %	1987 N	1987 % Responses	1987 % Respondents	1987 Orientation	1987 N	1987 %
Freudian	100	34.2	292	34.5	57.9	Freudian only	132	22.3
Ego Psychology	35	12.0	37	4.4	7.3	Interpersonal only	81	13.7
Interpersonal	33	11.3	145	17.1	28.8	Object Relations only	51	8.6
Object Relations	27	9.2	135	16.0	26.8			
Neo-Freudian	15	5.1	9	1.1	1.8	Freudian-Interpersonal	43	7.3
Eclectic	14	4.8	91	10.8	18.1	Freudian-Object Relations	79	13.3
Modern	8	2.7	38	4.5	7.5			
Self (Kohut)	6	2.1	50	5.9	9.9			
Kernberg	5	1.8	—	—	—	Mixed Other	207	34.9
Jung	4	1.4	7	.8	1.4	Total	593	100
Adler	4	1.4	2	.2	.4			
Erikson	3	1.0	—	—	—	Interpersonal only plus	124	21.0
Mahler	3	1.0	—	—	—	Freudian-Interpersonal		
Grenson	3	1.0	—	—	—			
Developmental	—	—	7	.8	1.4	Object-Relations only plus	130	21.9
Existential	—	—	6	.7	1.2	Freudian Object Relations		
Psychotherapy	—	—	5	.6	1.0			
Horney	—	—	5	.6	1.0			
Gestalt	—	—	1	.1	.2			
Behavior	—	—	1	.1	.2			
Contemporary	—	—	1	.1	.2			
Other	32	11.0	14	1.7	2.8			

training, considering that only 8% of the institutes were regarded as offering Object Relations training. For Freudian and Interpersonal orientations, there were more men than women (65% and 61% respectively).

About 70% of those considering themselves to be Freudian and 66% of those labeling themselves as adherents of Object Relations reside in the mid-Atlantic region, 84% of the Interpersonalists are located there with only 16% practicing elsewhere in the country.

Theoretical Orientation and Analytic Practice

Inspection of Table 4.9 reveals few surprises except that a sizeable portion of those who identify themselves as only Freudian report a once, twice, or three times a week analysis, most in the latter category. Most Interpersonalists (59%) report a three times a week analysis. Of the Object Relationists 37% indicate a four or five times a week analysis as compared to 56% of the Freudians and 16% of the Interpersonalists. Thirty-six percent of those listing Freudian and other orientations, or just other orientations, were also in analysis four or five times a week (see Table 4.9).

Theoretical Orientation and Orientation of Supervisors

Table 4.10 shows that somewhat more than half of those analysts who identify themselves as Freudian (54%) have seen Freudian supervisors only. About 39.5% of those respondents who deem themselves to be Interpersonal in orientation have seen supervisors who are also Interpersonalists and 1% see supervisors whose orientation is Object Relations. Of the latter group of analysts, 11% consult supervisors who are Freudian only, 5% consult supervisors who are Interpersonal and 17% consult those with an Object Relations orientation, although 21% of the Object Relations psychologists also report seeing Freudian–Object Relations supervisors. About one third (31%) of the "mixed other" group had supervisors of "mixed" orientations.

TABLE 4.9
Own Theoretical Orientation and Weekly Frequency in Analysis

	1X		*2X*		*3X*		*4X*		*5X*	
Orientation	N	%	N	%	N	%	N	%	N	%
Freudian only	6	50	9	24.3	40	40	43	61.4	29	87.9
Interpersonal only	3	25	17	46.0	45	45	13	18.6	0	0
Object Relations only	3	25	11	29.7	16	15	14	20.0	4	12.1
Total	12	100	37	100	101	100	70	100	33	100
Other	9		92		129		86		19	

TABLE 4.10
Own Theoretical Orientation and Supervisors' Theoretical Orientation

	Supervisor Orientation									
	Freudian Only		Interpersonal Only		Object Relations Only		Others		Totals	
Own Orientation	N	%	N	%	N	%	N	%	N	%
Freudian only	72	54.5	1	0.8	5	3.8	54	10.9	132	22.3
Interpersonal only	9	11.1	32	39.5	1	1.3	39	48.1	81	13.7
Object Relations only	6	11.8	3	5.9	9	17.6	33	64.7	51	8.6
Others	103	31.3	29	8.8	11	3.3	186	56.5	329	55.5
Total	190	32	65	11	26	4.4	312	52.6	593	100

Theoretical Orientation and Orientation of One's Analyst

The relationships between one's own orientation and one's own analyst seems even more direct. About 93% of those regarding themselves as Freudian have Freudian analysts, 81% of Interpersonally identified psychologists have Interpersonal analysts. Only 35% of Object Relations psychologists have Object Relations analysts, whereas another 38% chose Freudian analysts and 25% have Interpersonal analysts (see Table 4.11), but it should be noted that Object Relations as a delineated orientation is a relatively recent phenomenon and there are fewer analysts who define themselves as such.

Of all the analysts seen by the respondents, regardless of their own orientations, 43% are characterized as Freudian. About one fifth of the respondents—17%—choose Interpersonal analysts, and 6% choose Object Relations analysts. The remainder—one third (32%)—saw analysts of other or of several

TABLE 4.11
Own Theoretical Orientation and Analysts' Theoretical Orientation

	Analysts' Orientation									
	Freudian Only		Interpersonal Only		Object Relations Only		Others		Totals	
Own Orientation	N	%	N	%	N	%	N	%	N	%
Freudian only	89	93.7	5	5.3	1	1.0	37	28.0	132	22.3
Interpersonal only	7	12.1	47	81.0	4	6.9	23	28.4	81	13.7
Object Relations only	12	38.7	8	25.8	11	35.5	20	39.2	51	8.6
Other	150	45.6	44	13.4	22	6.7	113	34.3	329	55.5
Total	258	43.5	104	17.5	38	6.4	193	32.5	593	100

TABLE 4.12
How Many of Your Patients Do You Consider Psychoanalytic

# Patients	N	%	# Patients	N	%	# Patients	N	%	# Patients	N	%
1	21	7.4	6	16	5.7	11	3	1.1	16–20	17	6.0
2	49	17.4	7	18	6.4	12	15	5.3	21–25	9	3.0
3	38	13.5	8	16	5.7	13	5	1.7	26–28	2	0.0
4	24	8.5	9	14	5.0	14	4	1.4			
5	18	6.4	10	20	7.1	15	8	2.7			

persuasions. Less than half (44%) of the respondents identify themselves as being exclusively of one of the three major theoretical orientations.

Number of Psychoanalytic Cases

Although there is no comparable data in the 1980 survey or anywhere else that we could discover, the 1987 respondents consider one of three patients to be psychoanalytic (see Table 4.12). This inference was drawn from the observation that the median respondent reported about 15 patients and considers 5 to be psychoanalytic. On the other hand, 25% of respondents judge that 10 or more of their patients are psychoanalytic. Among Freudians 62% regard between one and five of their patients to be psychoanalytic. Interpersonalists and Object Relations psychologists tend to regard a higher portion of their patient load as psychoanalytic (see Table 4.13).

Definition of Psychoanalytic Treatment

We made an attempt to clarify this controversial issue by asking the respondents to list their criteria for defining a psychoanalytic situation (see Appendix A). The responses were categorized in a twofold paradigm, relegating certain

TABLE 4.13
Own Theoretical Orientation and Number of Patients Considered Psychoanalytic

	Number of Psychoanalytic Patients									
	1–2		3–5		6–10		11–28		Totals	
Own Orientation	N	%	N	%	N	%	N	%	N	%
Freudian only	17	24.6	26	37.7	16	23.2	10	14.5	69	32.7
Interpersonal and Freudian Interpersonal	8	12.7	17	27.0	25	39.7	13	20.6	63	29.9
Object Relations and Freudian Object Relations	21	26.6	16	20.3	24	30.4	18	22.8	79	37.4
Totals	46	27.8	59	28.0	65	30.8	41	19.4	211	100

TABLE 4.14
Technique and Theory Criteria for Defining
a Psychotherapy Situation as Psychoanalytic

Technique	N	% of Respondents	Theory	N	% of Respondents
Couch	133	33.3	Transference	283	61.7
Frequency	254	55.3	Counter-Transference	18	3.9
Free Association	110	24.0	Trans. Counter-Trans.	29	6.3
Abstinence	33	7.2	Unconscious	89	19.4
Neutrality	45	9.8	Genetic Reconstruction	35	7.6
Delay of Gratification	7	1.5	Resistance	120	26.1
Interpretation	74	16.1	Other Theory	22	4.8
Dream Interpretation	87	19.0	Diagnosis	34	7.4
Length of Session	10	2.2	Psychological-Mindedness	38	8.3
Length of Analysis	26	5.7	Character Change	36	7.8
Depth of Analysis	62	13.5			
Other	42	9.1			

questionnaire responses into a technique category and others into a theoretical category. Technique refers to frequency, use of the couch, dream interpretation, abstinence, neutrality, and so on. Theoretical refers to responses such as use of transference, countertransference, genetic reconstruction, resistance, and so on. There was a variation in the number of responses each respondent gave, ranging from one to six. The data reported (see Table 4.14) reflect the percentage of respondents who listed the various criteria.

Most frequently mentioned in the technique category were frequency (55%), use of the couch (33%), free association (24%), use of dreams (19%) and interpretation (16%). Neutrality and abstinence were cited by 9% and 7%, respectively. In the theory category, 61% of the respondents thought that transference analysis was significant, followed by resistance analysis (26%). The only other criterion mentioned by a relatively large number of respondents focuses on unconscious processes (19%). Genetic reconstruction, diagnosis, psychological-mindedness, and character change were listed by 7% to 8% of the respondents. With the current emphasis on countertransference, it was surprising that only 10% listed countertransference or transference–countertransference as salient features of the analytic situation.

Table 4.15 shows that 62% of Freudian respondents and 61% of Object Relations respondents indicated that frequency was a criterial factor, but only 40% of Interpersonalists did. Likewise, 43% and 35% of Freudian and Object Relations respondents, respectively, mentioned use of the couch as a defining characteristic of the analytic setting, but only 17% of Interpersonalists did.

It is also noteworthy that in most other dimensions such glaring differences did not appear. For example, with respect to abstinence and neutrality, use of

TABLE 4.15

Technique and Theory Criteria for Defining a Psychotherapy Situation
as Psychoanalytic and Own Theoretical Orientation

Criteria	Freudian		Interpersonal		Object Relations	
	N	%	N	%	N	%
Technique						
Couch	116	43.1	22	17.5	43	35.5
Frequency	169	62.8	51	40.5	74	61.2
Free association	79	29.4	28	22.2	26	21.5
Abstinence	29	10.8	12	9.5	6	5.0
Neutrality	33	12.3	11	8.7	12	9.9
Delay of gratification	9	3.3	1	0.8	3	2.5
Interpretation	38	14.1	17	13.5	19	15.7
Dream interpretation	54	20.1	35	27.8	14	11.6
Length of sessions	8	3.0	3	2.4	4	3.3
Length of analysis	25	9.3	7	5.6	4	3.3
Depth of analysis	44	16.4	14	11.1	18	14.9
Other	33	12.3	7	5.6	11	9.1
Theory						
Transference	162	60.2	81	64.3	74	61.2
Countertransference	2	0.7	9	7.1	6	5.0
Trans–Countertrans.	151	5.6	11	8.7	6	5.0
Unconscious	45	16.7	23	18.3	23	19.0
Genetic reconstruction	17	6.3	16	12.7	9	7.4
Resistance	66	24.5	34	27.0	29	24.0
Other theory	8	3.0	7	5.6	8	6.6
Diagnosis	23	8.6	6	4.8	8	6.6
Psychological mindedness	17	6.3	12	9.5	10	8.3
Character change	15	5.6	14	11.1	7	5.8

interpretation, free association, transference, resistance, and the unconscious, there do not seem to be any significant differences among the three orientations. A higher percentage of the Interpersonalists list countertransference than do Freudians or Object Relationists (15% vs. 6% and 9%, respectively) and more Freudians consider diagnosis to be important than do either Interpersonalists or Object Relationists, but all are low figures. Surprisingly, 27% of the Interpersonalists regard dream interpretation as a valid criterion, whereas only 20% of the Freudians and 11% of the Object Relationists do. Also surprising is the finding that 12% of the Interpersonalists listed genetic reconstruction, whereas only 6% and 7% of Freudians and Object Relations advocates did.

The 1980 survey asked a similar question: ''What three areas of psychoanalytic theory and/or technique are most important to you? (see Table 3.24). Transference (linked to countertransference) was the most frequently mentioned item.

CRITERIA FOR TRAINING IN PSYCHOANALYSIS

Personal Analysis

Table 4.16 asks the question, "should the candidate have previous analysis?" About 43% thought it should be mandatory, 40% thought of it as desirable, and 17% considered it to be optional. The median number of sessions per week suggested was 2.5, indicating a real split between those who advocate a once or twice frequency as sufficient and those who insist on three or more sessions a week. Only 15% of the respondents thought that one's personal analysis should entail four or more sessions a week.

Should the candidate have postdoctoral therapy experience? About 42% said this should be mandatory, 39% felt it would be desirable, and 19% thought it should be optional. The median time span would be slightly less than 2 years.

TABLE 4.16
Admission Criteria for Psychoanalytic Training

Specialty Area		N	%
Counseling	Yes	278	87.4
	No	40	12.6
School	Yes	224	74.7
	No	76	25.3
NP, Develop.	Yes	283	79.5
	No	73	20.5
Social, Experimental	Yes	333	71.8
	No	131	28.2
Previous Personal Analysis			
Mandatory		175	42.7
Desirable		164	40.0
Optional		71	17.3
Previous Analysis (Frequency) per Week			
1X		89	22.9
2X		107	27.5
3X		132	33.9
4X		51	13.1
5X		10	2.6
Postdoctoral Therapy Experience			
Mandatory		185	42.1
Desirable		171	39.0
Optional		83	18.9
Postdoctoral Experience			
1 yrs.		32	11.6
2 yrs.		147	53.1
3 yrs.		40	14.4
4 yrs.		24	8.7
5 yrs.		34	12.3

TABLE 4.17
Training Analysis Requirements

Training Analysis	N	%
Concurrent with Program		
Yes	326	88.3
No	43	11.7
Entire Time in Program		
Yes	102	17.2
If not, No. of Years		
1	44	14.4
2	95	31.0
3	104	34.0
4	47	15.4
5	16	5.2
Frequency per Week		
1X	10	2.9
2X	68	20.1
3X	156	46.0
4X	81	23.9
5X	24	7.1

Should additional analysis be concurrent with training (see Table 4.17)? Eighty-nine percent said yes, and 17% said it should continue for the entire time the candidate is in the program. An additional training analysis should be for about 2½ years (median), should involve about 300 hours (median), and should take place three times a week (median).

About one half of the respondents (48%) thought that the training analyst should be a graduate of a recognized psychoanalytic training program and should have various years of additional clinical experience; 50% thought 5 years was suitable, another 33% thought 10 years was needed. Only 12% thought the training analyst should have varying years of experience, but did not have to be a graduate of a recognized training program. Only 10% of the respondents indicated that the training analyst needed to be a graduate of a program in the same orientation as the candidate.

Supervision

Considering suggestions for psychoanalytic supervision (see Table 4.18), a requirement of 4 years was the mode, 3.6 the median. With regard to hours, the results were parallel in that the mode was 200 (or 4 years). The minimum number of supervisors was three (mode), although 30% thought it should be four. Three of every five respondents (61%) said that 50 hours per supervisor was sufficient, but the remainder (39%) thought 100 hours or more would be desirable.

TABLE 4.18
Training Requirements for Supervision

Supervision	N	%
Number of years		
1	27	8.4
2	37	11.5
3	87	27.1
4	134	41.7
5	28	8.7
6	6	1.9
8	1	0.3
9	1	0.3
Number of supervisors		
1	1	2.4
2	109	24.2
3	191	42.4
4	139	30.9
Minimum hours per supervisors		
40–50	274	61.0
80–100	113	25.2
More	62	13.8
Frequency per week patient should be seen		
1	21	4.2
2	111	22.2
3	222	44.3
4	123	24.6
5	24	4.8
Years patients should be seen		
1	13	4.4
2	99	33.6
3	132	44.7
4	48	16.3
5	3	1.0

How many hours per week should candidates see patients? About one quarter of the respondents (26%) said once or twice, 44% said three times a week, and 29% said patients should be seen four or more times a week. Almost two thirds of the respondents (62%) specified that patients should be seen for three or more years by candidates.

Curriculum

In response to a question regarding what types of courses should be taught (see Table 4.19), most respondents agreed on clinical case presentations (95%), technique (93%), and transference–countertransference (93%). Eighty-eight percent would want courses in dreams, 74% would like courses in symbolic

TABLE 4.19
Curriculum Requirements

Courses Should Include:	N	%
Clinical case presentation	462	95.3
Technical	451	93.0
Transference–Countertransference	449	92.6
Dreams	427	88.0
Symbolic communication	361	74.4
Development	329	67.8
Clinical entities	289	59.6
History	280	57.7
Metapsychology	256	52.8
Other	213	43.9
Minimum No. of Courses		
8–12	109	29.5
12–16	87	23.6
16–20	166	45.0
More	7	1.9

communication, about 68% want courses in development with fewer choosing clinical entities, history, and metapsychology. How should courses be taught? The vast majority favored small group seminars (94%), with lecture (55%) second. Concerning the number of courses or years of training required, 45% of respondents suggested 16 to 20 courses or 4 years (45%). However, 29% of the respondents thought that 8 to 12 courses or 2 years would be sufficient, whereas 23% chose 12 to 16 courses or 3 years, a surprising number (more than half) opting for less than a 4-year training program. A required sequence of courses was preferred by 69% of the respondents.

The Diplomate

The questionnaire included a few queries about criteria for admission for an ABPP examination in psychoanalysis. Should one be a graduate of an analytic institute? Fifty-seven percent said yes. Should someone obtaining equivalent training in a noninstitute setting where institute training is not available be admitted for possible ABPP diplomating? The response was 64% yes, but only 54% were in the affirmative where institute training was available but not sought. What about having postinstitute experience? About 58% of the respondents thought 2 or 3 years should be the criterion for admission (see Table 4.20). As in 1980, when Meisels and O'Dell noted the intense feeling of the membership regarding certification, there is still a wide divergence of thought about who should be considered as a psychoanalyst and about the diplomating process.

TABLE 4.20
ABPP Requirements

Candidate Should be Graduate of Institute	N	%
Yes	200	57.3
No	149	42.7
Have Equivalent Training		
Yes	230	64.4
No	127	35.6
Have Equivalent Training Where Institute Training Is Available		
Yes	156	54.0
No	133	46.0
Have X Years of Post Institute Experience		
1	15	9.0
2	57	34.3
3	40	24.1
4	10	6.0
5	41	24.7
more	3	1.8

CONCLUSIONS

How do we resolve such issues? Freud recommended talking, claiming that civilization was invented by the first people who hurled words, rather than spears. We think the results of this survey communicate a wide domain of agreement among psychologist-psychoanalysts. For all the diversity in theory and in practice, there is strong agreement about what analysts should know and how institutes should teach.

REFERENCES

Cummings, N. A. & Lucchese, G. (1978). Adoption of a psychological orientation: The role of the inadvertent. *Psychotherapy: Theory, Research and Practice, 15*, 323–328.

Herron, W. G. (1978). The therapists' choice of a theory of psychotherapy. *Psychotherapy: Theory, Research and Practice, 15*, 396–401.

Steiner, G. (1978). A survey to identify factors in therapists' selection of a therapeutic orientation. *Psychotherapy: Theory, Research and Practice, 15*, 371–374.

APPENDIX A

SURVEY OF PSYCHOANALYTIC TRAINING AND PRACTICE

I. Background and Practice

A. Age _____ Sex M _____ F _____ How long practicing as a PsA: _____ years

B. *Graduate Training:*
School: _____ City and State _____
Psy D: 19 _____ PhD.: 19 _____ Ed D: 19 _____ Other degree (Specify) _____: 19_____
In what discipline (i.e., clinical, counseling, school, etc.) _____

C. *Post Graduate Training:*
Institute: _____ City and State _____
Date(s): _____ Certificate/Degree: 19 _____
Orientation _____
If not graduate, courses taken?
Number _____ Where _____

D. *Personal Analysis:*
From 19_____ to 19_____ total years _____
Frequency per week: _____ x
Orientation of your PsA:
(essentially Freudian, interpersonal, object relations, Gestalt, Kleinian, Jungian, Adlerian, Modern Freudian, self psychology, existential, other (specify) _____

E. *Psychoanalytic Supervision:* Years _____ Approximate hours _____
Number of supervisors _____
Orientation(s) _____

F. *Current Practice:*
Total No. of individual treatment patients _____
No. of patients in individual treatment seen 1x _____ 2x _____ 3x _____
4x _____ more x _____ a week
Do you work with groups: Yes _____ No _____
Do you work with families: Yes _____ No _____
Do you work with couples: Yes _____ No _____
Are you involved in teaching PsA Yes _____ No _____
or in supervising PsA Yes _____ No _____
How would you characterize your own psychoanalytic orientation _____
Of your individual patients, how many would you consider to be psychoanalytic patients? _____
Briefly, indicate your (technical) criteria for defining a psychotherapy situation as "psychoanalysis"
1. _____
2. _____
3. _____
4. _____
5. _____
Of what other APA Divisions are you a member?
List: _____
Of what Division 39 sections are you a member?
I _____ II _____ III _____ IV _____ V _____

II. Training Standards

In your opinion what would constitute minimum standards for training as a psychoanalyst?

A. *Admission Criteria for Psychoanalytic Training*
Should candidate from one or more professional specialities be admitted:

Clinical only   Yes _____   No _____
Counseling   Yes _____   No _____
School   Yes _____   No _____

Should candidates from newly emerging areas seeking specialty status be admitted (e.g., neuropsychology, developmental/applied). Yes _____ No _____
Should candidates from other academic specialties (e.g. social, experimental, developmental) be admitted. Yes _____ No _____ If so, which? _____
Should candidate have previous personal analysis?
mandatory _____ desirable _____ optional _____
If yes, minimum hours required _____ frequency _____ x per week
Should the candidate have post doctoral therapy experience?:
mandatory _____ desirable _____ optional _____
How many years? 1 _____ 2 _____ 3 _____ 4 _____ or more _____

B. *Training Analysis:*
Should additional analysis be concurrent with training: Yes _____ No _____
If yes, then for the entire time in program _____ or for specified no. of years:
1 _____ 2 _____ 3 _____ 4 _____ or more _____
Minimum hours required _____
Frequency (sessions per week) _____

C. *Training Analyst:* Analyst should be: (check one or more)
a) Graduate of a recognized psychoanalytic training program
b) Have _____ (no. of) years of psychoanalytic experience but not necessarily be a graduate of a recognized psychoanalytic training program
c) Be a graduate of a recognized psychoanalytic training program and have _____ (no. of) additional years of experience
d) Be a graduate of a recognized psychoanalytic training program in the particular orientation of which the candidate is being trained
e) Other (please specify)

D. *Psychoanalytic Supervision:*
No. of years/hours required: ____ /____
No. of supervisors: 1 _____ 2 _____ 3 _____ 4 _____ more _____
Minimum no. of hours per supervisor: 40–50 _____ 80–100 _____ more _____
Minimum no. of patients to be seen for graduation: no. _____
Minimum no. of hours per week patients to be seen for graduation:
1 _____ 2 _____ 3 _____ 4 _____ more _____
Minimum no. of years patients to be seen for graduation:
1 _____ 2 _____ 3 _____ 4 _____ more _____
Should more than one supervisor be consulted if patient load is more than
1 _____ 2 _____ 3 _____ 4 _____ more _____ not necessary _____

E. *Curriculum:* Which courses should be included:
a) Development ____ b) Metapsychology ____ c) Clinical entities ____
d) History ____ e) Clinical case presentations ____ f) Dreams ____ g) Transference-countertransference ____ h) Symbolic Communication ____ i) Technique ____
j) Other courses (Specify): _____
How should courses be taught: a) Lecture _____ b) small group seminar _____

c) experimental _____ d) tutorial (independent study) _____ (check one or more)
Comments: _____
_____

Should there be a minimum no. of courses required:
a) for formal training (at a recognized institute): Yes _____ No _____
If so, how many: 8–12 or 2 yrs ____ 12–16 or 3 yrs ____ 16–20 or 4 yrs ____ more ____
b) for informal training: Yes _____ No _____; if so, how many:
8 _____ 12 _____ 16 _____ more _____

F. *Other requirements:* (for formal training at institutes)
Should there be a theoretical/clinical/paper/presentation as a graduation requirement?
Yes _____ No _____
Should there be a prescribed course sequence? Yes _____ No _____
Are there other psychoanalytic training requirements you deem essential?
Specify _____
_____

G. *Criteria for Admission for ABPP examination in PsA*
a) Graduation from an analytic institute Yes _____ Not necessarily _____
Specify _____
b) Obtaining "equivalent" psychoanalytic training in a non institute setting where institute training is not available
Yes _____ No _____ Where institute training *is* available?
Yes _____ No _____
c) Additional years of post-institute experience: none _____
1 _____ 2 _____ 3 _____ 4 _____ 5 _____ more _____
d) Other (Specify): _____
_____
_____

II

The Work of Committees

If the number and achievements of committees is an indication of the potency of an organization, then Division 39 has been seminal indeed. Generally, our committees have operated autonomously, and the great amount of work accomplished has been a function of the initiatives of the chairs and the requirements of the task at hand. We have been fortunate to have attracted a large number of devoted members who have been stalwart in developing and enlarging the Division's functions, activities, and productivity. The five major achievements of our committee structure may be summarized as follows:

- The development of an effective Publication Committee that has expended great effort in providing the Division with a journal, a journal of abstracts, a newsletter, and a forthcoming book series.
- The Program Committee, for running the annual Spring Meeting of the Division, one of the major annual psychoanalytic conventions held in the United States.
- The Qualifications Committee and the Division Board for developing criteria for qualification in psychoanalysis, this in the face of enormous diversity in the membership (see chapters 2, 10, 22, and 26).
- The Local Chapter Committee, for laying the foundation for the chapter movement;
- The Division Board, serving as a Committee of the Whole, in supporting, financing, championing, advocating, and overseeing the GAPPP lawsuit.

Although these five committees appear as the brightest stars in our firmament, there have been other stellar committees as well. The finance committee and the work of the treasurer is an enormous, time-consuming task, as is the production of our Directory, editing of our Journal and Newsletter, or planning the Division 39 presentations at the annual APA convention. There have been numerous ad hoc committees that have come and gone, and sometimes prodigious amounts of work have produced meager results. (Who now remembers the inordinate efforts about APA Peer Review in the mid-1980s?)

What follows are chapters detailing the functioning of committees.

The History of the Publications Committee

Robert J. Marshall

The following history was compiled from the author's personal experience as Chairperson of the Publications Committee from March 1986 through August 1991, perusal of minutes and publications, and discussions with persons who experienced the early, formative years of the Division.

The history traces the development of personnel, structure, and function particularly in regard to: the journal, *Psychoanalytic Psychology*; the newsletter, *Psychologist-Psychoanalyst*; the abstract service, *PsycSCAN: Psychoanalysis*; and the proposed book series.

The Beginning

In August 1979, pro-tem President Reuben Fine appointed Marvin Daniels and Robert Lane Co-Chairs of the Publications Committee and Co-Editors of the Newsletter. The Publications Committee later evolved out of the Journal Committee, chaired by Max Rosenbaum in 1979 and Sydney Smith in 1980, with Helen Block Lewis and Martin Mayman as members appointed by Gordon Derner.

Once the Board of Directors decided that a journal would be supported by the Division, the committee was disbanded and Robert C. Lane appointed Sydney Smith, Chair of the Publications Committee. As of March 25, 1982, no guidelines for the functioning of the Publications Committee had evolved. Sydney Smith requested guidance from APA and President Lane put the Publications Committee, "in charge of all publications (of the Division). The Newsletter and Journal should function autonomously, but they do come under the aegis of the Publications Committee" (July 6, 1982 letter to S. Smith).

THE JOURNAL: *PSYCHOANALYTIC PSYCHOLOGY*

On March 2, 1982, the Board of Directors approved the publication of *Psychoanalytic Psychology* to be published by Lawrence Erlbaum Associates. President Lane appointed Helen Block Lewis editor for a 5-year-term on May 16, 1982. Lewis (1982) commented, "The journal hopes to represent the best of both clinical and experimental work in psychoanalytic psychology" (p.15). The goal of the journal was, "to serve as a focal point for the publication of original articles that broaden and enhance the interaction between psychoanalysis and psychology. It represents an effort by psychologists to contribute to the development of psychoanalysis and the discipline of psychology as a whole" (Annual report, May 23, 1982). The Publication and Communications Board of the APA approved the proposal to publish a journal in June 1982. A call for papers brought in a flood of fine material. A system of blind peer review soon produced a rejection rate of more than 50% of proffered manuscripts.

On October 27, 1983, Helen Block Lewis reported highly positive prospects for the newly published journal. In particular, she cited her experience with Lawrence Erlbaum as being uniformly excellent in developing the new journal.

When Sydney Smith retired as Chair of the Publications Committee, Nathan Stockhamer appointed Arthur H. Feiner in August 1985. Bringing his experience as an author and editor of *Contemporary Psychoanalysis*, Feiner formed a committee consisting of Sydney J. Blatt, Darlene Ehrenberg, Nicholas P. Dellis, Dorothy Evans Holmes, Rita Frankiel, Gloria Friedman, Zanvil Liff, and Ruth Formanek. Ex-officio members were Edward S. Penzer, Irving Solomon, Eric Singer, Helen Golden, and Helen Block Lewis.

In March 1986, Feiner resigned and President Stockhamer appointed me as Chairperson. Using the already formed committee including Feiner, I began to draw up the organizational structure and function of the Publications Committee. In 1987, Murray Meisels, newly elected Division President, restructured the Committee. Ehrenberg, Frankiel, Friedman, Holmes, Dellis, and Blatt left the Committee, and Laura Barbanel, Arthur H. Feiner, and Elaine Caruth were added to the Committee. In practice, as chair, I continued to define the boundaries and powers of the Publications Committee.

In May 1986, guided by the organization of the APA Publications and Communications Board and the APA Rules of Council, the structure and function of the Publications Committee was spelled out on paper and submitted to the Board of Directors as follows.

Structure

The Committee shall consist of nine members of the Division. The Committee shall include the Treasurer of the Division and the Editors of the publications as ex-officio members. At least one member shall be knowledgeable in the technical aspects of journal management, printing, and production.

The Chairperson of the Committee shall be designated by the President of the Division in consultation with the Board of Directors. The Chairperson, in turn, and with the approval of the President, shall select the members of the Committee in order to maintain at least nine members with staggered terms of 6 years. In the selection of Committee members, every effort will be made to provide optimal representations of the Division in terms of affiliation, location, and section. Issues arising for a vote shall be resolved by a one person-one vote majority decision.

Purposes

In general, the Publications Committee is an analog of the Publications and Communications Board (P&C) of the APA and is oriented by the guidelines for the P&C Board as they appear in the APA Bylaws and Rules of Council of 1984. For example, Article X, Section 8 states that the function of the P&C Board is "to make recommendations on current and innovative plans and policies on the acquisition, management, initiation, or discontinuance of journals, separates, and related publications and information services." Moreover, Article V, Section 9 states, "The management and editing of such journals shall be supervised by the Publications and Communications Board. . . ."

It shall be a function of the Committee to recommend new Editors of Division publications to the Division President. The Committee shall set up a search committee 2 years prior to the expiration of an editor's term as outlined by Eichorn and VandenBos (1985).

According to the bylaws of Division 39, "The Publications Committee shall develop and monitor the publications of the Division." The key word "monitor" is taken to mean observing, supervising, and recommending. These policies must be carefully delineated from the areas accorded to the editors of publications. The following are considered to be within the recommending purview of the Committee:

1. number of pages of the publication;
2. number of editorial pages;
3. expenses of editors;

4. honoraria for editors;
5. journal subscription prices;
6. fiscal, managerial, production, and contractual agreements;
7. a shift from commercial to self-publishing;
8. measurement and evaluation of the degree to which publications are meeting the professional needs of the membership;
9. promotions of sales of publications;
10. liaison with PsycINFO; and
11. conduct of search for editors.

As founding editor of *Psychoanalytic Psychology*, Helen Block Lewis established standards of dedication, integrity, and excellence that served to evolve a respected professional journal over a short period of time. She was especially mindful of minorities, gender, and age. Some felt that Lewis leaned too heavily toward the psychological side of the psychoanalytic–psychological spectrum, whereas most believed that she truly represented the vast interests of the Division membership.

As a consequence of the unexpected, tragic illness and death of Helen Block Lewis in January 1987, several steps were taken. Gerald Stechler was appointed as interim editor. As a testament to Lewis' capable stewardship, Stechler found it easy to maintain the journal during his term. The backlog that did build up resulted in the journal size being increased from 96 to 128 pages.

A search Committee was formed in January 1987 to find an editor for *Psychoanalytic Psychology*. The Committee, consisting of Helen Gediman, Sydney Smith, Arthur H. Feiner, Joseph Masling, and Co-chaired by Zanvil Liff and me, selected Bertram J. Cohler from an impressive array of 50 candidates, many of whom had very superior qualifications in editorship, publication, scholarship, psychoanalytic training, and clinical practice.

Bertram J. Cohler received his PhD in Clinical Psychology in 1967. Among his considerable honors and scholarships, he has held the William Rainey Harper Chair at the University of Chicago since 1978. Among his varied clinical positions and consultantships, Cohler had been Director of the Sonia Shankman Orthogenic School and graduated from the Institute of Psychoanalysis of Chicago. At the time of his selection, Cohler was the author of more than 60 articles and chapters and was on the editorial board of four journals.

The process of the search was described by Marshall (1988, p. 26). Cohler assumed his duties in April 1987 for a term of 6 years. Cohler (1989) further elaborated on his wish to reflect the professional interests of the Division, and his reliance on extensive blind peer review of submitted articles. The Publications Committee is pleased to see positions explicitly taken, along with open critique and rebuttal rather than snide and surreptitious corridor comments.

The Publications Committee issued a charge to the Editor of *Psychoanalytic Psychology* in November 1988: The purpose of *Psychoanalytic Psychology* is to explore the interface between psychology and psychoanalysis. A central and unclear issue regards the definition of psychoanalysis and psychoanalytic psychology. The boundaries are not always clear and agreed on. The editor of the Journal and to some extent the editor of the Newsletter implicitly define the province of psychoanalytic psychology each time they publish or reject an article. Too narrow a definition steers the journal in a parochial or cultist direction. On the other hand, an excessively expansive definition may result in making the journal indistinguishable from other journals.

For the present, we are left with the position that the editors, in consultation with their staff, are prime determiners of the boundaries of psychoanalytic psychology and perhaps of the term psychoanalysis. The editors are significant fence makers and gatekeepers of our divisional realm. Therefore, we recommend that the editors create and maintain dialogues with and within the membership in order to continually sharpen the definitions.

Besides determining whether a manuscript is in the province of psychoanalytic psychology, the editors are charged with determining the quality of the article. How are the merits of a manuscript judged? In part, the answer is a function of the judgment of the editor in accepting or rejecting a manuscript for review. Another part of the answer is inherent in the judgment of the editor in his selection of associate editors and the editor's decision about which reviewer(s) to use for a given manuscript. A third part of the answer rests in the judgment of the designated reviewers as they appraise the paper. A fourth part lies in dialogue among reviewers, editor, and author. A fifth and implicit judgment is made by the audience of membership readers. If the opinions of Division members play a role in determining the quality of an article, there should be a feedback system whereby the editor continually and directly is in touch with the judgments of the members. In time, a questionnaire will be distributed to members to poll them on their evaluations of the publications. Until that time, we encourage a free and open dialogue among editors, authors, and readers.

The editor is also charged with publishing manuscripts that are representative of the diverse interests of the Division. "Without yielding to changing political and theoretical tides, the editor has the task of choosing articles that reflect the interests of sections, chapters, researchers, developmentalists, theoreticians, clinicians, among others. Given this diversity and spectrum of interests that the editor must address, we also hope that the readership will help create the dialogue that we value" (Memorandum to Publications Committee, May 1988).

From time to time the issue arises concerning the Journal having the right of first refusal of papers presented at Division meetings. Advocates suggest that this system would assure the Journal of the selection of the best papers. Opponents declare that such a system would frighten away persons who wanted their papers published in other journals. It is of interest that Helen Block Lewis, as she assumed the editorship of the Journal, requested the right of the first refusal for all papers at Division 39 meetings.

There have been unending negotiations with publishers, including the APA, who are interested in publishing our journal. At each juncture, LEA Publishers manages to stay competitive with other offers in terms of distribution, publicity, support systems for the editor, and quality of publishing. At the same time, we have been constantly considering the merits of self-publishing.

The Publications Committee believes that the journal holds a unique and significant position in the professional literature of psychoanalysis because it is successfully pursuing its goal of publishing those papers that explore and integrate the interface of the rich fields of psychology and psychoanalysis. Some measure of the journal's value is that institutional subscriptions increased from 41 to 117. Also, we note that individual subscriptions have remained at about 125 over 7 years, and that these individual subscribers tend to become Division members.

THE NEWSLETTERS:
PSYCHOLOGIST-PSYCHOANALYST,
ROUND ROBIN, AND *FORUM*

After several stimulating editions of the newsletter pioneered by Marvin Daniels and Robert C. Lane, Lane appointed Edward S. Penzer and Irving Solomon as coeditors in August 1982. Penzer initiated a column entitled "Psychomedia" that abstracted articles from news media that impacted on psychologist-psychoanalysts. With a very limited budget and in a very short period of time, Penzer and Solomon found the way to produce a newsletter with magazine-quality paper, editing, proofreading, printing, and mailings. In addition, they enlisted the services of a world renowned calligrapher who crafted a magnificent cover page. Adding Bernice Barker, Susan Hans, and Burt Grossman as editorial assistants, there was increased coverage of Board meetings and conventions.

Penzer and Solomon attempted to report faithfully and judiciously the conflicts that frequently arose during this formative era. "As Division 39 progressed and became larger, the confusion over disparate concepts of what is psychoanalysis and who is a psychoanalyst mounted. The Division was not only attempting to be a cohesive coterie, but also to become a unified scientific and professional group of psychologists from various psychoanalytic perspectives. We warned of divisiveness in the Division. Unfortunately, at times, diversity prevailed apparently fostered by an expanding sectionalism" (E. Penzer, personal communication, February 6, 1991). While reporting the increasing sectionalism, Penzer and Solomon, personally, were adamantly opposed to separate section newsletters. They believed that all news of the Division belonged to all members in one newsletter. They argued that not only were the additional expense and duplicated efforts wasteful, but that the lack of mutually shared information could lead to increased disharmony. As a consequence of the potential proliferation of newsletters and with the possibility that each section would have its own newsletter, Penzer and Solomon resigned the editorship of the Division newsletter after they published the Winter 1985–1986 issue.

In 1985, Helen Golden founded *The Round Robin*, the newsletter of Section I, the Section of Psychologist–Psychoanalyst Practitioners. Named after Otto Fenichel's own round robin letters, *Die Roundbriefe*, circulated in the 1930s, Section I's newsletter has been under the able editorship of Mary Libbey since 1986. Judith Hanlon served as Associate Editor from 1987 through 1988 while Gil Katz served as Associate Editor from 1987 to 1990 and has been Co-Editor since 1990.

Its mailing list extending 200 past its 400 Section membership, *The Round Robin* owes its popularity to its unique format. It is a timely report with a wide spectrum of topics including psychoanalytic perspectives on popular films, economics, computers, and current American culture. Four lively and regularly featured columns developed by Mary Libbey and her editors are: "Distinguished Member's Commentary"; "Psychoanalysis and Contemporary Life"; "New York, New York"; and "Being an Analyst in Different Places," the latter initiated by Helen Golden.

Another newsletter, *The Forum*, was born in early 1988 when Donald Milman, second president of Section V, asked Susan Hans to give voice to the fledgling section of Division 39. After a modest beginning, the newsletter took on a professional appearance and has continued to grow in format, size, and content. A feature of the newsletter is a book review with accompanying interview of the author. Spyros Orfanos, assisted by Mark Gerald, assumed editorship for the spring 1991 issue.

The Round Robin and *Forum* were the first two section newsletters of note. Actually, some local chapters had started newsletters in the early 1980s, and, by now most sections and local chapters publish newsletters.

As a consequence of the resignation of Penzer and Solomon as Editors of *The Psychologist–Psychoanalyst*, new coeditors Eric Singer, Peter Buirski, and Arnold Schneider were appointed by Nathan Stockhamer on March 19, 1986. The new Editorial Board worked diligently to maintain the integrity and tradition of the newsletter and report the news of the Division. However, the coeditors resigned as of January 1, 1988. Penzer was slated to reassume the editorship of the newsletter, but in December, 1987, he withdrew from that position. A Search Committee chaired by Robert J. Marshall and consisting of Helen Gediman, Zanvil Liff, Sydney Smith, Arthur H. Feiner, and J. Masling recommended to the Board that James W. Barron be appointed as Editor of the *Psychologist–Psychoanalyst* for 6 years.

Barron was selected over several qualified applicants for his background in

English literature, his editorial experience with two newsletters, and an extremely active commitment to psychoanalytic psychology. Under Barron's direction, the newsletter has expanded in many directions. He has consistently filled 40- to 48-page editions with news that has attracted the attention of increasing numbers of readers. The newsletter has been published in collaboration with APA since 1989.

PSYCSCAN

On March 2, 1981, in the first recorded contact between Division 39 and Psyc-SCAN, Toni Bernay and Dorothy W. Cantor, Co-Chairs of the Public Information Committee requested *PsycSCAN: Clinical Psychology* to include eight psychoanalytic journals in its search. A psychoanalytic abstract was the vision of Dr. Lane since the formation of the Division, and when he became president he invited Dr. Susan Knapp of PsycINFO to address the Board of Directors. Dr. Lane then appointed Dr. Edward Penzer and Ruth Formanek Co-chairpersons of a committee on psychoanalytic abstracts to work with the APA Publications Board to bring this dream to reality.

PsycSCAN: Psychoanalysis is now a publication co-sponsored by APA PsycIN-FO and Division 39, and has rapidly developed into a valuable research and informational tool. The APA P&C Board voted to establish *PsycSCAN: Psychoanalysis* in 1986. First published in January 1987, *PsycSCAN: Psychoanalysis* now abstracts journals, journal articles, and has incorporated a book and book chapter abstract service. Beside psychoanalysis, scholars in all fields adjacent to psychoanalysis have found increasing merit in this publication.

BOOKS AND THE BOOK SERIES

We observed the collaboration between Division 39 and the APA in publishing a centennial book describing the interface of psychology and psychoanalysis over 100 years. That book coedited by James Barron, Morris Eagle, and David Wolitsky, was published in time for the centennial celebration.

Another centennial book, *A History of the Division of Psychoanalysis in the American Psychological Association* (this book) will shortly be published.

In less than 12 years, the Publications Committee of Division 39 evolved from a Journal Committee to a growing organization that has been continuously defining its structure and function. As the Division has grown, the Committee, in trying to sense the informational and communicational needs of the Division membership, developed and monitored several types of publications that have major impact on the psychoanalytic world. Recognizing the growing interest in the interface of psychology and psychoanalysis, the Publications Committee seeks to foster continued growth of meaningful and quality publications.

ACKNOWLEDGMENTS

I am especially grateful to the following persons who have contributed information and/or helped clarify the manuscript: Laura Barbanel, Ester S. Buchholz, Helen Golden, Susan Hans, Robert C. Lane, Mary Libbey, and Edward S. Penzer.

I want to express my appreciation to the many persons who evolved themselves in the growth of the Publications Committee, especially the current members who provided a steady source of good counsel, technical expertise, and emotional support: Laura Barbanel, Elaine Caruth, Robert C. Lane, David Mac Beth Moss, Donnel B. Stern, Jane Tucker, Joseph A. Turkel; ex-officio—James W. Barron, Bertram J. Cohler, Helen K. Golden, and Bertram P. Karon.

ADDENDUM

In August 1991, Charles Spezzano, PhD, was appointed by Jonathan Slavin as Chair of the Publications Committee. A Division book series is being launched. The first title will be, *The Handbook of Psychoanalytic Psychology*. It will be aimed at graduate students and younger psychologists who seek an accessible and authoritative account of the history and current status of psychoanalysis. A survey of Division members regarding the journal is underway.

REFERENCES

Eichorn, D. H., & VandenBos, G. R. (1985). Dissemination of scientific professional knowledge: Journal publication within the APA. *American Psychologist, 40,* 1309–1316.

Cohler, B. J. (1989). Editorial policy of *Psychoanalytic Psychology. Psychologist Psychoanalyst, 9*(1), 4–6.

Marshall, R. J. (1988). Selecting editors of Division 39 publications. *Psychologist Psychoanalyst, 8*(5), 26.

Psychoanalytic Psychology, *1988–1992*

Bertram J. Cohler

Psychoanalytic Psychology is very much a mirror of the achievements and problems of the Division as a whole. The journal reflects both the successes and the enduring tensions that characterize both contemporary psychoanalysis and also our Division within APA. Problems confronting the discipline include the very definition of psychoanalysis, the relationship between psychoanalysis and psychotherapy, and the nature of scholarly inquiry concerning both study of process and outcome within psychoanalysis and also the means for applying psychoanalytic concepts and methods to the study of personal experience and social life. Over the course of the past half-century since Freud's death, important contributions to psychoanalytic theory and technique considerably expanded the scope of psychoanalytic intervention and inquiry.

DIVISION 39 AND THE DIVERSITY
OF PSYCHOANALYTIC INQUIRY

This expanding scope of psychoanalysis raised questions regarding both the theory of clinical technique and the nature of psychoanalytic contributions to disciplines ranging from psychology itself to history and the humanities. The journal of the Division should reflect both the diversity of inquiry and also the multiple perspectives on theory and technique that reflects the Division as a whole. The journal should also facilitate both clinical and empirical inquiry regarding process and outcome of psychoanalytic interventions, and should provide a means for fostering scholarly inquiry regarding clinical and theoretical aspects of psychoanalysis within human sciences and the humanities.

A major issue for the Division and its journal concerns the distinctive nature of the psychologist-psychoanalyst as contrasted with the medical-psychoanalyst. From the outset, the Division struggled to define a scholarly publication that would reflect the distinctive identity of the psychologist as psychoanalyst. The issue is compounded by the quite different definitions of the psychologist-psychoanalyst found across the Division. My goal as Editor has been to provide a forum in which this diversity of definitions would be represented in scholarly contributions. To a large extent, the Division was founded by psychologists trained on the East Coast in traditional psychoanalytic centers. Consistent with intellectual perspectives characterizing these established psychoanalytic training centers, initial submissions to the journal focused on issues of clinical process and technique. Over time, with increased interest in the work of the Division among psychologists not necessarily having been able to obtain formal psychoanalytic education, submissions to the journal increasingly concerned the application of psychoanalytic perspectives to study the psychotherapy process and outcome, as well as empirical clinical and personality research inspired by psychodynamic perspectives.

The Editorial Board tried to establish an identity for the journal that would differentiate it from medical psychoanalytic journals. The question of what is explicitly psychoanalytic about our Division is complex: the definition of what constitutes psychoanalytic inquiry and practice depends very much on whom one talks to. Division 39 appears to have at least three distinctive groups with explicit positions on these issues: those psychologists formally or informally educated as psychoanalysts, and identifying with particular psychoanalytic traditions, including contemporary Freudian perspectives, ego-psychological and interpersonal-humanistic perspectives; psychologists interested in psychoanalysis, who are largely involved in private practice of eclectic psychodynamic psychotherapy, and a small number of humanistically educated scholars of psychoanalysis, and investigators involved in systematic empirical research. The first group, formally educated psychologist-psychoanalysts, are most interested in papers discussing clinical psychoanalytic theory, whereas those whose careers are focused around psychotherapy seek expanded publication for case reports regarding innovations, problems, and solutions in the psychodynamically oriented psychotherapy of the more troubled patient (borderline personality disorders, narcissistic personality disorders, etc.). The third group seeks to read and report on empirical research in the area of psychodynamic psychotherapy and psychoanalysis, or to use psychoanalytic approaches in fields ranging from criticism to history.

As Division membership increased, and as psychoanalysis has become ever more diverse in both training possibilities and intellectual perspectives, the question of the intellectual focus of the journal has become an ever more pressing issue. Although a significant readership remains interested in a more traditional psychoanalytic publication similar to that of other leading psychoanalytic scholarly journals, another group of Division members seeks a journal focused more explicitly on issues particularly relevant to psychodynamic clinical psychology. This tension reflects the larger tension within the Division between those members practicing psychoanalysis as a specialty, and those members who joined the Division in the spirit of an interest group, and who are principally identified with an eclectic psychodynamic perspective regarding issues more traditionally of interest to clinical psychology.

EDITORIAL REVIEW AND PUBLICATION

Upon assuming the position of Editor, I created an Editorial Board composed of members of each of the extant sections of the Division. I was particularly concerned that the Editorial Board have a mix of men and women reflecting both geographical diversity and also reflecting the diversity of intellectual position and mode of practice that comprises the Division as a whole. The goal of the Editorial Board is to consult with the Editor regarding the merit of submissions for publication, to advise on matters of editorial policy, and to solicit possible contributions to the journal.

Whereas the Editorial Board participates actively in the review of submitted manuscripts, the volume of submissions requires the use of ad hoc editorial reviewers. Initially, all manuscripts were sent to members of the Editorial Board for review. However, with increased rate of submissions and increasing diversity of manuscripts, it soon became clear that we would have to reach beyond the Editorial Board to our colleagues both within and without the Division. Increased reliance upon reviewers from both the Division and from medical psychoanalysis has added to the vitality of the editorial review process and involved both medical and nonmedical colleagues in constructive dialogue regarding psychoanalytic theory and practice. Over the past several years, at a time of increased tension between APsaA and our own Division, the fact that colleagues from each group could join in a discussion of scholarly issues related to psychoanalytic theory and practice showed the possibility of greater collaboration more generally in psychoanalytic scholarship and practice. Involving medical colleagues in the review process also served to bring the journal to the attention of a larger group of colleagues as readers and as authors. I am particularly pleased that medical colleagues regard our journal as a particularly desirable place of publication.

Although reviewers' comments are advisory, the decision to accept a manuscript in which two or three reviewers concur in recommending that the paper not be accepted in its present form represents a difficult decision for the editor. In those infrequent instances in which there is disagreement among reviewers, we may send a manuscript for additional editorial review, ar ask members of the Editorial Board to weigh the several critiques and recommend a solution regarding publication. It is important for the Editor to make use of peer review and to avoid arbitrary decisions regarding publication, even if this means additional workload for some reviewers and that some less strong manuscripts might be sent out for editorial review. In the first place, reviewers are selected who are both familiar with work reported from a particular psychoanalytic persuasion or using a particular method of study. In the second place, reviewers are encouraged to be maximally helpful to the author in suggesting areas in which revisions might strengthen a manuscript. Generally, papers are accepted conditional on making suggested revisions or at least responding to editorial critiques regarding issues posed by reviewers.

Peer review is essential for a journal precisely because it provides an opportunity for colleagues to offer suggestions regarding the manner in which papers might further be strengthened in order to realize the greatest possible contribution. It is not assumed that authors will blindly follow all suggestions for revision. Rather, editorial review should be seen as another source of guidance and assistance in creating a manuscript designed to make a significant contribution to the field. It is certainly acceptable for an author to reject reviewers' suggestions and to show that the reviewer either misunderstood the author's point or was simply ill-informed regarding the issues. We do expect that authors will respond in good faith to reviewers' suggestions. The Editor and members of the Editorial Board then undertake the difficult decision of deciding on the adequacy of the author's response to editorial readers' inquiries and suggestions for revising and strengthening a manuscript.

Since 1983, when the first manuscripts were received by the journal to the present time, the number of manuscripts received by the journal has grown from 41 over the course of the year to 98 in the immediately past year. The number of pages published has grown accordingly from 356 to 576 in the past year. Consistent with APA policy, all manuscripts are sent out for blind review, and each manuscript is reviewed by at least two, and usually three reviewers. Manuscripts are only sent to reviewers who would be expected to be positive regarding the intellectual orientation of the author, the particular approach to clinical technique, or the particular method of study. Reviewers are asked to evaluate a paper in terms of its likely contribution to the field, including whether the reviewer would cite the paper in the reviewer's own writing and research.

The success of the journal depends on the adequacy of this matching process of author and reviewer, and on the cooperation of reviewers in providing timely return of manuscripts. Over the course of the past few years, several hundred colleagues have been involved in the peer review process; the names of all reviewers are printed in the last issue of each volume of the journal. We also now routinely include biographical information on each author whose paper is published in that issue of the journal in a section on "Notes on Contributors."

EDITORIAL INNOVATIONS
IN *PSYCHOANALYTIC PSYCHOLOGY*

Other changes introduced to accommodate the interests of an increasingly diverse Division membership include sections dedicated to papers on psychoanalytic psychotherapy, an increased effort to solicit empirical research related to study of psychoanalytic intervention and psychodynamic psychotherapy, bibliographies of literature relevant to psychoanalysis, and integrated reviews of the literature in particular areas. Initially, the journal did not include papers in psychoanalytic psychotherapy. The issue of publication of psychoanalytically informed psychotherapy case studies and the publication of empirical research are issues which have proven to be particularly complex. Upon assuming the position of Editor, a number of colleagues, members of the Division and readers of the journal, wrote regarding the problems they had encountered in realizing publication for papers reporting on innovations in psychoanalytic technique. Many of the journals have been reluctant to publish psychodynamically informed papers. While accommodating the interests of the membership, there have actually been relatively few submissions of such papers devoted to psychotherapy and even fewer manuscripts judged by reviewers working in the area of psychodynamic psychotherapy to make a significant contribution.

It has been somewhat difficult to obtain reviews of these psychotherapy papers. As might be expected, divergence of opinion regarding quality psychotherapy manuscripts is greater for psychotherapy manuscripts than for papers reporting systematic findings or papers focused more generally on the theory of technique. Although one reviewer might find a technical innovation helpful, or might find use for the discussion of the resolution of a particular impasse in psychotherapy, another reviewer may find the discussion to be of little value and is not able to recommend publication. We continued to solicit and publish the best manuscripts in the field concerning psychodynamically informed psychotherapy; often reviewer's comments are helpful in revising psychotherapy manuscripts for publication.

It has been particularly difficult to obtain empirical reports for publication. Clearly, one of the major differences between psychologists and others committed to psychoanalytic inquiry is the greater sophistication in the conduct of research within a field in which explicit research training is an integral part of doctoral education. Although we have been particularly committed to publishing research reporting on the psychoanalytic process and outcome, we have not been successful in encouraging a large number of submissions in this area. Increased publication of quality empirical papers remains a goal for the future.

A more difficult decision confronts the Editorial Board regarding publication of papers reporting on the use of projective tests in testing psychodynamic or other personality hypotheses. A number of manuscripts have been submitted documenting the use of scales for coding Rorschach protocols that have psychodynamic names, or which report on personality attributes presumably referring to concepts from ego psychology and other schools of psychoanalytic thought. It is sometimes difficult to determine the nature of the contribution to psychoanalysis as distinct from contributions to the validity of projective tests or of hypotheses based on particular theories of personality. Our criterion has been that the manuscript should make a contribution to psychoanalysis, either as a method useful in testing psychoanalytic propositions or as a tool for measuring process or outcome of psychoanalysis or psychoanalytic psychotherapy. For example, a study of the development of persons with borderline personality disorders would likely be of interest to the readership of our journal, whereas a projective test measure of a concept such as ego-strength, not more fully elaborated in terms of its possible significance for psychoanalytic study, might be most appropriate in a journal devoted to publication in the area of projective tests.

Other innovations introduced within the Journal over the past several years include a section of commentary in which readers respond to previously published papers in the journal (with an opportunity for the author to respond to the commentary), and dedicated issues, including those planned by Section III (women) on psychoanalysis and women, and one planned by Section II (children and adolescents) on child analysis. The journal would like to ultimately be able to publish dedicated issues focusing on the work of each of the sections within the Division. Pages for these dedicated issues are taken from the annual allotment of pages from the publisher, and are at the cost of somewhat greater publication lag time (currently about 8 months following acceptance of a manuscript). Dedicated issues provide an opportunity for in-depth study of a particular controversy within psychoanalysis from diverse perspectives and permit a wider readership to learn of the issues confronting sections within the Division.

Although at least some papers for these dedicated issues may be solicited, all papers are subject to the same editorial scrutiny as other papers submitted to the journal. Further, whereas dedicated issues may have defined editors, the Editorial Board of the journal maintains oversight over the process according to which these papers are selected for dedicated issues. We are particularly concerned that all papers, whether solicited or submitted, be subject to blind editorial review, and that reviewer's comments be considered by all authors of papers accepted for inclusion in the dedicated issue. Reviewers' comments may further strengthen a contribution which the editor soliciting a paper might be more hesitant to suggest. This blind editorial review must extend even to those papers written by the editors of these dedicated issues of the journal.

The journal would also like to include a larger number of papers and symposia accepted for presentation at both the spring meetings and the annual APA conventions. Unfortunately, too many of these papers are never published or are published in journals other than our own Divisional journal. Generally, papers presented orally require additional work prior to formal publication, and authors are not always able to devote time to such revision for publication. Over the past several years, a number of symposia first presented at Division 39 meetings have been published in the journal. Editorial review of the symposia is somewhat complex because we require that each of the contributions to the symposium be judged worthy of publication in its own right, and also that the symposium as a whole make a contribution greater than the sum of the included papers.

Finally, we explored a number of options regarding book reviews. It is difficult to determine the value of book reviews for our readership. There are a number of journals that now specialize in reviews of new books in psychoanalysis and allied fields. Book reviews require pages that could also be devoted to publication of submitted manuscripts. We attempted to identify those few books that are likely to make particularly significant contributions to the field, or which are of particular interest to our readership, and to recruit reviewers with expertise in the area to undertake reviews. In contrast to submitted manuscripts, where we attempt to find the most congenial possible reviewer, we seek book reviewers who have a definite position in the field with regard to the subject matter of the volume. The reviewer is encouraged to make his or her own biases clear in the review. Reviewers are encouraged to report on the author's own goal for the volume and the extent to which this goal has been realized. We have also begun to solicit reviews regarding classics in the field where recent developments might alter a previous understanding of a work, or where the work has become a classic which may either inform or mislead contemporary appreciation of a book.

FUTURE PROBLEMS AND PROSPECTS

As significant as the journal has been in making innovations both in format and coverage within the fields of psychoanalysis and psychotherapy, problems remain to be overcome. The first and most serious concerns the length of time taken by editorial review. The journal depends on a large number of editorial reviewers in order to obtain reviews of manuscripts. Use of multiple reviewers provides an opportunity for authors to obtain considerable assistance in revising manuscripts for publication so that the published paper may make a maximum contribution to the field. Although we are generally successful in obtaining timely reviews, greater promptness on the part of reviewers would lead to a reduction in time between receiving a manuscript and reaching an editorial decision regarding suitability for publication. Particularly in a discipline in which a majority of the readership is involved in practice rather than teaching and writing, finding the time to undertake editorial review sometimes becomes a burden.

The introduction of a formal peer review system has also increased the proportion of papers that are not regarded as appropriate for publication in their present form. In 1984, more than two thirds of all manuscripts were accepted for publication; nearly a decade later, about 30% of papers are accepted for publication. However, whereas more than two thirds of all submitted manuscripts are returned to authors with detailed reviews, when authors choose to resubmit, about two thirds of resubmitted manuscripts are ultimately published, often after additional editorial review and revision. Editorial reviews are generally quite complete; reviewers are asked to discuss the merits of a manuscript and to provide a detailed critique for the author. We also send copies of all reviewers' comments to each reviewer together with the editorial decision regarding the manuscript. Reviewers tell us that they learn a great deal from reading the comments of other reviewers.

Our goal is to provide a sufficiently detailed review that, in the event a paper is not accepted for publication, the author is provided with assistance in revising the paper for publication either in our own journal or elsewhere. Authors do not always realize that they have the option of responding to specific points of criticism by showing that the reviewer either missed the nature of the contribution or was not correct in some specific points of the critique. The Editor and members of the Editorial Board may decide that the author has successfully responded to a critique and that one or more aspects of the paper should remain as they are.

Over the past few years, the journal has been able to return some profit to the Division. However, the Division would clearly profit from a larger institutional subscription base for the journal than has been realized to date. Unfortunately, this is a time of greatly reduced library budgets; it has been difficult to convince college and university libraries to undertake purchase of additional serials at a time when they cannot afford present institutional subscriptions. Further, the clinical content of the journal may discourage some university libraries from subscribing. Although growth in institutional subscription may not be a practical goal at a time when most libraries are being forced to make significant cuts in funds available for journal subscriptions, additional advertising would foster increased profit from the journal with a readership of much the present size and may help to realize the goal of increased revenue for the division. Study of means for realizing increased advertising would directly benefit the membership of the Division and enhance the profit for the Division now being realized from sales of the journal.

PsycSCAN: Psychoanalysis *and*
The Psychologist-Psychoanalyst

Robert C. Lane

PSYCSCAN: PSYCHOANALYSIS

PsycSCAN: Psychoanalysis began publication in 1986, and has been expanded and improved. At the first meeting of the Editorial Board in August 1987, the number of journals abstracted was increased from 27 to 40, and is now over 50. The result was a more comprehensive and valuable survey of the world's literature on psychoanalysis. At the second meeting of the Editorial Board in August 1988, the number of issues was increased from two to four annually. The additional two issues cover selected core terms. There was no increase in the subscription rate for non-39 members, whereas Division 39 members went from $3.75 for two issues to $7.50 for four issues. When books and book chapters became the content of the fourth issue, this necessitated a rise in cost to $10.

The Editorial Board felt that the *SCAN* would not be regarded as a throw-away publication with the addition of an index. The merits of an annual versus a quarterly index were discussed, noting whereas individual subscribers might use a detailed quarterly index, an annual index would be preferred by institutional subscribers, because it would be more useful for systematically reviewing the literature. The Board concluded it would like to have an annual index in the December issue with revised and updated terms. It further agreed that all three types of indexing (subject, author, and title) were needed.

With regard to marketing our *PsycSCAN*, we engaged in exchange advertising, but have not yet initiated any further marketing plan. If *PsycSCAN* is to be marketed to non-U.S. subscribers, the index terms need to be revised and the Table of Contents' categories should be modified to reflect the current research in Europe and other parts of the world. APA's Gary VandenBos suggested that overseas promotion could begin as soon as the Index is added to the *SCAN*. Bertram Cohler felt there was a lack of awareness overseas of the *SCAN*, and recommended the creation of a flier showing *SCAN* journal coverage by language groupings. Promotion at the APsaA convention was also discussed, and it was suggested that a table be set up with free copies and subscription forms.

Several format changes were discussed. It was suggested that because the issues are different (i.e., books and chapters in March, journal-based in June and December, and term-based in September), readers need to have a fuller description in each issue of what will be covered throughout the year. The Board discussed whether it might be possible to list all journal titles and index terms on the second page of each issue. VandenBos said that the "front" presentation could be revised to provide more information on the year's coverage. It was agreed, however, that providing a full listing of terms in this section would be misleading because it would appear to constitute an index.

Additional $1 increases in 1993 and 1994 to cover the cost of the inclusion of the Index, was agreed on. Present circulation is more than 5,000 copies, and we would like to raise it to 10,000.

THE PSYCHOLOGIST-PSYCHOANALYST

Marvin Daniels (deceased) and Robert C. Lane, appointed by Reuben Fine, were the first editors of the newsletter. They were also the first Co-Chairs of the Publication Committee, and gave the newsletter its name, *The Psychologist-Psychoanalyst*. Lane designed the Division's logo. After publishing Volume I (Nos. 1 and 2) and Volume II (No. 1) in 1980 and No. 2 in 1981, Lane assumed the presidency of the Division. Feeling there might be a conflict of interest if president and simultaneously Co-Editor of the newsletter, he removed his name as Co-Editor. However, the newsletter was written on Sundays with both editors participating in the process and contributing to the next three issues (Summer of 1981, Winter of 1982, and Summer of 1982).

At first the newsletter was printed on 8½ by 11 paper and stapled together. It was newsy and contained what was happening in the Division, a president's column, articles and stories the membership submitted, credentials of those seeking office, and summaries of the minutes of the Board of Directors and of papers presented at conventions. The newsletter also contained a section on letters to the editor. Starting with Volume II (No. 1) the format was changed to a book form, and the newsletter was given a name. The cover varied, it could be pictures of outstanding analysts, pictures taken at the Mid-Winter Convention, a theme, or other topics. These three issues had many pictures of the members and the Board of Directors.

When Marvin Daniels accepted a position in Austin, Texas in August 1982, and Lane was to become Past-President of the Division, Lane secured the services of two close friends, Edward S. Penzer and Irving Solomon, to become the new Co-Editors of the newsletter. They improved the newsletter in many ways, making it more professional and less newsy, more magazine-like, and used glossy paper, which improved the appearance giving the newsletter a classy look. Penzer and Solomon published 14 issues including Volume III (Nos. 3 and 4), Volume IV (Nos. 1, 2, 3, and 4), Volume V (Nos. 1, 2, 3, and 4), and Volume VI (Nos. 1, 2, 3, and 4). Their first issue was in the Fall of 1982 and their final issue was the Winter of 1985–1986. They were Co-Editors during the administration of George D. Goldman, Ernest Lawrence, Helen Block Lewis, and Nathan Stockhamer. They instituted the four-issues-a-year policy. There were two issues yearly during the first 2 years, and we were to go to four issues in 1982; we published two issues the year Daniels resigned, and Penzer and Solomon also edited two issues in 1982.

In 1985, Nathan Stockhamer, the seventh president of the Division appointed Eric Singer along with Peter Buirski and Arnold Schneider Co-Editors of the newsletter just prior to his leaving office. They published seven issues, Volume VII (Nos. 1, 2, and 3) and Volume VIII (Nos. 1 and 2, 3 and 4). They were Co-Editors during the administrations of Nathan Stockhamer, Fred Pine, and Murray Meisels.

After Singer, Buirski, and Schneider gave up their editorial responsibilities for the newsletter, Edward S. Penzer was reappointed Editor of the newsletter by a Search Committee. Unfortunately, he could not pursue his appointed function. It was at that time (1988) that James W. Barron was appointed Editor of the *Psychologist-Psychoanalyst,* a position he still holds.

The newsletter under James Barron's editorship has become one of the APA's finest division newsletters. He edited Volumes VIII (Nos. 5, 6, and 7), IX (1, 2, 3, and 4), X (1, 2, 3, and 4) , XI (1, 2, 3, and 4), and XII (1 and 2 to date), and a special supplement in reaction to Desert Storm, *Psychoanalytic Perspectives on War* (Volume XI, Special Supplement, Summer 1991).

Barron rethought the purpose and scope of the newsletter and transformed it into a lively hybrid, incorporating features of both a newsletter and a journal, and publishing brief factual articles and longer reflective essays and commentaries. By actively seeking out contributions from members of sections and local chapters and from participants in the Division's scientific meetings, he significantly expanded coverage of Division activities.

In addition, he felt that the Division needed to look outward to the larger community and not repeat the insularity and elitism that had been the historic hallmarks of medically dominated psychoanalysis in this country. The Division had an opportunity, even a responsibility, to begin to articulate psychoanalytic ideas and their applications in a broad social context. Therefore, the newsletter began to include a variety of articles by prominent psychologist-psychoanalysts on important social issues. Following the war in the Persian Gulf, the newsletter published a special supplement on *Psychoanalytic Perspectives on War.*

The newsletter's robust expansion reflects the growth of the Division. When Barron began as editor, the newsletter averaged 4 to 8 pages. Under his editorship, it grew to an average of 48 to 52 pages, and generated advertising revenue in the range of $5,000 to $6,000 per year.

James Barron achieved what many of us feel was a monumental task, and has done it with grace and dignity. He corresponds with and accommodates all who contact him, and publishes everything of interest to our members. We feel our newsletter, like our journal and abstracts, is among the APA's proudest publications.

8

The Membership Directory

Murray Meisels

It is common for organizations to provide their members with directories, and our Division does so, but in our case it required a full decade for a directory to materialize. The history of this prolonged gestation is as follows: At the 1980 Business Meeting during the annual APA convention—the Division's first APA convention—a motion for a directory was approved by the colleagues in attendance. As Membership Committee Co-Chair, I proceeded to develop ideas and solicit cost estimates, which I presented to the Division Board in the Fall of 1980. A debate then ensued in which a number of Board members argued vehemently against publishing a Directory on the grounds that some psychologists might misuse it to claim qualification in psychoanalysis, or that some librarian might think it a list of actually certified psychoanalysts. Already, it was argued, some individuals were misusing Division membership as a claim to psychoanalytic competency, and so it was incumbent on the Division not to provide any further temptations to irresolute colleagues. On the other side, it was argued—rather weakly—that we had a right to know who we were. The result of this rather one-sided argument was a compromise formation, the 1981 Membership List, which consisted of a geographical listing of members: no addresses, telephone numbers, or affiliations were provided, just names. Thereafter, the issue of a Directory was dropped.

When I became president of the Division in 1987, I appointed Carol A. Butler to chair a Directory Committee. By that time, the emancipation of psychologists from medical domination had greatly advanced and no one voiced concern that we would be acting irresponsibly if we published a Directory. However, in 1987 the Division was confronted with a different issue, that of the controversy between Sections I and V. Even prior to publication of the Directory, an argument developed regarding whether to include section membership alongside the names and addresses of members, lest users of the Directory regard Section I membership as a privileged status. And, after the 1989 Directory was published, this controversy continued since then-President Zanvil A. Liff had written in the Forward that Section I was a practitioner group with "criteria and requirements comparable to international standards for psychoanalysis." Section V bridled at the statement, because it implied that the Section V position was not in accord with international standards.

For the 1991 Directory, with the able Carol Butler still in charge, the controversial statement about international standards was deleted. In addition, President Bertram P. Karon wrote in the Foreword that: "We hope our own members, other mental health professionals, as well as the general public make productive use of this Directory." Our 1980 fear that librarians might make use of our Directory has become a wish.

For comparison purposes, the 1980 Membership List consists of 36 typewritten pages with 1,371 names, whereas the 1991 Directory contains 191 printed pages, a veritable book, of approximately 3,000 members listed alphabetically with addresses, telephone numbers and section memberships, as well as a breakdown by geographical area and a listing of the membership of each section. The expectation is for a new directory every second year, and that the next issue will also contain information about state licensure.

Division 39 Programs: Annual Convention, Midwinter/ Spring Meetings, and Continuing Education Programs 1979–1991

Joanne E. Callan

Since its inclusion as the 39th division of the APA in 1979, the Division of Psychoanalysis (39) demonstrated an energetic commitment to developing and offering professional programs on psychoanalysis and related topics. Each year, the Division's leadership supported quality program offerings at two annual meetings, and, over the years, it also developed a formal Continuing Education (CE) Program, which offered professional workshops in conjunction with the annual meetings. This chapter presents information on the Division's program offerings from 1979 into 1991.

ANNUAL MEETINGS

Division 39, through its two annual meetings, functioned: (a) as a participant–contributor along with other APA divisions in the annual APA Convention; and (b) as the sponsor of what was initially referred to as Division 39 annual Midwinter Meetings and then became known as the annual Spring Meetings. Table 9.1 presents brief descriptions of program sessions and activities offered at annual APA conventions between 1980 and 1991, and Table 9.2 presents information on program offerings at the annual Midwinter/Spring Meetings (note that a shift in title occurred after a Board of Directors decided to hold the annual Division-sponsored meeting in the spring rather than in midwinter).

TABLE 9.1
Division 39 Annual Convention Programs (1980–1991)

Year	Invited Speakers	Presidential Address	Program Chair
1980	Martin Mayman	Reuben Fine	Robert C. Lane
1981	Herbert J. Schlesinger, Rudolf Ekstein	Gordon F. Derner, "The Psychoanalysis of Human Experience: Love, Grief, and Parataxes"	Robert C. Lane
1982	Helen Block Lewis, Sydney R. Smith	Robert C. Lane, "The Language of Dreams"	George Goldman, Joanne E. Callan
1983	Rudolf Ekstein, Sidney J. Blatt, Howard Shevrin, George Mandler, Allan Rosenblatt, Michael Posner	George Goldman, "Psychotherapy and Psychoanalysis: Are the Two So Different"	Ernest S. Lawrence
1984	Robert R. Holt, Jerome L. Singer	Ernest S. Lawrence, "The Object in Intrapsychic Conflict: Strategic and Clinical Considerations"	Helen Block Lewis
1985	Roy Schafer, Jay R. Greenberg, Louis Berger	Helen Block Lewis, "Psychoanalysis as Therapy Today"	Nathan Stockhamer
1986	Erika Fromm, Morris Eagle, Margaret Brenman-Gibson	Nathan Stockhamer, "Psychoanalysis from Any Point of View"	Darlene Bregman-Ehrenberg
1987	Bert Karon, Reuben Fine	Fred Pine	Murray Meisels
1988	Zanvel A. Liff, Bertram J. Cohler	Murray Meisels, "A Critique and Redefinition of Resistance in Psychoanalysis"	Co-Chairs: Zanvel A. Liff, Carol A. Butler, Harold B. Davis
1989	Aldo Carotenuto, Richard M. Jones, Robert C. Lane	Zanvel A. Liff, "On, Off and Beyond the Couch: Fifty Years After Sigmund Freud"	Co-Chairs: Ruth-Jean Eisenbud, Anna S. Leifer, Jerry M. Ritigstein
1990	Kerry Kelly Novick, Jack Novick, Hedda Bolgar, Carol Gilligan	Ruth-Jean Eisenbud, "Ego Dream Transformations During Psychoanalysis"	Bertram P. Karon
1991	Malcom Owen Slavin, Irene Fast, Charles Spezzano	Bertram P. Karon, "The Fear of Understanding Schizophrenia"	Co-Chairs: Maureen Murphy, Jonathan H. Slavin

ANNUAL CONVENTION PROGRAMS

Subsequent to the September 1979 action by the APA Council of Representatives that established a Division on Psychoanalysis as of January 1, 1980, the newly elected Division 39 officers began immediately to develop a professional program for the 1980 APA Convention, the first APA convention in which the Division was eligible to offer its own presentations, symposia, and invited addresses.

Correspondence among Division officers in 1979 and 1980 encouraged one another to promote interest in developing proposals for the Division's 1980

TABLE 9.2
Division 39 Annual Midwinter/Spring Meeting Programs (1980–1991)

Year	Featured Speakers/Events	Program Chair
1980	Presentation: Murray Cohen, Ruth-Jean Eisenbud, Rosalind Gould, Helen Block Lewis and Ernest Prelinger	Chairperson: Reuben Fine
1981	*Special Theme:* Psychoanalysis Today & Tomorrow	Chairperson: Stanley Moldawsky Co-Chairperson: Harriette Kaley
1982	*Special Theme:* "Contributions of Psychologists to Psychoanalytic Practice, Theory, and Research"	Harriette Kaley
1983	Special Presentation by Merton Gill	Co-Chairs: Zanvel Liff, Muriel Fox
1984	Presidential Forum: Ernest Lawrence	Chairperson: George Goldman, Carol Kaye
1985	President's Address—Helen Block Lewis—"Some Thoughts about the Process of Becoming a Psychologist: ANNO 1985"	Ava L. Siegler
1986	Presidential Address: Nathan Stockhamer—"Sex Without Drive"	Arlene Kramer Richards
1987	*Special Meeting:* "Anti-Trust Suit vs. the American Psychoanalytic Association"	Darlene Bregman-Ehrenberg Co-Chair: Carol S. Michaels
1988	*Invited Address:* Jay Greenberg—"Toward a 'New' Oedipus Complex" *Invited Address:* Rudolf Ekstein—"The Life Cycle of Transitional Objects and their Meaning in its Psychoanalytic Situation"	Co-Chairs: Samuel Gerson Maureen Murphy
1989	*Invited Address:* "Generational Consciousness"— Christopher Bollas, British Psychoanalytic Society *Special Presentations:* Distinguished Scientific Award: Bruno Bettleheim—"How I came to Psychoanalysis"	Co-Chairs: James W. Barron Jonathan H. Slavin
1990	*Special Award:* Division 39 Distinguished Scientific Award: "Beyond Phenomenology: The Illusion of a Separate, Integral Self"—Stephen A. Mitchell *Invited Address:* Section II Sponsored Speakers: "Some comments on Masochism and its Delusion of Omnipotence from the Developmental Perspective"—Jack Novick and Kerry Kelly Novick *Invited Speaker:* Section I Sponsored Speaker: "On the Nature of the Physical: Some Comments on the Trade Structure in the Analytic Exchange"—André Green	Co-Chairs: Gil A. Katz Mary Libbey
1991	*Special Invited Presentation:* "Psychoanalysis Transplanted to America"—John E. Gedo *Invited Address:* Cognition and Motivation in recent Psychoanalytic Theory"—Nigel Mackay	Oliver J. B. Kerner

convention program. Division 39's first president, Reuben Fine, wrote (December 19, 1979) to the new Program Committee urging them "to stimulate worthwhile contributions either from yourself or persons you know." As President, he wrote again to the Committee on January 7, 1980, pointing out the importance of the first impression to the APA and the psychological community "as to what the new Division of Psychoanalysis will present that is unique, stimulating, and on a high level," and challenged Committee members to come to the January 12, 1980 meeting with program ideas.

Program Committee meetings were held on January 12, 1980 and on February 16, 1980 to make final decisions on paper presentations and symposia. Attending the January Program Committee meeting chaired by Robert C. Lane and Reuben Fine were: Anna Antonovsky, Henry Bachrach, Albert Berenberg, Leopold Caligor, Kenneth Isaacs, and Stanley Moldawsky. A memorandum from Lane dated March 11, 1980 to those selected to be participants in the 1980 APA Convention in Montreal indicated an expanded Program Committee, adding the following names: Murray Cohen, Ruth-Jean Eisenbud, Rosalind Gould, Helen Block Lewis, and Ernest Prelinger.

The first actual convention program, as reported by Program Co-Chairs Robert C. Lane and Reuben Fine, included 15 papers presented in six sessions (from the 46 submitted); 8 symposia (from 16 submitted); 2 invited addresses, a presidential address, a business meeting, and a social hour. Executive Board Minutes (September 1, 1980) noted the excellence of Lane's work on the 1980 program. In an October 8, 1980, memorandum, Robert C. Lane acknowledged the success of the Division's program at the August 1980 meeting in Montreal and also encouraged Division members to join the 1981 Program Committee.

The 1981 Division 39 convention program included both CE offerings and Hospitality Suite presentations in addition to the 20 hours of regular program offerings, which were divided into eight 2-hour symposia and four paper sessions and included 14 papers. The Hospitality Suite workshops included several presentations. Gordon Derner's Presidential address was titled "The Psychoanalysis of Human Experience: Love, Grief, and Parataxes."

Table 9.3 presents information on the annual APA Convention Programs from 1980 through 1991, noting Division 39's Presidents and Program Chairpersons.

MIDWINTER/SPRING MEETINGS

Division 39 leaders deliberated frequently on options available for holding meetings additional and complementary to those held each year in conjunction with the APA conventions. They considered the nature of business and programmatic content for such meetings as well as member preferences on location, facilities, calendar, length of meeting, cost, and transportation. Division leaders also considered, even debated, whether to hold such additional meetings

TABLE 9.3
Division 39 Annual Conventions (1980-1991)

Year	President	Program Chair	Location
1980	Reuben Fine	Robert C. Lane	Montreal
1981	Gordon F. Derner	Robert C. Lane	Los Angeles
1982	Robert C. Lane	George D. Goldman and Joanne E. Callan	Washington
1983	George D. Goldman	Ernest S. Lawrence	Anaheim
1984	Ernest S. Lawrence	Carol Kaye	Toronto
1985	Helen Block Lewis	Nathan Stockhamer	Los Angeles
1986	Nathan Stockhamer	Darlene Bregman-Ehrenberg	Washington
1987	Fred Pine	Murray Meisels	New York
1988	Murray Meisels	Zanvil A. Liff, Carol A. Butler, and Harold B. Davis	Atlanta
1989	Zanvil A. Liff	Ruth-Jean Eisenbud, Anna S. Leifer, and Jerry M. Ritigstein	New Orleans
1990	Ruth-Jean Eisenbud	Bertram P. Karon	Boston
1991	Bertram P. Karon	Maureen Murphy and Jonathan H. Slavin	San Francisco

independently or to schedule them concurrently, if not collaboratively, with other groups, entering invitations to meet jointly with other APA divisions. Some members thought it would facilitate professional dialogue to meet alongside other groups of professional psychologists, for example, Divisions 12 (Clinical), 29 (Psychotherapy), 42 (psychologists in Independent Practice), and 43 (Family Psychology), and some members saw joint meetings as more economical in time and in dollars. Correspondence (March 24, 1981) from President Gordon F. Derner to Herbert Freudenberger, then President of Division 29, described the advantages and disadvantages of having "Division 39 and Division 29 meetings back-to-back," and correspondence (June 29, 1981) from Derner to Stanley R. Graham indicated that such back-to-back meetings would be studied by Division 39 but would not occur in 1981. Over the years, the content of the Midwinter/Spring Meetings was determined considerably by the Program Committee chairperson in collaboration with the Division president. In the early years, after 1980, the Program Committee often consisted of as many as 10 members, which allowed for broad input regarding program content.

The Division's first three Midwinter Meetings were held outside the United States, the first in Mexico and the next two in Puerto Rico. Planning required considerable effort on the part of Division leaders and outside consultants to arrange meeting and travel accommodations and also to assure compliance with IRS policies. For many reasons, including efforts to meet in conjunction with other groups (even though such collaboration did not actually take place), a decision was made to hold the fourth meeting within the United States, and arrangements were made to hold the 1984 meeting in San Diego, California, at the Hotel Del Coronado.

Among highlights of the first Midwinter Meeting (1982) were a movie about China's mental health facilities, presented in preparation for a 1983 divisional trip to China, and a special address on "Perspectives of Psychoanalytic Practice in Puerto Rico" by Victor Bernal y del Rio. Subsequent reports from some of the 160 participants indicated that they very much enjoyed learning about the history of psychoanalysis in Puerto Rico, about the challenges of practicing psychoanalysis in a smaller population center, and about the presence there of only two PhDs in psychology who had formal training in psychoanalysis.

The theme of the second Midwinter Meeting was "Contributions of Psychologists to Psychoanalysis: Practice, Theory, and Research," and highlights of this meeting, held in Puerto Rico, included four invited presentations (see Table 9.2). As at the first Midwinter Meeting, 160 participants attended the meeting, according to Division records, and the response to the program was highly enthusiastic. The location of the third Midwinter Meeting was a matter of considerable discussion among Division leaders, but a decision was made finally to return to Puerto Rico. A special session at the 1984 Midwinter Meeting was the Memorial Service for Gordon F. Derner. George Goldman chaired this session that honored one of the Division's founding fathers, and others who participated included Ernest Beier, Aaron H. Cantor, and Ernest Lawrence.

The 1985 meeting was scheduled in April and was the first, therefore, to be referred to as an annual Spring Meeting. Held in New York City, the attendance increased to 514 participants representing 15 states. The 1986 meeting was held in February in Mexico under the leadership of Arlene Kramer Richards, and the 1987 meeting returned to an April date, with Darlene Bregman Ehrenberg and Carol Michaels as chairs. At the 1987 meetings, President Fred Pine gave his presidential address on "Motivation, Personality Organization, and the Four Psychologies of Psychoanalysis."

The 1988 meeting was held in San Francisco, Chaired by Samuel Gerson and Maureen Murphy, and the 1989 meeting, whose theme was on "Current Controversies in Psychoanalysis—Theory, Practice, Research, and Training," was held in Boston and chaired by Jonathan H. Slavin and James W. Barron. These two meetings, as with the several preceding ones, included several invited speakers who added considerably to the theme and substance of the spring programs. The 1990 and 1991 Spring Meetings were held in New York and Chicago, respectively, and they, too, were characterized by comprehensive program offerings that included continuing education sessions, business meetings, invited speakers, and awards receptions.

CONTINUING EDUCATION PROGRAMS

The Division's sponsorship of continuing education (CE) programs on psychoanalysis and related topics was considered even before its founding in 1980, and specific continuing education workshops were proposed each year subsequent to the Division's establishment. In response to interest expressed by Division members for opportunities to learn through the presentation of clinical tapes, Milton M. Berger and Max Rosenbaum presented videotape programs at the 1980 Convention. Hospitality Suite presentations and featured contact hours with invited speakers at annual APA conventions were developed partially in response to continuing education interests.

The Division's first action to establish a formal continuing education program, is described in Executive Board Minutes of September 1, 1980, as an approval for a review of a proposed continuing education program to be held at coming meetings in New York City. Early supporters of the Division's efforts to develop and implement a Continuing Education program included the Division's first three presidents, Reuben Fine, Gordon F. Derner, and Robert Lane. Among other Division 39 supporters instrumental in advancing Division 39 CE programs were several members actively involved in established graduate and postgraduate education and training programs: Martin Mayman, Sydney R. Smith, and Ernest S. Lawrence.

In the November 1, 1980 Executive Board meeting, Martin Mayman gave an informal report in which he encouraged Division leaders to begin to conceptualize the continuing education programs. The ensuing discussion focused on whether Division CE programs would be a substitute for institute training or would be separate, independent offerings. After lengthy review, the Board passed a motion to postpone action until the Education and Training Committee could meet, presumably to complete its review. Within the year, however, a practice was initiated whereby the Division's president, with the support of the Executive Board, would appoint a chairperson of a CE Subcommittee that would function somewhat independently even though officially noted as under the umbrella of the Education and Training Committee. The Subcommittee's primary charge was to develop and offer CE workshops.

Martin Mayman was Chair of the CE Subcommittee for the 1982 Annual Spring meeting and for the 1982 APA Convention. CE activities offered at the Spring Meeting were subsumed in the full program. In a review of these first CE activities at the October 25, 1982, Board of Directors meeting, Reuben Fine called for longer and more formalized courses, responding to interest in CE courses. Also noted was the congruence of an ongoing Division 39 CE Program with the Division's commitment to advancing psychoanalysis. Although Division leaders had interest in CE opportunities for Division members, they were particularly interested in developing more formal and intensive psychoanalytic training programs. In discussions on these two different kinds of CE interests, distinctions were drawn between their different purposes and needs. Responding to strong interest in the development of intensive training institutes to educate and train psychologists as psychoanalysts, Division leaders, in the early 1980s, explored with APA's Committee for the Approval of Continuing Education Sponsors ways in which such a training program might garner endorsement from APA's sponsor-approval system. After several years of such exploration, however, leaders concluded that the pursuit of such endorsement might not be practical at that time.

Concurrent with explorations regarding the development of psychoanalytic institutes, the Division began dialogue with APA's Continuing Education Office and the Sponsor-Approval Committee to gain accreditation for its developing CE program. In a 1982 letter from President Robert C. Lane to Martin Mayman, as chairman of the Division's Education and Training Committee and also its Continuing Education Subcommittee Chair, Lane alluded to earlier unsuccessful efforts by the Division; however, he pointed also to the readiness of the Division to garner such approval in this remark: "I am sure this time that we will have no trouble gaining sponsorship approval." In a response dated April 12, 1982, however, APA's Director of Continuing Education, Barbara Hammonds, wrote that, based on a review of Division 39's most recent self-study and application for accreditation, the Sponsor Approval Committee had deferred action. She noted several criteria and standards on which further information was requested and advised that, if the Division could respond more fully on these points, the submitted response would be reviewed and possible action taken in the Committee's next meeting.

A convincing response to these concerns (e.g., how the evaluation of participant learning in the Division's CE activities was conducted) was forwarded to APA's Sponsor-Approval Committee by Martin Mayman, on behalf of Division 39's Continuing Education Committee that also included Marvin Hyman and Elaine Grimm. On July 15, 1982, correspondence followed from APA to Mayman, advising that the Division's CE program had received full approval for a 1-year-period.

The Division's first continuing education workshops offered under this endorsement by APA's Sponsor-Approval system were held at the 1982 APA Annual Convention on Sunday, August 12, 1982, as described earlier. Martin Mayman and his CE subcommittee were acknowledged by the Division's Board of Directors at its October 24, 1982 meeting. There was again a call for longer and more definitive CE courses, and Reuben Fine supported the further development of CE programs toward this end.

Correspondence from President George D. Goldman, in October, 1982 informed APA's Continuing Education Office that Martin Mayman would continue to serve as Chairman of Division 39's Education and Training Committee and that Muriel Fox would chair the Continuing Education Subcommittee. Fox developed a series of professional presentations with a group of "organizers" for the 1983 Midwinter Meeting, which was held in Puerto Rico on February 27–March 6, 1983.

The practice to connect, even subsume, CE activities with what were first referred to as the Midwinter Meetings but later came to be called the Spring Meetings was followed, off and on. Program Committee Chairs (or Co-Chairs) were influential in determining whether or not, and the extent to which, CE activities were offered in conjunction with both the annual meetings convention. Also, Division presidents and other officers exercised influence over how continuing education was viewed, advanced, and offered. As happens in membership organizations, especially in new ones, the establishment of a particular program and its continuing priority may fluctuate considerably. Division 39 archives indicate that an ongoing Division CE Program endured some ambivalence and some fluctuation in its first years.

Correspondence in 1983 between Martin Mayman and APA's Continuing Education Office indicates that Division 39 decided against reapplying for sponsor-approval status, partially because of structural issues and questions on Division priorities; thus, the initial 1-year approval from APA of Division 39's CE program ended. In 1983, Suzette Finkelstein, however, was appointed to chair Division 39's CE Program Subcommittee, and after offering CE experiences at the Hotel Del Coronado in San Diego in 1984, she corresponded with APA toward reinstating Division 39's approval. The response from the Sponsor-Approval Committee awarded retroactive reapproval of the Division's CE program for a 3-year period extending from 1983 to 1986. In an August 1984 Board of Directors' meeting, Finkelstein reported low attendance at the CE activities, despite efforts to offer attractive CE activities. Records reflect that she also submitted her resignation at that time.

In 1985, after being asked to lead the Division's CE Program, Joanne E. Callan sought to consolidate its sponsor-approval status, by gathering an ad hoc group to develop the next required annual APA report. Its review resulted in a 1-year approval status with specific requirements noted (some of which related to new criteria developed by the Sponsor-Approval Committee). To further sponsor-approval status from APA, the next task was to conduct a more comprehensive self-study that included a memberwide needs assessment survey, thus assuring member-responsive CE activities. Sydney R. Smith and Ernest S. Lawrence, stalwart and loyal subcommittee members for several years, worked with Joanne Callan, as did Mary Ann Houts, all contributing significantly to the survey development and to the larger self-study. APA's CE Office reviewed the 1987 Self-study and awarded full approval for 5 years to the Division's CE Program. The comprehensive nature of the 1987 self-study report and efforts to demonstrate learning acquired by workshop participants were noted with special praise.

Table 9.4 presents Division 39 CE activities from 1980 to 1991. It reflects locations, presidents, program chairpersons, and CE chairpersons for these years, during which time CE activities were offered as either separate but concurrent activities with the annual APA Convention and Midwinter/Spring meetings or subsumed into the larger programmatic offerings.

To advance the Division's CE program and its offerings, Callan recommended in 1987 that the CE Subcommittee be established as an entity apart from, although collaborative with, the Program Committee, asserting that long-term

TABLE 9.4

Division 39 CE/Mid-Winter/Spring Meetings

Year	Place	President	Program Chair	CE Chair
1980	Zihautatano, Mexico	Reuben Fine	Reuben Fine	Martin Mayman
1981	Rio Mar Resort, Puerto Rico	Gordon F. Derner	Stanley Moldawdy, Harrietee W. Kaley	Martin Mayman
1982	Palamas Del Mar, Puerto Rico	Robert C. Lane	Harrietee W. Kaley	Martin Mayman
1983	Hotel Del Coronado, San Diego	George D. Goldman	Zanvel A. Liff, Murriel Fox	Martin Mayman, Suzette Finkelstein
1984	Vista International, New York	Ernest S. Lawrence	Carol Kaye	Suzette Finkelstein
1985	Club Mediterraee, Ixtapa, Mexico	Helen Block Lewis	Ava L. Siegler	
1986	Vista International, New York	Nathan Stockhamer	Arlene K. Richards	Joanne E. Callan
1987	St. Francis, San Francisco	Fred Pine	Darlene Bregman-Ehrenberg, Carole Michaels	Joanne E. Callan
1988	Hotel Meridien, Boston	Murray Meisels	Samuel Gerson, Maureen Murphy	Joanne E. Callan
1989	Vista International, New York	Zanvel A. Liff	James Barron, Jonathan Slavin	Joanne E. Callan
1990	Hotel Weston, Chicago	Ruth-Jean Eisenbud	Gil A. Katz, Mary Libby	Joanne E. Callan
1991		Bertram P. Karon	Oliver J. B. Kerner	Joanne E. Callan

planning, including advance invitations to prospective workshop leaders, could not be extended without some independence from the larger Program Committee. The Executive Committee affirmed the request and reaffirmed that its CE Program would not be held responsible for generating extra funds even though expected to work toward a break-even fiscal outcome, thus underscoring its more important goals to meet Division members' CE needs and to promote nonmember interest in psychoanalysis. Through 1991, the Division's CE programs either broke even or generated additional income.

In the spring of 1991, Callan submitted her resignation from her several-year tenure as chair of the Division's CE Committee, to be effective as of the August 1991 Annual Convention. In August, 1991, Jaine Darwin, appointed by President Jonathan H. Slavin, assumed the post and responsibility for leading Division 39's CE Program.

SUMMARY

In the years from 1980 to 1991, both the annual meetings Division 39 held in conjunction with the APA Convention and the annual Midwinter/Spring Meetings, as well as the activities offered through its CE Program, developed into highly professional offerings (as reflected in the tables in this chapter). They were planned well in advance, offered comprehensive programming of high quality, and received increasingly positive reviews from both Division members and nonmembers. Division 39's leadership, all voluntary, demonstrated through the success of the many programs offered in the two annual meetings and the CE Program activities its commitment to advance psychoanalysis.

ACKNOWLEDGMENTS

Special thanks are expressed to Robert C. Lane for access to his personal correspondence; to Division 39 offices for access to archival records; and to APA's Offices of Continuing Education and Divisional Affairs for access to relevant files in the preparation of this chapter.

Professional Identity in Transition: Psychoanalytic Education and Training in the Division of Psychoanalysis

Jonathan H. Slavin

That a group of psychologists, whose professional organization is little more than a dozen years old, would undertake to publish a history of themselves, may be an act of immense self-importance. Yet, it may seem less so, if one takes into account that the decisions made by this group, and the political and psychological dynamics which shaped these decisions, have already had considerable effects in this country, and internationally, on how training in psychoanalysis is provided and to whom, as well as, more generally, on how and by whom mental health services are delivered. In this context, the history of Division 39's efforts to organize psychoanalytic training and the development of psychologist-sponsored, psychoanalytic training programs in various localities, provide a unique window through which we may view the issues affecting psychoanalytic psychologists as Division 39 was formed. The history also provides a striking picture of the dynamics involved in the effort of a largely excluded group to legitimate themselves in the psychoanalytic world.

BACKGROUND: THE DYNAMICS
OF EXCLUSION AND ALIENATION

In the United States beginning in the 1930s, psychologists had been systematically denied access to psychoanalytic training within the dominant, medically sponsored institutes of APsaA. Following World War II and the rise of professional clinical psychology as a consequence of the need for services engendered by the war, some psychologists were able to achieve training through the institutes of APsaA by means of the research waiver. Although the waiver permitted access to training for some, it repeatedly concretized, as each individual "research" candidate was given a "special" ticket in, the notion that psychologists were, in fact, not suited as a group to practice clinical psychoanalysis.

At the same time, especially after World War II, a number of psychoanalytic institutes outside of APsaA and IPA developed in New York City. Some were open to psychologists and provided training across the spectrum of psychoanalytic perspectives. However, in the minds of many, they functioned under the cloud of not being a part of the mainsteam psychoanalytic movement. No matter how rigorous their training program might be, or how well known their teachers and graduates might become, a certain mark of illegitimacy was associated with them. If they were not part of the established, "authoritative" structure of organized psychoanalysis, they were suspect in terms of quality and standards.[1] We return to the intermingling of the issues of legitimacy and quality later as psychologists began to try to launch new institutes across the country and had to contend with the anxieties of their more established colleagues, who were concerned about whether the new programs starting up outside of their purview would uphold what they felt to be essential standards.

Second, in addition to being excluded from the dominant psychoanalytic organizations, psychoanalytic psychology had not managed to find a hospitable home within its own professional body, APA. The alienation came from both sides. The APA was thought of by psychoanalytically oriented clinicians as the repository of anti-intellectual, native American behaviorism, rat research and a fundamentally negative attitude toward all clinical endeavors. And, from the other side, in its textbooks and in its scholarly journals, American psychology had repeatedly pronounced psychoanalysis both unscientific and dead.

No discussion of the history of psychoanalytic psychology can be true to its psychoanalytic roots if it does not take into account the effects of these two very profound experiences of exclusion and alienation on the identity and self-esteem of psychoanalytic psychologists. As I discussed in detail elsewhere (Slavin, 1989), exclusion leads the excluded group to internalize the perspectives and standards of the excluding group, in a rigid and harsh way: a form of identification with the aggressor. Individuals in the excluded group come to believe that they don't measure up and that the values, standards, and points of view of the excluding group are the only legitimate ones. Alternative perspectives generated by members of the excluded group come to be thought of as inevitably, inherently inferior. The wish to emulate, and ultimately become

---

[1]Clearly some institutes and individuals outside of the structure of APsaA and IPA had traditions and perspectives that conveyed a sense of their own legitimacy. Being trained by and belonging to institutes affiliated with these latter organizations were experienced by most as an insignia of quality and validity.

a part of, the excluding group can, and often does, become a powerful, almost obsessional motivator. In the process, one no longer sees oneself as shaping one's own destiny but rather looks, in a more childlike fashion, for legitimation from a group that becomes the arbiter of one's identity. A process of collusion begins, in which both the excluding group and those who are excluded come to believe that the excluding group possesses some corner on truth and on the correct interpretation of reality.

This chapter describes the the way Division 39, during its first decade, approached the question of providing psychoanalytic training for psychologists. Most psychologists were excluded from the predominant form of psychoanalytic training available in this country; it took a very long time to develop a sufficient sense of identity and mission to form a coherent group within APA; and the questions of legitimacy, quality and standards permeated most of the discussions of psychoanalytic training within the Division during its early years.

Events occurred both in the center of the Division's operations—in its Board of Directors and its Education and Training Committee—whose membership was drawn from individuals mostly trained and located in the New York City[2]

---

[2]How matters came to be perceived in geographical terms, at least by some of the participants, is worth noting. Of the original signers of the APA petition to form the Division of Psychoanalysis, more than 50% were from the New York City area. The preponderance of New Yorkers both in the Division and in its leadership in its early years was due in part to the fact that almost all the psychoanalytic training programs that would freely accept psychologists were located in New York. As a consequence, as more psychologists from other areas became involved in Division affairs, conflicts or differences between these newer participants and the established Division leaders tended to be perceived—at the very least by those from outside of New York—in geographical terms. Some of the readers of this chapter have taken issue with this perspective (all of them New Yorkers) while others have indicated that it meshed with their experience (most of them non-New Yorkers!). At the same time, it should be kept in mind that the New Yorkers were by no means a homogeneous group. Both Bernard Kalinkowitz (Section V) and Anna Antonovsky (Section I) pointed out, in their reading of drafts of this chapter, that much of the controversy I described in geographical terms can more accurately be understood in terms of the struggles between Section I proponents and Section V proponents. I believe they are partly correct in this assessment. However, the representatives from the local chapters who first became involved in the Division around the time of the White conference (1984) felt almost uniformly a sense of wariness if not a suspicion that emanated from at least the more conservative voices, who, as it happened, came mostly from New York. The minutes of the White conference taken by George Goldman and published in the Division newsletter (vol. VI, no. 1, p. 20–22) reflect the intensity of feelings on the part of local chapter representatives about the geographical issue. Goldman writes that in a "very emotionally charged meeting . . . the major message of the group seemed to be that the people outside of the New York area wanted to be as much a part of the Division as the New Yorkers were. . . . The major feeling of the group was that almost to the last person, they feel left out, unrepresented, uncommunicated with." In addition, the Section I–Section V controversy—in which there was basic disagreement on a number of issues of training and practice, especially regarding frequency of contact—was viewed by many of the newer local chapter representatives as an almost quintessentially New York affair. Among most local chapter representatives there was little quarrel with the frequency of sessions affirmed by the Section I proponents as essential, at least in training, nor did they quarrel with the need to be open to "relational" and other nonclassical ideas promoted in Section V.

area; as well as on the geographical periphery, in areas such as Chicago, Denver, Michigan, Boston, and San Francisco, where there were no formal training programs available to psychologists[3] (except for one in Los Angeles) and where the need for training was most urgent. Ultimately, programs began in all these locales.

The first decade of the Division's history with regard to training can also be framed in terms of what many consider to have been a watershed event, namely, a 2-day conference sponsored by Division 39 and held at the William Alanson White Institute in December of 1984. This conference brought together representatives from beginning local chapters and nascent training programs from around the country with many of the individuals most centrally involved in activities within the Division. The conference provided an intense sense of initiative and energy to the representatives from different localities who felt authorized by their contact with the Division to return home and begin to develop local chapters and programs of psychoanalytic training. However, the meeting also represented a confrontation of the Division's leadership with members from across the country who were interested in taking initiatives on their own behalf and did not feel necessarily beholden to established views. The local chapter representatives clearly wanted to make use of their identification with the Division but did not want to surrender any sense of autonomy to it. Both the Division leadership and the individuals from the "hinterlands," or "provinces," as they were termed at the time, were to be radically changed by this meeting and its aftermath.

THE EARLY YEARS: THE EFFORT
TO BEGIN A "NATIONAL PROGRAM"

In its first bylaws the Division established a standing Education and Training (E&T) Committee. The charge to this committee is broad and vague. It stated that the committee should "devote itself to the development of professional practice," and should be "responsible for devising whatever educational structure and curriculum seems appropriate," as well as "developing the means for this realization," subject to the approval of the Board of Directors. But what sort of educational structure and curriculum would be appropriate? And by what means would they be developed and implemented?

It gradually became clear that Division 39 would neither be permitted by APA rules to directly sponsor programs that would provide a certificate in psychoanalysis (although the Division could certainly sponsor educational courses and work-

---

[3]The Detroit Psychoanalytic Institute under the leadership of Richard and Editha Sterba did train psychologists and was cast out of the APsaA as a result. Subsequently, the larger Michigan Psychoanalytic Institute adhered to the practices of APsaA regarding the training of Psychologists.

shops) nor could the Division directly engage in accrediting psychoanalytic training institutes or certifying psychoanalytic practitioners.[4] All of the privileges of certification of individuals and accreditation of training programs were reserved for the APA itself and not for any of its divisions. Indeed, for many years it was questionable whether the Division could promulgate or recommend standards for psychoanalytic training. Nevertheless, the question of credentialing was a paramount issue in the early years of the Division, perhaps precisely because of the dynamics engendered by the experience of exclusion and alienation. Most of the members of the Division had either received their psychoanalytic training, if they had formal training at all, from institutes not recognized by the major national or international psychoanalytic bodies[5] or they had approximated some form of psychoanalytic training in a more informal, "bootleg" manner. None of this was designed to provide a sense of professional legitimacy and affirmation.

In establishing an Education and Training Committee, the Division mimicked APsaA in an apparent effort to address the issue of legitimacy. However, APA could neither establish nor accredit training programs. Thus, the Education and Training Committee was a committee in search of a mission and a way of implementing that mission, but without the clear means or authority to do so. As Murray Meisels put it: "It was a given. Obviously there would be an Education and Training Committee. The beginning feeling was we would be like the 'American' and have our own societies, but it didn't fit the facts because of our relationship to the APA."

Martin Mayman recalls that, in 1979, the E & T committee was thought of as offering workshops but not organized training programs. Reuben Fine, the first president pro-tem of the Division and the central force in its formation, proposed sending instructors affiliated with the Division around the country to teach and foster psychoanalytic education and training. This proposal was a precursor to the effort to establish some kind of a "national" training program.

Indeed, after that first proposal, the major initiatives to establish training programs consistently came from outside of the Education and Training Committee and from outside the primarily New York based leadership of the Division. The Division had the resources but the need was elsewhere. The impetus for the establishment of formal psychoanalytic training associated with Division 39 came from Oliver Kerner and a group of psychologists who had worked with Bruno Bettelheim in Chicago. The work with Bettelheim affirmed their sense of legitimacy as psychoanalytic clinicians in a way that enabled them to take further training steps on their own (Kerner, 1989, and chapter 32, this volume). In any event, the Chicago group was among the first to form a local chapter

---

[4]Although the APA indicated that the Division could establish sections that had different membership criteria than in the Division as a whole. It was on the basis of this provision that Section I, with specific training criteria for membership, was established.

[5]The William Alanson White Institute was recognized by the Academy of Psychoanalysis, but its psychologist graduates were excluded from membership in the Academy.

in 1980 and in 1982 they began working toward the establishment of a psychoanalytic training program. The process of first forming a local chapter, from which an impetus for training develops, became a historical pattern that was repeated with variations in Denver, Boston, northern California, and Michigan. Brief histories of these training programs are included at the end this chapter. In each of these instances the local chapter provided a vital psychological function in legitimizing discussion and planning of training programs in psychoanalysis outside of the umbrella of APsaA. It meant a great deal to be part of a national organization that gave some implicit imprimatur to one's plans. It was a major factor in counteracting the experience of being excluded and alienated and the attendant doubts about one's professional authority and competence. Despite the fact that the national leadership may have been skeptical about the capacity of their local colleagues to do something of sound quality without their direct assistance, the affiliation of these local groups with the Division on a national level provided a sense of authorization to move forward, even if it was not formally given. Indeed, this authorizing function was maintained despite the deep differences that began to emerge between the more conservative[6] views of some of the Division leadership and the local chapters who were pressing for the development of training programs under their own auspices. Whereas the divisional affiliation permitted them to plan their own programs outside of the authority of APsaA, these groups also wanted little to do with the authority of the Division itself.

In August 1981, Oliver Kerner and Bertram Cohler co-authored a response to a paper by Murray Meisels and Marvin Hyman of Michigan that dealt with a proposal for the Division to accredit psychologist-psychoanalysts and, secondarily, to provide some form of regional training. Kerner and Cohler regarded the Meisels–Hyman conception of training and credentialing as overly traditional and controlling. The Kerner-Cohler paper was a detailed proposal for the establishment of regional psychoanalytic education under the auspices of Division 39. In their memorandum Kerner and Cohler expressed their concern about a trend toward overly standardized and rigidified forms of psychoanalytic training and they urged, "a much less narrow specification or training and education, taking advantage of the diversity of understandings of psychoanalytic processes

---

[6]I am using the term *conservative* to represent a sense of concern on the part of many in the leadership that the new local groups, in their eagerness to launch programs of psychoanalytic education, would not maintain high standards (see chapter 2). As the controversy over Section V developed (which, along with other differences, did not endorse the frequency of sessions standard maintained by Section I) the question of local groups establishing their own programs, somehow outside of Divisional auspices and control,was seen as a potential additional threat to high standards. However, not all members of the Division leadership were equally skeptical about the local chapters or concerned about what they might do on their own. Some were particularly sympathetic with local groups (e.g., Goldman and Lane were part of a successful effort to revitalize the local chapter movement) while others (Kalinkowitz) saw them as potentially assisting in maintaining the Division's openness to alternative perspectives.

and the diverse interest and skills of possible faculty." They proposed an ad hoc committee to explore these proposals outside of the Education and Training Committee. They further proposed that the committee represent various theoretical perspectives and regions around the country. Although they do not say so explicitly, it seems apparent that they viewed the Education and Training Committee as either too conservative to deal effectively with their ideas or unprepared to move forward on these matters.

It is not exactly clear how this proposal, manifestly critical of traditionalism in training, and coming from individuals outside of New York, was received by those in the traditional institutes that operated in the shadow of the authoritative, medical institutes. The proposal repeats several times the need for a more flexible, less orthodox way of looking at training possibilities. Such statements, although reasonable, may have given birth to the suspicion that was later harbored toward the new local chapter groups. The more conservative leaders felt a need to reassure themselves that any programs begun under the Division's umbrella (even though the Division could not officially sponsor them) would live up to the standards they felt essential. Much of this concern reflected the broader concerns of the then recently established Section I, with which many Division leaders were affiliated, for the maintenance of what they felt were essential minimal standards for training.

This first initiative was followed nearly a year later by a request in the Division Newsletter from the Education and Training Committee to gather information about how individuals had been trained informally as psychoanalysts, with the goal of studying the feasibility of sponsoring some kind of "informal" training. Apparently there was a negligible response and little data was collected. At the same time, at the Board meeting of the Division during the APA meetings in August 1982, Kerner, then chair of the Local Chapters Committee, along with Meisels presented, according to the minutes, "a very extensive and thorough review of a proposal for a national program of psychoanalytic education." Specifically, they recommended that a study be undertaken to assess the feasibility of a national program of psychoanalytic education and to make recommendations about how such a national program could be organized, administered, and financed.

The proposal for a national program of psychoanalytic education was published in the autumn 1982 volume of the Division's newsletter. The proposal was the first to state openly that the Division was not simply, "an interest group within APA, but is a professional organization responsible for representing, organizing and developing policies pertaining to the present and future needs of psychologist-psychoanalysts." They proposed two models for the establishment of psychoanalytic training programs around the country. First, a traditional, local model where there were sufficient numbers of trained analysts, especially psychologists, to provide analyses, supervision, and faculty. In areas where there was not a sufficient concentration, they proposed a regional model. The personal analysis would be obtained locally, from a practitioner affiliated with one of the medically sponsored institutes, but the regional training center would provide course work on a seasonal basis. The problem of a continuous case conference was addressed by the suggestion of using locally trained analysts or flying in trained psychoanalysts form other areas. The proposal also mentioned the possibility of telephone conferences for seminars.

Although this program was never implemented, it is important historically because it attempted to begin to tackle the problems that the Division faced in fostering training programs, such as the difficulty in getting trained faculty, supervisors, and analysts. In most areas, the great majority of the trained analysts were psychiatrists affiliated with the medical institutes. They were generally reluctant to be openly involved, in the era prior to the lawsuit settlement, with the training of psychologists. The problem of finding teachers and analysts was real and had to be addressed at least conceptually before any proposal could be taken seriously. Thus, although regional training programs never developed, some of the ideas advanced were, in fact, later implemented by local initiative, first in the Denver area. This included, in Denver, flying in faculty for extended seminars; the use of telephone conference calls for seminars; and videotaping combined with conference calls from the distant faculty. All of these were factors that enabled the Denver program to get off the ground with little initial cooperation from the local, medical analysts.

Thus, the proposal by Kerner and Meisels (written in collaboration with Mayman) represents a seminal statement of some critical ideas. That it was pressed by individuals outside of the New York area where the established institutes were concentrated, and took shape under a special ad hoc committee suggests that the Education and Training Committee itself was already too caught up in difficult controversies around unresolvable issues of standards and accreditation to undertake this initiative. Instead, the initiative came from those members around the country most desirous, and in need, of Divisional support.

The Board of the Division approved the creation of a Committee on Psychoanalytic Education (COPE) co-chaired by Kerner and Meisels. Its membership included several other individuals from around the country such as Hedda Bolgar, who was already involved with the Los Angeles institute, and Charles Spezzano of Denver. Very quickly, the committee became involved in a political controversy about whether it would be an independent, ad hoc committee or would be placed under the aegis of the Education and Training Committee. George Goldman, then President of the Division, felt that under the bylaws it should be placed under the Education and Training Committee. Kerner and Meisels objected in a letter to Goldman and took the issue to the Board in its October 1982, meeting. They protested being placed under the Education and Training Committee and felt that Goldman's letter had changed the charge from one of developing appropriate models and making recommendations for psychoanalytic education to one of ''exploring the qualifications that various institutes have." Kerner and Meisels argued that the original charge to their committee had involved a program of policy planning in accord with their original proposal, while "the revised charge . . . involves a summary of the qualification of teaching and training analysis along with a summary of curricula." A struggle for control was beginning to take shape. The struggle foreshadowed the difficulties that were to develop later between the more conservative leaders concerned about maintaining standards and those from around the country who were interested in moving forward quickly to establish new programs. In this instance the matter was resolved by the Board and COPE was established as an independent committee. The Committee was asked to come up with a report by the April 1983 Divisional board meeting.

Through all of this the Division was beginning to be racked by the controversies regarding the establishment of Section I and the issues regarding the qualifications of who was a psychoanalyst. Proposals for training were understood as reflecting on that extremely controversial and divisive issue. Although many saw these questions solely in terms of the concrete professional issues at stake, much of the controversy, and the bitterness and passion it engendered, was an outgrowth of the excluded and demeaned identity that psychologists had suffered for a half century and their efforts to use the Division to repair it.

During the next several months, COPE concluded that the establishment of local training programs, even in those areas where there was a sufficient number of analysts capable of working with them, was likely to be a long way off due to struggles within local chapters around ideology and views of training. In its final report COPE emphasized the divisiveness that tended to crop up within local chapters and did not hold out much hope that these areas would be a source of significant new initiatives in psychoanalytic training in the near future. In this prediction they turned out to be incorrect. However, it may have been partly as a result of this Committee's work that this prediction proved too bleak.

The Committee also came to the conclusion that establishing regional training centers, which had been part of the original proposal, would not work. It was their estimation that it would be difficult to get psychologists to go to a regional center on a seasonal basis. Instead, they recommended that a national training program be established, in which intensive courses would be offered in conjunction with the Division's midwinter meeting and the summer meetings of APA which both candidates and faculty would attend. In conjunction with this the COPE report incorporated Charles Spezzano's proposal, which he had made in a letter to Kerner and Meisels, of flying in faculty to various local areas that were trying to establish training programs for week-end long seminars, workshops, and supervision.

The proposal for a national training program was submitted to the Board and the minutes indicate that it received a favorable response. However, it was never formally acted upon. Instead, during the Presidency of Ernest Lawrence, Donald

Kaplan was appointed to succeed Mayman as Chair of the Education and Training Committee. Apparently, what arose out of Board discussions was a decision to have the Education and Training Committee, which had been kept apart from these developments, meet with the COPE committee to jointly hammer out some proposal. The question of control was coming up again. More fundamentally, embedded in the question of control were all the anxieties and suspicions about what sort of training programs would be developed, how individual orthodoxies would be protected, and how legitimation and validation would be achieved. Consistently incorporated in the rhetoric of these struggles was a question of standards and a definition of what was truly psychoanalytic. But in reality there were very few differences in substance. No one disputed a tripartite model of psychoanalytic training or the necessity of intensity in treatment. That disputes could center in professional discussions around whether "true" psychoanalysis was done two, three, or four times a week was perhaps more a symptom of the profound anxieties and sense of illegitimacy engendered in an outgroup of psychologist-psychoanalysts who never felt that they truly were validated, than it was a serious intellectual or professional question. In any event, a joint meeting of the COPE and Education and Training Committee was called by Kaplan and held in February, 1984. It is reported in a follow-up memo from Kaplan that the question of standards was repeatedly raised. It seems that the major conclusion was that a recommendation was presented to the Board to create a Standing Committee on Education and Training for a 5-year period to provide continuity. This is a perplexing outcome given that there was already a standing Education and Training Committee! In effect, it seems, matters were tabled. Shortly, thereafter Lawrence was succeeded as President by Helen Block Lewis.

THE WHITE CONFERENCE AND ITS AFTERMATH:
THE ROAD TO CLARK

Helen Block Lewis came from a different mold than her predecessors in the leadership of Division 39. Although she had received self-directed psychoanalytic training (with supervision that had to be kept secret because she was a psychologist) as had many of the other senior psychologist-psychoanalysts, and she was a training analyst at one of the most traditional psychologist-oriented New York institutes (the Institute for Psychoanalytic Training and Research), she had truly radical ideas about psychoanalytic training and practice. And she was committed to the dissemination of these ideas. She and Meisels, who was developing a reputation for dogged perseverance, began to see some common interests. Meisels was committed to the development of local groups and the training of psychologist-psychoanalysts. His work in the COPE committee led him to view some kind of a national training program as a vehicle for accomplishing these aims. Although the Board had never formally approved the development of a national training program (it had gotten lost in the anxiety about standards), Lewis appointed Meisels as Chair of an ad hoc National Program Committee, despite opposition from some members of the Board. Lewis wanted to develop new models for psychoanalytic practice and training and saw a national training program as a means toward these ends. At the same time she appointed Anna Antonovsky, who held more conservative views about training, as the new chair for the Education and Training Committee.[7] She also appointed George Goldman and Robert Lane to Co-Chair a revitalized Local Chapters Committee in order to promote the development of local chapters within the Division.

Lewis and Meisels joined with Goldman and Lane to organize what was to become a very significant and transformative event: the White Conference. They decided to call a meeting of representatives from the developing local chapters around the country and of other individuals interested in psychoanalytic psychology throughout the United States who might be interested in the development of psychoanalytic training in their areas. Antonovsky and some members of the Board were initially opposed to this meeting, but, following a Board meeting in the Fall of 1984, the Education and Training Committee agreed to participate. Thus, the meeting was a combination of proposals by the local chapters group, spurred by Goldman and Lane, the effort of Meisels' National Program Committee to try to initiate a national training program, as well as the skeptical Education and Training Committee, which wanted to provide expertise as well as insure high standards to any programs that might develop. At the same time that Lewis was able to bring these forces together, the lawsuit against APsaA and IPA was about to be filed under the leadership of Bryant Welch, Nathan Stockhamer, and Ernest Lawrence. A historic confluence of forces had occurred, at least in terms of our psychoanalytic world.

The purpose of the White Conference, as announced to the Division Board in October 1984 was to: "1) learn about local needs; 2) determine particular ways the Division could facilitate the educational task of local groups; and 3) discuss the feasibility of regional and/or national course work." Many key figures who were to later play prominent roles within the Division and within its developing local chapters attended the two day White conference. Meisels, who chaired the conference,[8] and Lewis addressed issues of training; Goldman and

---

[7]Given the differences that later followed in the views of Antonovsky and Lewis, the questions of why Lewis made this choice has often been asked. There is no clear answer, except the suggestion made by some that the appointment of Antonovsky was a compromise with Section I members who were concerned about where Lewis and Meisels might take the Division. Lane suggested that Lewis was not simply interested in pushing her agenda but was committed to fair representation of all points of view.

[8]As noted earlier, minutes of the conference taken by George Goldman were published in the Division newsletter, *The Psychologist-Psychoanalyst* (Spring, 1985, Vol. VI, No. 1, pp. 20–22).

Lane spoke to local chapter issues; and Nathan Stockhamer talked of the development of a diplomating process for psychoanalysis. In addition to the speakers, those in attendance included: Ester Shapiro, Jonathan Slavin, and Muriel Weckstein from Boston; Maurice Burke and Oliver Kerner from Chicago; Sue C. Finkelstein from Cleveland; Myron Lazar from Dallas; Charles Spezzano from Denver; Murray Meisels, Marvin Hyman, and Bert Karon from Michigan; Milton Eber and Antonio Virsida from Florida; Robert Aguado and Ernest Lawrence from Los Angeles; Frederic Levine and Michael Kowitt from Philadelphia; Murray Bilmes and Philburn Ratoosh from San Francisco; Susannah Gourevitch, Rochelle Kainer and Irving Raifman from Washington, DC and others.

The atmosphere in the meeting was electric. People who had been on the periphery of the Division, but thinking in some embryonic way about local chapters or psychoanalytic training were energized by the opportunity to meet colleagues from around the country who shared similar passions, fantasies, hopes, and concerns. At the same time, the presence of the Division's leaders all talking about training and building local chapters provided a sense of affirmation and validation to those who had felt isolated in their efforts to create psychoanalytic cohesion in their local area. Even though tensions were immediately apparent (regarding anxieties about whether the Division or its Education and Training Committee would somehow take control of the training process), the vitality within the Division was an enormous boost for those in attendance. Here were a group of psychologists, and a charismatic leader like Lewis, talking of planning national training programs, filing law suits against powerful psychoanalytic organizations, and promoting local development. In addition, those in attendance were to learn that some areas had already managed to begin training programs, as in Chicago and, especially Denver, which had gotten started despite extremely limited local assistance. As a result, some representatives returned to their home areas almost manic with energy and enthusiasm.

It was fortunate they returned this way, because the struggles that followed might have served to dampen their persistence and enthusiasm. At the White conference a plan was developed to hold a follow-up conference to further discuss training issues and plans. Helen Block Lewis announced the possibility of a grant from the Exxon Foundation to support a major conference on training, which she hoped to hold at some point at Clark University in commemoration of Freud's visit and lectures there earlier in the century. A tentative plan to hold an interim conference in Ann Arbor in June 1985 was made and was brought to the Board of the Division for its support at the Spring Meeting in New York City in April 1985.

At the Board meeting all of the pent up anxieties within the Division generated a good bit of mutual suspicion. In addition, the struggles within the Division around the establishment of Section I, and the beginning effort to form Section V by those who disagreed with Section I's views, were also beginning to come to a head. The local chapters and their efforts to begin training programs became inevitably enmeshed in these battles. Many in the Division saw the local chapters as a radical development, somehow associated with the movement to launch a Section V. The concern about "standards" became a rallying issue for those who objected to the plans to establish a Section of Local Chapters or to launch new training programs in association with those chapters.

The concern about standards was reasonable, but it can be suggested that some of those who were most concerned about the problem of standards, with no evidence whatsoever that these local groups were in any way intent on lowering or changing standards, were playing out the dynamics of exclusion and alienation.[9] One can speculate that, having been kept out of the predominant psychoanalytic organizations, nationally and internationally, and having been considered by others—and, perhaps, by themselves—as second-class psychoanalysts, they now enacted the legacy of these professional injuries on a new group.

At the Board meeting the proposal for the Ann Arbor meeting was the subject of lengthy and heated debate that culminated in a straw vote to see which way opinions leaned. The straw motion to support the Ann Arbor meeting was defeated. At that point Charles Spezzano of Denver made an impassioned plea. He candidly called attention to the fact that members of the Board seemed to be treating the local representatives as though they were outsiders, rather than as colleagues who were equally serious about establishing high quality chapters and training programs in their areas (indeed, some Board members referred to the local chapters as the children); and he made it clear that members of the Division across the country would establish new institutes with or without the Division's help. Spezzano challenged the Board members to consider who or what they thought they were protecting by slowing down the formation of new institutes for psychologists who did not now have any kind of access to formal psychoanalytic training and who sincerely desired it: psychoanalysis? future analysands? future candidates of these new instititutes (could they be turned into less competent therapists through psychoanalytic training?). He asked why it would be assumed that psychologists interested in psychoanalysis would opt for a lesser standard of training after battling for years to gain access to what they perceived to be the best available training. A second, on-the-record, vote was taken. Two members of the Board switched their votes and the motion to support the Ann Arbor conference passed.

This was an important turning point. Although deep divisions continued to fester and play themselves out, especially around the establishment of Section

---

[9]Interestingly, almost all of the new programs thus far established maintained the frequency standard of four sessions per week (with one adhering to the three session minimum of Section I) and have veered not at all from a comprehensive 4- or 5-year curriculum or the tripartite model. At the same time, some of these programs, particularly in Boston, Denver, northern California, and Chicago have espoused a comparative curriculum rather than a more narrow ideological one and have made modifications in the traditional training analyst role.

V and in the planning of the Clark Conference, the local chapters movement and the associated new training programs became, as a consequence of this decision, differentiated from those struggles. Thereafter, instead of suspecting its local chapters, the Division was able to find a way to embrace them and, increasingly, to provide guidance, personnel, and money to promote the development of local training programs.

The Ann Arbor meeting and a subsequent one in the fall of 1985 in Washington, DC, continued a process in which members of local chapters were able to come together to form their own Section (IV) and develop an increasingly clear identity as psychoanalytic psychologists. The two meetings enabled representatives from around the country to articulate their own vision of training in a supportive group context that empowered them to take further initiatives. They began to identify the issues at stake in initiating their own professional advancement with a group of like-minded colleagues from other areas. And, despite political infighting, they were able to do this in the context of being identified with a national organization, which was also supporting a major lawsuit against the dominant psychoanalytic group that had kept psychologists out of the psychoanalytic mainstream. This was no small source of a sense of power and pride. At the Washington meeting, papers were presented by Stephen Appelbaum, Myron Lazar, Jonathan Slavin and Charles Spezzano. Each paper addressed the question of psychoanalytic identity and the degree to which those seeking psychoanalytic training had the professional and personal authority to undertake such training and arrange it as they saw fit. Similar issues had been addressed in the Ann Arbor meeting in talks by Bertram Karon, Marvin Hyman, Susannah Gourevich, and Rochelle Kainer.

THE CLARK CONFERENCE:
NEW INSTITUTES ARE FORMED

The excitement and momentum generated at the White Conference, the Ann Arbor, and the Washington, DC, meetings were maintained as planning continued for the Clark Conference on psychoanalytic training to be held in October 1986. In the interim, the newly formed Section of Local Chapters (Section IV) had its first spring meeting in April 1986 in conjunction with a conference sponsored by the Colorado local chapter. This further spurred the development of local, psychologist-sponsored training programs. Representatives from other localities were able to see first hand how a small chapter had managed to sponsor a serious psychoanalytic training program with little or no cooperation from the local medical analysts. If it could be done in Denver, it could be done in Boston and elsewhere.

A second watershed event in the history of training within Division 39 was the Clark Conference (see chapter 11, this volume), which took place in October 1986. A separate chapter in this volume details more of the substance of that conference, and a volume of the papers and discussions at those meetings has been published (Meisels & Shapiro, 1990). What may be most important to note here is that Helen Block Lewis, with the assistance of Shapiro and Meisels, was able to use the event to sponsor the articulation and legitimation of new visions of psychoanalytic education and training,[10] especially in the symbolic context of holding the meeting at Clark University, where Freud had spoken decades before. Indeed, the conference program tackled just about everything. Views about psychoanalysis and psychoanalytic training from the most traditional to the most radical were represented and discussed. Those who attended, and there were many from chapters around the country, found a heady air of excitement, ferment and open debate that few had expected to characterize a psychoanalytic conference. Questions were raised about the traditional models of psychoanalytic training, forms of training, the interface of psychoanalysis with other approaches to treatment, the educational and symbolic role of the training analyst and training analyses, the nature of the curriculum, the role and nature of supervision and other issues. The quality and openness of this debate proved very inspiring to those who were thinking not only of establishing training programs in their areas but especially about the possibility of doing things differently. It was especially important to our Massachusetts group that the conference was held in their state. Many members of the Massachusetts local chapter were in attendance and for many whose only contact with psychoanalytic issues was through the traditional medical institutes, it was the first glimpse that fundamental questions about psychoanalytic training could be asked and discussed in this way. There is no question that it enabled the individuals involved in forming a training program in Massachusetts to begin to take these fundamental questions as their own, instead of feeling that they had to begin with the forms and models of training that already existed. And some of the most senior psychologist-psychoanalysts who spoke encouraged the representatives of local groups to begin their own programs and not wait for the medical institutes to open their doors.[11]

THE DEVELOPMENT OF LOCAL INSTITUTES

The remainder of this story is perhaps best told in terms of developments in the local chapters and the new institutes that formed around them. As the White conference confronted the Division with a recognition of its local affiliates, and

---

[10]Kernberg's (1986) often cited critique of the organization and construction of psychoanalytic education was published shortly thereafter.

[11]I have a personal recollection of Stephen Appelbaum urging me to not wait until other leadership arrived to develop a program in Massachusetts and specifically using a civil rights metaphor that we not sit in the back waiting for an invitation to move forward. It was the kind of spur for us to take our own authority that individuals in many local areas needed from the senior people identified within the Division. Many others were later to contribute the same kind of authorization to various local groups establishing their own program.

spurred a certain trepidation about what these outsiders were going to do, the Clark conference marked the beginning of a resolution in the Division's concerns. Indeed, it began a period of active support financially and programatically in the development of local training programs. Within months of the Clark conference the Education and Training Committee, chaired by Antonovsky, funded the visit to Boston of Charles Spezzano and Marvin Hyman to discuss the kind of programs that they established in their areas and to assist the Massachusetts local chapter in the development of a new training program. Some months later, the Board made a grant of funds directly to the newly developing Massachusetts group after they had demonstrated a fundraising capacity of their own.

When Murray Meisels became President of the Division in August 1987, he appointed Marvin Hyman as the new chair of the Education and Training Committee. Under Hyman's tenure one of the primary roles of the committee became the review of requests for financial and other assistance from developing training programs. The first to seek such funding through the committee process was the group developing a program in the San Francisco Bay area, followed later by Philadelphia and Pittsburgh. This new role for the Education and Training Committee continued when Jonathan Slavin became Chair during the Presidency of Ruth-Jean Eisenbud and when Hyman again chaired during the Presidency of Bertram Karon. When Jonathan Slavin became President of the Division in 1991, he appointed Stuart Pizer as the chair of the Education and Training Committee with a specific charge to expand on the role Hyman had begun, to support developing training programs, and to encourage initiatives to start new programs. In less than a decade, initial concern, indeed suspicion by the Division and the Education and Training Committee had been transformed into direct support. In fact both in the Division Board, among its officers, and on the Education and Training Committee, many of the original representatives from the local chapters now played central roles.

In this context it should be noted that the Division Board's decision to schedule its spring meetings in major cities where there were organized local chapters (instead of in resort areas where they had been held earlier in the decade) spurred the development of a sense of group cohesiveness and identity in these chapters and the growth of the important organizational infrastructure to proceed with a training program. Thus developing training programs coincided in time with Divisional spring meetings in San Francisco, Boston, and Philadelphia.

As of the writing of this chapter, five psychoanalytic training programs—in Chicago, Denver, Boston, San Francisco, and Michigan with one more group in formation in Philadelphia—developed in conjunction with the local chapters in their areas and in affiliation with Division 39. Each of these programs obviously reflect some of the unique issues of their locality and the individuals who were most centrally involved in organizing them. However, an examination of their development also suggests certain striking commonalities that say much about the psychological and political dynamics that are involved in the effort to establish a psychoanalytic training program. As I suggested earlier in this chapter and elsewhere (Slavin, 1989,1990), the establishment of psychoanalytic training programs by psychologists who do not have formal training in an "authorized" institute, and have had to overcome a legacy of exclusion, is not a simple matter. The impact of exclusion may leave a corresponding doubt about one's authority and capacity to organize one's own training and raises the question of where the authorization to move ahead will come from.

The process of establishing a psychoanalytic training program, which almost always included modifications of traditional educational structures and curricula, were experienced by the organizers as providing them with a new and profound sense of personal authority and control over their professional destiny. The intense sense of exhilarating liberation often experienced by the participants in this process, may suggest that psychoanalytic training has been burdened through the years by a rigidity, even authoritarianism, that engenders both difficulty in making change as well as a sense of freedom when one has overcome the constraints on change. The sources of such authoritarianism in the history of psychoanalysis, and the hold it has on the identifications of many who have trained in this field, is beyond the scope of this chapter. However, this question may be important to address if psychoanalysis is to continue to grow and be enriched by new ideas. In any event, in the remainder of this chapter I offer an account of the evolution of the first set of the new psychologist-initiated training programs.

CHICAGO

The pre-history of the Chicago Center began in 1957 when a group of psychologists (including Maurice Burke, Oliver Kerner, Irving Leiden, Joanne Powers, and Johanna Tabin) established a study group. Beginning in 1959 the group was led by Bruno Bettelheim. In large measure, the study group functioned as an analytic "control" seminar. A parallel situation occurred in Boston where the establishment of a training program coincided with and was fostered by a group of relatively senior clinicians who began to study psychoanalysis and discuss treatment cases outside of a formal institute program. In these instances, actually doing and studying psychoanalysis played an important role in conveying a sense of empowerment to develop a formal program. In his account of the history of the Chicago program, Kerner (1989) made clear that the association with Bettelheim imparted a powerful sense of psychoanalytic legitimacy and identity to the participants and played a major role in enabling them to later take the initiative to establish an independent training program outside the aegis of the local and very powerful medical institute.[12] We see later how each of the new groups

---

[12]In his *Round Robin* account (1989) Kerner stated: "The sense of inner identity as psychoanalysts, which was provided to each participant in their work with Bruno Bettelheim served

dealt with the question of finding the personal authority and sense of legitimacy to take this kind of initiative.

Many of the same clinicians who had originally participated in the Bettelheim study group now became involved in the Organizing Committee of the newly formed Chicago Center. The first classes began in 1983 and the program was formally incorporated in 1984. It has been functioning since that time.

DENVER[13]

Unlike Chicago, which enjoyed the benefit of the presence of a figure like Bruno Bettelheim and the sense of authorization that he was able to convey, when Charles Spezzano arrived in Denver, there was no such authoritative figure, or even a coherent group of psychoanalytic psychologists. Spezzano had come to Colorado for his internship following graduate training in New York City and stayed on. His experience in New York was one that he described as, "every psychology graduate student walking around with the catalogues of the various psychoanalytic institutes considering which ones they might apply to." This was not the case in Denver where the only analytic institute, the one associated with APsaA, had graduated essentially no psychologists in the years prior to the lawsuit. Spezzano had been an early member of Division 39 and entertained the hope that the Division, in undertaking the sponsorship of local chapters, could also become the catalyst for promoting the development of training programs around the country that would be open to psychologists. Spezzano agreed with the view of Meisels and Kerner, that the Division should not simply be yet another organization that sponsored an annual meeting, but should use its resources to promote the training of psychologists in psychoanalysis. Spezzano wrote to Robert Lane, then President of the Division, asking for support and also contacted the six individuals in the state of Colorado who were members of Division 39 to try to organize a local chapter and think about launching some kind of training program. Although five of these individuals responded, their discussions over a period of several months went no further and they eventually disbanded. In addition, nothing further regarding initiatives for training seemed to be taking place in the Division.

Disappointed but not dissuaded, Spezzano decided to take matters into his own hands. It was clear from his discussions with the medical analysts in Denver that significant or overt help from them would not be forthcoming. Instead

---

to involve each person in . . . the drive and the will to work towards the day when clinical psychologists in Chicago would have their own house, free from medical domination."

[13]As becomes clear, the developments in Denver and the individuals involved had a very direct impact on the Boston group. In turn, what transpired in Massachusetts directly influenced developments in San Francisco. These influences are crucial aspects of this narrative and they are therefore dealt with in sequence in this discussion.

he inquired carefully among the various nonmedical institutes in New York about who on their faculties were good teachers and would be willing to travel to spend a weekend conducting intensive seminars as part of an initial series of workshops focused around a first year psychoanalytic curriculum. In March 1984 Spezzano sent a letter to all APA members in the state of Colorado announcing the formation of a local chapter of Division 39 and inviting everyone to attend an organizational meeting. At that meeting, 35 people applied for membership in the Division and Spezzano announced that a workshop series of nine week-end seminars had been set up for the coming year. Those who wanted to register for it were to write checks in the full amount of $1,500 or a minimum of $750 as a nonrefundable deposit. Spezzano left that meeting with more than $22,000 and the first year curriculum of the future Colorado Center for Psychoanalytic Studies was launched.

One of the first to sign up for the seminars at that meeting was Karen Rosica who was to become the second President, after Spezzano, of the local chapter in Colorado and one of the leaders of the newly established training program. As was repeated in other areas, the close collaboration and colleagueship between Spezzano and Rosica provided the necessary sense of mutual support that was psychologically essential to being able to carry out such a significant organizational and psychological undertaking. At the same time, the Colorado situation was in many respects different from that of Chicago or from the other areas where programs were launched. In Colorado, Spezzano fundamentally authorized himself to take the initiative despite the absence, initially, of any support or authorization from local colleagues, senior mentors, or the Division itself. But the support was soon forthcoming. Among those who conducted the first set of week-end seminars were such venerable figures as Reuben Fine as well as the young psychologists Jay Greenberg and Stephen Mitchell, who had already become well known for the book they co-authored on object relations in psychoanalysis. Other individuals who taught these early seminars were Lloyd Silverman, Elliot Adler, Ruth-Jean Eisenbud, and Donald Kaplan.

In addition, Spezzano ultimately had some help first from one local medical analyst, Henry Coppolillo (and soon from others, especially George Hartlaub and Peter Mayerson, once the program had been launched). Spezzano was also successful in arranging for telephone supervision for participants with several of the people who also had served as instructors for the weekend seminars. As a result, the refusal of local analysts to supervise did not stifle the development of the training program at the outset. The phone supervision was sustained by periodic visits of the instructors to Colorado to teach their seminars and visits by the supervisees to New York for intensive in-person meetings.

As a result of the success of his efforts, Spezzano and the Colorado undertaking served as a catalyst and model for similar undertakings in Boston, San Francisco, and Philadelphia. That a successful and serious psychoanalytic training program could be started in Denver with no initial assistance from the medical analysts and no support from senior psychologists in the local area, was clear evidence that a program could almost certainly begin in these other, potentially more fertile, settings. One could no longer claim to be held back because there would be no local support! For psychologists outside of New York interested in establishing independent psychoanalytic institutes the founding of the Colorado Center for Psychoanalytic Studies by Charles Spezzano was the shot heard "round the country."

BOSTON

The question of whether to develop a psychoanalytic training program, and what kind of program, quickly became the subject of extensive, often heated, exploration. If such a program were to begin at all, it would have to be initiated by a group of senior clinicians in positions of relative prominence in the community. Most of them had not undertaken formal psychoanalytic training, largely because of the discriminatory policies of the medical institutes. As the discussion of a new training program evolved, many of these experienced clinicians formed a study group to actively and openly study psychoanalysis together. Somewhat later, several also began a control seminar led by Paul Myerson, a senior, medical, training analyst.[14] The study group and control seminar played a crucial role in cementing a sense of a psychoanalytic identity and of a capacity to be the creators of one's own professional education.

Some of those who were in a position to initiate a program—including myself, Malcolm Slavin (no relation), Ester Shapiro, James Barron, Richard Geist, Gerald Stechler, and a few others—had a very distinct point of view about psychoanalytic training. We felt that if a new program were to begin, it would have to be founded on a different conceptual basis than those of the existing programs. In briefest terms, we believed that psychoanalytic training should be based on sound educational principles. For example, it was evident that psychoanalysis, after a period of somnolence, was bursting with controversial and divergent perspectives in both theory and practice. In our view, a serious study of psychoanalysis required that those controversies and competing perspectives be presented from the outset to individuals training in psychoanalysis. A comparative curriculum that would challenge the thinking of candidates, rather than one that would impart a particular vision of what psychoanalysis was, seemed educationally essential.

Our thinking about using fundamental educational considerations, rather than simply relying on traditional forms, extended beyond the curriculum to the role

---

[14]It is fair to say that the Boston group encountered no significant institutional opposition from the medical institutes and a warm and sometimes enthusiastic welcome from individual members of those institutes. There has never been a problem recruiting senior faculty or supervisors from among them.

of the personal analysis and the way in which candidates were to be evaluated. Although we subscribed to the tripartite model of training, including a substantial personal analysis, we believed candidates should be evaluated on the basis of the most observable ingredients, such as the reports of their teachers and supervisors about their work. We felt it was critical to confront difficult educational decisions about candidates by building it into the evaluation process, and not hope that problems would somehow be resolved in the personal analysis. We also felt that candidates should be treated as mature, professional learners, capable of having a vital say in the organization of their own professional training. This view extended to the admissions process, which we felt should stress evaluation of one's readiness and capacity to learn and benefit from further clinical education.

Despite these intentions, it was not at all clear where those with the clout to actually launch a program would fit into the process. That these senior clinicians had the ability and standing to carry it off was clear. We were officers in our local chapter, directors of respected clinics and psychology training programs, and senior supervisors in major training settings. What was missing was some conception of what these individuals would be doing as part of the process. Would they be teachers and supervisors, even though they weren't formally trained as analysts? Would they be candidates? Many felt, that to sit in the introductory Freud course, to learn the basics of psychoanalysis, after studying and practicing it for 15 or 20 years, would be a charade not worth considering.

The effort to begin a program was stalled by the uncertainty of where the senior clinicians who could launch it would fit in. Charles Spezzano suggested, "a separate program for 'advanced' candidates who could later become the teachers and supervisors in the new program." It was a very creative idea that fit well with the perspective of looking to the real educational issues. If we really believed that psychoanalytic training should be dealt with on a common sense educational basis, with evaluations done on the basis of observable educational ingredients, the same thinking should apply to the situation of these senior clinicians. It was in this manner that a very successful program for "advanced candidacy" at the Massachusetts Institute for Psychoanalysis was first conceived. The success of this program meant that an entire generation of very experienced psychologists[15] could now complete their psychoanalytic education and offer something to the next generation of psychoanalytic clinicians.

In evaluating the backgrounds of prospective advanced candidates there was a serious effort to exercise common sense in our educational judgments. A clear, concurrent educational justification for what would be asked of the advanced candidates was necessary. At the same time, there would not be differential

---

[15]The Advanced Candidates program soon attracted the interest of several senior psychiatrists and clinical social workers who had not, or could not undertake psychoanalytic training earlier in their careers.

standards between what was expected of advanced and regular candidates. Thus, advanced candidates were asked to complete all the requirements for psychoanalytic training the same as regular candidates, including a substantial personal analysis, the equivalent of 4 years of course work in psychoanalytic theory and practice, and the treatment of three control patients, at least two of whom would be seen four times a week on the couch. However, a process for evaluating these advanced candidates was established for the purpose of crediting them with up to about half of what was required of all candidates. Thus, all advanced candidates would be required to have had a substantial personal analysis—but would not be required to be in one concurrently—unless there were indications from their supervisors that they needed further treatment. The question of further analysis was treated as an educational decision.

All advanced candidates would also be required to take 2 years of control seminars and a 2-year theoretical seminar. In addition, if the evaluating committee felt that there were areas of specific deficiency, they could require additional tutorial courses. Advanced candidates could also be credited with up to half of the 200 hours of required control supervision, if they had control experience. At least half of the control supervision required of regular candidates had to be completed under the auspices of the institute. In this manner, the basic tension between recognizing the real accomplishments of advanced candidates, making genuinely relevant educational decisions, and yet not simply awarding a certificate for work not accomplished under institute auspices, was resolved.

To evaluate advanced candidates, a committee of senior clinicians was selected, mostly from Division 39 and outside the local area, so distance and prominence made it clear that judgments would not be influenced by the status of the advanced candidates in their home community. Among those original evaluators from Division 39 who contributed to this unique program were: Nathan Stockhamer, Ruth-Jean Eisenbud, Jay Greenberg, Helen Golden, and Zanvil Liff. Andrew Morrison and Paul Russell from the local medical institute also contributed.[16]

The advanced candidates program was only one facet of an extended process in formulating a new program in Massachusetts. A series of committees was established to take a fresh look at all facets of training, including admissions, curriculum, administration and finance, as well as advanced candidates. A separate psychotherapy track was rejected.

The members of the Organizing Committee included Jonathan H. Slavin as Chair, James Barron, Murray Cohen, Betty North, Ester Shapiro, Malcolm Slavin, and Muriel Weckstein. Each chaired or participated in one of the special committees.

---

[16]Prior to taking the Freud Chair at the Hebrew University in Jerusalem, Bennet Simon played an active role in helping to formulate the Advanced Candidates program.

SAN FRANCISCO

The development of a training program in San Francisco illustrated both the role of Division 39 as catalyst for the launching of a program and the function external figures may play in providing a sense of empowerment and authorization. The first step in this process, as had been the case in Chicago, Denver, and Boston, was the formation of a local chapter. Under the leadership of Maureen Murphy and Samuel Gerson, the chapter undertook sponsorship of the Division 39 Spring Meeting in 1988. The immense success of that meeting programmatically, financially, and in terms of attendance created a clear sense of a cohesive organizational identity. In addition, one of the programs at the Spring Meeting stimulated a great deal of energy and enthusiasm among several clinicians in the Bay area who were later to provide the initial leadership in organizing an institute.

That program consisted of a panel of speakers who spoke about the psychoanalytic training programs they had begun in their areas. The speakers were Karen Rosica from Colorado, Jonathan Slavin from Boston, and Marvin Hyman from Michigan (see later). Charles Spezzano and Ester Shapiro, who had been active participants in the development of training programs in Denver and Boston were in the audience and participated in the discussion. Members in attendance from the San Francisco area were catalyzed by this panel. They saw groups in three different localities that had managed to successfully launch training programs of their own design and on their own initiative. The programs they heard about were both successfully launched and, in many ways, highly innovative. It conveyed a sense that perhaps in the San Francisco area something similar could be accomplished.

An interdisciplinary group consisting of Maureen Murphy, Samuel Gerson, Jill Horowitz, Rachael Peltz, Stephen Seligman, Justin Simon, and Gayle Wheeler began to meet and discuss the organization of an institute. As their plans evolved they consulted regularly with Jonathan Slavin, who was asked to spend an intensive weekend discussing the full range of issues with them in January 1989. That weekend retreat provided the final stimulus for moving ahead. Adapting the process that had been developed in Boston, the organizing committee established a number of working committees to examine in detail all facets of starting a training program. Although they had access to the reports on curriculum, admissions, advanced candidates and other areas that had been developed in Boston, and used some of the ideas generated in these reports, a thorough reworking of each aspect of the future program was undertaken. This process, although laborious, gave the individuals involved—both in Boston and San Francisco—a powerful sense of having created something original and very much their own, even when the outcome paralleled existing forms of psychoanalytic training. Nothing was accepted in a rote way and each aspect of the program was debated by serious professionals who were in the process of designing their

own training, rather than someone else's. As in Boston, the various committees were composed, quite deliberately, of individuals representing a broad range
of views regarding psychoanalytic training with a charge to arrive at a consensus that would reflect the best interests of, and educational needs of prospective candidates.

Having moved much more quickly from the period of initial discussions to
a formal beginning than had any other group, the Psychoanalytic Institute of
Northern California was officially launched in October 1990. As in Boston, the
San Francisco program began with a group of advanced candidates, whose background had been assessed, much as had the Boston group, by prominent outside evaluators affiliated with Division 39, including Hedda Bolgar, Nathan
Stockhamer, Jay Greenberg, Karen Rosica, and Charles Spezzano.

MICHIGAN

Development of a Division 39 affiliated training program in Michigan had its own
unique character, in many ways quite specific to the situation there. Long before the founding of Division 39 there was a psychoanalytic institute in
Michigan—the Detroit Psychoanalytic Institute—which had been started by
Richard and Editha Sterba after they came to this country during the rise of
the Nazi regime in Germany. They carried with them both their own very substantial contributions and reputations as psychoanalysts, as well as the aura of
having been Viennese analysts who worked with the founder of psychoanalysis.
The Detroit Psychoanalytic Institute, however, was decertified by APsaA because it continued, in defiance of the APsaA, to train nonmedical analysts. Three
of the individuals who were among the leaders in the establishment of both the
local chapter of Division 39 in Michigan and the training programs that developed, Marvin Hyman, Murray Meisels, and Bertram Karon, all had their training either formally at the Detroit Psychoanalytic Institute or more informally
through the mentoring of the Sterbas.

For the first several years of its existence, until the late 1980s, the local
chapter in Michigan sponsored an affiliated educational program that enabled
individuals to construct, with the advice of supervisors and advisors, their own
psychoanalytic curriculum and training. The program did not issue formal certificates, but did inform its students about the standards that had been promul-
gated by Section I of Division 39 as well as by other groups, such as the IPA.
Those who enrolled in courses and took supervised cases could work toward
meeting those standards, if they chose. The construction of a training program
on this less formal basis reflected the radical but very cogent views of Marvin
Hyman, who stood staunchly against the creation of a professional school model
of psychoanalytic training.

This model of training remained in effect for several years. However, eventually a split began to develop in the local chapter between those who wanted to continue psychoanalytic education in this manner and others who wished for a more formal training program that would lead to a certificate and other formal ways of recognition as a psychoanalyst. Discussions and debates of this question were carried on in the chapter for some months. Eventually, a group led by Murray Meisels and Bertram Karon formed the Michigan Psychoanalytic Council that recognized, for psychoanalytic certification, the training of those who had completed the equivalent of Section I requirements through the more informal training program the chapter had sponsored as well as in more formal programs elsewhere. They established a new, formal program in psychoanalysis that reflected what they felt was a centrist position about what psychoanalytic training should consist of. The curriculum included an immersion in contemporary psychoanalytic thinking with special emphasis on issues of gender.

Looked at from the point of view of the meaning and dynamics of the wish for certification, it appeared that the sense of recognition and approval that one could get from being involved in a group which identified with the views of people like Sterba and such very senior individuals as Marvin Hyman could keep the quest for more formal certification at bay only for a time. In the end, the wish for formal, institutional affirmation, apart from its concrete, practical meaning and potential benefits, won out in Michigan as it did elsewhere. Psychoanalysts, like everyone else, generally need to feel that what they are doing is legitimate, and thought of as legitimate, by others. Informal legitimization appears to be insufficient for a sense of continuing professional self-esteem and development. Beyond the structure of a formal curriculum, it seems clear that psychoanalysts, like most people, want to know that they have clearly, and in a documentable way, graduated from something.

ACKNOWLEDGMENTS

Thanks to the following individuals who spent time interviewing for this chapter and/or reading and correcting drafts: Robert Aguado, Anna Antonovsky, Barbara Goldsmith, Leopold Caligor, George D. Goldman, Bernard Kalinkowitz, Oliver J. B. Kerner, Robert C. Lane, Martin Mayman, Murray Meisels, Maureen Murphy, Karen Rosica, Charles Spezzano, and Nathan Stockhamer. The author is solely responsible for the content.

REFERENCES

Kernberg, O. (1986). Institutional Problems of Psychoanalytic Education. *Journal of the American Psychoanalytic Association, 34*(4), 799–834.

Kerner, O. J. B. (1989). The Chicago Center for Psychoanalytic Psychology. *The Round Robin*, Newsletter of Section I, Division 39.

Meisels, M., & Shapiro, E. (Eds.), (1990). *Tradition and innovation in psychoanalytic education: Clark Conference on psychoanalytic training for psychologists.* Hillsdale, NJ: Lawrence Erlbaum Associates.

Slavin, J. (1989, August). *The dynamics of exclusion and emancipation: Psychoanalysis and civil rights.* Paper presented at the annual meeting of the American Psychological Association, New Orleans.

Slavin, J. (1990). Authority and identity in the establishment of psychoanalytic training: Questions regarding training models. In M. Meisels & E. Shapiro (Eds.), *Tradition and innovation in psychoanalytic education: Clark Conference on psychoanalytic training for psychologists.* Hillsdale, NJ: Lawrence Erlbaum Associates.

11

The Clark Conference on Psychoanalytic Training for Psychologists

Ester R. Shapiro

The Clark Conference on psychoanalytic training for psychologists, organized by Helen Block Lewis during her presidential year and co-chaired by her and Murray Meisels, was held October 24–27, 1986 at Clark University in Worcester, Massachusetts. The Clark Conference was the outcome of a series of meetings on psychoanalytic training initially called by Lewis and Meisels to establish a National Training Program. Analytically informed readers immediately understand the Division's choice of Clark University in Worcester. In 1909, Sigmund Freud visited the United States at the invitation of Clark University president, G. Stanley Hall, a founder of APA and one of the first members of the scientific community to recognize the importance of Freud's work. There is, in fact, a little-known but instructive story behind the location of the conference at Clark University. In 1984, on the 75th anniversary of Freud's visit, Clark University held a symposium to commemorate this event. Most of the participants were medical analysts and although APsaA was included in planning the event, the Division of Psychoanalysis was not. When Helen Block Lewis heard of this, she called her friend and research co-author Seymour Wapner, Chair of Clark's psychology department, to inquire why Division 39 was excluded. According to Lewis, Wapner responded that his oversight had occurred because it was APsaA that had been traditionally associated with psychoanalysis in the United States.

Chagrined and apologetic about having excluded Division 39 in the anniversary symposium, and further moved along by Helen Block Lewis's righteous indignation, Wapner agreed to redress the exclusion by promising Clark University, free of charge, as the location of a Division conference on psychoanalytic education for psychologists. These circumstances speak well to the pervasive and pernicious effect of the medical monopoly on psychoanalytic participation among psychologists, which both the antitrust lawsuit and the Division's activities in the area of psychoanalytic education were designed to redress.

To symbolize that psychology was ready to reclaim its historic position as a discipline that fully participated in, and would help transform, the psychoanalytic enterprise we gave the conference presenters two photographs as mementoes: one of the presenters at our own 1986 conference, and one of Freud and his colleagues at the 1909 lectures from the Clark University archives.

At the same time that Bryant Welch and others launched the antitrust lawsuit against APsaA, Division 39 and its local chapters began to explore the kind of psychoanalytic training we would design for ourselves. We were especially interested in openly and critically addressing the existing problems in medical institutes.

In initially calling for a National Training Program, Division 39 was drawing on the familiar centralized models of the IPA and APsaA. Whereas those of us helping to organize local chapters found the support of Division 39 essential, we were reluctant to embrace any centralized authority that would dictate educational programs and standards, and bypass the unique interests and needs of our different communities.

Representatives from the new local chapters of Division 39 began to critically discuss existing psychoanalytic institutes and to create interdisciplinary training programs that would not be mirror images of the existing medically dominated institutes of APsaA. The Clark Conference began, with this internal conflict as a central theme: in what way could the Division support the development of psychoanalytic training for psychologists, and promote high standards for the quality of training, without immediately structuring a curriculum and imposing requirements that would restrict the full exploration of the widest range of educational options? It was our very capacity as a Division to engage in the open exploration of this institutional and educational conflict—between the supportive traditions of a community and the freedom for individual innovation—that enabled us to transcend the self-protective impasse that has paralyzed progress in psychoanalysis.

With financial support from the Division and an additional grant from the Exxon Foundation, the Clark Conference brought together a diverse group of teachers, theorists, and researchers in psychoanalytic psychology and other disciplines. Their purpose was to review the problems of existing psychoanalytic training programs and the training models we as psychologists would design for our own education.

The conference participants came predominantly from groups within the Division that formed the local chapter section and the future Section V. The conference was virtually boycotted by a subgroup of members who anticipated that the conference would not value traditional standards of psychoanalytic education. However, both speakers and participants included a wide range of perspectives on psychoanalytic training models, and the diversity of perspectives contributed significantly to the conference's success.

The conference achieved both a high level of scholarship and a productive atmosphere of respectful collegial exchange. Through programmed talks and unprogrammed interpersonal engagement the participants offered, considered, and debated new ideas about training.

The conference was attended by 180 participants, 40 of whom were invited faculty. Participants came from all over the country, and brought with them a diverse range of backgrounds in psychoanalysis that enriched the discussions. Even the coffee breaks and lunches hummed with the constant sound of animated conversation, reflecting the enthusiasm with which participants responded to the issues presented in the formal talks.

The small-group workshops, which met four times during the conference, tested the reality of our commitment to offer flexible, participant-centered learning and to place educational concerns over institutional concerns. Most of the faculty were listed in the original program as available to lead either general discussions of presentations, or focused discussions relevant to a particular interest group such as Jungian or child analysis. Each of eight workshops included some permanent, core participants as well as a changing group who sampled several.

Participants agreed that the conference "holding environment" had successfully provided a setting where participants transcended their customary positions and learned from each other in exciting, open-minded, mutually enhancing ways. I believe the success was based on a structure for learning, which itself mirrored the conference recommendations for creating psychoanalytic training programs that encouraged diversity and dialogue in a mutual rather than hierarchical fashion, and did not locate educational authority in the hands of a few expert faculty.

The Clark Conference was experienced by many as vital and timely, because it took place just when local chapters were beginning to launch their own training programs. Because the conference was attended by participants from local chapters all over the country who were at different stages of their own development, the critiques of psychoanalytic training influenced the creation of new educational forms. The proceedings of the Clark Conference were edited by Meisels and Shapiro and published in *Tradition and Innovation in Psychoanalytic Education: Clark Conference on Psychoanalytic Training for Psychologists*, a volume distributed to all Division 39 members. The Clark Conference articulated a critical perspective on psychoanalytic education that has supported the ongoing, creative development of local chapter training programs.

THE CLARK CONFERENCE
RECOMMENDATIONS: CHANGING THE
DEFINITION OF EDUCATIONAL AUTHORITY

The Clark Conference, with its diverse presentation of papers from different psychoanalytic backgrounds, offered process as well as content in expanding the definition of psychoanalytic education. The organization of the conference reflected the realization that exploration of many points of view, a process of dialogue across differences, could lead to a diversity of educational visions that would enrich rather than threaten the future of psychoanalysis. The title *Tradition and Innovation in Psychoanalytic Education* implied the goal of including the wisdom of the past while permitting the creativity required for a future of continuing growth. Too often in the development of individuals, families, or institutions, tradition and innovation are polarized as mutually exclusive categories, such as orthodoxy and heresy or conservation and revolution. Most intellectual disciplines, including psychoanalysis, treat dualities as irreconcilable alternatives. In his paper for the conference, Appelbaum suggested that the hallmark of a first-rate mind is the capacity to tolerate paradox, and extend one's thinking by exploration of contradictions. He proposes that psychoanalytic theory needs to tolerate the tension generated by opposing polarities and integrate these into a more complete psychoanalytic theory including human development and gender differences.

Although we had not planned it from the outset, the Clark Conference papers implicitly offered a view of psychoanalytic education from a dialogic and dialectical developmental perspective, in which the tensions created by the open-minded exploration of differences or conflicting points of view are themselves the stimulus for shared intellectual growth. In this spirit, the papers offered a perspective on a process of learning rather than a specific educational form or outcome. Consistently, presenters at the conference addressed the question: how does the training institute's relational organization impact on the vision of psychoanalysis that is integrated by the candidate? From the developmental vantage point described earlier, the Clark Conference papers could be seen to explore consistently the qualities of educational relationships, institutional and interpersonal, that enabled the greatest personal autonomy while retaining the supportive nurturance of an experienced, established educational community.

As I discussed in the concluding chapter of the Clark Conference volume, the formation of psychoanalytic educational institutions took place under conditions of overwhelming political and personal trauma in Central Europe between the two world wars. These historical conditions significantly contributed to the creation of institutions that emphasized strict control of psychoanalytic education as a means of preserving psychoanalysis for the future. Although it seemed to the first and second generation of psychoanalysts that they needed to protect their ideas from premature dilution, this approach has isolated psychoanalysis from other intellectual and clinical disciplines.

Although psychoanalysis has long struggled with legitimate questions concerning psychoanalytic theory and practice, critical scientific discourse has been impeded by a long-standing fear that intellectual exploration would lead to diluting the "pure gold" of psychoanalysis and was therefore forbidden as heretical disloyalty. Its educational forms had evolved toward conservative self-protection, restricting the use of self-criticism necessary for continuing adaptive change.

The Clark Conference papers confronted this ultra-conservative attitude. In his introductory chapter, Meisels noted the importance of the Division as a home for psychologist psychoanalysts that has supported new development without homogenizing differences. The volume of proceedings is dedicated to Helen Block Lewis, who died January 18, 1987, shortly after the conference. Her theoretical contributions to the field of psychology and psychoanalysis, and her conceptual contributions to the Clark Conference, are summarized in a memorial chapter by Shapiro. The book also includes Lewis' presidential addresses to the Division, which describe her views on psychoanalytic education. Helen Block Lewis' theoretical contributions on the superego emotions of shame and guilt focus explicitly on the nature of relationships with inequality of status, and the intrapsychic consequences of interpersonal dominance or exploitation by authority.

Anne Marie Sandler's keynote address discussed the costs and benefits of a requirement-oriented system: This creates a supportive community offering a sense of certainty, in which the faculty takes educational responsibility and the students are compliant. She compared it to an independent-study system that allows more autonomy and creativity, but more uncertainty and revolt. A series of papers on open and closed psychoanalytic training systems followed with the question: What is the proper balance between creating a supportive, experienced community while preserving the autonomy and creativity of its participants? Charles Spezzano's paper noted that because psychologists in the United States have been excluded from training in medical institutes, we have overemphasized the quest for legitimacy and have sought to find or create some overarching authority (a national certificate, the IPA, etc.) to which we could then submit in return for a feeling of external validation. This echoed Meisels' and Slavin's statements that the quest for external authority interferes with the active self-definition required for change.

The papers on the components of psychoanalytic training, personal analysis and supervision, argue that when the training analysis is an institutional requirement, defined as the most important dimension of the psychoanalytic educational process, candidates become extremely vulnerable to conscious and unconscious coercion to become analysts in the image of their training analyst or institution. Panelists addressing the candidate's theoretical learning, "Becoming a psychoanalyst of one persuasion or another," emphasized that psychoanalytic learning at its best involves a relational process of communication of diversity and systematic exploration of differences toward unique personal integration. Exploration and integration of differences in a supportive relational climate not only enhances the analyst's capacity for relatedness as a clinician, it also offers the best chance of advancing the growth of psychoanalytic theory.

The papers on the relationship of psychoanalysis to other forms of therapy and outcome research suggest that psychoanalysis has failed to develop, both technically and theoretically, through its isolation from other disciplines and from scholarly and experimental challenge of its established assumptions. The discussion of the relationship between the Division and local chapters emphasized the importance of active self-determination. For example, initiating the lawsuit against the APsaA, or creating our own educational programs, or in promoting the autonomous self-definition of psychologists as psychoanalysts. Finally the concluding papers were on the contribution of family theory and research—psychology of women, child development, infant research, and family systems theory.

In summary, the Clark Conference papers convey the hopefulness that psychoanalysis can recapture some of the innovative spirit that characterized psychoanalysis in its early years. It is no coincidence that these critiques were generated by Division 39, a psychoanalytic group outside the established groups of the IPA and APsaA. When Division 39 was launched in 1979, it created an important community of reference in which psychologists could explore their own, self-directed participation in the psychoanalytic enterprise. Psychologists in the United States—however they achieved their training—had previously been forced to define themselves as psychoanalysts in relation to the educational and institutional structures of the medical psychoanalytic institutes, which claimed that medical practitioners were the only true keepers of the psychoanalytic flame. Because of systematic exclusion, many psychologists in Division 39 operated outside the rules of family or organizational loyalty.

However, as a number of presenters noted, we cannot yet afford to congratulate ourselves. We outsiders are family members also, and we need to learn as much as we can from the psychoanalytic family history, which is ours as well, lest we too repeat it. What will it take to change our problematic psychoanalytic history toward a less authoritarian, more collaborative future? Hopefully the settlement of the antitrust lawsuit and the Division's creation of new interdisciplinary institutes will provide new opportunities for dialogue which will further the integration of the previously fragmented psychoanalytic community. However, we now have to watch ourselves closely, as we become authorities in the new psychoanalytic establishment, to ensure that we do not idealize any entrenched ideas.

12

The Financial History of Division 39: A Brief Review

Helen K. Golden

The Division of Psychoanalysis (39) was established as an unincorporated, not-for-profit, educational organization in August 1979 with 864 signatories, an annual assessment of $10 per member, and George Goldman as its first treasurer. At the end of its fledgling year it boasted a gain of 250 members and a net worth of $5,933. Twelve years later, under the successive financial stewardships of Ernest Lawrence, Sydney Smith, and Helen K. Golden, and following a membership expansion unparalleled in the history of the APA, it has become the fifth largest division in the Association. Its income, generated primarily by membership dues and increasingly by the registration receipts of its internationally recognized spring meetings, led to a net worth, at the end of 1990, of approximately $300,000. In addition to this, approximately $300,000, held in escrow by the attorneys for GAPPP, remained from the settlement of the antitrust suit against APsaA and IPA. As the moral force behind the commencement and maintainence of the lawsuit, and having contributed substantially to its prosecution and to the continuing needs of its Settlement Enforcement Commission, the Division holds a contingent interest in whatever will remain of these monies.

It is often said that "money is program," and the Division is justly proud of the program it has been able to support. Let me outline its major undertakings, most of which are described in fuller detail in the reports that comprise the main substance of this history.

From the beginning, our single greatest financial commitment has been toward publications, both the official organs of the Division and ad hoc others that have furthered its diverse goals. In 1990 this subsidy, in excess of $108,000, amounted to almost 50% of the total annual disbursement. The Division's journal, *Psychoanalytic Psychology*, founded in 1984 by the late Helen Block Lewis, is currently under the editorship of Bertram J. Cohler and is subsidized at $13.77 per volume for each member. Our publisher, Lawrence Erlbaum Associates, believes that its growing reputation, its widening subscription base outside the Division, and proportionally decreasing costs by virtue of volume will enable a growing return of this extended subsidy beginning with Volume 8 in 1991.

The quarterly Newsletter, *The Psychologist Psychoanalyst*, founded by Marvin Daniels and Robert C. Lane in 1979 and currently edited by James Barron, costs about $20,000 annually. It currently attracts sufficient advertising to offset this subsidy by over 25%. The Newsletter's value as a timely publication of widespread interest to the membership continues to grow, and as increasingly sophisticated production techniques keep costs in bounds, the financial burden it represents to the Division is expected to diminish.

PsycSCAN: PSYCHOANALYSIS, a quarterly journal of abstracts of the national and international psychoanalytic literature, has been a cherished project of the Division. It was developed in conjunction with APA's *SCAN* team, and is produced as part of its highly acclaimed *SCAN* series. It had originally been subsidized at $7.50 per member and is $10 at present. Its usefulness as a reference has led to an extensive subscription beyond the Division. We believe that the Board's recent decision to underwrite the development of an annual index will further enhance its scholarly worth.

The official Membership Directory, in its second edition under the able supervision of Carol Butler, provides an up-to-date listing of the membership, its geographical distribution, as well as the rosters of its seven sections and the officers and locations of its 26 local chapters.

In addition to these regular publications, the Division contracted with Lawrence Erlbaum Associates to publish the proceedings of the Clark Conference at a cost of about $19,000. This 300-page archival volume, *Tradition and Innovation in Psychoanalytic Education*, edited by Murray Meisels and Ester R. Shapiro, was distributed gratis to the Division's membership and was made available to an interested public. We believe it represents a major and significant contribution to contemporary thinking about psychoanalytic education.

The Clark Conference itself, which was held in Worcester, Massachusetts in 1986, was initially endowed by a $25,000 grant from the Exxon Corporation that was awarded to the Division through the efforts of the late Helen Block Lewis. The conference was granted an additional $29,000 by the Division over the several years of its planning primarily to cover expenses of invited overseas participants, of audio taping and transcription of the proceedings, and finally, of the publication mentioned earlier.

The Division also published two books in honor of the APA Centennial year.

The second book published by the Division, *Interface of Psychoanalysis and Psychology*, edited by James W. Barron, Morris N. Eagle, and David Wolitzky was budgeted by monies allocated by the Centennial Committee and subsidized by the APA who published the book, *A History of the Division of Psychoanalysis in the APA* edited by Robert C. Lane and Murray Meisels was budgeted $21,500 for distribution to the membership.

A second area in which continuing financial support has furthered a paramount divisional goal has been the development of local chapters of Division 39 in areas of the country where opportunities for professional involvement in the psychoanalytic enterprise has been limited or nonexistent for psychologists. The Division has directly funded the expenses of consultants, speakers, and a variety of organizational startup activities through annual budgetary grants to Section IV (Local Chapters) and to the standing Education & Training Committee. In addition, the Division has made contributions to the several new psychoanalytic training institutes that have developed as natural outgrowths of several of the local chapters.

A third major area of financial support has been in the prosecution of the GAPPP antitrust lawsuit against APsaA and IPA. In 1985, the Board voted to increase the annual membership assessment by $15 to be earmarked for this purpose. In the 5 years following, almost $175,000 was forwarded to GAPPP as a direct consequence of this action. In addition, the Division mounted a campaign for voluntary contributions from the membership, an effort which garnered an additional $56,000 for the lawsuit warchest. The ultimate disposition of any remainder of the settlement monies must, of course, take into account those sources of financial support deriving outside the Division.

A fourth ongoing commitment was initiated in 1988 with the establishment of a Development Fund, an enforced savings of $10,000 annually to be sequestered from the working capital of the Division. These monies are currently invested in high yield certificates and represent not only a financial cushion against unforeseen expenses, but also a nestegg for future educational and research goals.

Let me close this review of the Division's larger involvements with a brief summary of some of its newer and perhaps less well-known activities. In 1990, two important conferences were inaugurated. The Federation Conference, initiated by past-president Murray Meisels, was designed to explore, with representatives of psychoanalytic training institutes and local chapters around the country, the feasibility of forming a federation of such educational groups to further those individual and common interests that lie outside the domain of the Division. The Bethesda Conference was a research meeting held in conjunction with, and equally supported by APsaA. Its historic mission was to explore the possibility of discovering genuine areas of mutual interest and potential liaison in the area of psychoanalytic research. As with the Federation Conference, this joint exploration continues. In a somewhat different vein, the Division has just completed a substantial 5-year pledge of support to the Freud Museum at Maresfield Gardens in London. Its position as a patron of the museum is prominently acknowledged on a plaque in the lovely garden room where Freud spent the last weeks of his life. The appointment of a new curator for the museum has caused us to delay full renewal of this pledge as we await clarification on potential changes in policy. In a similar spirit, in 1991 the Board made a 5-year pledge to the American Friends of Hebrew University in support of its Freud Center whose program promotes, in a multitude of ways, psychoanalytic study and research in Israel. And finally, the Board has recently established and funded a Committee on International Relations. Its aim is to sponsor contact with psychologists from the Soviet Union and emerging iron curtain countries whose desire for contact with American psychologists is recognized as being mutually enriching.

Let me now turn to the ways and means by which this program has been realized in little more than one brief decade. First and foremost, the unprecedented growth of the Division has defied the growth curves of each division preceding it. It expanded by an average of 16% annually in its first 5 years of existence and has continued to grow at an average rate of 8% to this time—an astonishing fact in view of the dire commentaries on the future of psychoanalysis. Thus, from a founding membership of 864, our latest figures indicate a membership of 3,433. The original assessment of $10 was increased to $25 in the second year with gradual increments over the next few years as the Division struggled to get on its feet and to inaugurate the program that I reviewed. In August 1985, at the time this reporter began a 6-year term as treasurer, the assessment was increased to its current $60 primarily to support the antitrust suit. Gross income has grown from $10,605 at the end of the first year largely through membership assessment and contributions to $229,432 10 years later through membership assessment, contributions, the mid-winter meeting, interest income and Newsletter advertising.

Let me turn now to that fluctuating but substantial source of the Division's revenue—its midwinter meeting. This meeting was originally conceived as an opportunity to combine the purposes of a scientific convention with a brief vacation break for interested members. Thus, five of the first six meetings were held in warm weather resort areas. However, the fifth meeting, held in New York City, had an enormous attendance and generated a profit that accounted for almost 20% of the income for the entire year. It was clear that part of this success could be attributed to the large proportion of the membership that resided in the New York City area. However, a closer analysis of the registration distribution suggested that the high costs of attending a meeting in Mexico or Puerto Rico discouraged many members, and positively prohibited attendance by the graduate students and analytic candidates who were so abundantly and enthusiastically present in New York. A reassessment of the purposes of this meeting pointed to the choice of a site that would be both affordable and located in

TABLE 12.1
Midwinter Meeting Income, 1981–1991

Year	Location	Net Receipts
1981	Mexico	324
1982	Puerto Rico	(192)
1983	Puerto Rico	
1984	San Diego	4,590
1985	New York City	26,776
1986	Mexico	7,286
1987	New York City	27,726
1988	San Francisco	20,948
1989	Boston	47,000
1990	New York City	100,191
1991	Chicago	26,126

an area that would facilitate the participation of the youngest members of the Division—its student affiliates. Table 12.1 indicates the wisdom of this shift in concept although it does not attempt to do justice to the many variables that account for as encompassing a figure as the net receipts presented in the last column.

One final note concerning contributions. Approximately 7% of the members of the Division have reached the status of Life Member in the APA. As such, they are dues-exempt in the parent organization as well as in any of the divisions to which they may belong. This group has consistently contributed to Division 39 and has gone a long way in carrying the costs of the many benefits that accrue to them as members. At the other end of the curve are the student affiliates, a group of about the same size, and whose membership the Division gladly subsidized in exchange for their anticipated contribution to the continuing development of psychoanalysis. In any case, I believe it safe to say that the Division is thriving and well able to sustain the quality of diverse program briefly outlined here. The support of its older members, the dedication of its leadership, and its ability to continue to attract vital new members gives testimony to its strength of purpose and the health of its treasury.

13

Membership

Stuart A. Pizer

There are many stories to tell about Membership in the Division of Psychoanalysis during the decade of the 1980s. One story would be about those individuals who labored as membership chairs in the first years of our Division's life, contributing the "nuts and bolts" work that established the set of procedures on which our membership's growth and maintenance now depends. But, although this work was indeed important, its narration does not make an epic saga. So, with our Division's succession of membership chairs and their dedicated efforts remaining in the background (as, indeed, did their creative and pragmatic work along the way), the focus of the story here is the Division's membership itself.

The central themes of the Membership story are growth, change and diversification. Table 13.1 details the growth of Division 39 membership in the years since 1980 (according to data obtained from APA Membership Registers and Directories).

In August 1980 the Division's membership numbered 926. By August, 1991, our membership expanded to 3,280. A sampling of membership growth in the intervening years shows that in each year our division grew by roughly 200 members, until 1990–1991 when we enjoyed a growth spurt of 507 new members. In 1987 we received 535 requests for membership applications; in 1990 we received 1,686. Last year Division 39 was the fastest growing Division in the APA, and the third largest. There seem to have been two bursts of membership growth in the 11-year history of our division: one at its birth, and the other in the period of the lawsuit settlement, the burgeoning of new psychoanalytic

TABLE 13.1
Division 39: Division of Psychoanalysis, Membership History

	Members	Associates	Total
1980	926	—	926
1981	1,175	—	1,175
1982	1,355	—	1,355
1983	1,544	—	1,544
1984	1,748	—	1,748
1985	1,910	39	1,949
1986	2,066	50	2,116
1987	2,222	72	2,294
1988	2,356	79	2,435
1989	2,470	113	2,583
1990	2,669	104	2,773
1991	3,158	122	3,280
1992			3,433

training institutes nurtured by local chapters across the country, and the remarkable renaissance of interest in psychoanalysis.

Impressive as this sheer numerical growth has been, the expansion of Division 39 has rendered notable changes in the membership profile that can be summarized in a word: diversification. The Division of Psychoanalysis has developed a membership base increasingly diverse in its geographic and professional distribution. For example, a survey of Division 39 members conducted in 1980 by Murray Meisels and Jerry W. O'Dell led them to conclude that "our Division is dominated by New Yorkers." Fully 54% of the membership lived in the New York City area. In the 1989 Membership Directory, the percentage of Division members living in the same geographic area had shrunk to 41%. By August 1990 the New York City area accounted for roughly 37% of the Division's membership. Meanwhile, membership in Illinois, Michigan, and Pennsylvania had doubled; membership in California, Connecticut, and the Washington, DC area had nearly tripled; Massachusetts quadrupled and Colorado quintupled. Thus, the Division of Psychoanalysis, in the course of 10 years, has approached a more broad and even geographic distribution of membership as local chapters and local institutes have proliferated outside the New York area. The geographic spread of membership in the Division of Psychoanalysis now extends to Canada, France, Mexico, and South Africa. In 1990 Division 39 received requests for membership applications from West Germany, Argentina, Puerto Rico, and India. And, with the profound historical changes of 1991 we received membership requests from eastern Europe and the former Soviet Union.

The same 1980 Membership Survey reported by Meisels and O'Dell stated that 89% of the membership was involved in private practice, and that for 61% private practice was their sole professional position. College and university affiliations represented 40% of the survey's respondents. This survey led to the inference that "we are, in sum, practitioners and teachers. We are not consultants, researchers, administrators, or government workers." Whereas the preponderance of our membership may well be similarly distributed in 1990, it is relevant to note here that Division 39 now has a Section on Research and a Section on Groups.

Finally, as of August 1991, women constituted 51% of the membership of Division 39. This makes the Division of Psychoanalysis the third ranking division in APA in percentage of female membership (after the Division of the Psychology of Women and the Division of Developmental Psychology).

In summary, between 1980 and 1991 Division 39 has witnessed a dramatic growth in membership, a wave of investment in psychoanalysis that has rippled across the country among psychologists, and spread beyond the cadre of graduate analysts who originally gathered to discuss whether the new Division of Psychoanalysis should be a credentialling body with restricted membership or an interest group with open admission to members of APA. Who knew back in 1979 what beast had come slouching toward Manhattan to be born?

14

A History of the Awards Committee

Harold B. Davis
Helen W. Silverman

The history of awards within the Division reveals a natural evolution although an uneven one. Its history can be divided into two time spans, prior to 1987 and since then. Prior to 1987 various ad hoc committees with various names (e.g., research committee or awards committee) suggested specific awards or names for awards from the Division and from APA. As far as can be ascertained from existing records and reports, there was no consistent procedure or committee for making awards. Periodically the names for awards or a suggestion for a specific type of awards was made. The interesting point is that the type of awards suggested in the earlier time frame were very similar, though with different names, to those independently developed by the recent committee. Thus, the Division has always sought to recognize significant contributions to scholarly work as well as contributions of service (i.e., primarily professional activity). In addition there had already been a suggestion by a research committee for an award for the best publishable paper by a senior or junior psychologist. As the Division has become more developed and organized, the Awards Committee has coordinated what was previously done, though in a more consistent and structured way.

The Awards Committee of the Division is an ad hoc committee that serves a specific and limited function. The chairperson is appointed by the President on an annual basis. Originally the Awards Committee, under varying names, was appointed on an intermittent basis, selected an awardee and disbanded. The Committee's original purpose was to honor a specific individual for scientific contributions, however, in recent years the number and types of awards have increased. Since 1990 the Committee has been regularly reappointed by each President and has functioned on a regular basis. This change to a more consistent existence though still on an ad hoc basis, reflects the advancement of the Division, and the desire of the Division to acknowledge the contributions of its members on both a national and local level.

The Committee has met regularly in the last 3 years and several awards are now offered on a yearly basis. The main award is the Distinguished Scientific Award, which is given to someone for a lifetime of work or a major contribution to psychoanalytic thought. Another major change in the last 3 years is the increased autonomy of the Division in selecting the awardee. Previously the Committee made recommendations to APA for the granting of its awards. The final judgment was made by APA whose criteria reflected a greater emphasis on the contribution to general psychology rather than to psychoanalysis proper, although the individuals who received the awards had also made contributions to psychoanalysis. The award was APA's and not the Division's and reflected a different emphasis as well as a lack of autonomy by the Division. For example in 1983 a committee chaired by Sidney Blatt recommended to APA Roy Schafer, Robert Holt, and Gordon Derner for awards. Other ad hoc committees presented awards for the Division to Rudolf Ekstein, Erika Fromm, and Lester Luborsky.

In the last 3 years the Awards Committee increased the number of awards bestowed in an attempt to recognize and honor people who made significant contributions to psychoanalysis in several categories. First, is the Distinguished Scientific Award whose nominee makes an address to the Division at the midwinter meetings, and then a Distinguished Service Award honoring a person whose contribution has been in service to psychoanalysis rather than scholarly contributions. This latter award is one that APA would not have readily accepted. This award recognizes that in psychoanalysis significant contributions may be made in the areas of service and training and are as important for the field as scientific achievements.

Second, a Postdoctoral Award and a Doctoral Award were instituted for the best paper submitted in each category. These awards were developed to recognize and stimulate contributions to the psychoanalytic literature by the younger generation of psychoanalysts. The former award was for the best paper by someone within 10 years of having received their doctorate. The latter award was for the best doctoral dissertation or paper contributed by a doctoral student. When the Committee originated these two awards it was unaware that a suggestion for similar awards had been made previously, but apparently not instituted. A research committee under the chair of Joseph Masling had proposed a junior and senior award for the best publishable paper in (a) clinical theory and practice and (b) research. Here is an illustration of the Committee's continuous basis for what previously was only suggested or intermittently executed.

Thirdly, the Division Board has recently authorized the Committee to make a special award to a nonpsychologist who has made a significant contribution to psychoanalysis. Because this award is to a nonpsychologist, it requires the approval of the Board. This award was the outgrowth of the Board's approval of an award to Merton Gill on the recommendation of Oliver Kerner. In the category of special awards, the Committee has been the agent of the Division Board in preparing the awards for those the Board wished to honor, such as to the plaintiffs of the lawsuit, and to Byrant Welch for his service with the lawsuit, and so on. Special awards have also included awards to individuals who have made long term contributions of service to the Division.

The recipients of the Distinguished Scientific Awards in the last 5 years have been:

Bruno Bettleheim, 1988	Morris Eagle, 1991
Stephen A. Mitchell, 1989	Jay R. Greenberg, 1992
Sylvia Brody, 1990	Irene Fast, 1993

The recipients of the Distinguished Service Award have been:

Bernard Kalinkowitz, 1988	Murray Meisels, 1991
George D. Goldman &	Jules C. Abrams, 1992
Robert Lane, 1989	Esther Menaker, 1993
Marvin Hyman, 1990	Bryant Welch, 1994

The recipients of the Postdoctoral Award have been:

David Anderegg, 1988
Lewis Aron, 1989
Brent Willock, 1990

The recipients of the Doctoral Award have been:

David J. Diamond, 1988
Steven Reisner, 1989
Lourdes Ochoa, 1990

The members of the Committee have been:

1987–1988   B. Karon, H. Nechin, R. Ochroch, and M. Pollak
1988–1993   G. Gerber, R. Ochroch, and H. Silverman

15

The History of the Ethics Committee in Division 39

Norma P. Simon

In the beginning . . . during the first year of the Division, there were the usual start-up struggles and decisions to be made concerning the structure and function of the various committees and task forces of the Division. The Standing Committees, including the Ethics Committee, were created by the bylaws of the Division and a chair was chosen for each standing committee by the President of the Division. The first elected president, Gordon F. Derner, chose George Stricker as the first Ethics Committee Chair. The original task of the Committee was to develop a charge and set an outline for its work. At that time, 1980, at APA, the role of ethics committees of the divisions was in a state of flux. To Stricker it was clear that the responsibility at the division level was to forward ethical complaints to the APA Ethics Committee, make a considered judgement about the various ethical questions asked of the chair and of the committee, and to provide an educational forum for ethical issues. The charge as Stricker wrote it was:

> The Ethics Committee has both passive and active functions. Its major passive function is to serve as a resource for the Division in the event that ethics questions are asked or ethics issues are raised. The active function which it currently has undertaken is to study the relevancy of the APA Code of Ethics for the practice of psychoanalysis and to construct a casebook of theoretical problems in psychoanalysis and their resolutions.

THE EARLY YEARS

The kinds of issues brought to the Ethics Committee in the beginning were such things as: Was it ethical to bring a patient to be observed with you at an ABPP examination? What are the limits of confidentiality? Was a license required to be a psychologist/psychoanalyst? In addition, the ethics committee provided information to the membership on current issues such as the revision of the *Ethical Principles in the Conduct of Research with Human Subjects*. During the early 1980s, APA was asking the divisions for information in this area. There were also many issues of social and ethical concern that were brought to the attention of the Division through the Ethics Committee. The development of a Committee on Gay and Lesbian Concerns was formed at APA to look into the issue of discrimination of both gay and lesbian psychologists and of clients who were gay or lesbian. APA also formed a task force to develop guidelines for working with the physically disabled. This committee was to look into such things as provisions at conferences for the disabled. Divisions were asked to disseminate information about the work of these groups to their membership. Also of concern was the resolution pending in the APA Council of Representatives asking for the prevention of the use of painful stimuli to "control or modify the behavior of handicapped children." Though this issue has had many forums from its introduction in 1980 until the present, it has not been resolved by APA.

Another function of the committee in the early days was to survey the membership. During George Sticker's tenure a survey was conducted asking for, "critical ethical incidents which illustrate dilemmas which arise in practice." Stricker remembers that few members responded. The Ethics Committee continued to publish material and be available to the membership on ethical issues. Ruth Ochroch and Robert Keisner were the other members of the committee during the years of Stricker's chairship.

In 1983, during the tenure of Mark Grunes, the Ethics Committee mainly handled complaints against members concerning their conduct during the practice of psychoanalysis. These complaints were forwarded to the Ethics Committee of APA. (Seldom does the Division receive a reply from APA Ethics on the various complaints sent forward.) In addition, the membership continued to turn to the ethics chair for advice concerning the appropriate behavior of a professional psychologist/psychoanalyst. In 1984 Irving Solomon raised an issue in the *Psychologist-Psychoanalyst* that set off a lively topic for discussion and response that continues to the present. What are the motivations for publicly supervising another analyst and what are the ethical considerations in so doing? Solomon was specifically interested in the unasked-for supervision when a case presentation has been made and a discussant is responding to the material. This raised the larger issue of the ethical problems in presenting case material at open forums and what protection must be afforded to the patient in such circumstances. The lead article in the Newsletter in the Spring of 1984 was on this issue. Recommendations were made for the proper procedures to follow in case presentations and for obtaining a release of information from the patient where necessary. Also in 1984, the issue of the distressed or impaired psychologist was first brought to the attention of the membership. The APA Board of Professional Affairs was working on a dissemination plan to provide information to state associations and divisions about this problem. Stanley Gochman wrote in the *Psychologist-Psychoanalyst* that "Division 39 should provide more input, assist in setting up helping criteria, and should be actively represented on the VIP Board and in the program, both in a preventive and in a helping role." The issue of peer review was hotly debated at this time as well. Much was said in our publications about this. Analysts were some of the prime movers to get APA to look at this issue and give greater protection to their patients as well as to the analysts themselves.

In 1985, during one of the most unpleasant times in the history of the Division, Nathan Stockhamer, President of the Division sent a note to "all board members, committee chairs, guests, observers and all Division 39 members who were present at the November 16, 1985, Division 39 Board of Directors meeting." This note indicated that some members received "insulting anonymous notes regarding divisional and related issues." Stockhamer went on to remind the members that this was reprehensible. He also reminded the note-writer that such behavior was grounds for an ethics charge before the APA Ethics Committee. Clearly this was a low point for the Division.

THE PRESENT

During the presidency of Murray Meisels in 1987, I was invited to be the Chair of the Ethics Committee. Meisels made it clear that the appropriate role of the committee at this point in time was primarily educational. Additionally, to give advice to members on ethical issues and to develop materials to make it possible for the Board of Directors to make determinations on the unethical behavior of members that might need to be forwarded to the APA Ethics Committee. Nina Fieldsteel was appointed to serve with me on the committee. We decided to write a column for the *Psychologist-Psychoanalyst* entitled "Ethical Dilemmas." In this column we presented ethical issues that either we had experienced or that had been brought to us by members of the community. We raised these dilemmas without answers with the hopes that we would receive reports back from the membership on how such dilemmas were being resolved. We did receive some responses in writing. One in particular from Lynn Means was published as a response to our dilemma on what to do when an airline pilot tells you he has been using cocaine. Other dilemmas raised were: What do you do when you have knowledge of HIV positive blood serum in a patient who is sexually promiscuous? What do you do when the analyst is sick or dying? How do you prepare and handle the records of an analyst who has died? What do you do for a patient whose analyst has died or is dying? We also commented on breach of confidentiality, both in cases of duty to warn and child abuse, as well as the therapist's breach when supervising, giving lectures and providing group treatment.

During my tenure as Chair, I was also asked to comment on ethical issues in training institutes and worked on the draft of a model ethical code for training institutes. Nina Fieldsteel and I decided to broaden this to ask current institutes to tell us what kind of a code they have, what issues need to be developed and how useful a code would be for them. The Executive Committee of the Division allocated money for us to develop a questionnaire and to work on the code. Fieldsteel has taken over the development of this during her tenure as Chair of Ethics (1990–1991).

Another issue that has come to prominence since the founding of the Division that seriously affects our work and the stature of psychologists in the public eye is that of sexual misconduct by psychologists. I believe that this has become an illegal activity in almost all of the states and provinces of Canada. A number of articles appeared on the subject in our publications over the years. In New York and in most other states, there have been a number of cases brought before the State Board for Psychology. In the majority of cases, a disciplinary loss of license is the strongest penalty that can be imposed on a psychologist if found guilty of such a charge in an administrative hearing. Many are also charged in a court of law. Sydney Smith wrote a column in the Newsletter on this topic in 1988. He discussed the Minnesota law of 1986 that became the model for other legislation. The Division has responded by having programs at both midwinter (or spring) meetings and at the APA convention where the issue of sexual impropriety on the part of the therapist-analyst has been highlighted. The concern for the patient, the effect on the patient's fragile ego resources, and the effect on the patient's family have been discussed. This issue, more than any other, has been the one that has continued to plague the entire mental health community. The knowledge that this behavior, like the incidents of sexual abuse of children, is far more prevalent than we would like to believe, is a sobering thought. What do we have to do in our graduate training programs and in our analytic programs to identify those persons we believe would violate the patient's trust in such a manner? What can we do to not only teach ethical behavior, but to insure ethical behavior? How do we proceed from here in our Division to continue to work on this and all of the ethical issues that have been raised over the years? Our profession will rise or fall on the trust the public has in the professional psychological-psychoanalytic community. We in our Division, have the added obligation as analysts to not only understand the issues but see to it that our membership is as informed as possible about all of the ethical and legal implications of our very sensitive roles in the lives of others. This continues to be the mission of the Ethics Committee for the Division.

16

Psychoanalytic Psychology: Its Place in Identifying Social Issues and Guiding Solutions Through Humane Public Policy

Erwin R. Parson
Stanley I. Gochman

AN AGENDA FOR CONTEMPORARY "CIVILIZATION AND ITS DISCONTENTS"

Psychologists within APA's Division of Psychoanalysis are in the enviable position of being able to substantively effect social change, and one available vehicle for this may be the Committee on Social Issues and Public Policy of the Division. There is an opportunity to influence the development of population-sensitive service delivery models (e.g., for the ethnic minorities and the ethnic majorities; for needy populations in America and in other countries of the world—particularly children affected by war and violence in their communities, etc.).

Additionally, conditions that result in high mortality can be managed through change in behavior and lifestyle. We believe psychoanalytic psychology can be advantageous because it deals with the underlying conflictual forces related to the why of high-risk behavior. For example, the rapid and alarming explosion of Acquired Immune Deficiency Syndrome (AIDS) in American youths appears highly resistive to public education. Perhaps an existing cultural, unconscious destructive drive is so powerful in today's youths that mere education directed to offer information (or cognitive education) is not enough. Psychologist-psychoanalysts can assist in helping youths educate the unconscious mind and emotions.

If psychologists are to be successful in applying their skills to contemporary and future society, psychologists' professional skills must be buttressed by a restructured state of mind and perspective. Without this occurring, the ideal move from tradition to innovation (Meisels & Shapiro, 1990) will not be possible.

Psychoanalytic psychology should move proactively toward image-revitalization and change, and toward the ameliorating of socialized expression of both libidinal and aggressive drives. The culture-directed profusion of violence in movies, the increase of violence against women (in terms of physical abuse and rape), the wanton disregard for family and social values, sexual promiscuity, the exposure of children to sexual abuse, increase in adolescent suicides, and mass and near-mass murders, constitute evidence that libidinal and aggressive drives have gone totally out of control, to the detriment of society.

It is noteworthy that early psychoanalysts showed great enthusiasm and hope that psychodynamic thinking would be applied to broad social issues and to public policy, as far back as the 1920s at least. Alfred Adler (1933/1964), for example, introduced the concept of Social Interest, or the significance of concern for a wider human community, beyond oneself, as an indicator of sound mental health and interpersonal interaction, and healthy normal development. Social Interest carries significant implications for the understanding of current social problems and social deviance and for the building of wholesome policies and human communities.

CONTEMPORARY DISCONTENTS AND CULTUROSOCIAL PERIL

Our society and world today exhibit a multiplicity of problems from both natural and manmade origins. Assaulting the integrity of family life, the heart of civilized existence, are child neglect and abuse, the normative cultural narcissism, which sanctions forms of subtle child neglect in the interest of parental narcissistic pursuits, family violence, severe economic pressures, absence of health insurance for over 37 million Americans, high infant mortality (especially among African American and other minority groups), and unrelieved family stress. In the corporate arena there is a widespread crisis in moral and ethical values and conduct. And, in society at large, discriminatory practices against people-of-difference continue unvanquished, as in sexism, ageism, Vietnamism, racism, and general intolerance for multiethnic diversity.

Many of these conditions affect most people directly or indirectly. The absence of a workable social policy to address these personal and social forms of conflict has created the unfortunate scenario of severe psychological and social conditions and disorders. Among the problematic responses are: alcoholism, ACOS (adult children of alcoholics), drug addiction and other forms of impulse disorders (workaholism, compulsive gambling, manic binge shopping, shoplifting, sex addiction, and addiction to violent behavior or passive viewing or vicarious participation), wife-beating (mostly physical), husband-beating (psychological in form of manhood-diminution and humiliation), child physical and sexual abuse; steep rise in divorce rates (almost one in two), community violence, the horrific finding that almost one in four African-American males (between the ages of 20 and 29, or 610,000) are in the prison system, and the increase in epidemiology of anger mismanagement and psychological and social disorders.

From this array of conditions, several patient/client populations are identified: child victims of sexual and physical abuse, parents and children of the Holocaust, traumatized refugees, prisoners of war, war veterans, and survivors of massive psychic traumatization; for example, refugees from Cambodia, Vietnam, Central America, and other parts of the world. Psychoanalysis must find new models by which to overcome the "limitations of middle-class-oriented psychotherapy to achieve results" (Caligor, Zaphiropoulis, Grey, & Ortmeyer, 1971, p. 175).

PSYCHOANALYTIC ECOLOGY

We believe Levine and Levine (1971) were correct when they wrote that "Social change is too important to be left in the hands of politicians, the engineers, the economists, managers, and architects alone. The mental health professional [psychologist-psychoanalyst] is a necessary member of the planning team" (p. 43). Freud (1925) showed he was aware of the need to communicate clearly to the public when he wrote, "but we shall need to find the simplest and most natural expression for our theoretical doctrines" (p. 402). The Division's "shift from 'standards' to local chapters" (Meisels & Shapiro, 1990, p. 4) is one effective way of finding "... the simplest and most natural expression" of psychoanalytic principles for the public.

Psychoanalytic psychology must incorporate the elements of the real world, those factors that shape people's personality, contribute to psychopathology, and often point the way to recovery as well. Proposed here is the psychoanalytic-ecological perspective, which views health and pathology as originating in the transaction of internal-intrinsic and external-extrinsic factors. This view moves us beyond the medical model's exclusive focus on the person and on his or her needs as the nexus of pathology, and as the exclusive agent in recovery. Psychoanalytic ecology espouses the psychoanalytic and the ecologic, and so incorporates conceptual elements from ethnopsychoanalytical field research (Parin, 1972).

The concept of psychoanalytic ecology embraces the perennial problem of the traditional analyst working with inner city minority, and low socioeconomic status patients. It is well known that the concept of the *average expectable environment* is an important one in conceptualizing health and pathology. Psychoanalysis can now usefully address the problems that emerge from the equally important concept of the *nonaverage, nonexpectable, erratic, and chaotic environment* (Parson, 1980).

Psychoanalytic-ecology constructs a theory of understanding and intervening based on the knowledge and conviction that people are the product of transactions that they experience between their internal world and the external environment. This notion is not new at all; however, analysts tend to behave in ways that negate the relevance of this interdependence, in our theories and techniques. Recognition of this interdependence is important if analysts are to progress to applying a psychology of social action to society's problems (Gochman, 1981).

When viewed from the transactional vantage point, it becomes possible to understand classes of patients in a different light. For example, problems of African-American patients may be conceptually understood as a result of transactional processes that are dynamic and interactive. This takes into consideration the interactive psychic effects of personal-familial, ethnic-cultural, and socioeconomic factors, to include the adverse effects of racism and its derivatives (e.g., poverty, low self-esteem, absence of opportunity, etc.). Similarly, the traumatic self-pathology of the Vietnam combat veteran may be understood from a complex (rather than from a one-track) perspective that focuses not so exclusively on pre-war factors, but also accommodates the effects of war trauma on the mind, and the impact of collective stigmatization and narcissistic wounding on subsequent personality organization.

PSYCHOANALYTIC PSYCHOLOGY AND PUBLIC POLICY

The Committee on Social Issues and Public Policy was created by Division 39 President Robert C. Lane a decade ago. He appointed Stanley Gochman as its Chair and lead author Erwin Parson later as Co-Chair. The committee's natural "constituency" includes the poor, blue-collar workers, and other underserved populations often neglected and dubbed untreatable or unmotivated, in the spirit of Freud (1925) who advocated extending psychoanalytic treatment to large masses of people, and spoke of the rights of the poor man.

As noted by Parson (1992) and Thompson (1989), some contemporary analysts still view poor and socially traumatized patients as posing problems that are incompatible with the procedures and requirements of psychoanalysis. These analysts, however, may find they have something in common with these patients; namely, being targets of discriminatory practices by a powerful and often intimidating authority. Slavin (1990) pointed out that psychologist-psychoanalysts suffered due to the political situation constructed by the medical orthodoxy that resembles apartheid.

Greater tolerance and respect are needed for the so-called difficult patients (Parson, 1988), for example, low-income White, and minority group persons;

Vietnam veterans; child victims of physical and sexual abuse; refugees; AIDS victims, etc.). Some analysts are more Freudian than Freud. Freud himself refused to be a Freudian; he instead chose freedom to be creative and innovative.

THE COMMITTEE ON SOCIAL ISSUES
AND PUBLIC POLICY (COMSIPP)

As a functional and meaningful endeavor, COMSIPP represents a proactively organized group of psychologists who identify and highlight key social issues. But they go beyond: they seek solutions through society's chosen policy structures. COMSIPP's initiatives, activities, and achievements since the early 1980s dealt chiefly with the identification and definition of problems. Its general objective, basic functions, and structure are presented later. COMSIPP set out "to deal with all matters which have broadly social and public policy impact for psychologist-psychoanalysts" (COMSIPP Structure, Function and Vision Document, 1981, p. 1).

Committee members were psychologists from various parts of the United States: Hedda Bolgar, Gertrude Cooper, Eva Gubler Gochman, Bertram P. Karon, James Lassiter, Harold Lindner, Virginia L. Revere, and Cheryl L. Thompson. The Co-Chairs were Stanley I. Gochman and Erwin Randolph Parson.

Specialized subcommittees were organized to cover a broad spectrum of social issues: Children's Affairs, Primary Prevention, Homelessness (Child-Mother Pairs, Veterans, and the Mentally Ill), Multicultural Affair and Anti-Apartheid Forum, Victimology (of rape, muggings, etc.), Veterans' Affairs, Peace and Anti-War Programs, post-traumatic stress disorder (PTSD; victims or survivor of war, rape, physical assult, airplane crash, car accidents, occupational, and duty-related traumatic stress.

Most of COMSIPP's work was at the stage of of identification of problems. The Committee reviewed and studied a proposal requesting Division support by Marie Coleman Nelson, who at the time was in Nairobi, Kenya in Africa. In Nelson's words: "If Amani, the only psychotherapeutic training and treatment facility in East Africa, does not obtain funding by December, 1985, it will have to close its doors. Can Division 39 help us?"

COMSIPP recommended that the Division offer the requested fiscal support, which would be matched by an international organization that ensures mental health services in Third World countries. An announcement was to be placed in *The Psychologist-Psychoanalyst* to alert Division members of the Program's needs.

The Committee took a firm stand against *Psychology Today's* advertising of electro-shock treatments. Though the Committee recognized that some forms of somatotherapies are useful for some patients, the concern was that the widely propagated claims would further confuse the general public about the relative value of psychotherapy versus medication. As President of Division 39 at the time, Helen Block Lewis noted that *Psychology Today* had been involved in other noxious advertising ventures that required our attention.

With the solid support of Committee members, Stanley I. Gochman, Co-Chair of COMSIPP wrote a three-page letter to ABC-TV's "20/20" reporters bringing their attention to three programs the network had aired on the biological treatment of anxiety and depression. He asserted that, "It is particularly important to present a balanced view on such topics, especially by you ("20/20" people), who are looked up to as presenting unbiased, objective information." Gochman went on to state that, "All three programs on anxiety, medication research, and depression presented a biological/medical point of view. This by no means represents a consensus or majority view of the mental health, psychological, psychiatric, and scientific community, but an extremist view. They would lead one to believe that biology, medicine, and drugs are either now or would become, in the near future, the panacea for the psychological problems associated with stress, conflict, and living."

The Committee requested feedback from the Division's Board of Directors pertaining to a specially developed Questionnaire on broad social issues confronting our society and Division. The Committee also appealed for input in identifying pressing social issues in need of public initiatives.

The Committee sponsored symposia, white papers, and articles on a psychological approach to mental disorders in general, and to specific disorders such as schizophrenia and traumatic neurosis. It reviewed APA Monitor's story on gene specificity pertaining to manic-depressive illness, and took proactive steps to combat such potentially injurious and misguided information to the public. A subsequent public service article was written by COMSIPP members and published in the APA Monitor. The article titled, "Public Misled on Gene for Manic Depression," stated that "The public has been misled by recent reports stating that a manic-depression gene has been found . . . Four recent independent studies found four different genetic locations." None of these reported studies was replicated in any of the other studies. Therefore, it seems clear that a gene responsible for manic-depression has not been found, and probably does not exist. Rather, at most, some genetic factors have been identified that may be linked with, but cannot be said to cause, manic-depressive disorders.

Thus, Karon, Revere, Gochman, and Parson (1986) stated:

> Similarly, past studies of hereditary factors in schizophrenia have proven inconclusive. Since it is well-known that most, if not all, manic-depressive patients treated biochemically relapse, it is a serious mistake to reinforce an exclusively biological emphasis in research and treatment. Equal emphasis needs to be placed on psychosocial factors in dealing with these disorders. . . . Finally, the relationship between a genetic finding and a set of symptoms (physical, psychological, or behavioral) is much too complex to warrant simplistic causal conclusions. (p. 20)

Its Co-Chair participated in proposals of the APA Committee on Under-represented Groups in the Publication Process, aimed at increasing minority psychologists' involvement in the publication process.

The Committee supported George Albee's proposal to increase minority representation on the APA Council, and also supported the resolution opposing the use of painful stimuli with children. Its Co-Chair was invited by the Ohio Psychological State Association to present a paper on public policy, and published a paper in Stars and Stripes: The National Tribune. Its Co-Chair also became President of the National Consortium on Psychological Aspects of Social Change—an outgrowth of the Fifth Vermont Conference on the Primary Prevention of Psychopathology: Prevention Through Political Action, and Social Change.

COMSIPP's Subcommittee on Children's Issues advanced a proposal to secure APA approval to utilize National Family Week to highlight the application of psychological knowledge to family concerns around such issues as prevention in general, and in relation to incest and rape, and children of Vietnam veterans.

The Committee took a proactivist stance, as well, against the indignity that accompanied a sudden, unexplained firing of eight psychologists in a facility. This meant that 90 children and families, which comprised 3,200 visits per year, mostly African-American, Hispanic, and indigent White Americans, would be dropped almost immediately from care, without plans for continuity or followup of the children. A letter campaign was waged by COMSIPP directed to the facility Director and to public officials.

The Committee engaged in public testimony pertaining to, minority access to the professions in New York State; and engaged in lobbying efforts to secure Medicaid registration programs for New York City psychologists who were unfairly discriminated against in this area. Committee members also participated in a public hearing on professional credentialing in New York State for psychologists. The establishment of a system of indigenous mental health service providers was proposed, who would serve inner city families, and would be supervised by psychologists. Public testimony was also given in behalf of policy adoption relating to Vietnam veteran services nationwide. Target outcomes were observed chiefly in Veterans' programs.

SUMMARY AND CONCLUSION

The Committee on Social Issues and Public Policy set out to accomplish a number of critical objectives in behalf of the Division, the APA and the public. Models that integrate psychodynamic perspectives with sociological, economic, and political factors are few but existent. Psychoanalytic psychology can make a difference in assisting society to formulate a program of education. Psychologist-psychoanalysts can be instrumental in catalyzing an efficacious psychology of social action (Gochman, 1981). Integrating the study of human behavior with the science of unconscious mental life provides an unusual foundation from which to launch inquiries into the contemporary human condition.

REFERENCES

Caligor, L., Zaphiropoulis, M., Grey, A., & Ortmeyer, D. (1971). The Union Therapy Project of the William Alanson White Institute of Psychiatry, Psychoanalysis, and Psychology: A psychoanalytic venture in treating the blue-collar patient. In D. S. Milman & G. D. Goldman (Eds.), *Psychoanalytic contributions to community psychology*. Springfield, IL: Thomas.

COMSIPP Structure, function, and Vision document. (1981). Garden City, NY: Division 39 Central Office.

Freud, S. (1925). *The question of lay analysis. Standard edition.* London: Hogarth

Gochman, S. I. (1981). On the road to 1984: Twenty questions on the psychology of social action. *Journal of Community Psychology, 9*, 103–117.

Karon, B., Revere, V., Gochman, S., & Parson, E. (1986). What gene? *APA Monitor, 17*, 20.

Levine, M., & Levine, A. (1971). Social change and psychopathology: Some derivations from "Civilizations and its discontents." In D. S. Milman & G. D. Goldman (Eds.), *Psychoanalytic contributions to community psychology*. Springfield, IL: Thomas.

Meisels, M. (1990). Introduction: The colorful background to the Clark conference. In M. Meisels & E. Shapiro (Eds.), *Tradition and innovation in psychoanalytic education*. Hillsdale, NJ: Lawrence Erlbaum Associates.

Meisels, M., & Shapiro, E. (Eds.). (1990). *Tradition and innovation in psychoanalytic education*. Hillsdale, NJ: Lawrence Erlbaum Associates.

Parin, A. (1972). *A case of "brain-fag" syndrome: Psychotherapy of the patient Adou A. in the village of Yosso, Ivory Coast Republic*. Hillsdale, NJ: The Analytic Press.

Parson, E. R. (1980, Summer). NYSCP's commitment to minority psychologists and patients. *New York Society for Clinical Psychologists Newsletter*, 14–16.

Parson, E. R. (1988). Notes from the Editor. *Journal of Contemporary Psychotherapy—A Special Issue: The Difficult Patient—Psychotherapeutic Strategies, 19*(2), 77–81.

Parson, E. R. (1993). Post-traumatic narcissism: Healing traumatic alterations of the self through curvilinear group psychotherapy. In J. Wilson & B. Raphael (Eds.), *The international handbook of traumatic stress syndromes*. New York: Plenum.

Slavin, H. (1990). Authority and identity in the establishment of psychoanalytic training: Questions regarding training models. In M. Meisels & E. Shapiro (Eds.), *Tradition and innovation in psychoanalytic education*. Hillsdale, NJ: Lawrence Erlbaum Associates.

Thompson, C. (1989). Psychoanalytic psychotherapy with inner city patients. *Journal of Contemporary Psychotherapy, 19*(2), 137–148.

The Public Information Committee

Susan Kavaler-Adler

The Division 39 Public Information Committee was originally founded by Toni Bernay and Dorothy Cantor, in 1980. The committee was to act as an agent for informing the public about the nature and practice of psychoanalysis. However, even more importantly, as the media presentation of psychotherapy and psychoanalysis became dramatically negative, the committee was looked to as an avenue for transforming the media image through public relations efforts.

In 2 years of service as the Public Information Committee's Chairperson, from 1986 through 1988, the following efforts toward these goals were made. The writer wrote an article printed in the Division newsletter entitled "Public Information Campaign: To Be or Not to Be?" The committee, Olga Marlin, Carol Butler, Aphrodite Clamar, Ona Robinson, and Rafael Javier, gathered together the articles that attacked and devalued the practice of psychoanalysis, such as an article appearing on the cover of *New York Magazine*, in which a patient was tied to a chair in an analyst's office, implying that patients were imprisoned by their analysts' resistance to termination. The Committee gathered information on public relations services and fees. The Committee began public lectures at the Mid-Manhattan library on psychoanalytic treatment. The writer corresponded with Dan Goleman to comment on his negative bias against both psychotherapy and psychoanalysis (particularly in his article on obsessive-compulsive disorders), and to offer ideas that would support a positive view of psychoanalytic treatment. Proposals were made for a liaison with other divisions that might have similar interests in public relations efforts. Attempts were made to work with the APA Practice Directorate in Washington concerning media coverage.

In addition, the writer wrote a proposal for a book on psychoanalytic practice, and consulted an agent who thought it would sell to the public. This proposal created a good deal of discussion, and much dispute about the need for public relations and controversy about the value of such a book. The Division Board did not support the book as a Division project, but many were in favor of the idea.

Historical review of the archives of the public information committee revealed that a successful campaign by a professional public relations consultant was waged by Tony Bernay and Dorothy Cantor. However, funding for the evolving campaign, with its press contacts and press packets, was curtailed by the Division Board before its fruition. Such a decision to curtail funding needs to be reviewed by the Division Board in order to assess the potential undermining of future public information campaign efforts. The curtailing of funding in this case is particularly noteworthy because the public relations consultant was a highly qualified professional who was willing to work for an extremely low fee due to a former close affiliation with APA.

The Newsletter article, "Public Information Campaign: To be or Not to Be?", would have better served its purpose as a letter to the membership. Its text would have invited financial contributions for such a campaign that might offset the financing required by the Division Board. The article stated:

> We would like to know if you think that our Division of Psychoanalysis should be investing in employing a public relations firm to pursue public relations activities. What can you yourself contribute to such a campaign? Would you be willing to be interviewed for articles through the APA Media Panel? Would you be willing to write an article either for the in house APA publications of Psychology Today or the APA Monitor, or for other magazines, and newspaper publications. Do you have access to research information on psychoanalysis that would be circulated to the public either through magazine articles or through a booklet specifically written to provide basic information about the practice of psychoanalysis to the public? Think about it. We all need your concern.

The earlier part of the article read as follows:

> As psychologists and psychoanalysts, we start out with two strikes against us in media representation. First we have the one just described, which relates to the neglect of funding from our own organizations towards any form of meaningful public relations project, which could enhance the public's view of clinical psychologists. Second, we have the overall bad press that psychoanalysis and long term psychotherapy has been receiving on a repeated basis from broad sections of the media. There has been much concern recently about the ongoing biases against psychoanalysis, which have been in the media, and about the related distortions and misconceptions which have been attributed as well to long term therapy in general. When APA met in New York, such articles proliferated even beyond the

ongoing norm. For example, *New York Magazine* came out with a front page picture of a patient chained to an analyst's couch. Many who never read the article still were apt to see this picture, and the inside story was not much better. Therapeutic addiction, rather than resolution of unconscious addictive yearnings was touted as the "nature of the beast." In response to this slew of media slants, or what we might call our "bum rap," many of us in the Division of Psychoanalysis have become concerned. We want to start a campaign to present a positive image of psychoanalysis and its related modes of treatment to the public.

I see the depletion of all our psychoanalytic practices being directly correlated to the lack of investment in public relations by psychologist-psychoanalysts. An article in the 1990 Newsletter of the New York Society of Clinical Psychologists states the case well:

> Psychology in New York state is limping badly these days. With few exceptions, stories I hear are of diminishing practice hours, and ever stingier insurance plans. Psychiatrists do not pose a significant threat to practices. The latest fads in insurance do. Yet to the best of my knowledge APA does not have one single program on the drawing boards directed towards the real adversary, the growth of HMOs, PPOs and managed care in NY state. Not one. Zero. Zip. Nada. If we're going to be in court at all, we ought to be battling managed care plans. And if we're going to be conducting letter-writing and public relations campaigns, we ought to be warning the public about the limitations on their right to therapy under managed care plans. . . .

The Public Information Committee could have a significant impact on initiating such a campaign, if sufficient financial support were provided by a combination of membership contributions and Division Board funds. Many in the Division who began to place faith in the Committee might not just be misguided in their assumption that "something is finally being done about it."

Minority Involvement
in Psychoanalysis

Dorita Marina
Antonio R. Virsida

Beyond numerical references, the word "minorities" carries connotative meanings that include allusions to difference, socioeconomics, and prestige. To discuss the relationship between psychoanalysis and minorities requires the appreciation that we are discussing the presence or absence of several minorities within a past and present context of a minority. It is well accepted that as psychoanalysis' founder and patriarch, Freud, splendidly experienced himself as isolated. As a minority, whether professionally or ethnically, Freud's personal charm, charisma, intellectual and linguistic brilliance, the value of his work as well as his belief in the importance of these theories and empirical discoveries, attracted many likeminded thinkers who found the majority "old order" of understanding to be lacking. Born and raised in the culture of the turn of the century Europe and Vienna, Freud and many other Jews and psychoanalysts were familiar with prejudices, socioeconomic harassments, religious stereotyping, and the application of political solutions to social and psychological conflicts. Acquiescence and divergence from mainstream assimilation has been a pressure experienced from both external and internal sources since psychoanalysis' beginnings. Out of desires and needs for safety, identity consolidation and differentiation, as well as economic survival, psychoanalysis has often been theoretically conservative and the political structure of training institutions and societies have been paternally prejudiced. Compared to the psychoanalysis of Vienna, France, England, and Latin America, the North American acculturation of psychoanalysis was paradoxically conservative. Tensions within the North American psychoanalytic community between "the old" and "the new" were subtly intensified through the absorption of refugees from the Central European psychoanalytic community before and during World War II. Additionally, Freud's antipathy toward the U.S. probably created a reaction contributing to the medical and scientific emphasis of the United States version of ego-psychology.

Medical and nonmedical psychoanalysis historically have been a male dominated profession. These trends are changing as evidenced by the large number of women who are members of Division 39. Although women cannot be numerically considered a minority, women have faced prejudiced attitudes and have struggled with identity conflicts. It is reasonable to assume that similar dynamics have been and are active in psychoanalysis' relation to persons of other differences, that is, minorities.

As Erik Erikson once said, psychoanalysis may be at its best when it is dealing with those forces that are troubling a society at a given time. Psychoanalysis, thusly described, has always existed in an uneasy position within society. Whereas psychoanalysis can be credited with creating a special method and context for its work, free from society's rule about conformity in thought, feeling, and word, outside of this special context of the consulting room, psychoanalysis has remained markedly conservative. The theoretical and clinical debates, which fill our journals regarding what is psychoanalysis, its components, and declarations that one or another method is not psychoanalysis; sound much like prejudice and elicit rhetoric similar to the rhetoric of nationalism and false pride. It is curious and perhaps theoretical to posit that parallel pressures have been occurring. Does psychoanalysis' scientific, theoretical, and clinical conservatism, acquiescence and conformity have a sociocultural-socioeconomic parallel? Does this attitudinal posture affect the relative presence and/or absence of minorities interested and/or active in psychoanalysis? Although our responses to these questions derive from impressions based on observation and anecdote, we believe that the apparent lack of involvement of minority persons as analysts and analysands is real and relatively ignored.

A review of Division 39's directory and the directory of APsaA yields few Asian, Hispanics, Native American surnames, not to speak of African Americans that we are unable to identify by name. At both meetings and social gatherings of Division 39, few of these minorities can be identified by appearance or languages spoken. Whether this is similar to or different from the larger cultural-social-ethnic trend in society, or in the APA, is difficult to determine. However, the fact that there is not facile access to this information suggests that the issue is largely ignored. It is our impression that there are fewer minority psychologists in Division 39 than in other divisions of the APA. Illustratively, only one of the recent members of APA's Board of Ethnic Minority Affairs identifies herself as working from a psychodynamic perspective.

European psychoanalystic roots certainly have a multiply-determined origin. Psychoanalysis was born and raised in the turn-of-the-century Vienna bourgeoisie and exported and sought refuge during World War II in England, France, Latin America, Canada, and the U.S. Separation, individuation, and the development and exercise of individual abilities and power, masculine acculturated motives, have long been prominent components of psychoanalysis' implicit prescription for health. In the United States, psychoanalysis became a tool for economic and professional prejudice when it became, consistent with Freud's prediction, a branch of the powerful and wealthy medical profession. The relationship between the definitions of a sense of self and a sense of a group identity are intertwined. Whether that of an individual or of a group, the sense of self is intertwined with a sense of ethnicity and nationality. Under the impact of political or transient crisis an individual or group of individuals adheres even more stubbornly to a sense of ethnicity or a sense of the familiar.

The Apportionment Ballot: Division 39's Representation on the APA Council

Robert C. Lane

On or about the first of November of every year, the apportionment ballot is mailed to every APA member eligible to vote. Each eligible member is given ten votes to be apportioned to any of the Divisions, States, or Coalitions. Thus, there are many possible recipients of votes. Seats on the Council of Representatives, the governing body of the APA, are allotted according to the number of votes Divisions, States and Coalitions receive on the apportionment ballot.

The number of seats to which an organization is entitled is determined by Article IV, Sections 4 & 5, of the APA Bylaws, which follow.

Section 4—Each APA Fellow, Member (or Voting Associate) shall choose the Division(s) or State Association(s) through which he/she elects to have his/her interests represented on Council by allocating at the time of the annual dues statement, a total of ten (10) votes to the Division(s) and/or State Association(s) though which he/she wishes to be represented the following year. However, any Fellows, Members (or Voting Associates) of the Divisions or State Associations so designated will be allowed to nominate and elect their Council Representatives.

Section 5—The size of Council shall be set at approximately 115, including the Board of Directors and Officers. The number of Representatives from a Division or State Association shall be determined annually as follows:

Less than 0.5%	0
0.5 to 1.4%	1
1.5 to 2.4%	2
2.5 to 3.4%	3

Council Representatives are elected for a term not to exceed 3 years, and terms are staggered so that an equal number of terms expire each year. One year between terms in any organization is required, although this ruling does not apply to any organization other that the one a representative just served on.

In 1979, the Division of Psychoanalysis received greater than 1.64% of the APA votes, which gave us two Council Representatives. These were Gordon F. Derner and Reuben Fine, our first two presidents, who joined Council in 1981.

For 1980, 47.1% of the APA voting members cast apportionment ballots. Division 39 was twelfth in the voting, receiving 2.48% of the votes counted. We missed having a third Council Representative by .02% of the vote. These results indicated that the Division of Psychoanalysis was the fastest growing division in APA (see Table 19.1).

The Division of Psychoanalysis received 2.24% of the apportionment ballot in 1981, an amount sufficient for the retention of our two seats on APA Council, but .24% less than the Division received in the last ballot. In 1982, the Division received 2.65% of the apportionment ballot, an amount sufficient to allot us three representatives on APA Council. These seats went to George D. Goldman, Harriet Kaley, and Robert C. Lane who joined council in 1984. This per-

TABLE 19.1
Division 39 Representation on APA Council

Apportionment Year	Apportionment Votes Received (%)	Number of Representatives	Names of Representatives
1979–1980	1.64	—	—
1980–1981	2.48	2	—
1981–1982	2.24	2	Derner, Fine
1982–1983	2.65	2	Derner, Fine
1983–1984	2.46	3	Derner, Fine
1984–1985	2.84	2	Goldman, Kaley, Lane
1985–1986	2.93	3	Kaley, Lane
1986–1987	2.97	3	Kaley, Lane, Stockhamer
1987–1988	2.67	3	Goldman, Lawrence, Stockhamer
1988–1989	3.45	3	Goldman, Kaley, Stockhamer
1989–1990	3.45	3	Bernay, Goldman, Kaley
1990–1991	3.02	3	Bernay, Kaley, Meisels
1991–1992	3.64	3	Bernay, Meisels, Stockhamer
1992–1993	3.65	4	Barbanel, Liff, Meisels, Stockhamer
1993–1994		4	Barbanel, Liff, Karon, Stockhamer

centage was .41 more than the Division received in the previous ballot. Most important to the success of this ballot is the allotment of all "10" votes to Divisions or States. Although 11th in the ballot, the Division was 7th in attaining "10" votes (282—up from 200 the previous year).

In the November 1983 apportionment ballot, the Division lost one seat on Council. This resulted in George D. Goldman going off Council following the Winter, 1985, meeting of Council. In the 1984 apportionment ballot, Division 39 received 2.84% of the vote giving us back the lost seat on Council. The elected representative, Nathan Stockhamer, assumed his seat in 1986. Division 39 continued to gain strength in the APA apportionment ballot in 1985, moving from the 8th largest vote getter in 1984 to the 5th. The Division received 2.93% of the vote cast in 1985 as compared with 2.84% in 1984. Harriet Kaley and Robert Lane went off Council and were replaced by Ernest Lawrence (1987-1988) and George Goldman (1987-1990). In order to stagger the terms, one elected representative was for 3 years, George Goldman, and one was elected for a 1-year term, Ernest Lawrence.

Division 39 retained its three Council Representatives in the 1986 APA Apportionment Ballot. The Division received 2.97% of the vote cast in 1986 as compared with 2.93% in 1985. We continued to be the fifth largest vote getter among 47 Divisions, 35 States, and 7 Coalitions participating in the election. The Division went from fifth to fourth among participants in the number of "10" votes received.

The results of the APA Apportionment Ballot for Council Representative for 1987 indicated our Division had retained its three seats. We had three Council Representatives during the legislative year 1987. These were Goldman, Lawrence, and Stockhamer. Harriet Kaley (1988-1991) returned to Council in the 1987 election, replacing Ernest Lawrence. The results of this vote show clearly that the membership of Division 39 is very interested in the active representation of its needs. The seriousness and loyalty of the membership in supporting the goals and purposes of the Division is strongly stated in this vote. Division 39 has gradually moved up in the balloting and is presently in the top six or so divisions in percentage of votes and in the number of "10" votes attained.

The Division of Psychoanalysis was 4th in the percentage of total votes among the 47 Divisions in the 1988 ballot. The results reveal a further rise in the placement of Division 39 among the divisions. Our Division missed getting a fourth Council Representative by .05% or 142 votes. We were third among the divisions in "10" votes. Toni Bernay was elected, her term running from 1989-1992. Our three representatives were: Toni Bernay, Harriet Kaley, and George D. Goldman in 1989. Murray Meisels (1990-1993) was to replace George Goldman, and Nathan Stockhamer was reelected for the years 1991-1994.

In the apportionment election in 1989, Division 39 received 3.45% of the vote, or .05% short of a fourth representative. Our 9,487 votes were the most the Division ever received. We were fourth among the divisions. As only 50% of eligible voters vote in many elections, members were urged to make sure to vote in every apportionment ballot, and to give Division 39 all "10" votes or a substantial number of them.

The 1990 apportionment election resulted in a strong drop in Division 39's vote. We went from 9,487 or 3.45% to 7,830 or 3.02% of the vote, a drop of .43%. We also dropped to fifth place in the ballot, fourth in the number of "10" votes. We retained our three representatives on the Council. These were: Toni Bernay (1989–1992), Harriet Kaley (1988–1991), and Murray Meisels (1990–1993).

Our 1991 apportionment vote rose to 3.64% or 9,496 votes, resulting in our attaining a fourth representative for the first time. In this election we were again fourth in the ballot, and third in the number of "10" votes. Zanvil Liff and Laura Barbanel were elected to the Council. At the time of this report, our present representatives are: Laura Barbanel, Zanvil Liff, Murray Meisels, and Nathan Stockhamer. In the 1992 Apportionment Ballot, the Division received 3.65% of the ballot. This placed us third among divisions, with four representatives. Bertram Karon will replace Murray Meisels in 1993.

Perusal of the aforementioned reveals our continuing growth, from 12th in 1979 to 3rd in 1992. Our representation is approaching that of the largest division. We can look forward to further success in the apportionment ballot as our membership approaches 4,000.

The following Division 39 members have served, are serving, or are going to serve on Council: Laura Barbanel (1992–1995), Toni Bernay (1989–1992), Gordon F. Derner (1981–1984), Reuben Fine (1981–1984), George D. Goldman (1984–1985; 1987–1990), Harriet Kaley (1984–1987; 1988–1991), Bertram Karon (1993–1996), Robert C. Lane (1984–1987), Ernest S. Lawrence (1987–1988), Murray Meisels (1990–1993), Zanvil Liff (1992–1995), Nathan Stockhamer (1986–1989; 1991–1994).

The Bylaws, Structure, and Organization of Division 39

Ruth Ochroch

Division 39 is subject to the bylaws of its parent organization, APA. One bylaw of the APA requires that each division promulgate its own set of bylaws. This became one of the first tasks of the Division.

Robert C. Lane wrote the first set of the Division 39 proposed bylaws in 1978 and they were passed in 1979. The first Bylaws Revision Committee, consisting of Reuben Fine, as Chair, and Gordon F. Derner as Member, was formed in 1980. Their work was continued by Martin Wagner. The first amendments to the bylaws were passed in 1981. These amendments made it possible for the officers and Board members to conduct the affairs of the Division more effectively, established new standing committees, provided for a yearly Midwinter Meeting and permitted the Division to publish psychoanalytic monographs. In addition, these amendments provided for the formation of specialized sections and of local chapters. These were and continue to be the main springs of the vitality and growth of the Division.

It was not until 1983, however, that established Sections were able, each, to send one voting representative to the Board of Directors. This set the structure of the Board as consisting of the elected officers, nine Board Members-At-Large, plus Section Representatives.

The establishment of sections is fairly common within the larger divisions of APA. As is usual, Division 39 requires each section to have its own set of bylaws. Section bylaws may not contradict the bylaws of the Division, which as mentioned earlier, are subject to the bylaws of APA. The Sections are free, however, to establish their own procedures, form their own committees, collect their own dues, publish their own newsletters, and pursue their own programs. This degree of autonomy makes for the vitality of the sections and of the Division. Another contribution to the vitality and growth of the Division emanates from the local chapters. Section IV (Section of Local Chapters) was charged with the responsibility of developing local chapters and presenting them to the Board for acceptance as affiliated groups. These local chapters now number 26, exist throughout the United States and Canada, and bring a breadth of perspectives and activities to the Division.

The bylaws continued to be amended in 1984, 1988, and in 1990. These amendments dealt with the limitation that a member may hold only one elected Division office at a time, the limitation on the number of terms a member may hold an elected office, the charge, composition and length of terms for members on divisional committees, and procedures for amending the bylaws. In 1986, the position of parliamentarian was established to ensure that the Board acted within the bylaws.

The latest amendments to the bylaws in 1990 dealt again with the sections of the Division and were necessitated by two groups requesting the formation of two new sections. These amendments state the procedures and requirements for the formation of new, and the continuation of established, sections and for a section to have a voting representative on the board of Directors.

As of this writing there are discussions of new divisional bylaw amendments and by the year 1998, 20 years after the first bylaws were passed, Division 39 bylaws will and should be substantially refined. In keeping with the philosophy as to the purpose of the bylaws, it is imperative that our bylaws allow for and enable the growth and effectiveness of Division 39.

The Division 39 Committee on APA Liaison

Norma P. Simon

At a number of the Board Meetings of the Division, the issue of APA politics was raised. One of the things noted was how few Division 39 members were on APA Boards and Committees and those that were, were not there as a result of the efforts of the Division or with the Division's help. It was therefore decided by the Board of Directors in 1988 that a committee on APA relations would be established. This committee was chaired by Ruth Ochroch and had as its members George Stricker and Norma Simon.

The Committee drew up a list of plans to:

1. Request advanced notice from the APA governance office of Board and Committee openings.
2. Target specific Boards and Committees in which our members would be interested.
3. Call the staffs of these Boards and Committees to get more information on the qualifications that the Board or Committee is seeking in candidates.
4. Review rosters of all the 39 Divisional leadership for candidates for these openings, select appropriate candidates, and present them to our Board.
5. Contact the membership of the specific Boards and Committees to push our candidates for their slates.
6. Network with the other practice divisions mutually to push each other's candidates or to concur on a candidate both for inclusion on a slate and on the APA Council's vote for Board and Committee memberships.

7. Educate our Division membership on the way in which Board and Committee members are selected.
8. Develop opportunities for Division members to become active in the Division and encourage them to do so.

The Committee held two conference calls. The first was to plan our approach and the second to decide the nominees we would recommend to the APA offices. Consultations were held with the President and other officers of the Division. A list of the major Boards and Committees we felt to be relevant to the Division were circulated to the Board of Directors and nominees names gathered. In March 1990, a letter was sent by Ruth Ochroch to the Division 39 leadership giving the major Boards and Committees and the requirements of each. The request was made for nominations. A list was gathered and the people nominated were contacted. Vita were collected and a list of our nominees was sent to the APA Governance Office. This procedure was followed in 1991 as well. It has been difficult to assess the impact of the Committee's efforts. There are more Division members on Boards and Committees; however, most of these people are active in other divisions as well. The procedure needs to be streamlined and carried out throughout the year in order for it to be more successful.

III

The Sections

The Division of Psychoanalysis has achieved its remarkable organizational success in part by identifying and utilizing the best features of its two parent disciplines, psychology and psychoanalysis. The APA structure is that of a large central organization (which deals with broad psychologist issues such as membership, journal publication, national conventions, etc.) and a host of divisions, such as ours, which represent narrower substantive areas. The Division of Psychoanalysis has adopted this model, and it too is comprised of a central organization that represents broader issues for psychologist-psychoanalysts (practically the same list applies, i.e., membership, journal publication, meetings, etc.) and subdivisions, called sections, which represent narrower substantive areas. The sections are national and even international in scope, have great autonomy, raise dues, hold meetings, publish newsletters and organize committees. It is surely the case, for example, that the Board of Section II, Childhood and Adolescence, will do more to develop this area of psychoanalysis than the Division Board could ever have time for, or that a Division committee could ever have authority for. Most sections have derived from committees when it appeared that the scope of a committee was too limiting for the purposes at hand.

Note that other national and international psychoanalytic organizations do not have such a structure. Rather, those organizations are comprised of a central body and a network of local institutes. The Division has emulated this model as well, and has developed a network of 26 local chapters. In the end, we are the only division in APA with a network of local chapters, just as we are the only psychoanalytic organization with a substructure of sections.

165

Organizationally, all of the sections and local chapters are semi-autonomous associations that operate under the auspices of the Division, just as Division 39 is a semi-autonomous group in the APA. APA and Division 39 policies provide defining parameters for sections and local chapters, but within those parameters the sections and local chapters have great autonomy and scope for action. It is noteworthy that what is being discussed here is a totality of 34 organizations—26 local chapters, seven sections and one Division. Each has a Board and committee structure, and most produce newsletters and hold scientific meetings, so that in the aggregate there must be literally hundreds of psychologists who are involved in some way in the governance of the Division. If each of the 34 organizations has 20 active participants in its governance, then 680 psychologists, or 20% of the total Division membership, are involved in sharing Division 39 authority. Add to this the colleagues who chair and present papers and symposia (there were about 200 presenters at the 1992 Spring Meeting in Philadelphia) and who participate in our offshoot institutes, and the number probably doubles. It appears that part of the success of the Division has been to share its authority (with sections and local chapters), and that by so doing it has given the opportunity for hundreds of its members to be active participants in its growth. Further differentiation, and further empowerment of colleagues, is to be expected in the future.

It is also noteworthy that even though psychoanalysts are usually identified by theoretical perspective (e.g., ego-psychologists, interpersonalists, or object-relationists), the sections are not so organized. Rather, they are organized by substantive areas. The chapters following present relevant perspectives on all seven sections.

22

Section I: Psychologist-
Psychoanalyst Practitioners
A History: 1982–1992

Ernest S. Lawrence

The Section of Psychologist-Psychoanalyst Practitioners of the Division of Psychoanalysis was constituted by the Division's Board of Directors at the 1982 Mid-Winter meeting of the Division held in Rio Mar, Puerto Rico. It was the first section to be established within the Division and remains the largest of the Division's seven Sections with well over 400 members.

Gordon F. Derner, the second president of the Division (1980–1981) and the Division's Board of Directors were concerned with the definition of psychoanalysis and with the qualifications that distinguish a psychoanalyst from other psychotherapists. Although recognizing that the Division basically must be an interest group, Derner felt that it was the responsibility of the Division to the public, to professional psychology, and to psychoanalysis to define standards: "to determine for American Psychology the basic education and experience requirements for someone to be identified as a psychoanalyst. . . . We will need some attempt at the evaluation of the training programs which prepare psychoanalysts." He was worried that the "continuation of questionable groups and inadequate training (would) be viewed as acceptable" (The President's Column, *The Psychologist-Psychoanalyst*, Summer 1981, newsletter of Division 39).

The history of Section I can only be understood against the background of the attempt of the organizers and the first group of members and officers of the Division to identify those psychologists qualified to be called psychoanalysts, whose education, training, and experience were equivalent to the most rigorous currently accepted standards within the psychoanalytic community, nationally and internationally.

A Qualifications Committee was appointed by Gordon F. Derner to respond to the questions that had been raised. Its members were: Anna Antonovsky, Leopold Caligor, Rita Frankiel, Kenneth Isaacs, Ernest Lawrence, Martin Mayman, Murray Meisels, and Nathan Stockhamer. Prior to the formal convening of this committee, an informal meeting of Lawrence (who had been appointed Chair of the Committee), Frankiel, Mayman, Meisels, and Stockhamer was held with Derner and Lane, the President-Elect of the Division to clarify the charge and to establish the ground rules under which the Qualifications Committee would function.

These general agreements remained in force throughout the Committee's work up and until the completion of the Committee's report and its submission to the Division's Board of Directors. The understanding may be summarized as follows: The Division should continue to welcome all psychologists interested in the study of psychoanalysis; there should be no requirements for membership in the Division except interest in psychoanalysis from whatever viewpoint or model, whether from the perspective of research, teaching, professional training or practice. However, there appeared to be a strong need within the membership to have groups (sections) that were more or less homogeneous—whose discourse around clinical issues effectively would be on a peer level, recognizing that the Division's membership itself was quite diverse in terms of training, practice, and experience.

It was generally agreed that while the structure of the Division would be a preoccupying issue for some time, the Qualification Committee's charge should be focused on defining the necessary credentials of the journeyman-level psychoanalyst. A compelling factor was that as a result of the essential exclusion of psychologists from the training institutes of APsaA, many psychologists had managed to get ad hoc training for themselves in the late 1940s and throughout the 1950s, in particular before most psychological and interdisciplinary psychoanalytic institutes were established; that is, they took courses and seminars, formed study groups, bought supervision, and had a personal analysis. The dedication and commitment of this group of psychologists to psychoanalysis had not only to be honored, but their qualifications had to be fully acknowledged.

The work of the Committee almost immediately became involved with the question whether we are, or should be, evaluating competence and, if so, what standards should be applied. How can we judge practice, experience, and knowledge in operational terms? An examination procedure would come dangerously close to being regarded as certifying and/or credentialing and that was clearly outside the scope of APA's policy guidelines.

There are, however, precedents in APA for Divisions to set standards for membership higher than APA requirements and for Sections of Divisions to set membership requirements more stringent than those required for membership in the Division. This information was contained in a communication to the Division from Michael Pallak, at that time the Executive Officer of APA.

Issues that the Committee struggled with was the need of many psychologists to have some sort of sanction beyond licensing as a psychologist in order to work as practitioners of psychoanalysis. Serious attention was paid to professional rivalries and antagonisms within psychoanalysis, both intraprofessionally and interprofessionally, professional and organizational developments in the United States and internationally, and questions regarding the future thrust of psychoanalysis: a general psychology or an autonomous specialized profession?

Very strongly felt and expressed was the conviction that psychology's formal organizational entrance into psychoanalysis on a national scale through the admission of the Division into APA should not serve exclusionary functions. There are reasonable publicly and professionally desirable reasons to set standards and recognize expertise; that these criteria could serve narrow guild interests. To best serve the community, professional psychology, and psychoanalysis, standards should be clear, understandable to the public, and sufficiently uniform and unambiguous to the professional community; wherever and whenever specifics and particulars are available, they should not be obscured by vague language or indeterminate standards rationalized as being open and pluralistic.

It was in that spirit—at that point in time—that the Qualifications Committee committed itself to defining the minimum credentials in education and training for psychologists to practice psychoanalysis, abjuring such general terms as intensive or depth and other qualitative terms which put the discipline in danger of sounding like Humpty Dumpty, "When I use a word, it means just what I choose it to mean—neither more or less." Apparently even Humpty Dumpty finally had to yield to some quantitative standard, however grudgingly.

Among other recommendations, the Qualifications Committee proposed that the Division sponsor Sections (where sufficient interest is expressed) in any area of psychoanalysis, and that each Section be autonomous with its own set of bylaws and officers although broadly bound by the Division's bylaws. Diversity of interests would thereby be accommodated and the many voices of psychoanalysis find expression. Section I represents a position that its members find professionally meaningful and theoretically congenial.

Because the Qualifications Committee was primarily concerned with the trained professional practitioner of psychoanalysis, its further recommendations concerned the establishment of a Section on the Professional Practice of Psychoanalysis :

1. That the Board discharge the Qualifications Committee and reappoint it as a Steering Committee to establish such a section with permission to write its own bylaws and invite founding members.
2. That the Steering Committee establish standards of membership in the Section for psychologists engaged primarily in psychoanalytic practice.
3. That membership standards be established on the basis of demonstrated competence as a practicing psychoanalyst, and that the Steering Com-

mittee explore methods of implementing evaluation procedures for qualification.

4. That the Section respect the varying points of view and orientations within psychoanalysis while, however, clearly delineating what is and what is not considered psychoanalytic practice.
5. That membership in this section may be linked to the recommendation of an acceptable training program and/or demonstrably qualified psychoanalytic work.

By May 1981 when the complete report was accepted and endorsed by the Board of Directors as well as the passing of a bylaw authorizing Sections and finally, the 1982 official acceptance of Section I as the Section of Psychologist-Psychoanalyst Practitioners, all the organizational work was accomplished and 82 founding members formed the Section. The Chair of the Qualifications Committee was turned over to Nathan Stockhamer, who continued in this position for the Division well after the Section was formed.

Additionally, during this period, a set of training requirements was worked out for membership in the new Section and accepted by the Board of Directors of the Division as a reasonable standard for the definition of a psychologist with the qualification to practice as a psychoanalyst. It was after lengthy and vigorous discussion that the operational mechanism to determine qualification was eliminated for reasons that have already been presented. Similar to other professional models, the requirements for membership in the Section were based essentially on education and training. An operational model to determine competence would have to await an external certifying or diplomating organization.

The specifications were based on what seemed like a reasonable compromise between the standards of the IPA, APsaA, and a number of interdisciplinary institutes in this country on the one hand, and what could be considered as essentially intensive psychoanalytic therapy programs on the other hand. The standards finally arrived at proved to be quite similar to the training requirements of the William Alanson White Institute in New York City, which had trained many psychologists. The interpersonal psychoanalytic orientation of White was irrelevant to the issue; it was the educational and training process that was meaningful. The requirements that follow would be subsequent to the doctoral degree, licensure, internship, and acceptance as a member of APA and the Division:

Four years minimal study leading to a certificate in psychoanalysis to include:

1. Personal analysis:
   a. 300 hours minimally at three or more times per week.
   b. Previous analysis acceptable.
   c. Analysis concurrent with training strongly recommended.

2. Supervision: 200 hours minimally with at least three supervisors with patients seen at least three or more times per week. At least one supervision should be on an ending phase case.
3. Curriculum:
   a. Four years each of theory courses, case seminars, and technique, plus electives.
   b. Orientation of instruction may be determined by individual and/or institute.

The major purpose of the training outline was to assure the kind of explicitly intensive experience that distinguishes psychoanalysis from other therapies. Although frequency of contacts is not a sufficient condition to guarantee the intense involvement likely to lead to rich and viable transference phenomena with the potential to be successfully worked through, it was the judgment of the Committee and the Board of Directors at that time that in almost all instances this minimal level of intensity is a necessary condition for the achievement of a successful analysis.

Psychologists who had not received formal training but were practicing psychoanalysts and had been equivalently trained were not to be penalized; their evaluation would be based on the functional equivalence of their varied experiences.

The formation of the Section and its standards was met with enthusiasm by many members of the Division, and quickly grew, although not without criticism of rigidity, slavish adherence to numerical requirements, elitism, establishment bias, being exclusionary, catering to the criteria of the medical profession and the APsaA, and adherence to formalities rather than an appreciation of professional diversity and pluralism.

You will note elsewhere in this volume that the qualifications that were accepted by the Board of Directors in 1982 when the formation of Section I was approved, were revised in 1990 as the leadership of the Division shifted to psychologists with a significantly broader and less quantitative definition of psychoanalysis and its training requirements. As a qualitative statement, there can be no quarrel with these more recent recommendations. Section I's requirements simply add what it believes to be a necessary quantitative dimension.

The requirements for membership in the Section were and are completely and entirely concerned with minimal conditions of education and training. It has never spoken to theoretical orientation or the technical aspects of practice. The membership represents psychologist psychoanalysts whose theoretic framework occupies the entire spectrum from humanistic to classical ways of thinking and working. In later sections of this chapter one may note the contributors and topics in the many programs that have been presented by the membership and invited guests. There is only one shared caveat: That we fully experience in our training that basic and heightened intensity that increased frequency of contact between analysand and analyst brings to the psychoanalytic process. How one then uses that training is completely up to the psychoanalyst.

The first President of the Section was Leopold Caligor followed by Anna Antonovsky, Rita Frankiel, Ken Isaacs, Ernest Lawrence, Sydney Smith, Nathan Stockhamer, Robert Lane, William Greenstadt, Ira Moses, and currently, Oliver Kerner. Parenthetically, it should be noted that since the founding of the Division of Psychoanalysis in 1979, that in the following 12 years, 10 of the Division's presidents were Section I members. The current President of the Division (Leopold Caligor) was the first President of Section I.

In 1985, a newsletter entitled *The Round Robin* was launched under the editorship of Helen Golden. Because the choice of the name reveals a sense of the spirit that founded the Section and continues to energize it, Helen Golden's words of explanation from the first issue on why the title was selected is worthy of a second reading.

> During the 1930s when premonitions of war scattered the early analysts, Otto Fenichel realized that they would need to stay connected in order to survive as a professional group with a clear identity. Periodically he loaded his portable typewriter with as many sheets of paper and carbons as it could hold and reported everything he felt would interest, guide and sustain his distinguished readers. He urged correspondence from them and then summarized their varied communications in his next letter. He reported and commented on new theoretical ideas and on the analytic activities of his readers.
>
> He passed along the political rumblings that came to his attention and detailed conversations with analysts whom he was able to see. He reviewed current publications. He was not averse to gossip. And he always spoke of his hopes and plans. These documents, dog-eared and often only faintly legible, were circulated among the group and became known as Die Rundbriefe. Today we would call them round robin letters—and they are both a source and a part of the history of the psychoanalytic movement.
>
> In admiration for Fenichel's devotion to the survival of the group, we name our fledgling newsletter *The Round Robin*.

Two issues were published in 1985 under Golden's editorship, and twice more in 1986 under its second and current editor, Mary Libbey. In the summer of 1987, Judith Hanlon became Associate Editor and Gil Katz Consulting Editor, Libbey continuing as Editor. That same year *The Round Robin* began publishing three times a year and continues with this frequency. In December 1988, Katz became the Associate Editor. Since the Spring 1990 issue, the Newsletter has been jointly edited by Libbey and Katz.

Lively, engrossing and innovative, *The Round Robin* not only reports the ongoing activities of the Section and its members, but has inaugurated stimulating and often provocative columns such as, Distinguished Members Commentary, Being an Analyst in Different Places, New York, New York, and Psychoanalytic

Views of Contemporary Life. Feature articles, special reports, guest editorials and reviews appear from time to time. The newsletter is meticulously edited and in a creative and energetic manner represents the tone and spirit of the Section. More than a Newsletter, it serves as a sort of reflective gazette of contemporary psychoanalysis for the psychologist-psychoanalyst practitioners of Section I.

Contributors to *The Round Robin* (in no particular order) have been Rita Frankiel, Sydney Smith, Milton Eber, Alan Cooper, Roy Schafer, Kenneth Isaacs, Doris Silverman, Ernest Lawrence, Donald Kaplan, Norbert Freedman, Martin Nass, Sheldon Bach, Isaac Tylim, Max Rosenbaum, Mark Grunes, Elaine Caruth, Philburn Ratoosh, Richard Lasky, Gil Katz, John Fiscalini, Peter Lawner, Helen Gediman, Andrew Druck, William Greenstadt, Moss Rawn, Louise Kaplan, Judith Hanlon, Karol Marshall, Oliver Kerner, Fred Pine, Richard Karmel, Robert Lane, Irwin Hirsch, Marylou Lionells, Ruth-Jean Eisenbud, Paul Lippmann, Shelley Rockwell, Alan Roland, Daniel Paul, Rudolf Ekstein, Helen Desmond, Bryant Welch, Howard Shevrin, Jonathan Slavin, Anna Antonovsky, Frederic Levine, Charles Spezzano, Sidney Blatt, Nathan Stockhamer, and Ira Moses.

Each year the Section presents two programs under the auspices of the Division: One at the annual Convention of the American Psychological Association and the other at the annual Spring meeting of the Division. Participants have included Ernest Wolf, Ernest Lawrence, Donald Kaplan, Alan Cooper, Rita Frankiel, Sydney Smith, Marvin Hyman, Susan Bram, Mary Libbey, Lawrence Epstein, Roy Schafer, Elaine Caruth, Nathan Stockhamer, Zanvil Liff, Joanna Tabin, Robert Lane, William Greenstadt, Jeffrey Golland, Louis Lauro, Norman Oberman, Estelle Shane, Evelyn Schwaber, Marion Oliner, Linda Brakel, Henry Bachrach, Martin Mayman, Jean Schimek, Zenia Fliegel, Anna Antonovsky, and Andre Green.

Among the topics at these meetings have been, Analysis in the Face of Massive Resistance, The Training Analysis, Seduction of the Female Patient, From Psychotherapy to Psychoanalysis, The Analyst's Self-Disclosure, Vulnerabilities and Stress Points in the Analytic Life, Analyzability, Current Controversies in Psychoanalysis, and Problems in Defining the Nature of Clinical Evidence in Psychoanalytic Treatment.

Beginning in February 1985, annual Study Group meetings on a national scale were introduced under the leadership of Ken Isaacs and Rita Frankiel. They were designed to offer Section I members a fairly relaxed and informal setting in which to regularly meet together in order to discuss subjects of common interest in clinical, theoretical, and research areas. Fifty-one members attended the 4-day initial meeting in Scottsdale, Arizona, assembling in eight groups with each member having the choice of participating in two different groups over the long weekend.

The topics of the groups at this first meeting were: Object Relations (Jay

Greenberg); Affect Theory (Ken Isaacs); Shame and Guilt (Helen Lewis); Female Psychology (Dale Mendell); Developmental Issues (Fred Pine); Resistance and Defense (Roy Schafer); The Abused Patient and the Abusing Therapist (Sydney Smith); Interpersonal Theory (Nat Stockhamer and Allan Cooper).

The second annual Study Group meeting was held in San Francisco on Fisherman's Wharf in May 1986. A more intensive experience was planned with four groups meeting for the entire weekend. The topics and leaders were: Object Relations in Psychoanalytic Practice (Greenberg); Developmental Theory and the Clinical Process (Pine); Aspects of Resistance (Schafer); Peer Group on Therapeutic Action of Psychoanalysis (Smith, Isaacs, Cooper, Stockhamer).

Following the aforementioned meeting Ricki Levenson took over as Coordinator of Study Group meetings. As an experiment, the 1987 meeting was scheduled for a full week in Mexico with only two group leaders: Merton Gill and Anni Bergman. Unfortunately, registration fell short and the meeting was cancelled.

The 1988 Study Groups meeting was held in Palm Springs, California and was organized by Carolyn Shadduck who chaired the Committee through the 1990 meeting. Thirty-six Section I members attended with 16 guests and a number of advanced candidates. Six study groups were organized: Borderline conditions (Rudolf Ekstein); Early loss of parents and siblings: Clinical reverberations (Frankiel); Masochism versus surrender (Emmanuel Ghent); The clinical use of dreams (Kaplan); Transference (Lachmann); Intersubjective approach to psychoanalytic therapy (Stolorow).

The fourth annual Study Group meeting was held at the United Nations Plaza Hotel in New York City in tandem with the Division's Spring meeting. Five groups met: Analyst's Self-Disclosure (Sabert Basescu); Implications for Psychoanalytic Technique in the Age of Object Relations (Bolgar); Transference, Character, and Working Through: A Comparative View (Cooper); Early Object Loss; Clinical Reverberations (Frankiel); Psychoanalysis More? Or Less?: Some Advantages of a Developmental Perspective in Dealing With the Difficult Patient (Siegler). The dinner speaker in 1989 was Brenda Maddox, author of *Nora*, the biography of the wife of James Joyce.

Santa Monica, California was the site of the 1990 Study Groups Meeting in February and featured Elisabeth Young-Bruel, author of Anna Freud, as the banquet speaker. Sixty-three participants and four study groups made up the program: Therapeutic Alliance and Therapeutic Impasse (Stolorow); Problems in the Application of Infant Research to Adult Psychoanalysis (Victoria Hamilton); Social, Cultural, and Historical Aspects of the Self: Clinical Implications (Roland); The British Independent Group And Object Relations Theory (Bolgar). The entire Study Group Program is currently being reevaluated by the Board of Directors of the Section.

The members of the Section were active in the formation of the Division and continue to play an active part in its scholarly and clinical programs, although less so in its political and governance activities. The members of the Section played a strong role in the class action antitrust lawsuit that established psychologists' right to psychoanalytic training and opened up membership in the International Psychoanalytical Association to psychological and interdisciplinary psychoanalytic institutes.

Among the current projects of the Section are arrangements with Institutes-in-formation to send experienced psychoanalytic clinicians to the local sites with clinical programs that will fit in with the needs of the local groups. These programs may be workshops, supervisory sessions, or any of a variety of experiences. The project is intended to help in the development and establishment of independent psychoanalytic training centers in the United States. The entire program will be financially underwritten by the Section.

At this point in time, it seems reasonable to say, the Section does not have a political agenda. From reading *The Round Robin*, one experiences the broad range of interests of the psychoanalyst members of the Section: Psychoanalysis and contemporary life, commentaries that use cinema reviews showing how psychoanalysis illuminates the ambivalent forces in our society, examinations of the work and struggles of psychoanalysts in different settings, cultural issues seen through the perspective of psychoanalysis, and of course, always issues of training and practice.

23

Section II, Childhood and Adolescence: Historical Reflections

Ava L. Siegler

Psychoanalysis began as a form of child psychology, an interest in origins that Freud shared with many scientists of his time. Although Freud's subject was the mental consequences of the psychic realities of childhood, his psychoanalytic method relied on the adult reconstruction of early memories. It took another 25 years before the thoughts and feelings of children themselves captured the scientific attention of psychoanalysts, and even now, despite the profound influence that developmental research has had on clinical practice, the study and treatment of children occupies a secondary tier in the psychoanalytic theater.

Given our history, it comes as no surprise then, that it was only after adult analysts had already gathered together to form a section devoted to their concerns (Section I, Psychologist-Psychoanalyst Practitioners), that a special section devoted to the study of children and adolescents (Section II) came into being.

Section II was conceived in August 1981, when Robert Lane, then president of the division, created a committee on Child and Adolescent Psychoanalysis. The Committee became a Section in October 1983, after being encouraged and supported by Presidents Lane, Goldman, and Lawrence.

At first, several of us met informally to discuss the feasibility of a special section on childhood and adolescence. A Steering Committee evolved from these early discussions, which included Sylvia Brody, Jan Drucker, Rosalind Gould, Anneliese Riess, Miriam Siegel, and Ava Siegler. Our objectives, as stated in the minutes of our first formal meeting in February 1982, were as follows:

176

1. To establish a network of Division 39 members whose primary theoretical and clinical interests are engaged in research with, and treatment of, children and adolescents.
2. To explore the contributions of psychoanalytic psychologists to psychoanalytic developmental theory.
3. To study those issues which are central to the training of psychoanalytic practitioners whose primary clinical responsibility is the treatment of children and adolescents.

Toward these ends, the committee decided to meet monthly, to request a travel budget that would allow us to meet with other child and adolescent psychologist-psychoanalysts throughout the country (denied), to request convention time for the presentation of a panel or workshop that highlighted a psychoanalytic study of childhood and adolescence (granted), and to hold special committee meetings at both the annual and the mid-winter conventions of Division 39, in order to reach out to our constituency.

By the summer of 1982, the Steering Committee had devised a special questionnaire to be mailed to all Division 39 members, surveying their interest in forming a special section of our new Division. Correspondence at that time revealed our hopes that once this special section was formed, "We could begin to address ourselves as a professional community to the ethical, theoretical, political, and educational issues that are of vital concern to those of us involved with the therapeutic care of children and adolescents."

Over 100 psychoanalysts, developmental researchers, and clinicians across the country, responded to our initial questionnaire, and became the founding members of Section II. Some of the most outstanding psychoanalysts in our field lent us their support in these early days. Among them were Anni Bergman, Bruno Bettelheim, Peter Blos, Sr., Rudolph Ekstein, Fred Pine, and Phyllis Tyson. We were also delighted to number researchers like Beatrice Beebe, Joy Osofsky, and Sebastiano Santostefano, among our founders.

On October 29, 1983, having received our petition, the Executive Board of Division 39 voted to approve the establishment of Section II: Childhood and Adolescence.

At the time of our beginning, controversy was still raging in the Division over the special membership requirements set by Section I (Psychologist-Psychoanalyst Practitioners) that defined who could qualify as a psychoanalyst and who could not. One of the earliest decisions made by the officers of Section II was our commitment to an open membership, based on current interest rather than prior qualifications. The minutes of our first official Board meeting state that, "Any members of Division 39 who are interested in psychoanalytic approaches to the psychology of childhood and adolescence are welcome to join Section II."

Members of our new-born Section emphasized the need for all of us to "simply think and talk together;'' to broaden rather than narrow our focus. The effort and energy that so many devoted to this humble goal was striking testament to its lasting vitality. Our "thinking and talking" ranged from the importance of promoting psychodynamic child training on undergraduate and graduate levels at our colleges and universities, to the need for psychoanalytically informed child advocacy, to the importance of applying psychoanalytic concepts to a variety of contexts outside of clinical theory and practice, to our own special "in-house" mission of converting adult analysts to the importance of the application of developmental theory to their clinical practice.

In these first few years, we worked very hard to pull together a viable group with shared interests in the New York metropolitan area. This, in itself, was difficult, but even more formidable was the task of creating an equally viable network of child practitioners across the country. At this point Division 39 was still in the process of forming local chapters, and there was no Section of Local Chapters.

It had seemed hard enough for us to bring together a group that would come to meetings, pay dues, vote in our elections, and attend our conferences. How were we going to mobilize local Section II off-shoots in California, Michigan, Philadelphia, Washington, and so on?

Participants in these early attempts to reach out to a more representative constituency included: Joy Osofsky at the Menninger Institute in Kansas, Sylvia Ginsparg, in St. Louis, Jack Novick and Irene Fast in Michigan, Muriel Weckstein, in Massachusetts, and Elaine Caruth, in California. But it was hard work. The more we attempted to extend our network, the more aware we become that practitioners of child and adolescent psychoanalysis or psychoanalytic psychotherapy were few and far between. Only a handful of us had been able to receive any formal analytic training, and most child psychologists across the country had been even more severely limited than adult analysts, by the lack of training opportunities of any kind.

It was clear that we needed to add an Education and Training Committee to our Section, one which would focus on developing the specialty training we believed was so essential to the psychoanalytically informed treatment of children, adolescents, and their families. The first members of this committee were Ava Siegler, Sylvia Brody, Carol Michaels, and Irving Steingart. We began to formulate our ideas about an ideal curriculum for a child and adolescent psychoanalytic training program over the next few years. At the same time, committees on bylaws, scientific program, public policy, and membership were formed. By 1985, our ranks had steadily grown to a high of almost 200 members. A Nominating Committee was formed to select a slate for our next election.

In July of 1985, Ava Siegler passed on the responsibilities of the presidency of Section II to Carol Michaels. Joining Michaels as Secretary was Elisabeth Kaestner, Ester Buchholz was Treasurer, and Members-at-Large included

Phyllis Ackman, Marsha Levy-Warren, Irving Steingart, and Susan Warshaw. Carol Kaye was named President-Elect, while, as Past-President, Ava Siegler became the representative to Division 39's Executive Board. Section II, blessed with a propitious birth, was now enjoying a healthy and vigorous infancy.

In her first letter to the membership, Carol Michaels pledged her "commitment to further the development of Section II as forum, resource, and communal enterprise for those interested in psychoanalytic work with children and adolescents." She also took note, with sadness, of the death of one of our founding members, Rosalind Gould. A panel was presented at the Mid-Winter meetings in Toronto, Canada, entitled, "Interpretations of Fantasy and Play: Comparative Approaches to Child Analysis." David Abrams, Anni Bergman, Hugh Griffith-Clegg, and Carol Michaels participated. Ava Siegler was honored to dedicate this panel to Rosalind Gould's memory.

The following year, psychoanalytic child psychology sustained another loss. Margaret Mahler, a psychoanalyst whose observations of the separation-individuation phases of child development had captured the imagination of adult analysts throughout the country, passed away. Section II dedicated their panel, "Paternal Representation in Girls," to her memory. Carol Michaels chaired this panel, which presented the work of Katherine Rees, Linda Gunsberg, and Rose Marie Balsam. Laura Helms Tessman was the discussant.

In the 1980s, the work of psychoanalytic developmental researchers, theoreticians, and clinicians was moving center stage in psychoanalysis, and Section II was also gaining momentum. Members of our section were active in the affairs of the Division, and represented the concerns of our membership on the Board of Directors. They participated on national committees and chaired national conventions.

On January 10, 1987, over 150 members and guests from the northeast region attended Section II's first Scientific Conference to hear Lawrence Aber and Arietta Slade present their joint work on "Attachment Theory and Research: A Framework for Clinical Intervention."

In that year, the presidency of Section II was taken on by Carol Kaye. That summer, Section II's panel at the APA's annual convention captured the spirit of our section, "Alive and Kicking: Psychoanalytic Theory's Heuristic Value in Child Work." Ester Buchholz, President-Elect, chaired this panel, which included contributions from Dorothy Griffiths, Stephanie Smith, and Susan Warshaw. Elaine Caruth was the discussant.

Ester Buchholz went on to become the fourth president of Section II, where her high visibility as the author of the section's "Byline" in the Division 39 Newsletter, stimulated her readers to think about such matters as the impact of cultural issues on the psychoanalytic treatment of children and adolescents, difficult aspects of clinical work with parents, and risk-taking as a normal aspect of adolescent development.

Our early insistence on paying psychoanalytic attention to the psychological needs of real children in the real world, had now been maintained through five administrations.

Ed Corrigan, Section II's current president, has also made one of our most challenging concerns his most pressing task: How to create a section that is nationally representative? His administration has come closest to this goal which we have all shared over the years. Bertram Cohler, the new President-Elect, is from Chicago. Miriam Green and Pearl-Ellen Gordon, Secretary and Treasurer, respectively, are both from New York, and Members-at-Large include. Carol Kaye and Carol Michaels, from New York, Ruth Resch from Washington, Peter Shabad from Chicago, and Ira Schaer from Detroit. Bertram Cohler will be Section II's first president from outside of New York, so we are definitely growing up and beginning to leave our home base.

I am confident that both Section II and Division 39 will continue to pursue their goals, into this, the second century of psychoanalysis, and I am proud to have served as Chair of the Founding Committee and the first president of the Psychoanalytic Division's Special Section on Childhood and Adolescence.

The History of Women and Psychoanalysis: Section III

Dale Mendell
Harriet Kimble Wrye

PART I: THE ORIGINS AND DEVELOPMENT OF SECTION III, 1981–1985 (WRITTEN BY DALE MENDELL)

The history of Section III is intimately connected with the history of the women's movement both inside and outside of psychology and psychoanalysis. The last quarter of a century has witnessed a resurgence of interest in the psychology of female development, with emphasis on early mother–child interactions, the nature of early identifications and the formation of gender identity. Much of this interest was initiated by the social and cultural questions posed by the larger women's movement, which challenged the mental health profession to examine its practices toward women. Within APA this challenge was met by the establishment of the Committee on Women in Psychology and by Division 35: Psychology of Women. Division 35 established a Task Force on Clinical Training to activate the clinical divisions to bring about change in theory, practice, training and research regarding women and to encourage women to participate in APA governance structures. By the time Division 39 was formed, there were established sections for women within the other practice divisions.

From the perspective of many of these groups, as well as a growing number of critics outside of the field, psychoanalytic theory and consequently psychoanalytic practice, was viewed as phallocentric and denigrating to women. Because many analysts themselves were having a difficult time reconciling their conviction and clinical experience with the Freudian view of femininity as a secondary, defensive formation, it seemed imperative that the newly formed Division of Psychoanalysis create a Committee on Women to examine essential theoretical, clinical and research issues pertinent to women's development and psychodynamics.

Barbara Claster, as Co-Chair of Division 35's Task Force on Clinical Training and Practice, was the primary initiator of the group which eventually became the Section on Women and Psychoanalysis. As the result of her contact with George Goldman, President-Elect and Robert Lane, President of Division 39, Lane contacted Dale Mendell and asked her to chair an ad hoc committee on women's issues in psychoanalysis to ascertain whether such a committee would be of interest to members of the Division. Ruth Formanek was selected as co-chair. On May 7, 1982, a committee consisting of Dale Mendell, Ruth Formanek, Barbara Claster, Bernice Barber, Carole Dilling, and Suzanne Phillips held its first meeting.

Although the ad hoc committee first met less than a decade ago to deal with issues around the changes in psychoanalytic theory and practice, there has been a good deal of progress since then, in part as a result of the work of the Committee and the Section which was its outgrowth. For example, the effect of gender on the process of analytic treatment, rarely considered at that time, is frequently addressed in the current analytic literature. It is worthwhile to recall the concerns of the Committee on Women in Psychoanalysis (CWP) and of interested members of the Division, in the summer of 1982.

At the first open organization meeting of CWP at the 1982 meeting of the APA in Washington, DC, the following areas emerged as major concerns among approximately 45 members of Division 39:

1. Concerns regarding equality included: the over-representation of male supervisors and training analysts at training institutes; the lower incidence of referral to female than to male analysts; the relative lack of women in positions of power in the Division.

2. Concerns regarding theory included: the phallocentric view of traditional psychoanalytic theory; the gender-blind construction of much clinical theory; the lack of attention to issues unique to women, such as the pregnancy of the patient and of the analyst; the relatively small number of female analysts revising and modifying theory.

3. Concerns regarding professional identity included: conflict between being a feminist and an analyst and the need for a group with dual identifications; apprehension over being identified with anti-analytic, self-dubbed "feminist therapists" by colleagues and patients.

4. Concerns regarding patients included: lack of recognition of the negative effects of cultural stereotypes on women's self-esteem; the too-frequent unconscious hostility toward women evinced by male therapists; the trend for

female patients to seek alternative therapies due to the public's image of psychoanalysis as negative to women.

During the 1982 meeting of the APA, members of CWP met with delegates of inter-divisional women's committees, including representatives of Divisions 29 and 35 and of the Committee on Women in Psychology, to learn about their experiences in organization and their opinions as to pertinent issues in the field. Among the many important and helpful ideas proposed, CWP immediately implemented several: writing a column concerning CWP or women's issues for each Division 39 Newsletter; forming local chapters in various geographic areas; co-sponsoring programs for APA meetings with other divisions' committees for women; keeping abreast of on-going activities concerning women and psychoanalysis and disseminating this information to our members; and becoming involved in the organization and politics of our division.

In the Fall of 1982, Ruth Formanek, Dale Mendell, and Bernice Barber wrote the first of a continuing series of columns for *The Psychologist-Psychoanalyst*. Aptly titled, "What Do Women Want?," this initial article announced the first meeting of CWP, summarized member concerns and called for additional members to join newly forming subcommittees. The Program Subcommittee, chaired by Helena Harris, had the goal of encouraging women to submit papers, ideas for panels and symposia for Division 39 meetings. The Research and Theory Subcommittee, under the direction of Joan Zuckerberg, functioned as a forum for members who were interested or involved in writing. Several published papers resulted from this forum, as well as a panel at the 1985 spring meeting of Division 39 in New York City; in addition, Joan Zuckerberg edited a volume that emanated from meetings of the Research and Theory Subcommittee.

The Subcommittee on Education and Consumer Affairs, chaired by Sheila Kaplan, focused on women's roles in training institutes and with the public's image of psychoanalysis and women. The Subcommittee on Rap Groups, chaired by Bernice Barber, organized information and discussions on the personal and professional role of the woman analyst.

While CWP originated in the New York area, geographic diversity and representation had always been considered a major building block for the organization. The earliest and strongest branch of CWP was its West Coast Chapter, based in Los Angeles, founded and Co-Chaired by Toni Bernay and Harriet Kimble Wrye. The West Coast group's focus emphasized study groups, speaker's forums and publishing a directory of members. Programs on analytic issues relevant to women, such as gender-specific countertransference problems, attracted a good deal of interest. Due to the newness of many groups there was often some overlap between Division 39 local chapter activities and the activities connected with CWP. This was true in Boston, according to Anne Thompson and Susan Adelman, and in Washington, DC, as reported by CWP members Susannah Gourevitch and Rochelle Kainer, where the major focus was on encouraging writing and publication among group members. Jean Apperson encouraged programs in women's issues in the Ann Arbor area.

After CWP had been in existence for less than a year, it became clear that there was sufficient interest from members of the Division to justify a more permanent organizational structure than that of an ad hoc committee. The Board of Directors of Division 39 was therefore petitioned to accept Women and Psychoanalysis as a Section of the Division. That petition was accepted unanimously by the Board on October 29, 1983. The petition read in part:

> The purpose of the Section shall be to promote interest in and provide a forum for communication on research and theory concerning gender differences and women's issues, to encourage women to participate actively in the Division of Psychoanalysis and to modify the current public image of psychoanalysis as negative to women.

With the change from an ad hoc committee to a Section of Division 39, the focus of Women and Psychoanalysis temporarily shifted to the necessary task of creating organizational structures. The President-Elect took over the function of Program Chair. The Bylaws Committee, consisting of Carole Dilling, Bernice Barber, and Helena Harris, based Section III's document on the bylaws of the Division; they were passed by section members and approved by the Board of Division 39 in December 1984. The Nominations and Election Committee, which was chaired by Barbara Claster and included Judith Butt, Barbara Counter, and Cheryl Kurash, wrote a procedural document for nominations and elections. The first elections took place in August 1984; the results were as follows: President, Ruth Formanek; President-Elect, Dale Mendell; Secretary, Aphrodite Clamar; Treasurer, Sheila J. Kaplan; Representative to Division 39, Toni Bernay; members-at-large Bernice Barber, Carol A. Butler, Susannah Gourevitch, Helena Harris, Rochelle G. K. Kainer, and Harriet Kimble Wrye.

In line with Section III's stated purpose of encouraging women to participate in the political process both inside and outside of the Division, a representative to the Division 39 Board of Directors was elected, and a representative to Division 39's Committee on Women in Psychology was appointed. Judith Butt was appointed representative to Division 35's Task Force on Clinical Training and Practice. An attempt was made to involve Section members in as many Divisional committees as possible, and Section III member Bernice Barber became the editorial assistant of the Divisional Newsletter.

Other, internal activities of the newly formed Section III included the compilation of a membership directory in March 1985 by Carol Butler, the membership secretary, and the publication of a Newsletter in April, 1985, edited by Helena Harris. In addition, an impressive 325 page bibliography of women's mental health issues, entitled *Female Psychology: A Partially Annotated Bibliography*, edited by Carole Dilling and Barbara Claster, was published in 1985 by the

New York City Coalition for Women's Mental Health. Several Section III members worked on this project. Due to her untimely death in October of 1984, Carole Dilling was not able to see the completion of the document. Her memory was honored by dedicating the Section's 1985 convention presentation to her.

The major strength of Section III in these early years was in program development, both for the annual convention and for the midwinter divisional meetings. In this way, concerns of women about psychoanalysis were explicitly presented to the entire Division. The Section III Board requested that the Division 39 Program Committee include a Section member to do blind review for each convention. In addition, Section III initiated the idea that each section of the Division be guaranteed time-slots for each convention and the right to solicit and review programs for that slot, without going through divisional blind review. A good deal of persuasion, hard work and political maneuvering was necessary to convince the heads of the Division Program Committee to relinquish a portion of their programming power to the Section on Women and Psychoanalysis.

PART II: SECTION III REFINES AND DEVELOPS ITS IDENTITY AND DIRECTION 1986–1991 (WRITTEN BY HARRIET KIMBLE WRYE)[1]

With Section III formally launched by its core group of founders and its first two Presidents, Ruth Formanek and Dale Mendell, and with the first set of bylaws in place, we set ourselves to the task of the development of membership, the refinement and implementation of our founding philosophy, broadening of our geographic base, and the further development of noteworthy programs that would consolidate our identity among our members and enhance our reputation in the division.

The majority of the original Board members were from the East Coast and most were also active in study groups. Bernay and Wrye who had co-founded the first West Coast Chapter of Division 39, Section III in Los Angeles in 1983, were influential in furthering the trend to broaden geographical representation and to foster the formation of Women and Psychoanalysis Chapters across the United States.

To this end, the 1986 Board voted to restructure the frequency and length of Board meetings. Whereas in the earliest days of the Section's founding, with most of the key members residing in the New York area, it was possible and fruitful to have frequent midweek evening meetings to take up the issues of the new Section, this format had to be altered to facilitate broader national representation. Thus, to this end, the 1986 Board voted to restructure the

---

[1]With editorial assistance by Helen Desmond, Section III President, 1989–1990.

frequency and length of Section III's Board meetings to correspond with Division 39's midwinter and APA's annual convention.

The activities during the middle phase of our development were directed by the then stated purpose of Section III, according to the bylaws: "The purpose of the Section shall be to promote interest in and provide a forum for communication on research and theory concerning gender differences and women's issues, to encourage women to participate actively in the Division of Psychoanalysis, and to modify the current public image of psychoanalysis as negative to women."

One of the truisms of the management and organization of Division 39 was that it often appeared to operate as a Good Ole' Boys' Club. The Section III Board agreed that if we were to implement our goals, we would have to forgo operating according to a stereotype as Polite Ladies Waiting to Be Asked and assert ourselves into the governance of the Division. To this end, we empowered the Section into becoming part of such key Division 39 committees as Programs and Publication, to assure that gender issues, female development, and psychology would be represented on any proposed diplomate exam. Aphrodite Clamar and Dale Mendell respectively represented the Section in planning and presenting a paper at the 1986 Clark Conference on Psychoanalytic Education. The aim was to highlight women's issues in training such as the development of curriculum and the selection of faculty. At that conference, we encountered the typical resistance to giving central importance to these issues—the speakers on women's issues were scheduled to speak at the end of the conference when most of the delegates had already departed. Similarly, it was necessary to take a strong stand to assert the Section's prerogative for timely inclusion in the Division 39 Newsletter, which became the Section's primary organ of communication to members and potential members across the country.

In 1987, the Board entered into a project to revise and expand the Section's membership directory under the leadership of Carol Butler, then Membership Chair, who went on to coordinate the publication of the entire Division 39 Membership Directory. Aware that we were undertaking some pioneering ventures and recognizing the importance of chronicling the history of the Section, we voted to develop and maintain archives under the tutelage of Cheryl Kurash. At the same time the Board instituted a number of Standing Committees with liaisons to the various Division 39 committees bearing the same name: Bylaws, Publications, Education and Training, Ethics, Research, Awards and Fellows, to honor distinguished women in psychoanalysis. Our delegates often had to struggle, not always successfully, to gain instrumental access to those Division 39 Board committees.

During the period 1985–1989 Section III also voted to send a representative to the Fund-raising Breakfast sponsored by Women's Coalition for Legislative Action (WCLA), now Women Psychologists for Legislative Action (WPLA), in conjunction with the annual APA conventions in August. Two distinguished female legislators who have been invited speakers to this forum are Congress-woman Bella Abzug and Representative Pat Schroeder. The Section also voted to honor one of its founding members by offering financial support for the Carole Dilling Memorial Lecture. This scientific meeting, established by the Training Institute for Mental Health and held periodically, addresses issues relating to psychoanalytic views of women.

During the same time, 1985 and forward, GAPPP began to take shape supported by Division 39, with the purpose of mounting a legal campaign to challenge the monolithic hold on formal psychoanalytic training exercised in the U.S. by APsaA. The decision to file an antitrust class action lawsuit was made. Two of the four plaintiffs to the suit, Toni Bernay and Helen Desmond, were active members of Section III, thus actualizing Section III's goals of active representation of women in the profession. The successful history of this GAPPP antitrust suit against APsaA is chronicled in detail by Arnold Schneider and Helen Desmond in Chapter 55, this volume.

Section III's dedicated purpose of the promulgation of psychoanalytic thinking favorable to women became the subject of one of the first significant philosophical and programming controversies the Section addressed during this period. Dissatisfaction with the status of women, both within the profession of psychoanalysis as well as within the theory, was an important reason for the original establishment of the interest group. Whereas feminist concerns have united the membership, differences in ideological commitment and adherence to theories have often emerged in discussion and program planning within Section III. At times, these differences have threatened to divide the Section. However, discussions of these issues and the nature and validity of psychoanalytic research, have led to a broadening view of programming beyond classical drive psychology to include a wide range of theoretical approaches, including examination of those construed as negative to women.

The programming policy that emerged invites free discussion among classical drive theorists, relational, and self-psychology and object relations theorists. Open and controversial dialogues and criticism of each emerging concept have been encouraged in the faith that negative conceptions of women would not long persist in such an open climate.

In 1988-1991, during the presidencies of Helena Harris, Helen Desmond, and Judie Alpert, and under the sponsorship of Helena Harris as Chair of the Bylaws Committee, the Section Bylaws were further revised. In addition to updating Section III's functions and procedures, the statement of purpose was modified as follows:

> The purpose of the Section shall be to promote research and theory concerning gender differences and women's issues, to increase the participation of women in the roles and functions of the profession, to promote and maintain high standards of practice in the psychotherapeutic treatment of women, to advocate on

behalf of women's issues, and to engage in collaboration with individuals, groups and organizations in the realization of these objectives.

The current psychoanalytic climate, in part resulting from the successful efforts of Section III, was deemed more enlightened with regard to women's issues. The phrase "to promote interest in" was deleted from the statement of purpose, reflecting the sense that interest in women's issues in psychoanalysis had successfully been generated during the early phase of the Section. The phrase, "to modify the current public image in psychoanalysis as negative to women," was now considered to be unnecessarily negative and thus deleted. The effort to increase women's participation in the Division was broadened now to aim at increased participation in the profession at large.

In fact, under the presidency of Judie Alpert, a Training Institute Ad Hoc Committee, chaired by Laura Barbanel, and a Political Action Ad Hoc Committee, chaired by Ruth Formanek, were formed. The purpose of the former committee is to consider means of facilitating women's degree of participation (both faculty and students) in training institutes, while the purpose of the latter committee is to engage in political action.

Another change in the bylaws, the addition of the phrase, "to promote and maintain high standards of practice in the psychotherapeutic treatment of women" reflects a move toward greater activism. The inclusion of this phrase reflects Section III's adoption of a form of Division 17's "Principles Concerning the Counseling/Psychotherapy of Women." Twelve principles focusing on psychoanalytic treatment of women were reported in *The Psychologist-Psychoanalyst* Vol VIII, No. 4. Fall, 1988. The principles reflect Section III's position that "Psychologist-Psychoanalysts should be knowledgeable about women with regard to biological, psychological, and social issues; should recognize evidence of sexism and oppression in themselves, in society, and in their patients, and assure that no preconceived limitations or biases are imposed in the treatment of women patients; and that they use nonsexist language in analysis, supervision, teaching, and journal publication."

The activist identity of the Section is reflected in the addition to the bylaws of the phrase, "to advocate on behalf of women's issues, and to engage in collaboration with individuals, groups and organizations in the realization of these objectives." There was debate at this time over changing the name and orientation of Section III from a primary focus on women's issues to reflect a broader focus on gender issues. The latter was considered by some as appropriate to raise the consciousness of men regarding gender issues—both masculine and feminine—and to generate the participation, and involvement of more men in Section III. A majority of the Board members however opposed this shift at this time, maintaining that the Section should continue its primary focus on women's issues and retain Section III's current name.

Another activist undertaking, during heightened religious and political debates regarding fetal rights and women's reproductive choice involved Sheila Kaplan's draft of a Pro-Choice Action Statement advocating preservation of women's legal rights to reproductive choice. This statement was endorsed by Section III and published in *The Psychologist-Psychoanalyst* (Vol IX, No. 3, Summer, 1989). In addition, in the wake of the Webster decision by the Supreme Court, a letter was circulated to the Division membership urging action and providing a state-by-state list of NARAL (National Abortion Rights Action League) members for use in securing information on working at the local level with state legislators.

Another recent development has been Section III's outreach to Section IV, Local Chapters, regarding the creation of local and regional study groups on gender issues. Marilyn Jacobs is chairing the National Study Groups Committee, formed in 1990. The intent is to develop a national forum for enabling local study groups to become aware of each other, to encourage communication and to foster networking among them.

Whereas during the early phases of the Section, the Board has fought to establish the right of the Section to a quality time slot on national programs, and the right to solicit and review programs for that slot, the actual arrangement of programs was the task of the President-Elect. This became problematic in that in many cases distinguished speakers' schedules are booked well in advance, and with time and experience, it became apparent that the President-Elect's lead-in time was insufficient to guarantee quality programs. Thus, in 1988 the Board established a Standing Program Committee that was charged with developing high-level programs that could be planned 2 years in advance. The philosophy of the Section has always been to provide first-rate programs that would be of interest to a large audience and would stimulate discussion and thinking about gender issues. This resulted in the establishment of Section III's reputation for providing consistently distinguished symposia at the Spring Division 39 and Summer APA meetings.

In addition to these formal programs, Section III established a policy to encourage its members to become accomplished journal writers, speakers and presenters, and to gain more experience and exposure through Women and Psychoanalysis conversation hours sponsored in the Division 39 hospitality suite and/or in the Section III President's hotel suite. With the increasingly competitive review process for the limited number of formal convention time slots, this policy was developed particularly to create fostering oral and written presentations and to encourage younger members' professional growth.

At this writing, under the presidencies of Judie Alpert and Carole Morgan, Section III continues to attract new and distinguished members associated with the concerns of female development, psychology, and psychoanalysis. Under the chairmanship of Adria Schwartz, of the Journal Ad Hoc Committee (1990), Section III is presently contemplating developing a journal as a wider forum for disseminating papers in the areas of interest for which the original Ad hoc committee was founded, thus promulgating the vision with which Section III was founded.

A Brief Personal Recollection
of the History of Section IV

Charles Spezzano

Section IV of Division 39, The Section of Local Chapters, was formed in 1985, 6 years after the Division itself had been formed. The origins of the Section, however, go back to at least 1980. In that year, a Committee on Local Chapters was established and was originally chaired by Jeffrey Binder from Nashville. According to a history written by Robert Lane in the Summer, 1988 Division 39 newsletter, Jeffrey Binder suggested a modus operandi that included the identification of a local organizer in each geographic area, the spreading of successful organizing ideas from one chapter to another, and the adding of a liaison role to the duties of the chair of the local chapters committee.

When Robert Lane became President of the Division, he invited representatives from five areas where communities of psychologists with an interest in psychoanalysis were beginning to identify with the Division (Chicago, Washington, DC, Michigan, Cleveland, New York) to meet for the first time in Chicago in October 1981. Oliver Kerner of Chicago hosted the meeting, with help from George Goldman who represented President Lane at that meeting. Oliver Kerner was elected Chair of the Local Chapters Committee and Murray Meisels was chosen to report on local chapters to the Newsletter, a task he carried out for several years in a popular column called "The Local Scene."

It was apparent at the Chicago meeting that training was on the minds of budding local chapters. Division members in areas that lacked suitable psychologist-psychoanalyst teachers and supervisors wanted to explore ways of importing them. Because training is an almost inherently conflictual issue, disputes within local chapters were already emerging.

When, in response to a letter that I wrote to the then Division President, Robert Lane, complaining of the Division's lack of attention to the needs of its members outside New York City, he invited me to attend a meeting of this Committee in Washington, DC in 1982, I met both Oliver Kerner and Murray Meisels, who was by then co-chairing the Committee. They encouraged me to start a chapter in Denver.

In 1983, Ted Reiss replaced Kerner and Meisels who were then jointly chairing the Committee. He served as Chair for 1 year. Then, in 1984, President Helen Block Lewis appointed Robert Lane and George Goldman as Co-Chairs and charged them with stepping up efforts to organize the chapters that were forming and becoming active and visible within their communities as centers of psychoanalytic interest and education.

The Local Chapters Committee, together with the National Program Committee and the Education and Training Committee, convened a nationwide conference at the William Alanson White Institute in New York City in December of 1984. Division members convened there to talk about how they might support each other, hopefully through the Division, and with its official support, to form societies, educational programs, and perhaps even institutes in places where psychoanalytic psychologists had felt no sense of community or identity. There was great excitement among everyone in attendance, but my memory of that excitement is that its source was not the same for everyone. For some Division members, often from New York City, the excitement seemed to come from the prospect of the Division spreading its sphere of influence around the country, growing and gaining new members. For others, often from the so-called hinterlands, the excitement came from the possibility that the Division would legitimize and perhaps help create training programs around the country. These two visions were at times in conflict.

This conflict intensified before it was resolved. Most of the participants at that 1984 meeting at White wanted to meet again, and what they wanted to discuss was training. There was little optimism that the money for such a conference on training would come from the Division, in which the prevaling power bloc of psychologist-psychoanalysts often seemed antagonistic to the idea that psychologists seeking training might simply create their own institutes. This antagonism, as I remember it, revolved around many variations on the theme that these new institutes would emphasize expediency over quality—a fear most memorably captured by a letter in the Division Newsletter, as I recall, that contained an odd and unconvincing analogy to the old idea from the history of economics that bad money pushed good money out of circulation. For some reason, it was feared, psychologists seeking psychoanalytic training, unlike other students at all levels of study in all other fields, would not want to get into the best schools but would flock to bad ones if these looked easy to get in and out of! Further, it seemed to have been feared, psychologists would go ahead and set up such institutes with inadequate quality controls over admission, supervision, personal analysis, and teaching. One specific form this embracing of inadequacy might take was a training standard of less frequency than three times per week for control cases and personal analyses. These were the core fears of some who opposed any further organization of local chapters—viewed now as launching pads for local institutes. So when local chapters expressed a desire to keep meeting, organizing and discussing training, this desire was often vigorously opposed.

Through a contact of Denver psychoanalyst Thomas Holman at Exxon, Helen Block Lewis was able to obtain a $25,000 grant for a conference on training. First a preconference was held in Ann Arbor in June 1985. Having been together twice now and judging organized opposition from other power blocs in the Division, Local Chapters decided to petition the Board to create a formal Section of Local Chapters with a representative on the Board to give voice to their concerns and desires. By that time I had joined Drs. Lane and Goldman in chairing the local chapters committee, which handled the ground work for the launching of the new Section. The Board approved the creation of Section IV in August 1985. I served as acting president for a year and then as the first official president of the Section during the 1986–1987 divisional year.

Local chapters were conceptualized as club houses where all Division members in a particular city or region could share their interest in psychoanalysis between national meetings. But a problem quickly arose. Should there be one local chapter in each area or should there be as many as people wanted to form? There were at least two hidden issues in the debate which evolved, during my term as President of the Section. The first was that, despite the fact that local chapters were not institutes, it was clear that they would spawn institutes and that these institutes would have, in their communities, a measure of legitimacy, derived from their perceived association with the Division and APA, not easily available to any institute which was not so associated in the minds of local professionals. So, if there were two or more groups within a local chapter with different favored models of training, they all wanted to have their own chapter to serve as a launching pad for their educational or training efforts, and to allow them separation from educational or training programs of which they did not approve.

The second hidden issue in the one-chapter-per-local-area versus multiple chapters debate was a possible last ditch effort by opponents of any self-generated training programs outside New York to stall the development of the new Section with the question of what exactly made a group of Division members a chapter? In reality, only the Division Board could designate a society of Division members an official local chapter of the Division. And the specter of every local faction setting up their own chapter was all the ammunition needed by anyone not supportive of local groups (perceived as launching pads for institutes that would not be forced to adhere to any particular training model or standards), to argue the Board into postponing any such official designations. There would be a Section IV with no member chapters! Many members of Section IV saw the best political route to be a clear initial presentation to the Board of the Division of a roster of local societies—one per area to eliminate any possibility of the Board using local dissension as reason not to designate official local chapters—of Division members seeking the Board's designation as official local chapters. Any such local chapter would then be a member chapter of Section IV. This was done and the Board did so officially designate all of the first group of societies presented to it as official Local Chapters of the Division. Nonetheless, some members of local societies who would have preferred to form a second or third local chapter apart from the large core chapter felt betrayed or disenfranchised. In some areas, such as Chicago and Washington, DC, additional chapters were supported by the Section and approved by the Board as an alternative to forcing incompatible local subgroups together against their will. Nonetheless, the basic principle was that, since local chapters are regional interest groups open to all Division members in the area and not ideologically defined training programs, only one chapter is needed in each area, this policy has been largely maintained over the years.

The newly formed Section IV held its first two official meetings separate from APA and Divisional meetings: one in Washington, DC in November 1985 and the other at the historic Brown Palace Hotel in Denver in April 1986, in conjunction with a scholarly conference sponsored by the Colorado local chapter. Since then, Section meetings have been regularly scheduled parts of Division programs.

I was succeeded in office by Robert C. Lane who served during the 1987–1988 Divisional year. At that time there were 15 approved chapters: two each in Chicago and Washington, DC, and each one in Colorado, Connecticut, Dallas, Massachusetts, Michigan, New York City, Philadelphia, Pittsburgh, Southern California, and Vermont.

In August 1988, Jonathan Slavin from the Massachusetts chapter took over as President of the Section from Robert Lane. A third Washington, DC chapter was added as well as one in southeastern Florida. The increasingly well organized Section sponsored a symposium on, "The Ideal Psychoanalytic Curriculum" at the Spring, 1989, Division meeting. By that time another chapter, in Austin, had been officially approved by the Board of the Division and had joined the Section.

James Barron, also from the Massachusetts chapter, succeeded Jonathan Slavin and served during the 1989–1990 year. He, in turn, was succeeded by Maureen Murphy and then Sam Gerson, both from the Northern California chapter, for the 1990–1991 and 1991–1992 terms.

The creation of local chapters in many areas greatly increased the visibility of the Division in those areas and drew many new members to the Division. In Denver, for example, Division membership jumped from about 6 to about 30 people within 1 year. Chapters such as the one in Boston and the one in the Bay Area have memberships rolls in the neighborhood of 500 members. Equally important, relationships have formed between some of the chapters, such as those in Denver, San Francisco, and Boston, which signal the beginning of a true national network of psychoanalytic psychologists who do not simply meet once or twice a year but collaborate on an evolving and continuous basis. As this happens, a sense of community is created. Members of chapters are increasingly invited to other areas to present papers or to be guest discussants at case conferences. It is now possible for members relocating from one region to another to find themselves welcomed as part of a professional community or even as extended family. In making recent moves from Denver to a year's sabbatical in Seattle and finally to a permanent resettling in San Francisco, I have been warmly welcomed by Division members who had learned of my plans and have received generous help in getting started in each new location. What a difference from 1984, when a colleague in Denver expressed his concern that by opting to train with the newly formed Colorado Center for Psychoanalytic Studies rather than the local medical institute, he would be giving up the opportunity to be affiliated with a national organization that would enable him to move to California one day, if he wanted to, with the prospect of being welcomed by other analysts there. Local chapters have definitely changed the psychoanalytic landscape to the advantage of psychologists across the country.

Addendum by Jonathan Slavin

I believe that Charles Spezzano's recollections are quite accurate about the development of the local chapter movement, although he is somewhat modest about his own role. Without his drive, clarity, and charisma, it is not certain that events would have moved as quickly and productively as they did. The Division clearly was of two minds about the question of local chapters. On the one hand, there was a clear wish to develop local chapters and spread the Division's influence. At the same time, as soon as the Division had successfully gotten people from all over the country together for the White Conference in December, 1984, there was a great deal implicit and often explicit anxiety about where these groups, made up of unknown individuals might go, using the Division's imprimatur. In chapter 10, I recounted a dramatic turning point, when the local chapters came to the Board in the spring of 1985 to ask support of the proposed Ann Arbor Conference. Although the Ann Arbor Conference was sponsored by the local chapters, it was also clearly a conference about the development of training programs. Spezzano's very effective appeal to the Board to be less suspicious of its local chapter colleagues managed to turn the Board vote around in support of this conference.

Another area that I would note is the role of the local chapters in the GAPPP lawsuit against APsaA and its codefendants. Local chapter members contributed financially, participated in the GAPPP Board and provided, when called on, extensive documentation of the discriminatory practices of the institutes of APsaA outside of the New York area. Local chapters also made direct contributions to the lawsuit and provided a forum for Bryant Welch and Nathan Stockhamer to promote the suit.

One of the primary recollections that I have from my Presidential year was that the Board accepted our recommendation that funding be provided on a regular, annual basis to assist local chapters in development. As a result, the Section's Membership Committee became the source for information about establishing a local chapter for individuals and groups around the country who were thinking of starting one. Individuals affiliated with the Division could apply for start-up funds that, if approved by the Section IV Membership Committee, were provided through the Division's treasury to support an initial organizing meeting and speaker, as well as other initial organizational costs. Almost all of the chapters that have become members of Section IV since that time have received funding in this manner. During my term, several new chapters were added including the Appalachian Psychoanalytic Society, the Austin Association for Psychoanalytic Psychology, the Connecticut Association for Psychoanalytic Psychology, the Western Massachusetts and Albany Association for Psychoanalytic Psychology, and the Southeast Florida Association for Psychoanalytic Psychology. We also heard from several new start-up groups in Cincinnati, Oklahoma, Toronto, and New Orleans, some of which have subsequently become local chapters.

During my term the Section maintained its tradition of sponsoring a program at the annual APA meeting and at the Mid-Winter Meeting related to psychoanalytic training. Although all of the Sections sponsor programs related to psychoanalytic issues, ours were specifically designed to address issues related to training.

There is one other feature of the local chapter movement that deserves mention. When the local chapters were forming and wrote bylaws for the Section, they included the possibility that clinicians from other disciplines as well as others interested in psychoanalysis could become involved. This degree of latitude, taken partly in response to the experience of exclusion on the part of the Societies of APsaA has enabled non-psychologists to become active and substantial participants in the affairs of several of the local chapters. In Massachusetts, for example, where non-psychologist clinicians were admitted first as associate members and later as full voting members, participation of clinical social workers and psychiatrists has enabled the Massachusetts local chapter (Massachusetts Association for Psychoanalytic Psychology) to become a professional home for psychoanalytically interested clinicians from all disciplines. It is the kind of unifying experience that has been sorely missing in many localities and have never been offered outside of the auspices of Division 39.

With Senate approval of local chapters in Austin, Texas, and Western Massachusetts—Albany, New York, Section IV became the organizational home to 20 chapters throughout the country. To facilitate continued growth, Section IV developed a Local Chapters Handbook to address questions regarding recruitment, bylaws, tax-exempt status, membership, fundraising, and organizational structure.

At the Division 39 spring meeting in Boston in 1989, Section IV sponsored a panel, "Reflections on the Lawsuit," to discuss the impact and implications of the settlement.

Section IV took an active role in exploring the proposed Federation of Psychoanalytic Training Programs, with James Barron and Murray Meisels co-chairing the first Federation Conference in May, 1989 in Washington, DC. Karen Rosica and James Barron co-chaired the follow-up Federation Conference in November of that year in Boston.

26

Section V, Psychologist-Psychoanalysts' Forum: A History (1986–1991)

Stanton Marlan
Joan P. Trachtman

The Psychologist-Psychoanalysts' Forum was founded to represent a broad spectrum of psychoanalytic schools and perspectives within the Division of Psychoanalysis. Members of the Forum are psychoanalysts and other psychologists committed to a pluralistic view of psychoanalysis. The Forum recognizes such orientations as Freudian, Jungian, Adlerian, Interpersonal, Existential, Relational, Lacanian and others, based on the criteria that have evolved within these respective traditions. The Forum focuses on clinical psychoanalysis. One of its objectives is to establish a place within the Division and the larger psychoanalytic community where practicing psychoanalysts of differing persuasions can meet to: (a) discuss clinical psychoanalysis from a variety of different approaches and schools; (b) disseminate information about both the training of analysts at different schools and the diverse types of psychoanalytic education and professional practice; (c) promote the development of dialogue between schools and approaches on clinical issues that encourage the interaction of members of different psychoanalytic orientations; and (d) contribute to the dialogue about, and assist in the development of, the highest standards in the practice of psychoanalysis and psychoanalytic training for newly developing schools.

The establishment of Section V within the Division was a long and difficult struggle against much resistance. Its development is best seen against the background of the emergence of the Division.

The Division was founded as an interest group but there remained a strong desire to identify qualified psychoanalysts. This mixture of interests set the stage for the formation of sections and for ways of identifying analysts. Murray Meisels

197

and Marvin Hyman put forth a proposal elaborating the need for a section of psychoanalysts that could award certificates of competency and elaborate training standards. They believed that this proposal would not cause controversy because psychologists who were not psychoanalysts fully understood that specialized training is needed to become one. It was reasonable to Meisels and Hyman that those who achieved such training be so acknowledged and that the section of psychoanalysts could serve such a purpose.

At the time, the definition of an analyst seemed clear to early organizers, and it did not seem as if the infighting of analyst against analyst would become an issue. In the Miesels/Hyman proposal the questions were raised: Who is qualified? and Who is to say what analysis is? The response boldly proposed was that the Division of Psychoanalysis would say who is qualified. On September 1, 1980, a motion passed the board that a committee be formed, with the task of developing a proposal for qualifications to be identified as a psychoanalyst. It was understood that no APA Division may do accrediting or credentialing but may set membership standards. The concern over credentialing was already fraught with controversy. What began as suggestions for standards or qualifications for the recognition of practicing psychologist-psychoanalysts ended up excluding a significant number of formally trained analysts of differing schools from membership in what was to become Section I, and did not, in our view, reflect the broad range of approaches in the field.

The establishment of Section I started the political fires that the Division was to struggle with for many years. Prior to the development of Section V, strong opposition to the criteria of Section I came from the postdoctoral university training programs in psychoanalysis at New York University (NYU) and Adelphi, each of which had graduated and were training a considerable number of psychoanalysts. In December 1982, Bernard Kalinkowitz sent a petition from the NYU postdoctoral community to George Goldman, then President of the Division, strongly objecting to the "methods used to establish Section I" calling them "ill-advised, hasty and in dubious accord with the precedent rules and regulations, and governance procedures of the APA." Similar objections were made by Don Milman, Director of the Alelphi postdoctoral program.

Kalinkowitz further stated that: "The effort of Section I of Division 39 to establish qualifications for a psychoanalyst was marked by an attempt to legislate by decree the answers to profound theoretical questions that perturb our whole field. The issues of what constitutes psychoanalysis, and what are the requirements for a psychologist to be entitled to the designation of psychoanalyst have a history of complex discussions, differing views, and the development of emergent new conceptions." He went on to say that: "Certainly these questions merit the most intensive and extensive exploration and discussion rather than a simplistic answer."

It is our view that the Division did not at that time create an intellectual forum for such explorations and the approach to the problems was decided by premature political action. The objections of the university programs had little effect once Section I was established. Section I represented the fulfillment of some members' original dream of validation, and at the time they did not envision that the Division had many analysts of different persuasions and schools. The unseen analysts were not yet politically organized and individual voices had little impact on the members of the Board and Section I, which had much overlap.

It is interesting now to reflect on the Summer, 1981 edition of *The Psychologist-Psychoanalyst*, which appeared with pictures of eight founding fathers and mothers of psychoanalysis, including Freud, Jung, A. Freud, Fromm, Horney, Adler, Binswanger, and Sullivan. It was comforting for many Division analysts who trained in the aforementioned schools to see their founders represented in the Divisional Newsletter, which seemed at the time to validate a broad approach to psychoanalytic practice. Even further, Gordon Derner began his presidential column with the idea that if a standard curriculum is developed, it was unclear whether it should be based on Freud, Adler, Sullivan, Jung or a variety of new and somewhat unusual theoretical models and procedures.

These words helped create the expectation that the Division would be a home for psychoanalytic practitioners of all schools. From Section I's perspective they were allowing diversity in acknowledging different schools, but in their zeal they rejected the definition of a psychoanalyst implicit in the traditions they professed to include. They did this by trying to establish uniform extrinsic standards to define the psychoanalyst, setting a standard of three times a week analysis as a membership criterion. This extrinsic standard was one of the main marks to distinguish Section I's membership standards, and a prime point of contention with other Division analysts. It was a standard held to tightly, because it was for this group a mark that distinguished analytic practice from intensive psychotherapy.

Rather than evaluating the subtle differences of clinical perspectives and what they achieve, proponents of three times a week analysis equated frequency with intensity and depth. The issue of three times a week versus once or twice a week got so polarized that differing schools came to represent one pole or another in the heat of political infighting. For many Jungians, neither once nor five times a week constitutes what is appropriate for analysis. Within the Jungian tradition, technique is intrinsically tied to clinical issues and variability of technique is highly regarded and not to be directed by standards external to the analysis.

The Jungian school is used as just one example. What was not appreciated by Section I was that the different philosophical orientations of the schools dictate different methodological and clinical approaches, putting into question and perspective such issues as frequency of sessions, use or non-use of the couch, and a host of other issues. Further, the differing clinical approaches are an intrinsic outgrowth of the way analysis had traditionally been practiced by the varying schools and differences will occur as change is occasioned by new innovations in analytic practice. From that perspective, trying to define psychoanalysis across the board by the extrinsic non-qualitative standards does not guarantee quality or depth, and serves to violate the training and practice traditions of a considerable group of analysts of other schools.

It is this perspective that set the stage for the organization of analysts from a variety of different schools who could join together to object to a simple externalized standard of quality. Stanton Marlan, one of the early voices of this perspective, contacted representatives of other approaches, and began to organize across schools, with the idea of creating another section of psychoanalyst clinicians. He first contacted Don Shapiro who was very sympathetic to this perspective, and who introduced Marlan to Maurice Krasnow. It is hard to remember the beginning of Section V without recalling the hard work and enthusiasm of Krasnow, who brought his expertise to work on bylaws and other tasks too numerous to mention. He served as a support to the development of Section V without which it is doubtful whether the Section would have come into being.

Those who worked for the development of the Section include Elizabeth Thorne, Don Shapiro, Stan Marlan, Bernard Kalinkowitz, and Don Milman. Though at the time they were not sure if moving toward a Section was the best way to resolve difficulties, they had already done much to promote a philosophy not unlike what the Section was to develop, and had hopes that the Board would come to recognize their perspective. As time went on and it became clear that their points of view were not going to change policy, they put their efforts toward a unified stand. Both Kalinkowitz and Shapiro were well known members of the Division and had the respect of a large number of Division members. Our Organization Committee was soon joined by Joan Trachtman, Rochelle Kainer, Harriette Kaley, and Ruth Ochroch.

As with all prospective new sections, we were required to present a formal petition to the Division Board, declaring our purpose, membership, and organizational bylaws. The presentation, typically pro forma, became for Section V, a political event. The Board raised many objections to our petition, though our petition met all formal requirements, and certain objections applied equally to other, already-accepted Sections. At two Board meetings, our petition for acceptance as "Psychologist-Psychoanalyst Clinicians" was rejected. Toward the close of a tumultuous third meeting, a third rejection was narrowly averted by our agreement (under pressure of imminent and perhaps final defeat) to change our name to "Psychologist-Psychoanalysts' Forum."[1] The change in name, as a political necessity, did not alter the heart of our fundamental position, i.e. that our psychoanalytic pluralism remains a challenge to any unimodel view of psychoanalytic theory and practice. Thus, on May 17th, 1986, Section V, "Psychologist-Psychoanalysts" Forum was born. The name did hint at our commitment to diversity. And, as subsequent history demonstrated, the struggle against premature foreclosure on these issues, under whatever name or banner, maintained its momentum and effectiveness.

---

[1]Editor's Note. It was Robert Lane who proposed that the Board caucus, at that critical junction, to develop an acceptable name. Some Section V people thought that if they had waited until after the Division elections they could have had the title of their choice.

The organizing Committee (Rochelle Kainer, Harriette Kaley, Bernard Kalinkowitz, Maurice Krasnow, Stanton Marlan, Don Milman, Ruth Ochroch, Elizabeth Thorne, Joan Trachtman) established an organizational structure for the new Section. Original petition signatories were invited into charter membership, and by mid-July over 170 became dues-paying members. The first Board of Directors was elected by this membership. Our first officers were: President, Stanton Marlan; President-Elect, Don Milman, Secretary, Esther Mullen, Treasurer, Joan Trachtman. Barbara Dusansky became treasurer in 1989–1990; Barbara Chasen became secretary in 1990–1991. There have been four presidents since: Don Milman, 1987–1988; Jules Barron, 1988–1989; Joan Trachtman, 1989–1990, and Marcia Pollak, 1990–1991. Esther Mullen, at this writing, is President-Elect, and Franklin Goldberg, President-Elect-Elect.

In an open letter to the membership, Stanton Marlan articulated our position: "Our general philosophy is that psychoanalysis should and does represent a broad and diverse spectrum of analytic theory and practice. . . . We welcome this diversity and feel psychoanalysis will be furthered by the rich ferment of ideas present in these traditions . . . It is our desire that these approaches be represented in our Section and that our programs reflect this richness. As psychologists and psychoanalysts it is important to talk to one another, to cross traditional boundaries, think, reflect, challenge and research the ideas and practices that have given much meaning to our lives and to those whom we treat. In this spirit, the section will promote the study of psychoanalysis through the interchange and recognition of the various schools of psychoanalytic psychology. . . . It is the intention of this Section to foster an appreciation of the clinical, epistemological and methodological contributions that arise from the diversity of orientations."

This clearly expressed our scholarly and ecumenical commitment; but it was clear that we had a political mission as well. Our Section had been born in response to a series of attempts to define the psychoanalytic perspective in quantitative terms, as the only acceptable model for training and practice, which shut out too many qualified analysts. Whereas the formation of the Section provided a scholarly gathering place for those with more diverse orientations, it was apparent that the attempts at ideological gatekeeping, which had galvanized us as a group, were continuing, and as we began to shape our identity and role, an inextricable mix of scholarly and political action seemed inevitable.

In the beginning, organizational matters naturally predominated. With our first Board of Directors in place, a set of bylaws was adopted, and a Committee structure established, with Executive, Membership, Program, Nominations and Elections, Finance, Publications and Bylaws committees. In addition, the Advocacy Committee (later renamed the Committee on Professional Issues) was established to coordinate our activities in the professional/political sphere, and a Liaison Committee (later subsumed under the Committee on Professional Issues) was organized to plan outreach to other Divisional Sections and to local chapters nationally on behalf of our Section V ethos. Stanton Marlan, as President and founder of the Section, was selected as our pro-tem representative to the Division 39 Board, and then formally elected by the membership to this position for a full 3-year term.

An immediately pressing priority was to establish our scholarly presence at the upcoming 1987 Mid-Winter meeting of the Division. Don Milman, as Section V program chair, arranged two panels: "Contemporary Views on Dream Analysis," developed and chaired by Stan Marlan and representing existential, interpersonal, and Jungian perspectives; and a special presentation on "Psychoanalytic Change: Existential and Relational Viewpoints," chaired by Dr. Kalinkowitz and held at NYU. And we continued to maintain a scholarly presence at all Divisional and APA meetings, with programs mirroring our perspective and reflecting cross-orientational viewpoints on clinical and theoretical issues. In 1989, after several years of presenting regular programs at Division and APA meetings, we added two permanent features to our scholarly programming. The first was the Section V Annual Scientific Meeting, envisioned as a presentation by a distinguished psychoanalytic scholar, inaugurated in the spring of 1990 by Robert Holt discussing his book *Freud Reappraised*, in which the basic theoretical structure and content of classical psychoanalytic theory was critiqued. The second was the formation of a Continuing Education Committee to sponsor CE programs, plus workshops and study groups through which we hoped to develop greater regional participation in our programs and wider dissemination of our pluralist philosophy. The inaugural event of this new project was a full-day program chaired by Barbara Eisold, "Child Abuse: Where Have We Come Since Freud?", which occurred in March 1991.

Previous attempts by the Division's ABPP Liaison Committee to promulgate restrictive standards for a diplomate in psychoanalysis had been one of the stimuli for the formation of Section V. In 1986, this Committee was disbanded and an independent corporation, ABPsaP was established. ABPsaP, however, continued recommending similar restrictive guidelines, and so Section V, now representing an organized constituency, made its position officially known. ABPsaP's recommendations implied a unified psychoanalytic position with consensus on training and practice criteria, and, by extension, criteria for diplomating. Section V underscored the existance of controversy and lack of consensus on these fundamental issues, and communicated its position to the APA Office of Accreditation, to ABPP, to the Division, and to ABPsaP. Our entry into this political controversy was joined by Bernard Kalinkowitz and Don Milman. After numerous meetings and apparent rapprochements, agreement on a diplomating examination has been achieved only recently.

In 1987, our committee on Professional Issues began work on a survey of professional practices and views on training. This study, sampling the entire Division membership, is reported in chapter 4 of this volume.

Also during our second year, plans to publish a Section V Newsletter coalesced. With Susan Hans as Editor-in-Chief, the premier issue of *Psychologist-*

Psychoanalysts' Forum was published. The *Forum* includes Sectional news, in-depth reporting of scientific programs, commentary on topics of professional and/or political concern, theoretical articles representing diverse psychoanalytic perspectives, and reports from regional representatives added to broaden our national coverage. Aesthetically and in substance, the *Forum* has evolved into a significant chronicle and clarion for Section V events and philosophy. In 1990, Spyros Orfanos, the Assistant Editor, picked up the reins as Editor-in-Chief to continue the development of the publication as the true professional forum.

In another major project, Marcia Pollak, as membership Chair in 1988, conducted a comprehensive informational survey of our membership, processed the massive amount of data collected, and was responsible for the design and execution of our first official Section V Membership Directory. A second, updated 1991 edition is at this writing being prepared by Robert Prince, current membership Chair, with additional information on the backgrounds, training and specializations of our members.

As we continued our watchdog function in relation to qualification and training issues, a new source of concern was the publication of the first Division 39 Membership Directory in 1989. The Directory Foreword implied that Section I was the sole practitioner group, and by highlighting Section I membership standards as comparable to international standards for psychoanalysis, the Directory seemed to confer sole legitimacy on this model. Section V lodged protests repeatedly, with successive Division presidents, to change this Foreword in the next Directory edition. After 2 years, a committee representing all Sections arrived at a consensus on the nonprejudicial Foreword that appears in the new 1991 Division Directory.

Meanwhile, the APA Task Force on the Scope and Criteria for Accreditation was considering the possibility of widening its scope of accreditation to include postdoctoral specializations. Task Force reports were routinely sent to interested parties for commentary, and Division 39 was already represented in this network. We immediately identified Section V as an interested party and joined this network. Through our Committee on Professional issues, Task Force reports and recommendations were studied, and official Section V responses were forwarded to the APA Office of Accreditation. Joan Trachtman served as liaison to the Task Force from Section V. We indicated support for the proposed expansion of accreditation into postdoctoral areas, and for the concept of recognizing new specializations at the postdoctoral level, of which we proposed psychoanalysis be one. We particularly highlighted the inappropriateness of the proposed internship model used in doctoral training, for training in psychoanalysis. We took strong exception to the apparent intention of APA to limit potential postdoctoral accreditation to institutes attached to universities or major health centers, stressing the absolute necessity of including free-standing institutes in their scope. This latter issue may well become a major point of controversy as accreditation plans continue. We are keeping abreast of developments in the planning of a proposed national conference on postdoctoral matters, now under the aegis of APA's Board of Educational Affairs. We have emphasized that in any such conference the full diversity of views within the psychoanalytic community must be represented fairly.

Since its inception, our Committee on Professional Issues, in addition to its other activities, had been working on the development of proposed Section V standards for accreditation of postdoctoral institutes training psychologist-psychoanalysts. Under the leadership of committee Chair Don Shapiro, a recommended set of standards was developed, embracing our ecumenical point of view and defining training components compatible with analysts of diverse persuasions. These standards were overwhelmingly endorsed by our Section V membership in the fall of 1988. At this writing, Edde Schreiber has assumed the professional issues committee Chair.

In August of 1988, at APA, the Division established an ad hoc committee to liaison with the APA Education and Training Committee (which would ultimately be receiving the Task Force recommendations), to acquaint them with special issues involved in psychoanalytic training. This ad hoc committee then began to develop an accreditation document for Division approval. The committee included Bernard Kalinkowitz, and Don Milman as Co-Chairs, Bertram Karon, and, as Division 39 and Section V representatives to the Task Force, James Miller and Joan Trachtman, respectively. As work on this document proceeded, the Section V position and philosophy was vigorously represented in committee discussions, and found increasing support in the group. When Ruth-Jean Eisenbud assumed the presidency of the Division in 1989, she gave high priority to settlement of the ongoing qualifications conflict that continued to fractionate the Division. She called a retreat for the Division Board to consider these issues. The special ad hoc Committee document became the center of discussion, and after several additional meetings, was approved by the Division Board. This document, published in its entirety in *The Psychologist-Psychoanalyst* (Fall 1990), recommends standards for the accreditation of psychoanalytic institutes training psychologist-psychoanalysts, including a generic definition of psychoanalysis, a tripartite model of training (i.e., personal analysis, supervision of patients and didactic curriculum), with recommendations stated in qualitative terms. These Division standards, quite congruent with the philosophy and approach of Section V, were submitted to the APA Office of Accreditation and the Board of Educational Affairs as the official Division 39 position on accreditation of psychoanalytic institutes training psychologist-psychoanalysts. This seemed the beginning of a healing process and of the possibility of renewed rapport and cooperation between previously alienated factions within the Division. In terms of the aims and goals of Section V, the acceptance of this document by the Division was a signal step in our struggle for an ecumenical viewpoint on psychoanalytic theory, training and accreditation.

Most recently, in 1991, there is some indication that ABPsaP, after a lengthy hiatus, has begun anew its activities toward the development of a diplomate examination in psychoanalysis. As of this writing, it is not yet clear what direction their activities will take . . . whether or not they will follow the spirit of the guidelines appearing in the Division accreditation document sent to APA, and how this will affect the current detente.

To be sure, the issue of accreditation in psychoanalysis is far from settled. While awaiting APA's actions in this arena, a Federation of Psychoanalytic Institutes is being formed independent of APA and the Division of Psychoanalysis, though with some financial support from the Division. Whether the Federation seeks to develop some role in the accreditation process remains to be seen. Another external group, NAAP, has officially applied to COPA (Council on Postsecondary Accreditation) to be established as the official accrediting body for psychoanalytic training institutes in the United States. And so, Section V's interest and philosophical position on these questions may yet again need vigorously to be represented.

Finally, moving from history and current activities, we have begun to look to the future with the establishment of an ad hoc Policy and Planning Committee in the spring of 1990. Chaired by Harry Sands, the Committee is concerned with long-term planning for the Section. Having reviewed and critiqued our organizational and programmatic functioning during our first half-decade, the group has completed the development of a 5-year Forward Plan for Section V. It is our hope that improved strategies for implementation of our fundamental ecumenical philosophy as psychologist-psychoanalysts will emerge from this effort.

ACKNOWLEDGMENT

We gratefully acknowledge the consultation and thoughtful contributions of Bernard Kalinkowitz.

A Brief History of Section VI:
The Psychoanalytic Research Society

Harold Cook

As best as the record indicates, shortly after the Division of Psychoanalysis was formed in 1979, Gordon Derner, the President of the Division, being very supportive of research, proposed a standing research committee of the Division. Derner appointed Joseph Masling as the first Chair of the Research Committee. Richard Billow, Sidney Blatt, Norbert Freedman, and Lloyd Silverman served with great enthusiasm as committee members. Masling chaired the committee until 1985 when Howard Shevrin was appointed Chair of the Research Committee, and he appointed Sidney Blatt, Philip Holzman, Lester Luborsky, Herbert Schlesinger, and Donald Spence as members. In 1988, James Eyman became Chair until 1989 when Harold Cook and Joseph Turkel were appointed as Co-Chairs of the Research Committee.

Throughout the formative years of the Division, the Research Committee attempted to draw attention to the scientific aspects of psychoanalysis, organizing research panels and papers for presentation at Division meetings and initiating research awards. The tireless efforts of the chairpersons and members of the Research Committee to sustain a research presence during those early years, occurred in an atmosphere of polite skepticism toward empirical research on the part of the overwhelming majority of the practitioner members of the Division. In general, the membership was mainly concerned with issues of clinical theory, technique, and professional practice.

In the Spring of 1989, the newly appointed Co-Chairs (Cook and Turkel) of the Research Committee invited a number of people to become members of the Committee. Their letter of invitation to prospective members of the Committee stated: "Our aim with your assistance is to establish some realistic goals for the Committee and perhaps a strategy and research agenda for the Division. We envision that almost any work we might do along these lines could impact the direction of future research committees and add saliency to the importance of psychoanalytic research for theory development and clinical practice." In response to this letter, an outstanding and widely respected group of psychologists agreed to become members of the committee, Co-Chaired by Cook and Turkel, membership consisted of Morris Eagle, Matthew Erdelyi, Irene Fast, Judith Kantrowitz, Lester Luborsky, Joseph Masling, Stephen Portuges, Howard Shervin, Herbert Schlesinger, and Hans Strupp.

It appeared politically that the time was right, and after several discussions, the Research Committee, functioning as an organizing committee, proposed (see Volume IX, No. 2, of *The Psychologist-Psychoanalyst*) a new Section of the Division. They were encouraged by the large number of members who responded to their solicitation of signatures to a petition to establish a Research Section. In the Fall of 1989, they submitted the petition to the Board of the Division requesting the establishment of the Section.

The cover letter stated:

> . . . The bylaws and publicity for the Division, state that the Division "is concerned with advancing scientific and public interest in the contributions of psychoanalysis to psychology as a science and a profession, and encouraging educational programs and research in psychoanalysis." It seems that "encouraging research in psychoanalysis" unfortunately has been a neglected objective of the Division.
>
> Thus, the establishment of *A Research Section* should be of vital concern and interest to the Division. It represents an opportunity for the Division to take an overdue, visible step in promoting the value and importance of psychoanalytically informed research, and its contribution to theory and practice. The section attempts to function as a catalyst in the development of a psychoanalytic research enterprise. At this historical junction, psychoanalysis is in need of well trained, thoughtful, dedicated research people who are psychoanalytically oriented to demonstrate the efficacy of psychoanalytic treatment and the viability of psychoanalytic theory. The section attempts to foster a research posture and attitude among psychoanalysts.
>
> Attached you will find: (a) A draft version of Bylaws for the proposed new Research Section; (b) A list of the names of almost 400 members of the Division (approximately 15%) who have signed a petition requesting a Research Section. About 15 more folks have signed the petition but have not yet been added to the list . . ."

With apparent pleasure and enthusiasm, on November 11, 1989, the Board of the Division approved the establishment and the Bylaws of Section VI—The Psychoanalytic Research Society with its stated purposes (Article II of Bylaws) being:

The Section subscribes to the general objectives of the American Psychological Association and the Division of Psychoanalysis. The overall purpose of this section is to promote psychoanalytic research of an empirical, theoretical and clinical nature. More specifically, this section shall further the development of a variety of research activities including the planning and conducting, as well as the dissemination of research findings. It will stimulate and support communication among researchers by the use of professional meetings and publications. In addition, it shall facilitate (1) the continual development and training of psychoanalytically oriented researchers; (2) the broadening of the role that psychoanalytic research plays in general psychology, with other related professional disciplines, and the public.

Subsequent to its establishment, the newly formed section, with pro-tem officers (Harold Cook, President; Joseph Turkel, Secretary-Treasurer; and Members-at-Large—Morris Eagle, Lester Luborsky, Howard Shevrin, and Hans Strupp) initiated a membership campaign. Within 6 months, 252 dues-paying members from throughout the States and from other countries became members of the new Section.

The Research Section was now firmly established and began to actively participate on the Board of the Division. It organized its first symposium at the Spring 1990 meeting of the Division—''Psychoanalysis as a General Psychology: Theoretical and Empirical Issues.'' The Section was influential in the Board's decision to recommend that the Research Section appoint a representative to future Divisional Program Committees. In addition, it conducted an empirical evaluation of the Division's Spring 1990 meeting, reported the results to the Board, who recommended that program committees of all Annual and Spring meetings conduct an empirical evaluation of their meetings. The Section also supported a request for funds from the Division to sponsor jointly, with APsaA, a conference—''Psychoanalytic Research: Education for Research Careers in Psychoanalysis—Dream or Reality?'' The conference, known as the Bethesda Conference, was attended by a small group of scientists, as well as several members of the Division.

In June 1991, the first contested elections of officers of the Section were held. More than 50% of Section members voted, electing Harold Cook, President; Joseph Turkel, Treasurer; Gwen Gerber, Secretary; and Peter Buirski, Morris Eagle, Carol Giesler, Nancy Miller, and Dennis Shulman, Members-at-Large. The new officers of the Section appointed a number of standing committees, established a format for a forthcoming Newsletter, *The Bulletin of the Psychoanalytic Research Society* (under Dennis Schulman's editorship), which was published in the Spring of 1992, and participated in discussions regarding the Division's co-sponsoring, with APsaA, a Joint Board for Psychoanalytic Research Training (JBPRT).

Although not without controversy, the Board of the Division initially responded positively to the JBPRT's request for additional funding, and charged the Research Section with an oversight function of JBPRT. Subsequently, further controversy regarding adherence to the lawsuit settlement dampened collaborative efforts with the APsaA. The funds were put on hold, and the Section was asked by the Board of the Division and Jonathan Slavin (the President) to provide recommendations to the Division regarding participation in JBPRT. A committee of the Research Section's Executive Board in discussing the complexity of issues recommended a delay in funding until several conditions are met, that is, (a) clarification of the oversight function assigned to the Section such that it includes a definition embracing "management, direction, control, and supervision"; (b) have the organizing committee of JBPRT provide a specific and concrete proposal with a detailed budget so that it can be realistically evaluated in light of the Division's and Section's interests; and (c) have the Section recommend five of the ten people to be appointed to JBPRT. These people should be first-rate in terms of either their research contributions or their experience in research training and be able to represent the interests of the Division and the Research Section. The Research Section is thus in the middle of a controversy involving the Division's relationship with APsaA. Any joint activity with APsaA appears at this time to involve a multilayered web of political, philosophical, and professional intrigue.

Hopefully, the Psychoanalytic Research Society will play an increasingly important and exciting role in invigorating psychoanalysis as a scientific, as well as a clinical endeavor. Inspiring the Division's membership to value, support, perhaps conduct and intelligently become consumers of research is an objective that should evoke the imagination and energetic participation of all of us who view psychoanalysis as a vibrant, intellectually stimulating and developing theory, and technique of treatment of human distress.

A History of Section VII:
Psychoanalysis and Groups

Marvin L. Aronson

Although a sizeable number of senior members have routinely combined individual and group analysis in their work with patients for at least 20 years, the Division manifested very little official interest in analytic group therapy until very recently.

In 1981, President Robert Lane did call on Leonard Horwitz and June Blum to form a committee on group therapy, but both tell me that they found little enthusiasm among the membership at the time. Some time thereafter, a workshop on combined therapy was offered at a Division 39 Annual Meeting at the Vista Hotel in New York. The workshop had three leaders: Judith Caligor, Nina Fieldsteel, and Marvin Aronson. Two registrants showed up for the occasion!

It was only in Zanvel Liff's presidential term, in 1989, that a Committee on Psychoanalysis and Groups was revitalized, with Marvin Aronson as Chairperson. One of the first acts of this Committee was to send out a questionnaire to the entire membership of Division 39 to explore their views on the interrelationships between individual and group psychoanalysis. The results of this questionnaire revealed that a substantial number of Division 39 members employed combined or conjoint analytic group therapy in their clinical practice, and, that many of these would be interested in joining a proposed new section on Psychoanalysis and Groups.

The Committee formulated the objectives of the proposed new section on Psychoanalysis and Groups as follows: To provide a forum to study : (a) the application of psychoanalytic thinking to the theory and practice of psychoanalytic group therapy; (b) the impacts of combined and conjoint psychoanalytic group therapy upon individual psychoanalytic processes; (c) the utilization of psychoanalytic concepts for understanding phenomena endemic to institutional and societal groups, and (d) to encourage the presentation of scientific papers at professional meetings of Division 39 and of Section VII.

The Committee designated the following individuals as pro tem officers of the proposed Section: President: Marvin L. Aronson; Secretary: Olga Marlin; and Treasurer: Emanuel Shapiro. It also designated the following individuals as pro tem Members-at-Large: Bruce Bernstein, Leonard Horowitz, Christine Kieffer, Desy Safan-Gerard, Peter Schlachet, and Antonio Virsida.

On November 11, 1989, the Executive Board of Division 39 voted in principle to form Section VII (Psychoanalysis and Groups). On April 6, 1990, the Board voted (at the Vista Hotel in New York) to accept the Section with voting privileges deferred until it met the membership requirement of 5% of the Division. The Board voted officially to admit the Section at its August 1990, meeting in Boston.

The first Scientific Meeting of Section VII, co-sponsored by the Psychoanalytic Institute of the Postgraduate Center for Mental Health, was held on January 9, 1991. At this meeting, the Asya L. Kadis Memorial Award Lectures were presented by two of the leading analytic group therapists in the United States: Henriette Glatzer and Alexander Wolf. The Section VII sponsored symposium at Division 39's 1991 Chicago Meeting was entitled, "Utilizing Group Therapy to Facilitate a Variety of Analytic Tasks." At the 1992 Spring Meeting in Philadelphia, Section VII sponsored a Symposium on "Gender Issues in Psychodynamic Group Psychotherapy." On May 27, 1992, Section VII co-sponsored a Scientific Meeting with the Postgraduate Center for Mental Health and the Eastern Group Psychotherapy Association. The speaker was Otto Kernberg. His topic: "Paranoiagenesis in Organizations."

The results of Section VII's first election, held in the Spring of 1991 were as follows: President: Marvin L. Aronson; Treasurer: Emanuel Shapiro; Secretary: Nancy Edwards; Members at Large: Bruce Bernstein, Barbara Dusansky, Peter Schlachet, and Antonio Virsida.

IV

Local Chapters

The local chapter movement is one of the premier results of the formation of the Division of Psychoanalysis. At first, it was largely a grass-roots movement among psychologists who had been long-frustrated by the psychiatry prerequisites in APsaA. Often enough, these new founders and leaders in the field of psychoanalysis were not qualified psychoanalytic practitioners. Still, their dedication and intensity led them to form local chapters, and after that, even institutes. It is noteworthy that the most senior and traditional psychologist-psychoanalysts in a given area usually did not participate in these organizational successes. Those psychologists who had been trained by APsaA were largely involved with APsaA, and the new creative leaders in the field came from elsewhere.

Two examples may illustrate this. The first example is Charles Spezzano, who almost single-handedly organized the Colorado local chapter and then the offshoot Colorado institute; the latter so that he could be formally trained in psychoanalysis, which is what he proceeded to accomplish. A second example is Arnold Schneider, who had received limited training at the Topeka Institute—limited training means that he completed coursework and a personal analysis, but that his petition for a waiver to receive supervision had been rejected—and who was so upset by APsaA's refusal to allow him full training that he joined the psychologist's lawsuit as one of the four plaintiffs. He was then ostracized at Menninger's and found a position in Tampa, where he is now organizing a local chapter. It is exhilarating to think that Spezzano and Schneider are now having a far greater impact on the field of psychoanalysis than they would have, had APsaA admitted them to full training. Stated differently, the era of helpless frustration with APsaA had passed, and psychologists now bent their energies to creative forms.

Once the Section of Local Chapters was formed in 1985, it exerted a great deal of energy to defining the requirements to become a local chapter, and actively recruited local Division 39 members to form new organizations. It continues to do so.

How have we done? Quite well! Table 1 presents the list of current local chapters along with their membership data, and some information about their professional and scientific activities. The data were collected in 1991 and 1992. As Table 1 indicates, the size of the chapters varies enormously, from 16 in the Potomac society to 500 in Massachusetts. Interestingly, Division 39 members only comprise about 33% of the total local chapter membership, while non-Division 39 psychologists comprise 26%. Psychologists altogether comprise 59% of local chapter membership, social workers, 20%; psychiatrists, 4%; and students, 13%. The total number of local chapters members is 2,887, a somewhat inflated number because some psychologists are members of more than one chapter. Still, subtracting the 958 Division members from the total local chapter membership of 2,887 leaves 1,929 colleagues who are affiliated with Division 39 even though they are not members of Division 39. Stated differently, the true impact of Division 39 is not only gauged by its membership count but also by counting the nonmembers who belong to its local chapters. The 3,433 members in May, 1992, are thus supplemented by an additional 1,929 local chapter participants, leading to a total psychoanalytic organization of 5,362 people.

The column on institutes in Table 1 refers to the presence of a psychologist institute in the geographical area. Local chapters have founded free-standing institutes in Chicago, Colorado, Connecticut, Massachusetts, Michigan, Northern California, Ontario, and Philadelphia, but other institute training opportunities have been developed as well. Southeast Florida psychologists have a training program at Nova University, Washington, DC, has a branch of the New York Freudian Society, and Oklahoma City has a branch of the Colorado institute. New York and Los Angeles have long had independent institutes.

Although formal training often takes place at allied institutes, local chapters are nonetheless active in education. Annually, they hold 130 scientific meetings (1–2 hours in duration), 66 workshops (one-half day or longer), 27 study groups, offer 38 courses, and publish 72 editions of newsletters.

Some multiplication will show the power and reach of the local chapter educational programs. The 21 chapters that present 130 paper sessions annually draw a median of 30 participants per paper, leading to a total of 3,900 individual participations. Each participation lasts at least one hour, for a total of at least 3,900 contact hours. Similarly, the 21 chapters that present 66 workshops have a median of 60 participants per workshop, leading to a total of 3,960 participations. Because each workshop lasts at least 3 hours, this yields a total of at least

TABLE 1
Local Chapter Membership and Educational Activities

	Year Founded	Year Entered Div. 39	Div. Members	Psychologists Not In Div. 39	Social Workers	Psychiatrists	Students	Other	Total Members	Papers Per Year	Ave. Attendance	Workshops Per Year	Ave. Attendance	Study Groups	Members In	Courses	Students In	No. News Editions	Institute In Area
Appalachia	1989	1989	23	27	5	3	2	—	60	4	18	1	25	—	—	2	9	4	—
Austin	1988	1988	16	16	25	8	5	—	70	7	35	2	100	—	5	—	—	—	—
Baltimore	1991	1991	10	35	40	5	5	—	95	—	—	6	63	3	6	3	—	3	—
Chicago CAPP	1980	1986	80	78	10	2	64	—	234	6	22	2	150	2	10	3	4	—	Yes
Chicago Open	1985	1985	8	4	20	5	7	1	45	4	8	2	—	—	6	4	—	4	Yes
Cincinnati	1991	1991	7	2	10	26	2	5	26	4	22	2	6	2	—	—	—	—	—
Colorado	1984	1986	58	10	44	—	—	14	152	5	25	—	—	—	—	—	—	3	Yes
Connecticut	1985	1986	60	20	40	10	8	2	140	2	—	4	70	3	10	—	—	3	Yes
Dallas	1982	1986	33	17	21	5	25	22	123	7	30	2	65	1	13	—	10	10	—
Georgia	1990	1991	10	8	2	2	5	8	35	4	20	2	20	—	—	4	—	4	—
Massachusetts	1983	1986	170	150	80	10	80	10	500	9	100	5	40	1	—	12	12	4	Yes
Michigan	1980	1986	50	30	25	5	20	20	150	8	25	2	65	1	5	1	10	3	Yes
New Mexico	1991	1991	9	21	4	9	14	6	63	1	40	2	100	—	—	—	—	—	Yes
New York	1986	1986	10	—	—	14	—	—	10	—	—	—	—	—	—	—	—	—	Yes
N. California	1986	1986	137	70	88	—	35	6	350	4	50	8	26	1	15	9	12	4	Yes
Oklahoma	1990	1990	5	3	19	2	—	—	29	11	18	1	50	—	—	—	—	—	Yes
Ontario	1991	1991	10	5	—	10	22	—	15	10	35	—	90	—	—	—	—	3	Yes
Philadelphia	1985	1986	50	66	2	—	—	—	140	5	30	4	60	3	6	3	—	—	—
Pittsburgh	1985	1986	10	6	3	—	8	—	28	10	20	8	40	1	9	3	8	—	—
Potomac	1980	1986	11	3	1	1	—	1	16	3	12	5	12	1	9	1	9	—	Yes
SE Florida	1987	1988	25	40	15	—	15	1	96	4	40	—	—	2	9	—	—	4	Yes
S. California	1984	1986	50	69	23	3	32	9	186	7	55	1	75	2	12	—	—	—	Yes
Vermont	1983	1986	3	30	20	5	5	5	68	—	—	—	30	—	—	2	8	2	—
WPSP, Wash, DC	1980	1986	73	19	20	1	4	4	121	10	45	2	100	3	8	—	—	4	Yes
WSPP, Wash, DC	1981	1987	25	15	40	1	4	4	80	10	20	4	20	4	12	6	10	2	Yes
W. MS & Albany	1986	—	15	3	20	4	8	5	55	9	15	3	45	2	6	2	15	8	—
Totals			958	747	577	120	366	119	2887	130		66		27		38		72	

11,880 contact hours. The 14 chapters that offer 27 study groups have a median of 10 members per study group, or 270 participations. If each study group meets an average of 15 times a year, and averages 2-hour sessions, this yields 11,100 contact hours. Finally, the nine chapters that offer 38 courses a year have a median of 10 people per course, or 380 participations. If each course is taught for one and one-half hours and lasts for 12 weeks, this yields 6,840 contact hours. Adding these numbers together provides a conservative estimate that the local chapter movement provides 33,780 hours of psychoanalytic education per year! The impact of Division 39 local chapters is actually far greater than this because of the educational activities of allied institutes. It is also proper to compare the 33,780 contact hours in 1992 with the number of contact hours prior to the establishment of the Division: That number was zero.

Besides quantity, the quality of the local chapter presentations was excellent, a panoply of current thinkers and theories. Indeed, many of the descriptions below were enriched with details of titles of papers and symposia, and panelists and presenters, most of which was perforce deleted because of space considerations. Overall, we are in the forefront of psychoanalytic thought.

In the following section, the local chapters, presented alphabetically, describe some of their history. These descriptions were mostly written by chapter founders, and the histories are certainly varied. Most chapters have experienced growth and integration, but several geographical areas have experienced dissension, and in Chicago and Washington, DC, this has led to multiple chapters. Some chapters are large, others are small; most are in urban centers, but some are dispersed around the countryside (e.g., Appalachia, Vermont). The 26 local chapters are in 23 geographical areas. Because the 1990 census lists 50 metropolitan areas with populations of 1 million or more, it is evident that there is room for growth. In the following chapters we document our accomplishments to date.

The History of the Appalachian Psychoanalytic Society

Stephen R. Friedlander

East Tennessee, as it turns out, has a relative abundance of psychoanalytically oriented mental health practitioners. This is due in part to the presence at the University of Tennessee of a psychology department where psychoanalytic theory and treatment techniques have been taught for a long time. Several generations of psychologists who were trained there elected to remain in the area to practice, and others committed to psychoanalytic thinking have been attracted here because an accepting milieu had developed.

Nevertheless, the call from Division 39 for the establishment of local chapters went unheeded here for several years despite the pool of potentially interested members. Members of Section IV, eager to get the ball rolling in unrepresented areas, encountered Stephen Friedlander by chance at the 1988 APA convention in Atlanta and urged him to organize a chapter. He discussed the matter with several influential psychologists in Knoxville, who acknowledged the desirability of having a local chapter, but declined, or at least demurred for the time being, to take any role in organizing it.

By coincidence, Paul Lerner, who completed his training and taught for several years at the Toronto Psychoanalytic Institute, moved to Ashville, NC, at about the same time. Lerner initiated inquiries on his own about starting a local chapter. Because Ashville and Knoxville were close, Lerner and Friedlander agreed to work together on starting it. A committee was formed to arrange an initial meeting at which interests and commitment to a local chapter would be assessed. Besides Lerner and Friedlander, the organizing committee consisted of Jeffrey

L. Binder, Eugene L. J. Cord, and James F. Murray. The first meeting of this committee took place on February 25, 1989, at the home of Eugene Cord.

The Committee, recognizing that people might have quite different visions of the desirable aims and operations of a local chapter, encouraged openness to divergent visions. Invitations to the initial meeting went to a large audience so that all those wishing to participate and have influence could be heard. As nearly as we could determine at the time, everyone from Ashville, North Carolina, to Nashville, Tennessee (a distance of over 300 miles), who might be interested was contacted by mail or in person.

The first meeting of what came to be known as the Appalachian Psychoanalytic Society (APS) was held at the Holiday Inn World's Fair in Knoxville on May 20, 1989. Section IV partially funded our start-up costs with a grant, and Jonathan Slavin, President of Section IV at that time, was our first guest speaker. He presented a paper entitled, "On Making Rules: Towards a Reformulation of the Dynamics of Transference and Influence in Psychoanalytic Treatment." He also shared his experience with beginning a local chapter in Massachusetts and his knowledge of how the task had been accomplished in other areas.

Twenty-two people attended the first meeting, coming from Nashville, Johnson City, and Ashville as well as Knoxville and its suburbs. Persons unable to attend but wishing to be involved were encouraged to say so. Those attending varied in depth of training and involvement in psychoanalytic work, but any interest in the discipline was welcome.

There was agreement on the desirability of forming a local chapter of Division 39, and those present took action on a number of important matters. They selected a name, adopted a tentative membership policy, which would continue to be broadly inclusive, set dues for the first year, and formed committees to attend to bylaws, elections, and similar matters. Dues were collected on the spot from most of those present, including our guest from Massachusetts, Jonathan Slavin. APS was a reality!

Some conspicuous absences from the first meeting served to remind us that the formation of a local chapter was taking place in a political climate resembling that of Division 39 and APA as a whole. We proceeded with our intention to encourage wide participation and free discussion of all the relevant issues, and a steady increase in membership since our opening meeting would seem to confirm the utility of this approach.

Lerner was the first President of APS, and other officers in the first slate included Cord (President-Elect), Murray (Secretary), and Binder (Treasurer). Other members of the original Executive Board were Friedlander, Larry Brown, Kenneth Carico, and Tommie Sue Slaydon. The Board's principal concern in the beginning was to obtain official status as a local chapter of Division 39. A Bylaws Committee chaired by Carrico drafted a preliminary version of bylaws, which were officially adopted by the membership after review and revision by the Board.

Friedlander headed a delegation, which included Murray and Joshua Williams, to present our application for official recognition as a local chapter to the Division at the 1989 meeting of APA in New Orleans. Following a brief oral history of the chapter and presentation of the bylaws, the board of Section IV recommended APS to the board of Division 39 as a local chapter representing the region of East Tennessee and Western North Carolina. We were duly accepted and proudly took our place as the 22nd local chapter.

Since its formation, APS meetings have been scheduled approximately every quarter. At least one a year is held in Nashville in conjunction with the annual meeting of the Tennessee Psychological Association. Our meetings typically consist of a prepared talk or case presentation followed by discussion. Guest speakers have included Sidney Blatt, Bernard Green, and Fonya Helm. APS members who made formal presentations include Hans Strupp, Jeffrey Binder, Eugene Cord, Stephen Friedlander, James Murray, Paul Lerner, Jerry Embry, Tommie Sue Slaydon, and Bruce Seidner.

The primary concern and activity besides clinical and scientific discussion has been to expand opportunities for psychoanalytic education. APS began sponsoring courses in the Winter of 1991, which are open to all professionals in the area. Paul Lerner and James Gorney, both certified analysts and members of APS, conducted the first two courses, which were devoted to transference and the elements of technique common to practitioners of varying theoretical orientations, respectively.

In response to suggestions from Cord regarding the distinction between education and training, we embarked on different paths to these objectives. Given the limited number of graduate analysts in the area, and other obstacles, we do not anticipate organizing an institute locally at this time. However, representatives from well-known institutes in other areas have indicated a desire to discuss training practitioners here. A committee is pursuing this project quite actively.

Within 2 years, APS membership had surpassed 50. Our members have been publishing and presenting at local, state, and national meetings. A major problem for us has been and continues to be the wide geographical distribution of our membership. At the time of this writing, Cord was President and Murray was President-Elect. Despite the difficulties mentioned earlier, there are indications for a bright future.

ACKNOWLEDGMENT

Thanks are expressed to Paul Lerner for his helpful suggestions in writing this essay.

The Austin Society for Psychoanalytic Psychology

Ricardo Ainslie[1]

Currently entering its fourth year, the Austin Society for Psychoanalytic Psychology began with discussion of the wish and need for a professional group which would promote education, training and dialogue regarding psychoanalytic theory, technique and treatment. Some Division 39 members living in Austin had attended meetings of the Dallas Chapter (DSPP) and/or the Division 39 Spring Meeting in previous years and it was in the hope of bringing together interested parties that initial discussion took place in early 1988. Assistance was offered by the Division and in particular by Dallas Chapter member Myron Lazar, who came to Austin to discuss with us both national and local chapter organization. Following the guidelines, all Division 39 members in Austin (and surrounding communities) were contacted, invited to initial planning meetings and polled for input in the months preceding Chapter acceptance at the August 1988, APA meetings. Founding officers were: Gemma Ainslie, President; Marvin Daniels, President-Elect; Richard Campbell, Secretary; Marsha McCary, Treasurer; Emelia Terr, Associate Member Representative. It was further decided that full membership would be open to Division 39 members, while Associate Membership would be open to mental health professionals of other disciplinary backgrounds and students in graduate level mental health degree programs.

Establishing an organizational year based approximately on the academic calendar, 1988-1989 ASPP's program included monthly meetings, during which

---

[1]In conjunction with Gemma Ainslie, Sharon Gorowitz, Peggy Bradley, Marsha McCary, and Margot Booth.

local members presented theoretical and/or clinical materials; the first year's program theme was Psychoanalytic Technique. After that first year, the group decided to include a Fall and a Spring Workshop/Conference in its annual programs. Speakers at these programs have included Dianne Martinez, Alan Sugarman, Morton Chethik, Otto Kernberg, Inge Bretherton, Joy Osofsky, and numerous local colleagues.

As we enter our fourth year as a formal organization, the Executive Committee is pleased with the success we have encountered in establishing for the first time a forum for discussion of psychoanalytic concepts and material in the Austin area. Our membership has risen yearly, so that currently we count approximately 20 Full Members and 65 Associate Members. Our monthly programs are attended by 25–40 persons, on the average, and our biannual conferences have attendance of approximately twice as many, culling people from surrounding communities as well as from both the Houston and Dallas areas. Austin has a small number of psychoanalysts and has neither an institute nor any other postgraduate training program in the field of psychoanalysis or psychoanalytic psychotherapy; these facts lead us to consider the establishment of some formal course offerings and to maintain avid interest in the development and support of such ventures through Division 39 throughout the country. Whereas we remain small in numbers and relatively young as an organization, we feel we have established a cohesive forum for our membership and its interests and we anticipate our continued growth and development.

The Baltimore Society
for Psychoanalytic Studies

John D. Gartner

In May 1990, I wandered into a meeting in Washington DC, chaired by Murray
Meisels to discuss the formation of a group to accredit psychologist-run psychoanalytic institutes. At that time, I was exploring different possibilities for
my own psychoanalytic training. What captured my imagination was the vitality
of Division 39, a movement based on the idea of people empowering themselves
to grow as analytic clinicians. When I discovered we did not have a local chapter
in Baltimore, I got fired up to start one. I spoke to my wife, who is also a psychologist, and we spoke to two other psychologist couples. This working group
of six: John and Alison Gartner, Lanz and Andrea Karfgin, and Paul Berman
and Katherine Killeen, founded the organization and became its first officers.
We spent the 1990–1991 academic year planning, and 1991–1992 was our inaugural year. At the end of that year we had 96 members.

As Division 39 has so often done, we filled a need among psychoanalytically
oriented clinicians in our community for further growth and collegiality. I think
this is one of the reasons for the rapidity of our growth. Also important, we
are interdisciplinary and draw members from all the mental health professions.
We meet on a bimonthly basis in a very spacious modern conference center
at Sheppard Pratt Hospital, an institution which is itself part of psychoanalytic
history, having had such luminaries as Harry Stack Sullivan and Harold Searles.
Our format is that we have an outside speaker give a formal lecture, which usually
includes a lot of interaction with the group, and a lot of time for coffee and informal interaction as well. We had teaching analysts from local and distant Institutes,

as well as respected non-analysts who published and taught in the area of psychoanalysis. An average of 50–75 attend each meeting.

The schedule for 1991–1992 included William Goldstein, Rochelle Kainer, Leon Wurmser, Charles McCormack, and Martin Ceasar. For 1992–1993, the schedule has Joseph Lichtenberg, Michael Stone, Sandra Boots, Harvey Rich, Charles Wasserman, and possibly Paulina Kernberg.

Our organization has facilitated the formation of informal study groups around the Baltimore area. Many of these smaller groups are currently forming. Two study groups have already begun. We are very grateful for the support from Division 39 and the Washington local chapters, as well as local chapter leaders in Connecticut, Massachusetts, and San Francisco who were consulted during our organization process. We found our colleagues to be without exception welcoming and supportive. In a similar fashion, the faculty of local institutes have been more than willing to come out and address our group. It's been a great year. We're tired but content.

The Chicago Association for Psychoanalytic Psychology

Lorraine H. Goldberg

The origins and development of CAPP, the Chicago Association for Psychoanalytic Psychology, are complex and can best be understood in their historical context—going back in time to the late 1950s when a small number of clinical psychologists, all psychotherapists, set up a study group for the purpose of deepening their understanding of all aspects of psychoanalysis. This small beginning eventually evolved into what became known as the Bettelheim Study Group. This was essentially a clinical case seminar devoted to the psychoanalytic process. In addition to its primary founder, Oliver J. B. Kerner, various others participated: they included Kerner, Johanna Tabin, Joanne Powers, Maurice Burke, and the late Irving Leiden. The Study Group set a precedent in seeking out psychoanalytic educators of reputation, talent, and accomplishment to meet with and teach them. These teachers included Thomas French, Heinz Kohut, Michael Serota, Edoardo Weiss, and Ernest Rapaport, all prominent medically trained psychoanalysts. When Bruno Bettelheim joined the group in 1957, the group had found a discussion leader and, in essence, a mentor. In this small beginning lies the origin of CAPP. The sense of inner identity as psychoanalysts, which was provided to each participant in his or her work with Bruno Bettelheim, served to involve each person in continuing psychoanalytic activities to this day, that is, not only in the development of the technical skills needed to conduct psychoanalysis as a treatment process, but in the drive and the will to work toward the day when clinical psychologists in Chicago would have their own house, free from medical domination. This Study Group went on weekly for 10 months out the year for 15 years, until Bruno Bettelheim retired in 1972.

With the advent of Division 39 in the late 1970s, three psychologists from Chicago—Oliver J. B. Kerner, Kenneth S. Isaacs, and Bertram J. Cohler—were invited to serve on the Steering Committee of the Division. One of the first orders of business at the Committee's meeting in New York City was to focus on the urgency of meeting the organizational and educational needs of psychologists outside of New York City, Los Angeles, and Topeka. Kerner, Isaacs, and Cohler were inspired by this historic meeting in New York to lay the groundwork for what in 1980 became CAPP, a local chapter of Division 39. Soon, 25 clinical psychologists, all of whom were in full or part-time practice, signed up as founding members of CAPP, dedicated to the development of psychoanalytic education and practice. An ambitious program of weekly and monthly meetings was mounted and step-by-step an organization grew: an early informal organization that ultimately became an approved nonprofit association dedicated to serving the profession as well as the public.

A variety of programs within the Local Chapter soon engaged the energies and interest of various younger clinical psychologists, such as Irwin Hoffman, Dale Moyer, Nell Logan, Lucy Freund, Lorraine Goldberg, Jane Wicklund, and Paul Sanders in addition to the continuing efforts of the earlier group: Kerner, Burke, Isaacs, Powers, Tabin, Cohler, and Leiden. All of these individuals served as leaders and officers of the Local Chapter.

Early on, CAPP set up a yearly symposium, which brought such psychoanalytic educators and clinicians to Chicago as Roy Schafer, Sidney Blatt, Martin Mayman, Rudolf Eckstein, Bruno Bettelheim, Hedda Bolgar, and Sydney Smith, among others, for all-day workshops and symposia. Such events brought out full audiences and succeeded in sparking the interest of the mental health community in and around Chicago. Attendants included graduate students, social workers, psychiatrists, and many clinical psychologists, both from the academic as well as the private practice communities.

After a few years, it became apparent within the governance of CAPP itself that a more permanent and concrete form of education was a necessity if clinical psychologists in Chicago were going to join the psychoanalytic community of psychologists as it was personified in New York City, where the majority of Division 39 members were concentrated. Therefore, in 1983, a small study group was formed that consisted of a carefully selected group of CAPP members. This group became the nucleus of what is now the Chicago Center for Psychoanalysis, a free-standing training institute, the first to have been established by psychologists outside of New York and California.

CAPP has continued to grow over the years, and now has a membership of approximately 255, of which over 100 are members of Division 39, plus 47 student affiliates. It celebrated its 10th anniversary in 1990. It continues to present monthly lectures given by prominent analysts in the Chicago area, such as Richard Chessick, Peter Giovacchini, and John Gedo; and twice yearly it presents a major program. Some of the individuals who have been brought to Chicago to speak on these occasions include Efrain Bleiberg, Jay Greenberg, Joyce McDougall, Fred Pine, Roy Schafer, Harold Searles, and most recently, Stephen Mitchell with Merton M. Gill as discussant, attended by approximately 200 people.

CAPP continues to reach out to mental health professionals who identify with the psychoanalytic approach to the understanding of human behavior and the treatment of emotional distress. It actively engages in outreach at the local universities and professional schools in the area, and tries to encourage interest in psychoanalysis. It continues to present monthly programs on clinical and scholarly issues for the membership and other interested professionals in the community. It sponsors a clinical research committee in which ideas are shared about research needs. It holds an annual meeting focused on third party reimbursement problems and issues.

Direct community services sponsored by the Association include: (a) A Referral Service that gives the name of a therapist in the caller's geographical area, who provides the therapeutic or diagnostic service of the type the caller seeks; (b) a Speakers Bureau that provides knowledgeable speakers to community hospitals, universities and other agencies on topics specified by the requester.

ACKNOWLEDGMENTS

The author wishes to acknowledge the assistance of O. J. B. Kerner and Maurice O. Burke who both provided information about the origins and the early history of CAPP.

33

A Brief Comment on the History of the Chicago Open Chapter for the Study of Psychoanalysis

David L. Downing

In ascending order of complexity and difficulty, the formation of psychoanalytic study groups, societies and training institutes within non-medical professions has been an arduous and even rancorous undertaking. In October of 1985, the Board of Division 39 approved the Section of Local Chapters (Section IV). This action gave the fledgling local chapter movement an important political and philosophical base within the Division and facilitated the growth and development of chapters throughout the country, thus helping increase the availability of various forms of psychoanalytical training. These local societies helped galvanize enthusiasm and interest in psychoanalysis as a research tool, a depth theory of personality, and a form of psychotherapeutic treatment. That such interest was already quite alive, healthy, and kicking is evident from early local chapter Senate Minutes, which indicate that chapters from Colorado, Boston, Chicago, Washington, Dallas, New York, Michigan, the Potomac Region, San Francisco, Connecticut, and Vermont were represented. It would only follow then, that these societies would function as springboards for more formalized training in psychoanalysis proper, within psychology's own house. The importance for psychoanalytically oriented psychologists not residing in New York or Los Angeles who had long-hoped to become psychologist-psychoanalysts cannot be over-stated. However, as mentioned in our opening remarks, such development was not without it difficulties.

Most of this combativeness had originated in the medical psychoanalytic ranks. APsaA had long opposed the psychoanalytic training and accreditation of non-medical professionals. However, a significant degree of internecine *Sturm und*

Drang further complicated the early years of the Division, its Sections, and its Local Chapters. The development of the Chicago Open Chapter for the Study of Psychoanalysis, then, represents a not-atypical coming of age, although in some respects, its history is rather unique.

Chicago has long enjoyed the distinction of being a center for innovation and change within the psychoanalytic movement. Scholarly activity and praxis here has led to the expansion of the parameters of what constitutes psychoanalysis and, in the process, to the extension of this form of treatment to populations once thought to be unanalyzable. The early years following the approval of the formation of the Division were marked by an aura of great optimism. However, as Murray Meisels and others have pointed out, adherents of more-or-less traditional notions soon began to clash on the question of who could be properly called a psychoanalyst and what could be properly called psychoanalysis. Schisms necessarily developed in the course of these conflicts, and as the lines of battle were drawn it was feared the Division itself might split. Yet, the ultimate recognition of the legitimacy and strength of diversity encouraged the accommodations necessary to keep these diverse constituencies within the Division.

Such was the case to an extent, in Chicago, where two Local Chapters emerged, and continue to thrive. The Chicago Open Chapter came into existence after the Chicago Association for Psychoanalytic Psychology (CAPP), though it was officially recognized and incorporated into Division 39 before CAPP, in May of 1986. The Chicago Open Chapter, the predecessor of the Chicago Open Chapter for the Study of Psychoanalysis (called the Open Chapter for short), was formed in June, 1985, in the wake of the Ann Arbor, Michigan, Conference of Division 39, largely through the organizational efforts of David Berndt. Berndt would subsequently go on to become the Chicago Open Chapter's first Division 39 Representative, to sit as one of the Founding Senators of the Board of Section IV, and to be elected as the second Secretary within the Section. The first officers of the Chapter at that time, in addition to Berndt, were David Hartman, President; James McGinnis, Secretary; and Christine Kieffer, Treasurer. As the Open Chapter made explicit, one of the center-pieces of its mission—indeed, its entire raison d'etre—was to actively encourage participation, dialogue, and engagement with members of all the health-service professions and social sciences. Thus, the Open Chapter maintained a very inclusionary stance, with only one type of membership, open to practitioners and theorists from different disciplines, promulgating greater diversity within the ranks. This policy helped the freer (and therefore perhaps much more heated!) exchange of ideas, as well as a questioning and objective stance toward things theoretical and clinical—a stance that discourages polemics and the dogmatic adherence to "-isms." Such a democratic and questioning ambience can hardly be expected to reduce tensions. Indeed, the erratic waxing and waning of the Chapter's vitality and cohesiveness in these formative years is probably testimony to its achieving its aims.

Unfortunately, attempts at rapprochement between the two local Chicago Chapters proved to be a far more elusive goal. Thus, whereas it is against current Section policy to give its imprimatur to more than one chapter in any one locale, the divergences between the Open Chapter and CAPP were deemed to be of sufficient degree to render one Chicago chapter unfeasible.

The Open Chapter prospered. Membership grew, such that in 1986, the year of its being officially incorporated into Section IV, it had 39 Division members. Chapter dues were kept at a nominal $10 per year, again in the service of making it accessible to many, including students with limited budgets.

In 1987, with the departure of Berndt from the Chicago Area, the Open Chapter languished. In January 1989, Lucia Villela-Minnerly began to contact former members and recruit new ones. Initially, this had the flavor of a grass roots campaign, but tapping the enthusiasm of the membership led, rather rapidly, to the development of ad hoc committees on membership, outreach, education, and business. Administrative help was secured so that a concerted and coordinated series of mailings publicizing the renaissance and activities could be effected.

These early gatherings furthermore proposed a change in the name of the chapter. "The Chicago Open Chapter for the Study of Psychoanalysis" made it quite explicit that the focus of its mission was psychoanalysis. Retaining "Open" in the name similarly made explicit the unique philosophical bent of the chapter. The first formal meeting of the newly reconstituted Open Chapter was held on June 9, 1989. The first elections further reflect the chapter's traditional commitment to diversity: Charles E. Turk, President; David L. Downing, Secretary; Gertrude Pollitt, Treasurer; Lucia Villela-Minnerly, Section IV Representative. The Members-at-Large on The Board consisted of: Lanny Johnson, Mary Hollis Johnston, and Anne Newman. Board members function as faculty at Chicago-area universities, professional schools, and the Center for Psychoanalytic Study; and /or are employed in private practice, and in hospital or out-patient settings.

The new bylaws formally adopted on June 9, 1989, reaffirm our origins and speak to our new agenda, an agenda that can now benefit from energies formerly committed to fighting for the legitimacy of multidisciplinary training in psychoanalysis and the early organizational issues discussed above. The purposes of the Chicago Open Chapter for the Study of Psychoanalysis were defined as (a) to promote the study of psychoanalytic theories of the mind, and of psychoanalytic theories and techniques of treatment; (b) to provide educational opportunities in the Chicago area through the sponsoring of conferences and/or small group meetings; (c) to serve as a clearing house for the formation of special interest study groups, such as those devoted to the study of specific theories, the scientific method in general, film and cultural issues. It was decided that membership should be open to all members of the Division, as well as to other licensed or registered professionals from psychology, psychiatry, social work, nursing, and pastoral counseling with a genuine interest in psychoanalysis. Membership shall also be open to clinicians from other disciplines (such as philosophy, anthropology, and literature) who have had training in psychoanalysis, and to nonclinicians from these disciplines who are interested in the philosophical, theoretical, or applied aspects of psychoanalysis (such as psychohistory, the analysis of films and literature, etc.). Graduate students from all of these disciplines would also be eligible. That is, we only have one type of membership and it applies to all who wish to join.

ACKNOWLEDGMENTS

Thanks are due to Lucia Villela-Minnerly who made valuable editorial suggestions in the preparation of the manuscript, and to James McGinnis and David Berndt for their comments and suggestions.

34

A History of the Cincinnati Society for Psychoanalytic Psychology

Lynn H. Pierson[1]

Background

Cincinnati is a small (about 500,000), conservative city with a geographical division of its people into East and West. Historically, Westerners believe in "pulling oneself up by the bootstraps" and tend to be wary (at best) or hostile (at worst) to psychotherapy. The idea that someone would see a psychoanalyst several times a week is probably incomprehensible to many Western Cincinnatians. Easterners fancy themselves to be far more sophisticated than their Western neighbors; though even today, many people on the East side are probably wary of psychoanalysis. The psychoanalytic community, therefore, is even smaller than one might expect in a city of this size. There is a concentration of psychoanalysts' and psychotherapists' offices in the part of Cincinnati near the University of Cincinnati College of Medicine and the Cincinnati Psychoanalytic Institute.

The Department of Psychiatry secured its reputation as a center for psychoanalytic teaching under the leadership of Maurice Levine. The Balints and, currently, Paul and Anna Ornstein are internationally known psychoanalysts associated with the Department. Going back at least to Maurice Levine's tenure as Chairman, psychoanalytic thinking held sway in the Department of Psychiatry. During that time, psychiatric residents often included psychoanalytic training and a personal analysis (obtained outside of the Department) as part of their

---

[1]With editorial help from Christine Dacey and Oliver Birckhead, III.

professional education, and the newly formed Cincinnati Psychoanalytic Institute was pleased to have them. Prior to the establishment of the local institute, Cincinnati psychiatrists received psychoanalytic training by commuting to Chicago. Many of the faculty of the Department of Psychiatry were also on the Staff of the Institute. Since Maurice Levine's death, the predominance of the psychoanalytic viewpoint in the Department of Psychiatry has declined relative to a biomedical orientation, although a significant number of faculty remain who are psychoanalysts.

Although the Cincinnati Psychoanalytic Institute is affiliated with APsaA, many, if not most, of the medical psychoanalysts here have been personally sympathetic and receptive to psychologists' interests in psychoanalysis. Most of the medical psychoanalysts probably favored the admission of psychologists to their Institute, although it would probably have been unthinkable for them to protest by terminating their affiliation with APsaA if it had won the lawsuit and refused to grant psychologists admission.

Hence, there has always been, for whatever reason, a rather friendly relationship in Cincinnati between medical psychoanalysts and psychologists interested in psychoanalysis. Many psychologists purchased supervision from medical psychoanalysts most of whom were pleased to have the brightest students they could find, regardless of their degree. Word has it that medical psychoanalysts' interest in admitting psychologists was correlated with their sense that the quality of psychiatric residents seeking psychoanalytic training was declining in recent years.

There are presently three psychologists who are candidates in the most recent class at the Cincinnati Psychoanalytic Institute. Of the three, two are members of the Cincinnati Society for Psychoanalytic Psychology. The third candidate lives in another city and is not a member. None of the three candidates has complained of any feeling that admission to candidacy was more heavily scrutinized for them than the medical candidates.

The Cincinnati Psychoanalytic Institute has graduated one psychologist as a clinical psychoanalyst. She was accepted before the lawsuit as a research candidate with the intention (since realized) of converting to clinical status.

In summary, it seems to be the case that with some exceptions there has been in Cincinnati far less of the acrimony between psychologists interested in psychoanalysis and medical psychoanalysts than in other cities. Until recently, psychologists seemed satisfied with, or passively accepting of, what was available from psychiatrist psychoanalysts.

Recent History

A core group of five psychologists was the driving force that led to the founding of the Cincinnati Society for Psychoanalytic Psychology. We had been meeting monthly in a peer supervision group for several years. The peer supervision group started as a result of our meeting each other while participating in a year long seminar led by the Ornsteins. We decided to keep meeting after the seminar ended. One of us began attending Division 39 Spring meetings and found the energy and comradery to be exciting. He shared with the other members his vision, tentative at best, of what a local chapter could be, and gradually a commitment to develop a shared vision emerged. Because we are such a young chapter and just getting to know all of our members, what we will become is still not clear. However, the initial response of local psychologists to the formation of a local chapter is heartening and suggests that there is a need for something more than has been available locally.

The first organizational meeting to found a local chapter of Division 39 took place on October 16, 1989 at Xavier University. Those in attendance were Oliver Birckhead, Christine Dacey, David Hellkamp, Lynn Pierson, and Shelley Rooney. David Hellkamp joined us for the first time and was especially interested in adding his expertise in getting new organizations off the ground. Todd Walker, the fifth member of our group, was not present but has been active in the formative efforts. Jonathan Slavin's active support of our efforts was especially helpful and noteworthy as he encouraged us to get some seed money to finance an initial open meeting. Preliminary bylaws were drafted and a slate of officers prepared for presentation at the initial meeting. Marvin Hyman, from the Michigan chapter, agreed to come to speak to the group.

The first open organizational meeting took place on September 12, 1990. The proposed bylaws were discussed, revised, and ratified. The task of legally incorporating as a tax exempt organization was assigned. Membership applications were circulated and the proposed slate of officers was presented. Nominations were accepted from the floor and the following were elected: President, Oliver W. Birckhead; President-Elect, Shelley A. Rooney; Secretary, Christine M. Dacey; and Treasurer, Lynn H. Pierson.

After dues were discussed, the remainder of the meeting was spent with Marvin Hyman telling us about the Michigan chapter's formative experience. He stressed that the programs were the raison d'etre for a society and that we should not hesitate to get programs going. We decided to have five meetings annually, each meeting to consist of a brief business meeting followed by a program.

At the time of the writing, Summer, 1991, our Society had three meetings. We had 27 members who have paid their dues, with several others who attended meetings but apparently remain undecided about membership. We are conducting a survey of our members to assess the wants and needs of the group, which will serve as a basis for developing program offerings for the coming year. Our hope is that in addition to the five meetings our Society can offer courses and seminars of interest to our members. Heretofore, the only offerings in town were the courses offered by the Cincinnati Psychoanalytic Institute. Although these courses were often interesting, their rigor tended to fall somewhere below the average level of sophistication of the class members, who were not screened. Some of us felt there was little available for those who had studied psychoanalysis rather extensively yet were not interested in entering candidacy. One of the challenges for our Society is to provide something of value both for the more experienced members, who have spent some years studying psychoanalysis, as well as for members who are seeking a place where they can begin to learn about psychoanalysis.

There seems to be no interest at this time in thinking about forming a competing institute, which seems to be a major issue in other Division 39 local chapters. Here there are very few psychologists with adequate training and experience who could staff such an institute. The staff would have to come from the Cincinnati Psychoanalytic Institute. Assuming that there would be a willingness to participate, there would be little point because what they would be offering at our institute is available by attending theirs. Recently, the Cincinnati Psychoanalytic Institute has made extra efforts at outreach to the larger mental-health community. There is a newly offered 2-year training program leading to a certificate in Psychoanalytic Psychotherapy, the curriculum planning committee for which included members of the psychology community including Oliver Birckhead, CSPP's President. Another factor in explaining the lack of interest in forming a competing institute may be that although all of us in CSPP are interested in psychoanalysis, at least among the founding members there is little interest in seeking certification in psychoanalysis. Reasons for this tend to be pragmatic: given the expense involved, given that most of us are in mid-life with families and other financial and time obligations, and given that our practices are unlikely to change much as a result of certification, we tend to prefer to contract as a group or individually for what we feel we need in the way of further psychoanalytic education rather than pay for a complete curriculum, aspects of which seem redundant and the adequate economic return for which seems doubtful. Our younger members may feel differently, but it seems that many of them lack sufficient background and experience to be viable candidates at present. We anticipate that for many of us our needs will be met by becoming more involved with Division 39, while remaining involved with the local sources that have sustained us in the past.

A Brief History of The Colorado Society for Psychology and Psychoanalysis

Charles Spezzano

The Colorado Society for Psychology and Psychoanalysis was one of those local chapters that formed before local chapters existed as official entities within Division 39. In the early 1980s, while members of the Division of Psychoanalysis in some regions were coming together and calling themselves local chapters, no such entity was officially sanctioned by the Board of the Division. Nonetheless, many psychologists with an interest in psychoanalysis were clearly starting to view the Division as a center of gravity for their identities as psychoanalytically oriented scholars and clinicians. In Michigan and Chicago, in particular—at least that's how it looked from Colorado—this was happening.

It was not, however, happening in Colorado. There, the handful of members of the Division attached very little importance to their membership in it. The only reason I became more interested was because I saw in the Division the possibility that psychologists with psychoanalytic training would be motivated to find new ways to bring the opportunity for training to other psychologists in the Division living outside of New York and Los Angeles. When, after a couple of years of membership, it became apparent to me that this was not on the Division's agenda, I wrote to then President Bob Lane and complained. He invited me to a meeting that Murray Meisels and Oliver Kerner were chairing to talk about local chapters.

I was moderately encouraged by what I heard, but discouraged that no clear sense of purpose existed within the Division for starting or even catalyzing institutes. Nonetheless, the Division seemed better than nothing. I returned to Denver and invited other members living in the Denver area to a meeting. About five or six of the eight or nine members came and wondered what good it would do to start a chapter. What would we do that we hadn't already done and tired of? We had all been in innumerable study groups and had tried various avenues of approach to medical analysts in the community to make available to us more systematic didactic programs, if not full-fledged training. What would now be different? It was, however, all right with everybody if we called ourselves a local chapter.

So, in stage one we went, in Colorado, from having no local chapter to having one that did nothing. As compellingly interesting as that was, I continued in conversations with two other psychologists, Thomas Holman and Richard Crager, to discuss ways a chapter might function as a focus for the identity and training needs of local Division members. Eventually, we named the chapter The Colorado Society for Psychology and Psychoanalysis, created a letterhead, and decided to send out an invitation to all APA members in the state with an interest in psychoanalysis to join the new local chapter.

It seemed clear to me that there was no interest in a society just for the sake of having a society. If there was to be any kindling of interest in the Division locally it would only happen when potential members saw something useful happening, something different than what had been available to them before. I decided that the announcement of the new chapter would be accompanied by an announcement of an educational program to be run by the chapter. This educational program had to be different from the usual seminar offered to non-analysts by analysts.

After numerous phone calls to New York, nine analysts with experience teaching courses in psychoanalytic theory and technique agreed that if I could drum up sufficient interest and money, they would come and teach one weekend seminar each. Overall, these seminars were designed to cover the topics that, it appeared to me from reading the catalogues of various institutes, were taught to first year candidates, and in the announcement I described them that way. My doing that raised concern among some Division Board members who either saw in such a statement a message that the Division was now in the business of providing psychoanalytic training or a message that because psychologists did, after all, have easy access to psychoanalytic training their lawsuit made no sense.

In any case, about 35 people showed up for that first meeting of the new CSPP in June of 1984. I had applications for them to join the Division and all did. They also joined the chapter and paid their first dues. By the end of the meeting about 20 of them handed me checks for either the full $1,500 annual tuition, or half of it to reserve space in the lecture series.

Early lectures by Jay Greenberg, Steve Mitchell, Elliott Adler, and Lloyd Silverman were not only informative but energizing. Here were psychologists who knew psychoanalysis. Within 6 months those members of CSPP who were interested in starting an institute had formed a new organization outside the

Division, The Colorado Center for Psychoanalytic Studies, to offer training to those qualified members of the local chapter who wanted to undertake it.

Both the local chapter and the institute were opened up to qualified social workers, psychiatric nurses, and psychiatrists. Both organizations remain interdisciplinary, although as a local chapter of the Division of Psychoanalysis, CSPP has a Board structure that maintains control by psychologists.

When the institute formed, the local chapter suffered an identity crisis. Much of the energy of the core leadership group shifted to the development of the institute and it became unclear what use the local chapter would be. Karen Rosica, who succeeded me as President of the Chapter, lovingly, but firmly, reshaped it from the single-leader outfit it had initially needed to be to make room for itself in the previously medically dominated psychoanalytic community. She made it an organization in which members gradually came to feel a sense of belonging to something meaningful to them. Even members who never attend any society functions continue to pay dues because the existence of the society affirms the legitimacy of their professional identity as psychoanalytic psychologists.

The Chapter now offers monthly meetings at which members can present papers-in-progress, clinical problems, or ideas to colleagues. There is an annual spring conference which draws anywhere from 100 to 200 people and features a nationally known speaker. When Fred Pine spoke at one of these recently, he made our members aware of the energizing influence that the Colorado experiment had on other local chapters around the country, something that the majority of members were moved by because they participated only locally, not nationally, and had been unaware that people in other places had been watching them and drawing ideas and inspiration from what they had done.

We also sponsored joint conferences with both the Denver Psychoanalytic Society and the state psychological association. So, we have clearly become a visible presence in our community. And, I believe, it is generally felt that the psychoanalytic community in Colorado was significantly changed for the better by there being "another game in town."

We are entering our 10th year as a local chapter. Judy Fox succeeded Karen Rosica and will, in turn, by the time this is in print, have been succeeded by Helen Hand. I no longer live in Colorado but continue to pay dues to the local chapter and to teach at the institute. The Board of the local chapter is composed now almost entirely of people who had little to do with the initial launching of CSPP. I see this as a good sign that CSPP has a life of its own beyond the agendas of its founders. It also affirms the idea that many psychologists who do not desire psychoanalytic training value psychoanalysis and feel identified with and interested in that brand of clinical psychology.

Further, professionals from outside the mental-health community have become members as a way to pursue their scholarly interest in psychoanalysis. A psychoanalytic scholarship track in the training program of The Colorado Center for Psychoanalytic Studies provides an avenue for them to rigorously study the psychoanalytic literature, and this nonclinical professional group of CSPP members is represented among candidates in what is now the third class progressing through the Center.

The bottom line is that today psychoanalytic psychology and, as a result, psychoanalysis, are thriving tn Colorado in a way that would have been unimaginable in the 1970s.

36

The Connecticut Society of Psychoanalytic Psychologists: A History

In 1982, Stanley Rosner was asked to organize a Division 39 local chapter in Connecticut. A list of psychologists in Connecticut who had expressed an interest in Division 39 was provided, and they were contacted. Then, several Sunday morning organizational meetings were held in Rosner's home in Weston, Connecticut. The nucleus of those attending these meetings were: Dale Ortmeyer, Leon Zeff, Ira Moses, Nancy Bronson, Wendy Stewart, Natalie Lurie, Harry Fiss, Michael Davies, Michael Fulco, Sue Bender, Phyllis Hopkins, Rosalie Greenbaum, Judy Epstein, and Patricia Houghton. These were primarily psychologists, some were graduates of psychoanalytic institutes, others were psychoanalytically oriented in their practice but not formally trained. One was a social worker. The following guidelines were established during these meetings.

1. A Connecticut local chapter of Division 39 was organized of mental-health professionals who were trained and/or interested in psychoanalysis. Bylaws of the Society was based on the Michigan model.
2. Membership was open to psychologists, psychiatrists, social workers, psychiatric nurses, and other mental health professionals and students interested in psychoanalysis.
3. Scientific meetings would be held and a Newsletter established.
4. An eventual, primary goal was to establish a psychoanalytically oriented training program.

The first slate of officers was: President, Stanley Rosner; Program Chairman, Ira Moses; Membership Chairman and Secretary, Wendy Stewart; Treasurer, Michael Davies. Since 1986, three to five scientific meetings have been held yearly. The locale for the scientific and business meetings is the New Haven Lawn Club, New Haven, CT, a central location for the state. Early speakers were Bernard Riess, Ernst Prelinger, and Leopold Caligor. Other speakers have been Dale Ortmeyer, Jay Greenberg, Fred Pine, Elisabeth Young-Bruehl, Stephen Mitchell, Hanna Segal, and Otto Kernberg.

A CSPP Newsletter has been published two to four times a year, starting in the spring of 1988. Rosalie Greenbaum and Michael Davies were the founding editors. The current editors are Rosalie Greenbaum and Barbara Marcus. The Newsletter features original clinical and theoretical articles; abstracts of scientific meetings; book reviews; reviews of Division 39 and National Federation of Psychoanalytic Programs meetings; and chapter news and notes.

Under the presidency of Dale Ortmeyer, our ad hoc training committee, chaired by Walter Spear and Sue Bender, in collaboration with representatives from the Connecticut Society of Clinical Social Workers, laid the groundwork for the Connecticut Psychoanalytic Psychotherapy Center (CPPC). By June 1990, the committees finished their intensive efforts; and the CPPC became an independent reality. The CPPC is now an independent, nonprofit, corporate educational center, founded to provide training in psychoanalytic psychotherapy to qualified clinicians in psychology, psychiatry, social work and nursing. The Center's 3-year training program aims to integrate understanding of psychoanalytic theory and its application to intensive psychotherapy. The four major theoretical schools of thought are taught in the curriculum, and represented on the faculty, Freudian, Interpersonal, Object Relations, and Self-Psychology. Attention is focused on a diversity of disorders and patients, requiring flexibility and creativity in clinical practice. The training integrates clinical supervision and coursework with the candidate's personal experience and personal psychoanalytic-psychotherapy. The faculty, curriculum, bylaws, and administration are in place. The date for the center to begin training its first year of candidates is in the Fall in 1991.

The second elected slate of officers for June 1988–1990, was Walter Spear, President-Elect; Wendy Stewart, Secretary; Michael Davies, Treasurer; Dale Ortmeyer, President. The current elected officers are President-Elect, Michael Davies; Secretary, Wendy Stewart; Treasurer, Ann Singer; and Walter Spear, President. As of the spring of 1991, the Connecticut Society of Psychoanalytic Psychologists has a membership of approximately 120 with attendance at scientific meetings averaging 50 to 60. The interest and growth of CSPP speaks for the investment in psychoanalytic psychology that is an active presence in Connecticut.

The Dallas Society for Psychoanalytic Psychology: A Brief History

Don J. Brix

Late in the summer of 1982 several of us were involved in a beehive of activity that was soon to result in the formation of The Dallas Society for Psychoanalytic Psychology. Someone suggested that we tell our local newspapers what we were up to. As a result, I undertook to write a press release, my first and, so far, only foray into journalism. It was never published because, for some reason, the idea was jettisoned before the item was ever submitted to the media. Now, 9 years later, I've discovered a use for it. Excerpting from it serves my present task nicely.

. . . More recently local chapters of the Division have been established in many major cities across the country. In concert with this trend a chapter was established in Dallas on September 11, 1982. Persons interested in learning more about the new chapter and investigating the possibilities of membership are invited to attend two organizational meetings to be held Saturday, November 6, during the Texas Psychological Association Convention at the Lincoln Hotel, Dallas. The first meeting will be at 9:30 AM, the second at 1:30 PM. The Dallas chapter will be hosting Dr.'s Oliver J.B. Kerner and Marvin Daniels. Dr. Kerner has been active in the Division since its inception, is currently Chairman of the Committee on Local Chapters and Co-Chairman of the National Committee on Psychoanalytic Education for the Division. Dr. Daniels is a psychologist/psychoanalyst now at the University of Texas at Austin. He was for many years associated with the Adelphi University postdoctoral training program in psychotherapy and psychoanalysis and until recently was Editor of the Division 39 newsletter.

By the time this announcement was written there was obviously a good deal stirring here in Dallas. Actually, a lot had been stirring for months previously.

It's likely that the Dallas Society for Psychoanalytic Psychology (DSPP) would have eventually been born even had Paul Munves not been finishing his training at William Alanson White in June of 1982. However, the question of how we came to be, when we came to be has everything to do with Munves' completion of his training and his decision to return to Dallas to establish a practice. Quoting from a letter Paul sent me February 15, 1982, "While I am anxious to establish another full-time practice, I also hope to facilitate the development of a local chapter of Division 39 of the American Psychological Association. Experience has taught me that psychoanalytically oriented psychologists need their own organization to nurture their continued development. I have enclosed a number of items that I hope will be of interest to you in this regard." He then proceeded to burn-up the telephone line between New York and Dallas for the next few months. Frequently Munves would call after I had retired for the evening and I would speak to him from bed. The conversation ended, I would begin to anticipate my slightly delayed long winter's nap when the phone would ring again. Again it would be Munves with another idea he wanted to check out with me. His enthusiasm for getting something off the ground in Dallas was unbounded. And get it off the ground he did.

As the aforementioned press release indicates, by the end of 1982 we had been paid a visit by Oliver J.B. Kerner whose enthusiasm for our project was unbridled. The late Marvin Daniels, who at the time was residing in Austin, visited us at the same time. Their visit was timed to correspond with the annual meeting of the Texas Psychological Association (TPA) which was occurring in Dallas that year. TPA allowed us to conduct a meeting during its convention at which Kerner and Daniels presented their thoughts on the merits of starting a local chapter as well as the merits of approaching patients with a psychoanalytic orientation.

Our first monthly Scientific Meeting was held December 1, 1982. A discussion of "The Non-Transference Relationship in the Psychoanalytic Situation" by Greenson and Wexler was led by Paul Munves along with long-time Dallas psychologists, Donald Giller and Ray McNamara. Malcolm Bonnheim, who would later be our third president, distributed the first draft of our bylaws; the result of the work of his ad hoc committee that had been assigned the task. Almost immediately we adopted a format of conducting one meeting per month from September through May. Two of these meetings are all day Saturday events (a few have included a Friday evening also) involving distinguished guests who are usually, but not always analysts. The remaining meetings are in the evening and are conducted by mental health professionals from the community, drawn predominantly from our own membership. The evening meetings are essentially designed to discuss papers that have been selected and made available to members by our program committee. Over the years the monthly presentations have ranged from rather faithful reviews of the assigned articles to the occasional reading of an original paper authored by a member. The amount of clinical material included in our monthly programs varies a good deal between presenters, but seems always to be well received by the group.

Paul Munves remained on as President until September 1984 when Myron Lazar assumed the position. During the time Munves was President we hosted Sydney Smith, Rudolf Ekstein, and Herbert Schlesinger. During Myron Lazar's term the Society inaugurated the practice of making available a photocopied collection of the curriculum articles for the year. Until that time, we had been relying exclusively on the Langs' edited *Classics in Psychoanalytic Technique* for our readings. During Lazar's term we enjoyed presentations by invited guests Anni Bergman and Roy Schafer. Our study foci was around Female Identity Development and selected papers by Roy Schafer.

By the 1985–1986 year, we began to reap the benefits of the practice of "training" our President by including a year of service as President-Elect. This enabled our "on-deck" leader to arrange his or her program well in advance, thus opening the way for considerably more latitude in selecting themes for the year's study. During the term of our third president, Malcolm Bonnheim, we hosted Louise Kaplan and Otto Kernberg. In preparation for Kaplan's visit, we studied Conceptions of Adolescence: Original and Contemporary, and around Kernberg's presentation we explored the narcissistic conditions. Division 39 was, by this time, involved in its own internal tensions involving criteria for membership in Section I. Malcolm Bonnheim served us well by his well-reasoned and even-handed interpretations—presented in our local Bulletin—of what the controversy going on at the national level potentially meant to us in Dallas.

Our fourth president, for the year 1986–1987, was Dale Godby. Invited guests that year were a Kohutian, Arnold Goldberg, and the noted psychotherapy researcher, Hans Strupp. Our themes were developed around the contributions to the literature of our two invited guests. Godby endeavored to augment the overall quality of our learning experience by looking critically at the process of discussion at our meetings. He instituted the practice of publishing discussion questions pertinent to the readings prior to each monthly meeting; a tactic that various presenters since have continued to find useful.

John Herman served us during the 1987–1988 season. Appearances by invited guest analysts, Stephen Appelbaum, and Jay Greenberg punctuated a wide-ranging look at object relations theory during our monthly discussions. The first combined meeting with the Dallas Psychoanalytic Society took place during Herman's term. Perhaps more than any other single officer throughout our history, John Herman urged us to think about where we were and where we were headed as a local chapter.

Aspects of the Psychoanalytic Process was our theme for 1988–1989. Our invited guests were Lawrence Friedman and Jacob Arlow. Our president was Marc Rathbun. At this date, Rathbun is assuming the Editorship of our *Bulletin*.

Over the years, his trenchant and erudite contributions to the Society, at all levels of discourse, have distinguished him as a genuine intellectual presence in our group.

Judith Samson shepherded us through a year of reexamination of the structure of governance in our chapter. We hosted E. James Anthony and Leo Rangell during her 1989–1990 term. Our topic of study was the Oedipus Complex.

Don Brix served as President during the 1990–1991 period. We devoted one "semester" to an investigation of Interpersonal Psychoanalysis and Psychotherapy. Philip Bromberg was our invited presenter. We followed his presentation with Harold Blum.

For the 1991–1992 season Richard Warshak was our President. Warshak and his Program Committee offered us a curriculum around the topic of trauma. Working with Warshak as President-Elect was Dale Roskos.

In 1984, Richard Warshak launched our *Bulletin*. The *DSPP Bulletin* is a professionally prepared Newsletter, which is published monthly during the active part of our year; less frequently during the summer months. It has been edited since its inception by Warshak. The *Bulletin* has received many compliments over the years both for the quality of its content as well as its top drawer physical appearance. Richard Warshak's willingness to remain in the editorship over an extended period has provided a subtle, unobtrusive continuity to the Society. His skillful management of this aspect of our functioning has contributed to the health and vitality of the organization in ways that are scarcely possible to measure. Over the years many individuals have contributed to the *Bulletin*. Warshak singles out three members whose contributions have been singular: David Faris, Anne Z. Hunter, and Marc Rathbun. The latter two persons took over as Editor and Associate Editor respectively as Warshak steps aside to become our President for the 1991–1992 season.

Beginning around 1987, DSPP began to sponsor extended courses on a limited basis. These offerings are separate from and in addition to our regular monthly meetings. An additional enrollment fee is also involved. Covering a variety of subjects and conducted by our own members as well as analysts from the community, the courses provide a more intensive examination of particular topics of interest to members. John Herman, Malcolm Bonnheim, and Jim Harris have been associated with this realm of the Society's activities over the years.

Several of our members have attended Division level meetings over the years. One individual, Mary Laurel Bass-Wagner, has emerged as our continuing presence in Division affairs. Bass-Wagner has, for several years, represented DSPP at national meetings and is currently serving as an officer in the Section of Local Chapters.

At this writing DSPP has logged close to a decade in pursuit of its mission. The mission is, simply stated: To facilitate the study of the psychoanalytic point of view so that our daily work as psychotherapists might be improved and enriched as it becomes informed by psychoanalytic theory and principle. So far, it seems to be working.

The Georgia Association for Psychoanalytic Psychology

David M. Moss III

Shortly after the 1988 APA Convention in Atlanta, an initial design for a Georgia chapter of Division 39 was sketched out by two members who had never met before. One was Maureen McGarty, a clinical psychologist who had recently moved from New York to Athens, and the other was David Moss, an Atlanta Episcopal priest whose postgraduate work included training at the Chicago Institute for Psychoanalysis.

During the Convention, David Moss hosted a party for the Division at his Buckhead home. The chief purpose of this event was to promote the International Campaign for the Freud Museum in London. Several other members of the Division took this opportunity to approach him about forming a local chapter.

The next day at the Convention's headquarters, Maureen McGarty became involved in a discussion with some colleagues from the William A. White Institute about the need for a Division chapter in Georgia. They encouraged her to contact Moss to see if their interests and talents were in tandem. She did and they were.

Moss and McGarty spent nearly a year gathering information about other chapters and recruiting potential members for a Georgia group. Then, early in 1990, 17 psychotherapists met at Moss' home to form the Georgia Association for Psychoanalytic Psychology. Most of these clinicians were from Athens or Atlanta, although a few others practiced psychotherapy in smaller cities scattered throughout the state.

With the encouragement of James Barron, President of Section IV, Moss and McGarty became Co-Chairs, Stephen Ziegler accepted the post of Secretary, and Gwen Bate took the position of Treasurer. These officers were appointed for one year—the length of time most members believed it would take to develop from a provisional position to a ratified chapter of the Division.

GAPP's first year was devoted to the development of institutional guidelines such as bylaws, membership standards and educational goals. David Moss' preparation of the bylaws was assisted by Maureen McGarty's consultation with Section IV officers during the Division's 10th Annual Spring Meeting in New York. One particular point made by these colleagues was the interdisciplinary nature of the membership in most local chapters.

From the outset GAPP's membership maintained a sound interdisciplinary character. Psychologists, family therapists, social workers and pastoral counselors came together eager to discuss psychodynamics in a peer group context. Eventually, this growing membership was enriched by the professional fields of law, education, financial planning, and the fine arts. In general, GAPP's educational activities clearly reflected this interdisciplinary interest.

By February 1991, GAPP reached a stage of institutional maturity that called for its next step toward ratification as an official chapter of the Division. Following the democratic procedure outlined by the approved bylaws, the officers who had been appointed for the provisional year were unanimously elected to their posts. There was only one modification to this process: The leadership shared by Moss and McGarty took a new shape, with the former President and the latter President-Elect. Other issues related to the Association's growth were also settled at that time (annual dues, standing committees, stationary design, etc.).

Shortly thereafter, David Moss presented a written account of GAPP's development to Maureen Murphy, the President of Section IV. In it he cited the opinion of a Division member who had practiced psychotherapy in Georgia for nearly two decades: "With a few exceptions, psychoanalytic psychologists have not had their own forum. We have been without an organizational base, which could bring us together as colleagues with a common theoretical orientation and clinical purpose. GAPP has the potential to help fill this serious void."

A month later, Moss went to Chicago to review this growth and its potential with the Division's Board of Directors. The occasion was the 11th Annual Spring Meeting. The Board was very enthusiastic about GAPP's development and its status as an official chapter was ratified.

Coincidentally, the first public announcement of this ratification occurred a week later at the Freud Museum in London. Moss was invited to be a Visiting Scholar of the Museum and during that tenure he led a forum focused on the continuing growth of psychoanalysis in the face of cultural resistance. He used the growth of GAPP as an example of creative tension and described three social factors that reflected a defensive attitude: poor public education; right-wing religious trends; and symptomatic or quick-fix psychological services. He went on to explain how these cultural features were some of Georgia's major symptoms of resistance to psychoanalytic psychology.

That same spring GAPP sponsored a workshop at the Annual Convention of the Georgia Psychological Association. Ira Moses, President-Elect of Section I, was invited to lead it. Entitled "Psychoanalytic Listening: A Comparative Study," his workshop concentrated on selected case protocols to show how clinicians can improve their listening skills. He also reviewed related theories that offered insights from developmental, interpersonal, object-relational, and structural perspectives.

The workshop was well attended and most participants joined GAPP members for lunch in one of the Hotel Nikko's private dining rooms. During this period, the subject of cultural resistance was addressed by Ira Moses. He noted that other chapters had experienced similar obstacles. As the conversation unfolded, it became clear to many members that the realities of poor education, religious rigidity, and superficial psychology presented important issues for GAPP to confront.

As GAPP continues to add more members to its group, these three features will be dealt with in one way or another. However, it is already clear that the Association is a vital organization with a definite desire to overcome such cultural resistance. In fact, this goal represents a central concern for GAPP during the closing years of the 20th century. And, whereas most agree that the task is challenging, their prognosis is positive.

A History of the Massachusetts Association for Psychoanalytic Psychology

James W. Barron
Jonathan H. Slavin
Muriel Weckstein

The Massachusetts Association for Psychoanalytic Psychology (MAPP) was founded in 1983 and grew quickly. After our first meeting we had about 100 members, and we now have almost 500. We have become a strong educational presence in psychoanalytic psychology within the greater Boston community.

MAPP'S ORIGINS

In the fall of 1982, Muriel Weckstein called six psychologists interested in psychoanalytic psychology and asked if they wished to meet to discuss organizing a chapter of Division 39 in Massachusetts: Richard Geist, Stephen Klein, Jonathan H. Slavin, Leonard Solomon, and Muriel Weckstein are still actively involved. They met for almost a year before deciding to hold an organizing meeting on November 14, 1983 at Tufts University.

Our initial task was to define goals:

1. To provide psychologists interested in psychoanalysis a forum for scholarly and clinical exchange, including study groups, regular chapter meetings for clinical and research presentations, and larger meetings with distinguished psychoanalytic clinicians and scholars.
2. To provide a forum for discussion of professional concerns and issues of interest to psychoanalytically oriented clinicians.

3. To provide a vehicle for psychoanalytic psychologists to improve their level of training and skill.

We did not publicly announce an interest in forming a psychoanalytic training program at that time, because we had not been able to resolve several controversial issues relating to formal analytic training and we did not see the creation of an institute as the first order of business. In addition, there was initial concern on the part of some that the formation of the chapter and discussion of training might alienate some of those involved with the medical institutes. In these early years in the development of the identity of psychoanalytic psychologists, the formation of a chapter was fraught with some anxiety about how other analytic clinicians would respond to it. However, we also envisioned an organization that would appeal to the largest group of individuals interested in the theory and practice of psychoanalytic psychology, and did not want a premature introduction of training questions to make the invitation more controversial.

We decided that we should have a program that would establish the highest level of analytic thinking that could be expected of MAPP meetings in the future. The Director of the Winnicott Archives, James Gorney, presented a paper on "Limits and Limit Setting in the Psychoanalytic Situation," while Richard Geist looked at the material from the viewpoint of self-psychology. About 110 people attended this first meeting. From the turnout and the discussion during the meeting we knew that the infant organization met a genuine need.

The discussion at the first meeting clarified the expectations of our potential members. They wanted study groups, meetings with speakers and an exploration of the issues involved in developing a training institute. By the end of the meeting, we had nearly 100 paid members. Shortly after the meeting, we added three members to the original steering committee, Harold Jarman, Elizabeth Rogoff, and Anne Thompson. Bylaws were written by a committee chaired by Jonathan Slavin and approved by the membership in April, 1984, enabling us to hold elections for officers.

DIVISION 39

In this early period we were well aware of the nourishment we, as an Executive Committee, were beginning to gain from our participation in the activities of Division 39, which provided us with a national community, and offered professional meetings and organizational ideas that guided our development. We wanted this affiliation. We were also aware of the dangers inherent in an overly centralized organizational structure where local chapters' growth might be smothered. We also felt the need for local autonomy, and wanted to stay clear of the Division's internal fights as we charted our course. In 1984–1985, Muriel Weckstein, President; Jonathan H. Slavin, President-Elect; and Ester Shapiro attended the historic conference at the William Alanson White Institute, which marked the launching of a Section of Local Chapters in the Division and sparked the later development of psychoanalytic training programs affiliated with local chapters. These meetings were useful in providing a forum to learn how other developing chapters coped with similar issues.

MAPP PROGRAMS

Muriel Weckstein chaired the Study and Peer Group Committee, which later became the Education Committee, with an assigned task of polling the membership to see what study groups would be of interest. When the first Board was elected with Muriel Weckstein as President, Betty North and Barbara Mandelkorn Coleman took over as joint chairs of this committee. By June 1984, nine study groups were formed each with an assigned coordinator.

In October 1984, our first officers were inaugurated: Muriel Weckstein, President; Jonathan H. Slavin, President-Elect; Stephen Klein, Secretary; Susan Adelman, Treasurer; Malcolm O. Slavin, Anne Thompson, Betty North, and Betsy Rogoff, Executive Committee members. Only members could vote. These distinctions reflected the Board's struggle with the issue of our status as a chapter within the Division and with our wish to include other professionals interested in psychoanalysis.

We were developing a favorable reputation within the community of psychoanalytically oriented psychologists, while providing an intellectual and collegial home for many practitioners interested in psychoanalysis both as a theory and as a clinical technique. For the first time, these individuals were part of a group they could shape and be proud of.

In April 1985, the Program Committee turned its attention to long-range planning. The committee, under the creative leadership of Malcolm Slavin, outlined an overall framework for MAPP program activities, which remains in place to this day. The format included:

1. General Meetings: a regular fall (November) and spring (May) meeting with an invited speaker, panel or symposium preceded by a brief business meeting.
2. Professional issues-oriented meetings several times a year.
3. Informal scientific meetings several times a year where members of MAPP could present work in progress.

During the 1985–1986 year, MAPP sponsored three major programs with Helen Block Lewis, Sherry Turkle, and Stephen A. Mitchell as speakers.

As MAPP matured, the Education Committee, led by Betty North and Barbara Mandelkorn Coleman, saw the need to offer courses in addition to study groups. Our next programming expansion occurred in 1987 when the committee, led by Ester Shapiro and Muriel Weckstein, added weekend workshops, similar to those developed by the Colorado Chapter. In these workshops we offered continuing education credits for psychologists and social workers. Our success with these 1- to 2-day workshops has been based on keeping them small, usually 20–25 participants, and on our ability to attract nationally known clinicians as teachers. The Massachusetts law mandating continuing education credits for psychologists helped us grow, but more importantly we were presenting psychoanalysis and psychoanalytic psychotherapy as an exciting field. In 1985–1986, we published a brochure listing 11 courses varying in length from 6 to 12 weeks. It was this kind of expansion of educational opportunities that maintained the strength of MAPP, and led both to its increased intellectual importance in the community as well as its growth in membership.

In January 1986, we published our first Newsletter with James Barron and Anne Thompson as editors. We now have a quarterly eight page newsletter dealing with organizational concerns, a summary of professional meetings, and special columns of interest to our members. Subsequent editors of the Newsletter have been Ava Penman, Jaine Darwin, Elaine Lang, and Gerard Donnellan.

MEMBERSHIP ISSUES

During the first few years of our growth, the issue of who was eligible for membership was frequently discussed at Executive Committee meetings. We wished to preserve our identity as members of Division 39, but we did not want to exclude nonpsychologists. We were mindful of the lawsuit against the APsaA and its co-defendants for denying training to psychologists. Though we were not denying training, we did not want to do to other professionals what had been done to us. Our original position was that voting membership within MAPP would be limited to individuals who were members of both Division 39 and MAPP. Membership without voting privileges but with equal access to meetings, study groups and other activities of the organization, would be open to all interested in psychoanalytic psychology. This policy had to be rethought because a number of psychologists chose to become members of MAPP and not of Division 39. Also social workers, psychiatrists, and nurses joined MAPP and did not want to feel they were second class citizens. Eventually we decided to open full membership in MAPP to all mental health professionals interested in joining. We retained a category of student membership.

DEVELOPMENT OF A PSYCHOANALYTIC
TRAINING PROGRAM

At the first open meeting we learned that some members wanted us to develop
a psychoanalytic training program. Some were primarily interested in psychoanalytic psychotherapy, whereas others were interested in becoming psychoanalysts. Some wanted to prepare for the expected ABPP exam; others
wanted an ongoing opportunity to study psychoanalysis without an institute. Some
wanted to help others receive more systematic professional training. All were
concerned that we continue MAPP's existing programs and activities and not
see these in any way diminished if we chose to develop an institute. The concern was that there would not be enough energy both to maintain MAPP's development and to develop an institute. It was clear that, within APA rules, an
institute could not be part of MAPP, but would have to be established as a
separate entity. More importantly, the issue was infused with concerns about
repeating the elitism and hierarchical structure engendered in the existing medical
institutes as well as concerns about offending those institutes by proceeding
with our own plans.

During 1985–1986 a Committee on Psychoanalytic Certification, co-chaired
by Jonathan H. Slavin and David W. Harder, explored the possibility of setting
up a training program in psychoanalysis. The committee sent a questionnaire
to the membership to assess the need for training and models of training the
members favored. Responses were substantial and indicated sufficient interest
for us to hold an open meeting in March 1986, chaired by Malcolm O. Slavin,
to discuss training models ranging from the open Michigan model to the more
formal Denver Institute model as well as other training issues. Speakers at the
meeting were Susan Adelman, Murray Cohen, Kenneth Lappin, Ester Shapiro,
Jonathan H. Slavin, and Muriel Weckstein. The next step was to establish a
committee to try to develop a model for a psychoanalytic training program in
Boston that would somehow pull divergent views together. In the Spring of 1986,
outgoing President Muriel Weckstein and incoming President Jonathan H. Slavin
agreed to jointly appoint a committee that would represent the broadest range of
views. Co-chaired by Murray Cohen and David Harder (and including Susan Adelman, Ginger Chappell, Stephen Cooper, Peter Lawner, Betty North, and Malcolm
Slavin), this committee worked for nearly a year to establish a training framework.

In developing our plans for a possible institute, we thought it was wise to
meet with representatives of the Boston Psychoanalytic Society and Institute
to assess the potential for cooperation. We met with a response indicating we
would meet with no overt opposition and might expect warm cooperation. Indeed, there has been considerable assistance from many individuals associated
with the medical institutes who have served as faculty and on committees, both
in our chapter and in our institute, and there has been no institutional opposition to our development.

Throughout the next 2 years Jonathan H. Slavin emphasized the necessity of putting aside individual, personal visions of psychoanalytic training in order to unite behind a common goal and common purpose. In addition, a series of regular programs were sponsored by MAPP in which the issues and questions at stake in developing a training program were openly discussed by the community. For example, in March 1987, we held an open discussion of "Psychoanalytic Training for Psychologists in Boston: Starting an Institute" with Marvin Hyman and Charles Spezzano as guest speakers, representing alternative models. At issue in these discussions were concerns such as how traditional the curriculum would be, how open it would be to comparative perspectives, how the question of training analysis and training analysts would be dealt with and many other issues.

The Training Proposal Committee, chaired by Murray Cohen and David Harder presented its report to the Executive Committee of MAPP in March of 1987. That initial report, which was accepted unanimously by the Executive Committee, served as the framework for the establishment of a future training program. Following the acceptance of this report, an Organizing Committee for the new institute was formed. It included Jonathan H. Slavin as chair, and James Barron, Murray Cohen, Betty North, Ester Shapiro, Malcolm Slavin, and Muriel Weckstein. The Organizing Committee, using the initial training report, formed another set of committees, chaired and co-chaired by all members of the Organizing committee, which ultimately involved more than 70 different people planning various aspects of the program including: Curriculum, Admissions, Advanced Candidates, Finance, and Psychotherapy Track.

The Organizing Committee formally voted to become a Board of Directors in March 1988. In the winter of 1989, the Advanced Candidates program of the newly named Massachusetts Institute for Psychoanalysis (MIP) began its first class and applications for a first general class, which began in September 1989, were received. In order to assure a continued close connection between the new training program and the local chapter that developed it, MIP bylaws require that the president of MAPP be a member of the MIP Board, to represent the views of the larger community of psychoanalytic clinicians.

CONTINUED GROWTH

In September 1986, Jonathan H. Slavin became the second President of MAPP. The Executive Committee now consisted of: Muriel Weckstein, Past President; David Harder, Secretary; James Barron, Treasurer; and Stephen Klein, Malcolm O. Slavin, Betty North, and Ester Shapiro as Members-at-Large. With this election there was both continuity and new faces in MAPP's leadership—a healthy development of a new organization. Jonathan H. Slavin, in his committee appointments, continued to bring new faces into leadership positions. By this time MAPP was a healthy adolescent. We knew we would survive and grow. The period in which Jonathan Slavin was president was also marked by continued growth in the size of the chapter which had begun to expand rapidly during the presidency of Muriel Weckstein. Chapter size increased from more than 150 to nearly 400 members. The program committee, chaired ably by Jaine Darwin, who was later to follow as MAPP's fourth president, brought in a number of interesting speakers who provided alternatives to traditional perspectives. In addition, the educational activities of the chapter expanded with a special workshop program described earlier.

In September 1988 James Barron became the third president of MAPP. MAPP continued to grow in size and complexity, providing a variety of collegial and professional opportunities to nearly 500 members. As a broad-based educational interest group, MAPP offered an array of study groups, courses, workshops, and scientific meetings.

As a chapter of Division 39, MAPP could not offer formal analytic training, but could help give birth to MIP, which began its first classes of advanced and regular candidates. Although MAPP was strongly supportive of these developments, many members were fearful that MIP would create an elite in-group split off from the larger MAPP community. We addressed these fears openly in various meetings and in the MAPP Newsletter. We strengthened the recognition that many of the same individuals were involved in both organizations, which could in fact enrich each other. We countered the polarizing tendencies by sharing resources and actively planning several joint educational activities. In addition to its other important contributions to the psychoanalytic community, MAPP is also serving as a society for graduates of MIP.

We began to reach out actively to graduate students by inviting them to participate in various MAPP seminars, and by providing a modest amount of financial aid. President James Barron appointed Lisa Kaplan as the first Chairperson of the Graduate Student Committee. Under her dynamic leadership we significantly increased student membership, established a monthly graduate student study group to discuss experiences at training sites, progress on dissertation research, aspects of clinical work, and involvement in the wider professional community. Graduate students met privately with presenters and discussants before MAPP scientific meetings, and also sponsored a highly successful open meeting on the supervisory relationship, including two graduate students as presenters. Most importantly we insured their ongoing involvement in the structure and functioning of MAPP by incorporating graduate students into important MAPP committees.

In September 1990, Jaine Darwin became the fourth President of MAPP. MAPP now had a membership of more than 500 members and had learned it could flourish with its training program sibling, MIP, without being jeopardized. An effort was made via a membership questionnaire and multiple discussions in the Executive Committee meetings to take stock. Were the needs of the members continuing to be met by the organization? Did the organization need to alter its goals after its first 5 years of existence? Were the extensive programs of scientific meetings, course, and workshops, satisfying the learning needs of the membership? The Executive Committee was gratified to learn that the membership continued to find a home for psychoanalytic thinking, learning, and collegial contact in MAPP. Further effort is being devoted to keeping the members more politically aware, to try to broaden thinking to deal with applications of psychoanalysis in the public sector, and to increase awareness of the multidisciplinary orientation of MAPP. Additionally, during this time, MAPP successfully collaborated with chapters in Washington, Denver, and San Francisco to sponsor a visit by two Russian psychoanalysts visiting the United States for the first time. It was consistent with the open stance our chapter has taken in welcoming fellow clinicians interested in psychoanalysis.

The Michigan Society
for Psychoanalytic Psychology:
A Brief History

Marvin Hyman
Gale Swan

The Michigan Society for Psychoanalytic Psychology was organized in 1980 by a group of psychologists active in Division 39. It is an interdisciplinary society comprised of professionals, students and others interested in psychoanalysis. Psychologists had long been active in the local community, but had never before created a society of their own.

In the 1940s and the early 1950s psychoanalytic activities in the Detroit area were dominated by the Detroit Psychoanalytic Society (the Detroit), at that time an affiliate of APsaA. A split in that group eventually occurred over the issue of nonmedical analysis. Richard Sterba, then a senior member of the Detroit, was charged with conducting training analyses and/or providing supervision outside of the Detroit Institute and, as a consequence, the Detroit was disaccredited. Sterba was prepared to bring suit against the APsaA, but was persuaded by Anna Freud that such action might be detrimental to psychoanalysis in this country. The Detroit split into several factions.

Richard and Editha Sterba (a psychologist) continued practicing independently and developed the Michigan Association for Psychoanalysis (MAP). A second group retained the designation as the Detroit and affiliated with the American Academy of Psychoanalysis. This group had difficulty recruiting physicians, experienced a new edition of the conflict over training, and has not taken new candidates in years. A third group, the Michigan Psychoanalytic Society (the Michigan), became the new affiliate of APsaA in 1958. Although many psychologists in the area have been analyzed and supervised by members of the Michigan, only a small number were formally institute-trained under the admissions policies of APsaA prior to the successful prosecution of the GAPPP lawsuit. Non-physicians in the area formed the Friends of the Michigan Psychoanalytic Society in the 1970s; the "Friends" was subsequently renamed the Association for the Advancement of Psychoanalysis and continues as an active organization. A majority of the psychologist candidates and graduates of the Michigan have not joined MSPP, Division 39 or Section I. Psychologists who had arranged their own analyses, supervision, seminars, and study groups in a program of self-directed training, and who were competent and experienced practitioners, were not recognized as psychoanalysts by members of the Michigan and, with few exceptions, were reluctant to refer to themselves as such.

The creation of the local chapter of Division 39, the Michigan Society for Psychoanalytic Psychology, provided psychoanalytic psychologists in Michigan with a professional home of their own. It was an exciting time, with a sense of camaraderie and adventure, tolerance for differences and a determination to work through obstacles. Colleagues no longer had to be just "Friends" of the Michigan or guests from related disciplines at meetings of a medically dominated group. MSPP met important needs and grew rapidly; the current membership is approximately 155, about half of whom are doctoral-level psychologists. The group disavows any orthodoxy and welcomes all significant viewpoints within psychoanalysis.

From the beginning the Society functioned as an interest group and there was lively interest in developing study groups, teaching, training and identifying qualified psychoanalysts within our ranks. In addition to holding monthly scientific meetings, one of the first activities of the Society was to form a Practitioners' Seminar in which senior members defining themselves as psychologist-psychoanalyst practitioners would meet to present case material to each other. The task we set ourselves was to talk about what characterized the work as psychoanalytic, and how we knew a transference neurosis when we saw one. There was also an early study group on countertransference, and one on object relations. Later, a technical seminar was organized as a more open version of the practitioners' group, to which all were invited. Technical issues were studied in the context of case presentations, often with process material, and secondarily through the literature.

The Society began offering courses in 1982 and in June 1986, established the Center for Psychoanalytic Studies. The purpose of the Center was to provide educational experiences in an organized but not formalized course of study for self-motivated individuals. The intent was to make available the opportunity to study respected theoretical positions and obtain technical training for those interested in the study of psychoanalysis as a body of knowledge and/or with the intention of achieving practitioner status. One aim was to offer sufficient course work to enable an individual to apply for Psychologist-Psychoanalyst Practitioner status with Division 39, Section I, or to be eligible for the planned ABPP exam in psychoanalysis.

MSPP accepted the Division's and Section I's standards as its criteria for identifying qualified psychoanalysts. In fact, early debate over the issue of standards was resolved with the formation of Section I. It was thought that the local organization would not need to become embroiled in the controversy over qualifications because psychologist members could apply for membership in Section I. The issue would be referred to the national organization. A number of our members were accepted into Section I and were regarded as the original cadre of psychologist-psychoanalyst practitioners. However, other members of MSPP were concerned with the training and credentialling of persons not eligible for Division 39 or Section I membership, and controversy grew over the question of whether MSPP would offer training leading to a certificate in psychoanalysis.

Interestingly, the matter of standards was not the issue that led to so much dissension within the local organization. Many of the senior members of MSPP had been analyzed on a four or five times weekly basis. Adoption of the Division's three times per week standard accommodated others, and the problem of numbers, which has so plagued the Division, and the efforts to establish an ABPP exam was never a source of divisiveness here. Rather, it was the matter of whether the local organization should certify qualified psychoanalysts and offer a training program which would lead to the granting of a certificate.

By 1985, there was growing pressure to offer formal training and to certify, and the membership began to divide more sharply. On February 1, 1986, an open forum was held to consider the issues. The Division's and Section I's concerns with the possibility of lawsuits over certification and the controversy over standards that led to the eventual formation of Section V brought matters once again into focus for the local chapter. Some then regarded the ABPP exam as a viable long-range solution until efforts to develop criteria for the exam bogged down, again over matters of numbers. Within our own organization there were essentially three positions represented.

One group regarded credentialling as a vital function of the organization. It was seen as a necessary part of the training process, as a means of recognition and acceptance of one's achievement by one's peers, and as an important step leading to integration of one's self-identity as a psychoanalyst. A second viewpoint saw the designation, qualified psychoanalyst, as a matter of self-definition and informal acceptance by one's colleagues; any formal process of evaluation was seen as unnecessary or counter to analytic ideals and, thus, counterproductive. Questions were also raised about liability insurance and the possibility of lawsuits should an applicant be denied a credential of the organization. A third viewpoint held that credentialling was desirable, but should be left to whatever mechanism would eventually emerge from national debate.

Two forums, one on training and one on credentialling, were planned for 1988–1989. However, in the Fall of 1988, Raymond Fowler, then President of APA, indicated in a letter to Jonathan Slavin of the Massachusetts local chapter

that accrediting is the sole province of APA. On December 11, 1988, the MSPP
Board voted unanimously to abide by APA policy and not accredit.

However, only eight days earlier, a group of MSPP members, frustrated with
the Board's reluctance to formalize training and credentialling by the local chapter, had voted to organize the Michigan Psychoanalytic Council (MPC) as a
separate organization for these purposes. Nine months later the group designated its first group of psychoanalysts according to Division 39 standards and
selected five new candidates. MPC is not an arm of the local chapter but an
independent nonprofit corporation. The institute continues the MSPP policy of
accepting all significant viewpoints in psychoanalysis. MPC also endorses the
Federation of Psychoanalytic Training Organizations, as does MSPP.

Meanwhile, MSPP has continued to meet professional and collegial needs
of its members by functioning as an interest group. In July 1991, it amended
its bylaws to reflect the current reality and eliminate the issues of formal training and recognition of qualified practitioners from its statement of purpose. Its
purposes now include: the study of psychoanalytic psychology and its promotion in the general and professional communities; the promotion and encouragement of the highest standards of practice; the providing of continuing education
and professional development opportunities for psychoanalytic practitioners; and
the expansion of psychoanalytic psychological services in the community.

Professional meetings are held on a regular basis; members are invited to
present papers, and professional development is enhanced through discussion
of theoretical and technical ideas. From time to time the Society sponsors meetings with invited speakers. We have also sponsored intensive, day-long workshops for the study of a particular area of interest. From its inception the group
has provided an opportunity for colleagues to form study groups and pursue
areas of common interest over an extended period of time. MSPP has also held
a number of Midwinter and Midsummer Institutes, usually in resort areas, where
colleagues could come together for a weekend of professional sharing, discussion and debate, social and recreational activities. An interest group on Wom-
en's Issues shares the purposes of Division 39, Section III, in promoting interest
and discussion concerning women's issues and gender differences, modifying
the current public image of psychoanalysis as negative toward women, and encouraging women to participate actively. MSPP also arranges group rates for
journal subscriptions and provides an information network for referral among
colleagues. It serves as an avenue of contact with other state organizations and
with the Division, and it helps in promoting interest in psychoanalysis among
students and training groups.

MSPP has contributed immeasurably to the professional lives of psychologists in Michigan who are interested in the study and practice of psychoanalysis. The excitement which accompanied formation of the original group reflected
the end of psychologists' isolation, and the hope and optimism accompanying
creation of opportunities to belong to a real psychoanalytic community. MSPP

members are no longer fringe members or outsiders, but full participants in all aspects of a mature and fulfilling professional life. Our development is ongoing and has not been without controversy, dissension, argument, and anger. We encountered no major difficulties over differences in theoretical orientation or over criteria for identifying qualified practitioners. However, a crisis arose over the issue of certification and, although APA's prohibition on accrediting marked a critical point in our debate, the fact is that we were unable to resolve differences in a way that preserved our unity while meeting divergent needs. The organization, which was enlivened by its variety of viewpoints, reached an impasse over the certification issue, and at this point there is a less than desirable overlap in membership between the Division's local chapter, MSPP, and the local interdisciplinary institute, MPC, with a number of psychologist members who are also active in Division 39. Hopefully, as we continue to evolve as a Society, psychologists will benefit from the resources and contributions of all who are active in the local psychoanalytic community, and diversity will again become a source of strength within our group.

A History of the New Mexico Psychoanalytic Society

Elizabeth J. Roll

For at least the past 20 years, various attempts have been made in Albuquerque to form psychoanalytic study groups for professionals to discuss case material and enhance their knowledge of psychoanalysis. Some of these have been more successful than others, but none has endured. However, the hunger to establish and bring a psychoanalytic current to New Mexico has sustained itself.

After the Division 39 meeting in San Francisco in April of 1988, several of us met together in Albuquerque in an attempt to form a chapter of the Division. One of the participants was Nancy Morrison who had been a student of Helen Block Lewis, and who presented a paper on shame at the conference. We organized a study group, which met for about 9 months, but had difficulty addressing the divergent levels of expertise in the group. Sunya Plattner, from Denver, came to one of our meetings and explained to us how they got their chapter started and also about the development of their institute. Some of our members wanted to establish a chapter and other members felt that we should put our efforts into establishing an institute. The result was that neither came to be.

After the Division 39 meeting in Chicago in the spring of 1991, several of us resumed the dialogue. Our enthusiasm had been rekindled to bring more psychoanalytic stimulation to New Mexico. This time we had the warm and consistent encouragement of Jonathan Slavin by phone and correspondence. Also, we had a useful manual, which was sent to us by Rona Eisner, and the welcome advice and consultation of Maureen Murphy. And this time we made it work.

We had three organizational meetings that summer each about 3 weeks apart. Approximately 12 people attended each of them with some overlap. We also met individually in between group meetings. One of our members agreed to chair a conference that we hoped to have with the financial assistance of the Division. We also established a bylaws committee. At our third meeting, we approved our bylaws, and voted for officers. Since then, we have had one Executive Board meeting and lots of communication between officers.

The most controversial issue was membership. There was a clear split between individuals wanting a professional organization of high caliber that would be inevitable and appropriately exclusive, and others that felt that an exclusionary policy was unnecessary, antiquated, and elitist. The majority felt that we should have two levels of membership: Full members who are licensed mental health professionals, and associate members would be students, non-licensed mental health professionals and other persons interested in psychoanalysis. We are committed to working toward a membership in which psychologists, psychiatrists, counselors and other mental health professionals can join together in the pursuit of a deeper understanding and utilization of psychoanalytic theory. Our membership committee has developed an application form that is being sent to a list of about 20 additional people who were interested in the chapter, but who are unable to attend meetings.

One of the most problematic areas for our chapter is the lack of professional resources at the senior level. We are very isolated. We have no psychoanalytic institute in the area. Over the years we have had no more than three analysts in the city at a time.

We are in the dilemma of having to bring in experts, which necessitates funding and greater member numbers. Most of our membership, about 25 at this time, would like a small group format for study and discussion. They are not eager to spend a great deal of energy planning conferences and raising money. Our senior clinicians already teach and have participated in helping to form the organization, so we do not feel comfortable demanding much more of them. The organization could easily become bottom heavy with graduate students in psychology and counseling, and residents in psychiatry.

We have many plans and possibilities. In October we are planning on having a panel with the working title: "Dora Revisited: Contemporary Application." In November we are starting a Journal Club and are now in the process of selecting articles. Eventually, several small study groups may emerge from the organization, which would be focused on a particular area or approach to psychoanalytic theory. In addition, we hope to have case presentations and discussions. We plan to make connections with our neighboring chapters in Texas and Denver. Once we are more grounded it may be possible to invite our neighbors in Arizona to join with us in some way.

Our history is brief because we are new. However, we do have one very precious older addition to our Chapter and she is Theodora Abel who has been a member of Division 39 since its inception. Although she is over 90 years old, she is always an enthusiastic and eager resource person. We plan to make her an honorary member.

The Mew Mexico Psychoanalytic Society Executive Board consists of: President, Elizabeth J. Roll; President-Elect, William Fishburn; Secretary, Karen Reubush; Treasurer, Ben Porter; Program Committee Chair, Nancy Morrison; Membership Co-chairs, Janet Robinson and David Landau; Representative to Division 39, Nancy Dodd; and Associate Member Representative, Judy Schuster.

The New York Local Chapter

Robert C. Lane

The New York Chapter, with many training centers in the area, and a large percentage of Division 39's membership (over 50% in the first survey), wanted to contribute in some manner to the local chapter movement. Whereas psychoanalytic education and training were nearly impossible to attain in many areas of the country, and was to become one of the major thrusts of the local chapter movement, this was not a problem in New York. The New York Chapter wanted to have an available pool of trained members, and members concerned with training, in order for the chapter and its members to serve as an advisory and resource center for emerging chapters throughout the country. Other purposes were to have a collegial forum, and to form a group with diversity of orientation representing a cross-fertilization, and offer dialogue and communication between the different groups via meetings, panels, symposia, workshops, and the like. At the time of the initial local chapter movement, in addition to New York, there were only a few states that offered psychoanalytic training to psychologists.

The initial local chapter movement was planned in New York when the administration of President Gordon F. Derner and President-Elect Robert C. Lane appointed Jeffrey Binder as the first chair of the Local Chapter Committee. Binder suggested (a) selecting from various geographic regions members willing to take on the responsibility for forming a local chapter; (b) asking persons who helped form existing local chapters to provide help and advice to interested parties; and (c) having the chairperson of the committee act as liaison among local chapters. Jeffrey Binder had also pointed out the goals of local chapters. These included scientific, clinical, and professional concerns. Binder also stressed the need for the Division to remain responsive to a "broad range of psychoanalytically oriented psychologists," and warned against the Division restricting itself to credentialling psychologist-psychoanalysts. Lane, when he wrote the bylaws for Section IV, the Section of Local Chapters, included Binder's goals and purposes. The thrust of the Chicago Conference of Local Chapters in October, 1981, pointed to the need for the development of training opportunities, including provision for consultation with an experienced group of teachers and trainers. The New York Chapter, represented by Ava Siegler and George D. Goldman, was ideally suited for this task.

There were several attempts to form a stronger New York Local Chapter. One such attempt came from Postgraduate Center and was led by Zanvil Liff. This meeting produced some 60 people, but there was never a follow-up to the meeting. Another attempt occurred in Long Island where several meetings were held. It appeared as if nobody wanted the responsibility of setting up meetings, writing to members, collecting dues, and planning scientific meetings.

George D. Goldman and Robert C. Lane continued to be the active members of the New York local chapter movement. Following Ted Reiss' appointment as Chair of the Local Chapter Committee (1983–1984), Helen Block Lewis appointed Goldman and Lane to Co-Chair the Local Chapter Committee. Both had a long history of involvement with the local chapter movement and were given the charge by President Lewis, "to revitalize the local chapter movement throughout the country and to enhance the flow of information between the various groups that have been formed or are in the process of being formed." Each was to be available as a resource person when needed. It was these Co-Chairs along with Murray Meisels, Chair of the Ad Hoc National Training Program Committee, and Anna Antonvosky, Chair of the Education and Training Committee, that planned the 2-day conference at the William Alanson White Institute on December 1 and 2, 1984. The purposes they set for this all-important conference of local chapters were: (a) to learn about local problems; (b) to determine scientific ways for the Division to assist in the educational needs of developing local chapters; and (c) to discuss the feasibility of regional and/or national coursework. Charles Spezzano was to join Goldman and Lane as Co-Chairs of the Committee, and these three Co-Chairs together paved the way for the acceptance of Section IV, the Section of Local Chapters.

On October 4, 1985, the two organizers, Goldman and Lane, petitioned the then Membership Chair of the newly formed Section IV, Myron Lazar of the Dallas chapter, for local chapter status. The principal members of the chapter were: Joseph Arleo, Peter Buirski, Leopold Caligor, George D. Goldman, Harriet Kaley, Bernard Kalinkowitz, Robert C. Lane, Carol Michaels, Donald S. Milman, Norma Simon, Susan Warshaw, and Zanvil Liff. Among these members were two founding fathers of the Division (Goldman and Lane), four who were to become presidents (Robert C. Lane, 1981–1982; George D. Goldman, 1982–1983; Zanvil Liff, 1988–1989; and Lee Caligor 1992–1993), an outstanding leader, statesman and trainer (Bernard Kalinkowitz), representation from the William Alanson White Institute (Caligor, Goldman, and Kalinkowitz), from NYU Postdoctoral Institute (Kaley, Kalinkowitz, Simon, and Warshaw), from Alelphi Postdoctoral Institute (Goldman, Lane, and Milman), from Postgraduate Psychoanalytic Institute (Arleo, Buirski, Michaels, and Liff), from NPAP (Milman), and from the New York Freudian Society (Lane). The group also contained a number of individuals who were to become active in APA governance. These included: Goldman, Kaley, Lane, Liff, Simon, and Warshaw.

To the best of the writer's knowledge, there were never any scientific meetings. The membership consisted of a group of highly visible people who volunteered to lend their services to chapters throughout the country. There was one meeting held on May 18, 1986, at Postgraduate Center. This meeting was advertised incorrectly in the *Psychologist-Psychoanalyst*, giving the wrong meeting address. In addition, the Newsletter arrived late, and the meeting was held on a very stormy evening. Despite the adverse conditions, Harold Davis, Magda Denis, George Goldman, Irwin Hirsch, Bernard Kalinkowitz, Bob Lane, Zanvil Liff, Catherine Masterson, Helen Silverman, and Bob Storch attended. The purposes of our local chapter were reviewed, and appear here:

1. To serve as a professional collegial alliance going beyond the philosophy of the institute one was trained in and one's orientation, thus offering a sense of professional identity and belongingness to its members;

2. To act as a forum in which psychologist-psychoanalysts can meet and learn from each other what is happening in the field professionally and politically, and in this manner participate more actively with one another in shaping our professional future;

3. To serve as a group that could become part of a cadre of trained psychologist-psychoanalysts who could participate in the training of other psychologists throughout the country, and also present a resource and information center for other chapters;

4. To offer a social as well as professional atmosphere.

Following the aforementioned meeting, there has been little further activity of the chapter, dues being paid by the two organizing members. In an attempt to revitalize the chapter, a letter has been sent to all members by Goldman and Lane at the time of this writing.

The Northern California Society for Psychoanalytic Psychology

Maureen Murphy

In February 1986, about two dozen mental health professionals responded to a widely circulated flier aimed at determining the feasibility of starting a local chapter in the Bay Area. A few enthusiastic hours later, we had a steering committee, a small treasury, and enough energy to build a thriving chapter and an institute over the next 5 years.

Background

A number of historical factors converged that permitted the rapid growth of our chapter. Dating back to the 1940s, a handful of nonmedical analysts, such as Seigfried Bernfeld, helped create an atmosphere that encouraged interdisciplinary collaboration. As a respected clinician and teacher, Bernfeld embodied the original notion of an analyst, and as such did much to dispel the medical bias in psychoanalysis in this area. This collaboration permeated the Mt. Zion Medical Center training program, which for more than two decades provided intensive psychoanalytic psychotherapy training to psychologists, social workers, psychiatrists, and nurses. Whereas medical graduates often went on to the San Francisco Psychoanalytic Institute, nonmedical graduates maintained an affiliation with the program as the only alternative cohesive psychoanalytic structure open to them. When financial pressures on the hospital occasioned the demise of this program in the mid-1980s, these well trained and by now senior clinicians, were left professionally homeless. It was no coincidence that several people from this group were among the chapter founders.

At about this same time, from 1984 through 1986, a group called the Committee for Lay Analysis, Co-Chaired by Jane Hewitt and Jill Horowitz, formed to launch a state-level suit parallel to the GAPPP federal anti-trust suit. This suit was based on the California Fair Practices Act that prohibits discrimination of equally competent individuals based exclusively on credentials. This suit took the position that licensed mental health professionals were just as qualified as physicians to practice psychoanalysis, and were being excluded from applying for training solely on the basis of their educational degree. When APsaA agreed to admit nonmedical applicants, the legal grounds for this suit were eliminated. Notwithstanding, the Committee brought together a diverse group of professionals interested in psychoanalytic education who were excited about the possibility of continuing to work together.

The evolution of professional schools within graduate education in psychology was another crucial component leading to the establishment of the chapter. In the Bay Area, the California School of Professional Psychology and the Wright Institute have been influential in generating a cohort of graduates, well-trained in psychoanalytic theory and practice. Nathan Adler, Kenneth Appel, Murray Bilmes, and Philburn Ratoosh were original core faculty at these schools as well as Division 39 members from its founding. This tradition continues to inform these clinical programs. Postdoctorally, this new generation of psychologists were looking for a way of maintaining their identity as psychoanalytic practitioners.

All of these factors both galvanized community interest in the formation of the chapter, and have influenced its continued success. As I describe the development of the chapter, the respectful collegiality and almost non-existent conflict that characterized this endeavor may seem like an anomaly within psychoanalysis. Usually such skepticism would be warranted. This time, however, there was a confluence of a trained, experienced, motivated group with a single goal that overrode the usual divisive factors, and provided a legacy in tone and spirit that carried the chapter well past infancy.

The Early Stages

The first year of the chapter was navigated by a steering committee co-chaired by John Fielder and Maureen Murphy and composed of Barbara Artson, Abbot Bronstein, Sam Gerson, Jill Horowitz, and Phyllis Kempner. By virtue of John Fielder's staff affiliation, we had access to space at the MacAuley Neuropsychiatric Unit of St. Mary's Hospital for committee meetings as well as scientific presentations. This was important for two reasons, one of which was financial. The more important reason was that we wanted to establish an identity separate from any of the existing training or graduate programs. In this neutral setting, we avoided being identified with any specific faction, and this permitted us to present ourselves as interdisciplinary and theoretically diverse.

During that time we drafted bylaws and held the first election of officers. Charles Spezzano, then president of Section IV, and Murray Meisels, provided invaluable and generous advice. The first officers were President, Maureen Murphy; President-Elect, Sam Gerson; Secretary, Dorian Newton; and Treasurer, Jill Horowitz. Originally there were two standing committees: the Program Committee, Co-Chaired by Barbara Artson and Annette Perry, and the Membership Committee, Chaired by John Fielder. The associate members were represented by Joanna Berg.

We made decisions regarding membership and program that influenced the direction of the chapter. The first was that full membership would be open to all licensed professionals. Any other position seemed to fly in the face of the GAPPP suit, and would have sounded an immediate divisive note in the community.

The program consisted of four scientific meetings and an annual lecture. In order to establish the value of our own work, and to underscore the important contribution of non-medical professionals, we decided that for the first few years the scientific presentations would come only from our own members. It was tempting to invite a well-known analyst with the belief that this would increase attendance and stimulate interest in the chapter. Without reliance on outside talent, we routinely had an attendance of 30 to 50 people. It would exceed the available limits of space to list all of the excellent presenters and discussants of the past 5 years. Suffice it to say we have no regrets about the decisions we made. The annual lecture was designed to provide a vehicle for inviting a distinguished analyst or analytic thinker from our community. These speakers have included Susan Quinn, Joyce McDougall, Elisabeth Young-Bruehl, and Roy Schafer. In both the scientific programs and the annual lectures, concern for gender balance has informed all of our choices.

Whereas we were still operating as a steering committee, San Francisco was selected as the site of the 1988 Spring Meeting of Division 39, with Sam Gerson and Maureen Murphy as Co-Chairs. This presented the challenge of staging a successful meeting outside of the North East Corridor. With a 500 person attendance, the largest Spring Meeting until then, the notion that there is analytic life outside of the East Coast was firmly established. Coming early in our existence, the Spring Meeting signalled our participation in a national organization. Other people were taking us as seriously as we were taking ourselves.

Established Chapter

By Fall, 1988, with the essentials of a chapter in place, we expanded in several directions. Phyllis Kempner agreed to chair the first Education Committee, which offered a variety of courses. In this first attempt at course work, various formats were tested. Some courses were one evening, others stretched for several weeks. Steven Walrod taught Freud's Vienna; Susan Sands, Self Psychology; Kenneth Appel, Dreams, Analysis, and Interpretation; John Curtis, Control Mastery: Theory and Practice; and Sam Gerson, Masochistic Phenomena and Their Treatment. In the past 3 years, under the leadership of Carol Drucker and Marilynne Kanter, the Education Program has evolved to a Fall and Spring schedule of more than 20 courses. In addition, there is a one-year intensive course in psychoanalysis that includes three courses per semester as well as a case conference. This intensive study group provides an in-depth experience for professionals as an alternative to institute training. The faculty for the first intensive study group included Adrienne Applegarth, Bryce Boyer, James Faircloth, Jay Greenberg, Joyce McDougall, Calvin Settlage, Justin Simon, Robert Stolorow, and Robert Westfall.

Dorian Newton organized the first Newsletter, and continues as its editor. The Newsletter, published biannually, includes Chapter and Division activities, summaries of the scientific meetings, book reviews, and professional accomplishments of our members.

Perhaps the most intrepid step taken by the chapter was the launching of a new institute. The question of whether or not to develop an institute had been raised at the very first chapter organizing meeting. After lengthy debate, it had been decided that we would start with a chapter, and depending on community response, move toward an institute. By the end of 1988, there was consensus within the chapter to proceed.

Psychoanalytic Institute of Northern California

In the Fall of 1988, the Executive Committee of the NCSPP appointed an organizing committee to develop an institute providing full psychoanalytic training to licensed mental health professionals of all disciplines. The organizing committee divided the task into three phases: (a) the development of principles and guidelines that would inform subsequent working committees; (b) the establishment of the working committees, administration, admissions, education and training; and (c) the appointment of a Board and directors, and the establishment of the institute as an entity separate from the chapter. The target date for completion of these tasks was October 1989. Once the Organizing Committee was established we looked to other chapter-established institutes for advice. Karen Rosica and Charles Spezzano in Colorado and Oliver Kerner and Jane Wickland in Chicago were extremely helpful to us. The Massachusetts Institute for Psychoanalysis saved us from reinventing the wheel by providing us with their committee reports and documents. Throughout this early stage, Jonathan Slavin was invaluable. He came to San Francisco and spent a weekend with us that served to organize our efforts.

The most frequently asked question about this project was, How will this Institute be different? The most succinct answer is that the Institute is organized on an educational model as contrasted to a guild model. The goal of the Institute is to create an educational climate that reflects the best in psychoanalytic training—dedication to rigorous critical thinking guided by the belief that psychoanalysis is a continuously evolving intellectual and clinical discipline. As such, the educational program will include the full range of psychoanalytic theories in the curriculum, and encourage interaction between psychoanalysis and other scientific disciplines.

The practical implications also include admission standards based on capacity to undertake the academic and clinical demands of psychoanalysis, and an evaluation system based on clearly stated criteria, and administered by faculty and supervisors in a way which is distinct from the personal analysis-training analyst model. Using these goals as a starting point, the various committees clarify the operations of the Institute.

The Admissions Committee was Co-Chaired by Jill Horowitz and Gayle Wheeler, and composed of John Curtis, Martha Rabkin, Kurt Schlesinger and Jeanne Wolff-Bernstein. The Psychoanalytic Institute of Northern California is committed to being a multidisciplinary center. As such, we welcome applications from licensed members of all mental health professions. The Institute looks for candidates who have a demonstrated commitment to psychoanalysis, a capacity for sustained academic rigor, and clinical capability, including the capacity to learn through self-reflection. A two-step process of a written application and clinical interview was adopted. In the second stage, applicants were seen two or three times by two different interviewers. Interviews cover both clinical presentations and broad personal and professional issues. The intent of the interview is to determine the applicant's capacity to undertake analytic training. These are not mini-analytic sessions. Nonetheless, we recognize that the tension between the personal and the professional—which is an aspect of all psychoanalytic work—will also exist in these interviews.

In addition to the general applicant, there was a category of advanced applicants. This category was developed to respond to the historical and political reality that qualified nonmedical professionals were until recently excluded from full analytic training. We recognized that there exists in our community a group of clinicians who have studied, supervised, analyzed, and contributed to psychoanalysis for many years without access to systematic training. This category applies to those applicants. The term advanced was not meant to be a qualitative evaluation, but rather as a description of a career stage. We envisioned this as a time-limited category, because the number of people currently qualifying was finite. The application process was the same as for general applicants.

The course of study at the Institute follows the tripartite model of coursework, supervised cases and personal analysis. This part of the program was designed by the Education and Training Committee, Co-Chaired by Rachael Peltz and Stephen Seligman, and composed of members Jean Harasemovitch, Jane Hewitt, Bruce Smith, Ron Spinca, and Robert Westfall.

The curriculum was designed as a 4-year course of study organized around theory, development, psychopathology, and technique sequences. Each year consists of four 8-week quarters. The first 2 years are more heavily weighted toward the didactic. There is increased opportunity to delve into areas of personal interest during the third and fourth year. Some courses are organized on the standard weekly basis, whereas others are offered on weekends in order to access out of town faculty.

With regard to supervised cases, the Committee recommended three cases, two of which are seen four times per week, and one of which could be seen three times per week. Two cases should use the couch. To avoid undue pressure on both candidate and patient, termination was not a requirement for graduation.

Who may supervise the candidates had been a major question. In broad strokes, a supervisor is someone who has graduated from a bona fide analytic training program or its equivalent, spends a substantial portion of his or her time doing psychoanalysis, is willing to participate in the evaluation of candidates, and complies with the ethical standards of the profession. Candidates propose their own supervisors in keeping with these guidelines.

What about the personal analysis? Personal analysis is conducted in such a way as to maintain the integrity and privacy of the psychoanalytic process. We are not a reporting institute. We hold that this value overrides the potential risk of uncovering personal pathology that would impede the clinical effectiveness of the candidates. As with the selection of supervisors, analysts are approved by the Institute using similar guidelines. Candidates currently in analysis, or those who have undergone extensive analysis, will not necessarily be expected to alter or resume treatment. Candidates with a previous or current analysis may apply for a waver of equivalency, which requires extensive personal evaluation and interviews.

The Administration Committee was the final of the three organizing committees. It was Co-Chaired by Maureen Murphy and Justin Simon, and composed of Barbara Artson, Victor Bonfilio, Suzanne Gassner, Phyllis Kemper, Robin Press, and David Stein. This committee was charged with developing a comprehensive blueprint for establishing a freestanding institute. The main tasks included defining the nature of the Board, appointing Board members, obtaining legal documentation, fund-raising, and miscellaneous logistical considerations.

The Committee recommended a Board that would provide representation from various sectors of the community, and be composed of individuals with previous administrative experience wherever possible. Each category of member would be selected by their own constituency, with a maximum length of term. In this way the Committee attempted to address issues of composition, stability, and entrenchment of power.

The first Board was seated in November 1989 and was composed of Barbara Artson, Hedda Bolgar, Victor Bonfilio, Wendy Everett, Sam Gerson, Jean

Harasemovitch, Jill Horowitz, Phyllis Kemper, Maureen Murphy, Rachael Peltz, Robert Westfall, and Gayle Wheeler. The first Admissions Committee was chaired by John Fielder, and Education and Training Committee by Bruce Smith. Twelve candidates were admitted to the first class, which began September 1990. Eight candidates were admitted to the second class in September 1992.

The Oklahoma Society for Psychoanalytic Studies

Stephen J. Miller

The Oklahoma chapter was the "brain child" of G. Michael Kampschaefer and Stephen J. Miller, who had been discussing organizing a local chapter for several years. In the Spring of 1990, Kampschaefer became serious about the task. An Organizing Committee consisting of G. Michael Kampschaefer, Stephen J. Miller, Stephen B. Hopper, Kay Ludwig, Joe Couch, and Champa Ranebenur was established in April 1990, and began meeting regularly. Bylaws were adopted in June 1990. We now hold monthly scientific meetings.

In August 1990, we began looking at several options for the establishment of a formal training program in psychoanalysis. One of our members, Martha Jo Shaw, was a senior candidate in the Colorado Society for Psychoanalysis. Through Martha Jo Shaw, we made contact with Karen Rosica, who came to Oklahoma City for a meeting in January 1991. Karen Rosica proved a godsend, and essentially single-handedly helped us establish an affiliation with the Denver program. We have 19 people who will begin coursework in psychoanalytic training through the Denver Institute in September 1991. Currently our local chapter officers are as follows: President, G. Michael Kampschaefer; Program Chair, Stephen J. Miller; Membership Chair, Champa Ranebenur; Treasurer, Stephen B. Hopper; and Secretary, Kay Ludwig.

A Pre-History of the Ontario Society for Contemporary Psychoanalysis

John D. Munn

The Ontario Society for Contemporary Psychoanalysis applied for and was granted Chapter status by APA Div. 39 in 1991. In forming this society our intent was to carry on and expand the work originally started by a small group of psychologists and students who founded the first psychoanalytic section within the Ontario Psychological Association (OPA) in 1985. Initially some reservations were expressed about the validity of forming a separate psychoanalytic section by the OPA, which was not surprising in that there had not been at that time a significant sustained psychoanalytic focus at the undergraduate or graduate levels in Ontario universities that could be considered sympathetic to psychoanalytic theory, except for the unique PhD program, directed by Otto Weininger at the Ontario Institute for Studies in Education.

However, there were rare occasions when psychoanalytic papers were presented at OPA conventions. These papers were usually very well received and regrets were expressed by members of the audience over the years that there was very little available to encourage and support an ongoing forum for psychoanalytic discussion and debate.

When the first meeting was called by John Munn to determine interest in the formation of a psychoanalytic section within OPA, a surprisingly large number of students, clinicians and academics turned out to offer their support for such a group. Most notably among the senior academicians and clinicians who added their enthusiastic support were Otto Weininger, Harley Wideman, Paul Lerner, and Morris Eagle.

With this support an Executive Committee was chosen as follows: John Munn,

Brent Willock, Art Caspary, Hazel Ipp, Rex Collins, Molly Weaver, Nira Kolers, Judi Kobrick, Margaret Kirk, Ricardo Harris, and Jack Kamrad. It was both gratifying and, as it turned out, a very good omen that so many were so eager to volunteer their time at this early phase.

In our formative years we put together a series of monthly scientific meetings to hear and discuss papers presented by eager graduate students and seasoned local psychologists with international reputations (Otto Weininger and Paul Lerner) and academicians involved in the psychoanalytic field (Phyllis Groskurth and Paul Roazen). Three ongoing study groups were also formed: to study in detail Freud's writings (led by Ahmed Fayek in Ottawa), to study the work of Lacan (led by Ricardo Harris), and later to study Object Relations (led by Ellen Greenberg and Julie Brickman).

Our aim in these early presentations and study groups was to attract new psychologists and students to the field, and to encourage the contribution of Ontario psychologists to the local and international scene. In keeping with this task, we have given an award of merit to an Ontario psychologist who our Section's Board decided has made a significant contribution to the development of psychoanalytic psychology. To date, we have given these awards to Otto Weininger, Paul Lerner, and Brent Willock.

During the mid 1980s we became the fastest growing Section of the Ontario Psychological Association, rapidly rose to a membership of more than 100, and as such, became a major group in OPA. Our Section has sponsored educational events since 1988, with such major contributors to international psychoanalytic psychology as: Sidney Blatt, Stephen Mitchell, Irene Fast, and James Fosshage presenting to multidisciplinary audiences.

Blatt, Mitchell, Fast, and Fosshage were notable to our history not only for the knowledge they shared with us, but also because of the enthusiastic encouragement they left us in respect to our fantasy of creating a psychoanalytic institute in Toronto, that would open more opportunities for psychologists and other professional groups who had until very recently been largely excluded from formal psychoanalytic training at the existing (medical) psychoanalytic institute.

Stephen Mitchell provided the significant spark that finally got us moving, and so in 1989, work began in earnest by John Munn, Brent Willock, Hazel Ipp, Art Caspary, and Nira Kolers to create this second forum for psychoanalytic training. To help us in our task, we enlisted the advice of others who had already successfully helped to form such programs, most notably Karen Rosica of the Colorado Center for Psychoanalytic Studies, Charles Spezzano of the Northern California Chapter, and Jonathan Slavin of the Massachusetts Institute for Psychoanalysis.

In 1992, we took steps to incorporate the Toronto Institute for Contemporary Psychoanalysis. An advisory board was formed consisting of Howard Bacal,

Leopold Bellak, Sidney Blatt, James Fosshage, Jay Greenberg, James Grotstein, Irene Fast, Morris Eagle, Ahmed Fayek, Stephen Mitchell, Jonathan Slavin, Charles Spezzano, and Otto Weininger.

The future aspirations for the new Ontario Society for Contemporary Psychoanalysis include using our affiliation with Division 39 to further foster interest in psychoanalysis, and to provide a home base in Ontario for Division 39 members and future graduates of the new institute. This new Society will also endeavor to bring with regularity to all students of psychoanalysis throughout Ontario the current scholarship evolving on the international scene by presenting symposia of the work of local and international contributions to psychoanalysis.

We look forward to a long and stimulating affiliation with our American colleagues within the Division of Psychoanalysis.

The Philadelphia Society
for Psychoanalytic Psychology

Michael P. Kowitt
Frederic J. Levine

THE SETTING

In the 1970s and early 1980s the atmosphere in Philadelphia was generally unfavorable to psychologists interested in psychoanalysis. Although there were several graduate departments in the city, only one, the Hahnemann PsyD program (now at Widener University) was invested in a psychoanalytically based model. Other departments, and the psychology community generally, were committed to academic research, family therapy, or to a variety of behavior therapy approaches. Nevertheless, scattered faculty and students in those departments, and a significant number of psychologists in hospital or practice settings around the city, were analytically oriented; and some members of the academic community were interested in psychoanalysis from a scholarly point of view. But there was no clustering of interest, no organization that could provide these individuals with a "home" or focal setting, and the analytically oriented psychologists often found the atmosphere professionally isolating and unsupportive.

Although there was no great interest among psychologists, the situation was quite different for psychiatrists. There were two well established local affiliate societies of the APsaA, which had high prestige and were very influential in psychiatric training and psychiatric hospitals. For the psychologists training in the Hahnemann PsyD program, there was good opportunity to learn from these medical analysts, in addition to the psychologists on their faculty. However, whereas there was this ready support by psychiatrist-analysts for psychology training at the graduate level, the familiar barriers that eventually culminated in the GAPPP lawsuit prevented most psychologists from obtaining formal training at the affiliate institutes.

In addition to the affiliate institutes, several other smaller institutes and interest groups developed over the years, and provided training and professional support for a few psychologists. These groups were of various orientations, and represented varying degrees of structure and rigor. Some were spinoffs from organizations in New York, but unlike New York, there was never a strong commitment by Philadelphia psychologists to advanced training in these institutes. They did not have high visibility or prestige in the psychological community, and many of their students came from nonpsychology backgrounds.

First Steps in Founding a Society

It was against this background and context that a small group of local psychologist-psychoanalysts welcomed the advent of Division 39 and its system of local chapters, and met in early 1984 to conceive the idea of forming a chapter in Philadelphia. This initial group consisted of Frederic Levine (chair), Jules Abrams, Michael Kowitt, Lester Luborsky, and Irving Shulman, all of whom were senior psychologists who had received analytic training, and were heavily invested in psychoanalytically informed clinical and academic work. At the second meeting, in March, of what was now called the Organizing Committee for the local chapter, the original group was expanded to include Deena Adler, Cheryl Biemer, Robert Kravis, and Jane Widseth—respected psychologists who were heavily committed to psychoanalysis. During the following months this group considered the potential role and functions of a local chapter, and quickly decided that the Philadelphia area desperately needed a forum where practitioners, students, researchers, and others could begin to communicate with colleagues who shared a similar clinical and theoretical perspective. More than anything else, the Organizing Committee hoped that the chapter could become a home for local psychologists of all persuasions and from all types of work settings, who were interested in the psychoanalytic approach to psychology. We also hoped that once it developed a membership and a visible presence, it could begin to exert a positive influence on the Philadelphia psychological community, enhancing the prominence of the psychoanalytic perspective among professionals and reaching out to interested students at Hahnemann and other institutions. A third important aim was to develop a political voice in regard to issues of insurance, peer review, public policy, and the like, on which psychoanalytic practitioners had particular points of view and special needs which were not represented by existing local psychological associations. At this early time, the members of the Organizing Committee of what was soon to be called the Philadelphia Society for Psychoanalytic Psychology had real doubt that the organization would find any welcome at all among its very dispersed, apparently passive potential constituency. We therefore made the conscious decision to shape the Society as only an interest group, and to limit its membership only to psychologists, with the view that this would give it the broadest appeal to psychologists as a non-controversial, but potentially high-prestige and high-quality organization. Because the extent of psychologists' interest in psychoanalysis was quite unclear, and so few of them had sought training at the institutes that were available, at the time it seemed highly premature even to consider establishing any kind of training arm of the Society (although from the first a study group program was planned). Furthermore, because a few prospective members were already affiliated with one or another of the existing analytic societies or institutes, the group decided to avoid seeming to compete for their loyalty by establishing a training program, and/or by privileging any particular theoretical perspective over any other. Despite the concerns of the Organizing Committee, the fledgling Society had an auspicious beginning on September 21, 1984, when its first open meeting was attended by about 50 potential members, who showed enthusiastic interest in the presentation of our first speaker, Stanley Moldawsky, and in signing up as members. The Society also received welcome support from several local institutions: The Institute of Pennsylvania Hospital, a psychiatric hospital with a long psychoanalytic tradition, offered seed money and secretarial services to help us get started, and permitted its facilities to be used for meetings. Eventually, the Institute became the de facto home of PSPP, with most scientific sessions and board meetings held there. The Hahnemann University Department of Mental Health Sciences also provided administrative help as well as moral and public-relations support; and later Haverford College played an important role by co-sponsoring major meetings with the Society.

In its initial year, 1984–1985, the Society quickly grew to a membership of 80 Members, 14 Associates, and 19 Students. During that year, we sponsored three major scientific programs (with presentations by George Goldman, David Sachs, and Stanley Moldawsky), initiated a Newsletter featuring articles by members and reports and announcements of local and Divisional activities, hosted a cocktail party, and began the process of organizing seven study groups. Two of those study groups—one on self-psychology and the other on Freud's life and its relationship to his early writings and theory development—have continued to function actively up to the time of this writing, whereas other study groups have varied during those years according to members' interests and availabilities. (The Freud History group has generated several panels at national Division 39 meetings and a series of publications by its members.) PSPP also became more involved with the Division, and often sent representatives to the national meetings. During that year the Organizing Committee gave intensive consideration to finalizing the Society's formal structure, by drawing up bylaws, appointing committees, and developing fiscal policies. We were grateful for the guidance of Division 39 chapters in other cities, especially Jonathan Slavin and the Massachusetts chapter, as PSPP felt its way through these unfamiliar organizational tasks and obstacles. By early 1986, the bylaws were passed, and formal elections gave us our first Board of Directors.

Further Growth and Activities

The first president of PSPP was Frederic Levine. He was followed by Deena Adler, Michael Kowitt, Robert Kravis, Laurel Silber, Linda Hopkins, and (1991–1992) Jane Widseth. From the first, candidates for the Board, officers and committee members were sought from all segments of Philadelphia's psychological community, in an effort to represent as many as possible of its analytic institutes, theoretical persuasions, and academic and professional institutions. This has resulted in a previously unheard-of collaboration between members of these diverse groups, and the development of increased feelings of solidarity, and improved personal relationships, among many of them. Through these several years, PSPP's major activities have continued to be its program of scientific sessions and study groups, and its Newsletter. The Newsletter, first edited by Cheryl Biemer, not only announced PSPP's activities, but also became a clearinghouse where all of the city's analytic institutes and societies could list their programs and calendars. Articles were published describing all of the existing training institutes, and eventually PSPP developed a subcommittee to provide information about these to members. Likewise, our study groups reflected the wide theoretical interests of our members and have, over the years, included everything from classical topics to the ongoing study group on self-psychology. Speakers at scientific programs have included invited guests such as Roy Schafer, Fred Pine, Selma Kramer, John Pradel, Peter Swales, Nathan Stockhamer, Jonathan Slavin, Beatrice Beebe, and Elisabeth Young-Bruehl; and there has also been opportunity for PSPP's own members to present their work. The latter have included Irving Schulman, Lester Luborsky, Jules Abrams, Frederic Levine, Michael Kowitt, Randy Milden, Douglas Davis, and Norman Schaffer.

A particular highlight among our scientific programs, which went far toward putting PSPP firmly on-the-map in Philadelphia was a 2-day meeting on February 20 and 21, 1987, co-sponsored with the Haverford College Department of Psychology. This symposium, entitled "Complex Femininity: Changing Views of Women in Psychoanalytic Thought," featured excellent papers by Irene Fast, Harriet Lerner, Donald Kaplan, and Carol Gilligan, which represented a broad, challenging and highly evocative range of current psychoanalytic thinking about women and femininity. The conference's audience of about 800 students, PSPP members, and other individuals from all branches of Philadelphia's scholarly and professional communities filled a large auditorium at the College, expressed its views with an emotional intensity and involvement which made this an unforgettable occasion, and added greatly to PSPP's reputation on the local scene.

Organizational Controversies and Questions

Perhaps one of the most crucial questions that has confronted PSPP from its inception—and may equally confront all local chapters—concerns the issue of defining membership requirements. For the reasons described earlier, that is, the desire to create an organization that would appeal to all psychologists as offering a home and a venue for scholarly activities of high quality, and that would not follow the pattern of several local institutes that had trained large numbers of individuals with sub-doctoral degrees—PSPP's membership standards were set up as parallel to those of the APA: Full members had to have doctoral degrees in psychology, and other categories of membership were restricted to psychology students and Master's-level psychologists. Almost immediately several well-qualified social workers (a few with analytic training obtained in other cities) expressed interest in becoming members, but (often with regret) it was decided not to offer these individuals formal affiliation. In the ensuing years, as PSPP has become well-established as an organization psychologists wanted to join, the early feeling that it was important to go to some lengths to maintain a psychology identity has seemed less important to many members, as compared to the vitality that might come from offering membership to well-qualified individuals from the broad mental health community. In addition, with the success of the GAPPP lawsuit against APsaA, many feel that the objections which were leveled at APsaA's exclusionary policies might now be applied to PSPP. These members found the then-current requirements to be a troubling bit of hypocrisy which had to be addressed, and membership has now been expanded to include these other interested professionals.

PSPP's achievement of a secure position as a viable organization, as well as the radical changes that have occurred nationally as a result of the success of the GAPP suit and the opening of new institutes in several cities, also caused several members to feel it was time to reevaluate PSPP's traditional goal of remaining strictly an interest group, with no involvement in or commitment to psychoanalytic training. Some other members were given pause by the fact that there was no ground-swell of potential candidates seeking admission to Philadelphia's two existing APsaA institutes that are now open to (and eager for) psychologist-candidates, or to the several non-affiliate institutes that are also available; and this led them to doubt that there was need for a new training program.

In light of these contrasting points of view, PSPP began to reconsider the question of training, beginning in 1989 by conducting a poll of the membership's views. The results of this poll showed sufficient interest to lead several members to begin work toward establishing a new training institute. Their first step was to consider whether to use a model similar to those used by current local institutes, or whether to do things differently, and hopefully better.

Following the questionnaire, the Training Committee sponsored two day-long conferences on training, to consider models. First, representatives from local institutes were invited to describe their programs; and in the second conference, representatives of the New York Freudian Society, the Massachusetts Institute for Psychoanalysis, and the Michigan Psychoanalytic Council presented their innovative models. Under the leadership of Barbara Goldsmith, the Training Committee has continued to meet regularly to evaluate needs and options, to develop a mission statement and program definition, and to explore possibilities of implementing a new program in the Philadelphia community. Although some PSPP members will undoubtedly continue to train at existing institutes, others clearly prefer a new, more open, psychology-run institute, and these individuals support the Committee's efforts.

Conclusion

In summary, the last few years have been remarkable for the number of challenges and changes confronting PSPP: The Society has become an established and respected part of the Philadelphia scene; it has offered important scientific programs, set up a viable program of study groups, and developed a large and loyal membership; its board had changed membership several times, with consequent significant changes in PSPP's policies and outlook; it is now considering reversing its initial policy of a psychology-only membership; and it is taking up questions of a new training institute. With the prospect of being the host chapter for Division 39's 1992 Spring Meeting, PSPP looks forward to further challenges and opportunities, and to continuing growth and success, in the coming years.

A History of the Pittsburgh Association for the Theory and Practice of Psychoanalysis

Stanton Marlan
Terry Pulver

The development of the Pittsburgh Local Chapter of the Division of Psychoanalysis began prior to its official formation. In psychoanalysis this should no longer be surprising; there is always a prehistory which is critical for the subsequent development of the known conscious, recorded history. For the Pittsburgh Association for the Theory and Practice of Psychoanalysis, some sketching of the scene of its prehistory is necessary in order to comprehend the official history which is to follow.

Until recently Pittsburgh had but one psychoanalytic institute, a traditional medical institute, neo-Freudian in orientation. For psychologists this institute long represented high quality clinical training. As has been typical, this admiration was tempered by the general exclusion of psychologists from full clinical training. Without the notorious waiver, a psychologist was restricted to becoming a research analyst. And, in a by now familiar psychological profile, many psychologists identified with the aggressor, as it were, assuming in an uncritical fashion a version of psychoanalysis at the expense of their own standing within the institute. Stringent rules, an air of exclusivity, an aloofness often passing over into a perceived arrogance, and the fact that physicians in the 1950s and 1960s still possessed the powerful positions in the medical institutions of the city, all worked together to establish the authoritative mythos of the traditional institute. In the hospitals and the community mental health centers, where many psychologists received their training, psychiatrists held the key positions of authority, power, and prestige. This of course only served to reinforce the impression that medical psychoanalysis was the ''only game in town.''

Adding to its authoritative mythos was the fact that the local institute had many older analysts on the teaching and training faculty. By their very presence they invited virtually spontaneous transferences of paternal and maternal imagoes. Replete with formidable matriarchies and patriarchies, and the as yet untarnished prestige and omniscience of medicine, the local institute enjoyed in Pittsburgh a period of dominance over both academic and medical institutional structures where the delivery of psychological treatment was concerned.

Then something happened. During roughly the same period a major event took place at the largest psychiatric research hospital in the region. A new administrator was brought in to run Western Psychiatric Institute and Clinic (WPIC). Up to the time of his arrival the analytic institute was housed at WPIC, and its analysts enjoyed prestigious positions in the hospital. What ensued was an overt power struggle; conflicts with the new administration, the latter with an eye toward new tendencies in federally funded research, eventually led to the withdrawal of the analytic institute—and many of its analysts—from WPIC, and ushered in the new age of biological psychiatry. So acrimonious was this change in direction that a number of senior analysts and their families moved to Houston in the aftermath.

The analysts of the traditional institute were forced to set up shop on a much smaller scale outside the net of prestigious institutional affiliations they had enjoyed. Nevertheless, the traditional institute survived as a free standing program, with a somewhat diminished visibility and influence.

For some, including psychologists, this institute still represented the highest level of clinical training to be had in the city. However, its prestige continued to plummet, and not always for the same reasons as were involved at WPIC. It should be said, for example, that not all psychologists in the city accorded such a positive value to psychoanalysis in the heyday of the medical institute. On the contrary, the graduate programs in psychology at Carnegie Mellon and the University of Pittsburgh stressed cognitive and behavioral approaches, and what exposure was given to psychoanalysis, was essentially to dismiss it as an unscientific and an historical anachronism.

The psychology program at Duquesne University represented a notable divergence from the academic and theoretical climate in psychology described earlier. Duquesne was one of the only programs in the country whose theoretical orientation was existential phenomenology. Duquesne was critical of the dogmatic assumption of mainstream American psychology, namely, that the natural scientific paradigm is the appropriate one for the human science of psychology. Rooted in the Continental intellectual tradition, the Duquense Psychology elaborated a searching epistemological and methodological criticism of naive empiricism and of psychology as a natural science. Duquesne questioned the prestige given to the nineteenth century physics experiment as the one and only royal road to valid knowledge, scientific or otherwise.

Ironically, with regard to psychoanalysis, the existential phenomenological perspective essentially castigated analysis for being *too* natural scientific and reductionistic. In other words, it criticized psychoanalysis for exactly the *opposite* shortcoming of what the other more mainstream psychology programs were saying about psychoanalysis, finding the lack of natural scientific experimentation to be damning. So, for diametrically opposed reasons, the various psychology graduate programs in the area essentially dismissed traditional psychoanalysis.

However, another shift began to occur in the late 1970s and early 1980s. Other psychoanalytic study groups outside the traditional institute began to form. One such group was organized around the work of Robert Langs with its close attention to transference-countertransference issues and the question of maintaining the frame of analytic treatment. Somewhat surprisingly, another group emerged out of the Duquesne program in conjunction with the growing influence of post-structuralism and the French psychoanalysis of Jacques Lacan. A rapprochement began between existential phenomenology and psychoanalysis, primarily through theoreticians such as Foucault, Derrida, and Lacan who offered an essentially transformed postmodern version of psychoanalysis, which was responsive to the existential and phenomenological critiques of analysis in Europe from the 1950s through the 1970s.

Perhaps the most institutionally developed movement outside psychiatric psychoanalysis in Pittsburgh was the founding and subsequent development of a Jungian analytic training program. At the same time that the Jungian training program was in the process of development, Stanton Marlan became involved in Division 39. He became the first president of Section V, and subsequently the first president of the local chapter. Bringing to the local chapter the same perspective of Section V, representing theoretical pluralism and a spirit of cooperation between the differing schools of analysis, Marlan gathered with a group of interested colleagues who were to form the nucleus of the local chapter. Then on September 4, 1985, the Pittsburgh Association for the Theory and Practice of Psychoanalysis was founded. The group began with a series of lively exchanges on a variety of psychoanalytic themes and issues from diverse theoretical perspective. Nancy Thompson ably represented the orientation of Robert Langs, while Ed Emery presented case material from a Kohutian perspective. Stan Marlan offered seminars on Jungian dream analysis and Terry Pulver taught a seminar on the psychoanalysis of Lacan. The group eventually decided to become an official chapter of the Division; letters were sent out to all members of the Division in the area and the group was opened to all interested in psychoanalysis. Officers were elected: Stan Marlan became President; Thomas Acklin, Vice President; Ronald Curran was the first secretary; and Nancy Thompson the Treasurer.

Meetings continued and the chapter began to sponsor and support a variety of activities, including the formation of formal study groups, invited lecturers, workshops, and committees for such projects as the formation of a new psychoanalytic institute. Thanks to a grant from the national body of Section IV, Murray Meisels was brought in as our inaugural guest lecturer from within the Division. He presented an original reformulation of the phenomena of resistance, which was very well received.

At the end of Stan Marlan's presidency, Terry Pulver assumed the position as the next president of PATPP. Bob Romano, who had been involved since the early meetings prior to the official formation of the chapter, became the new Treasurer. Sadie Strick, a tireless worker, contributed in many ways to the cause, and became the new Secretary. Richard Asarian, who eventually succeeded Romano as our next Treasurer, has been invaluable. As the director and founder of the Eylease Institute for Forensic Psychology, Asarian has generously made training resources available to the local chapter.

Terry Pulver, who had already been an active participant in the Lacan study group of Pittsburgh prior to his presidency of the local chapter, found PATPP a natural home for that group. In fact, a number of the members of the Lacan study group in addition to Pulver became active in the development and the forging of the direction for our local chapter. Glen Sherman, Carl Bonner, Mark Grabau, and George Cherico, to mention just a few, were integral to setting up a year long calendar of events as well as establishing traditions and institutions that will be in place for years to come. Some of the events over Pulver's presidency included presentations by Wynn Schwartz, Michael Arons, and Eugene Monick.

During the course of the year, Wilma Spice offered a monthly seminar in the psychoanalytic approach to fairy tales. There were also the ongoing case colloquium and the dream seminar of Marlan, and a seminar on Freud's *Interpretation of Dreams* by Pulver. Because of the strong indigenous influence of Jungian analysis and the psychoanalysis of Jacques Lacan, there had been a rare opportunity in our local chapter for an intense comparative dialogue and sustained exchange leading to critique and reassessment of Freud and Jung from post-structural and post-modern perspectives. Pulver and Marlan have been collaborating and working through a number of traditional impasses between the Freudian and Jungian schools. Bringing to bear the post-modern perspectives of Lacanian theory and Archetypal Psychology some common ground has been reached; namely the rediscovery of the symbolic function as the essential mediation of the psychoanalytic process. This dialogue has stimulated within the local group a reflection on the theoretical foundation of psychoanalysis. The psychoanalytic, Lacanian, Jungian, and Archetypal understanding continues to be reflected on and fosters a pluralistic spirit encouraging new ideas and developments.

The open spirit of the group has helped Dr. Marlan to establish the C. G. Jung Institute Analyst Training Program as a regional site of the Inter Regional Society of Jungian Analysts, which now has six candidates, two of which are in the control stage.

In addition, the local chapter continues to encourage membership from all psychoanalytic perspectives and fosters the formation of ideas and dialogue on the future possibilities of psychoanalytic thinking and practical developments in training. One such interest is in the development of an alternative institute based on the critiques mentioned previously and revisions of theoretical foundations of analysis.

On the whole, the chapter now contains members of classical Freudian, Jungian, Lacanian, and object relations perspectives; yet what distinguishes it is a lively and hospitable interest in critical dialogue, and the questioning of the theoretical foundations of all these perspectives.

A History of the Potomac Psychoanalytic Society

Irving Raifman
Hilda J. Weissman

Shortly after Division 39 was established, Irving Raifman and Sallyann Sack received requests from representatives of the newly founded Division suggesting that a chapter be organized in the Washington, DC, community. A meeting was held at Sallyann Sack's home in the fall of 1979 with a small group, including Fonya Delong, Nancy Miller, Joanne Miller, Rochelle Kainer, Stanley Gochman, Irving Raifman, and Marilyn Keilson.

There was genuine enthusiasm, and spontaneous interest, because the Washington, DC, psychoanalytic community was overwhelmingly medical and had been pretty much closed to psychologists who sought formal institute training. Some psychologists did obtain training informally and without institute recognition or acceptance: they were analyzed by medical psychoanalysts in the community in a combined therapeutic-training mode, arranged for analytic supervision of control cases, and took courses (and taught courses) at the Washington School of Psychiatry, which accepted all mental health professionals. The School was not recognized as a training center in psychoanalysis for this and other reasons of insufficient orthodoxy. Despite the School, the medical psychoanalytic community had a virtual stronghold on the field. The Washington Psychoanalytic Training Institute had admitted a small handful of research or university psychologists over the many years of its existence, as did the Baltimore Institute. In many cases these individuals were only allowed to go as far as taking courses and receiving analyses. Most were never allowed to take on analytic cases, receive analytic supervision, or be graduated as full members.

Given the large and enthusiastic number of psychologists in the Washington, DC, area, the stage was set for the development of a vital organization. In a short time, the meetings of the Washington psychologists were so well-attended that on a given night and with a given program, more than 30 people crowded into small spaces in the homes of its members. In the spring of 1980, Sallyann Sack was installed as the interim president of the group, by then known as the Washington Psychologists for the Study of Psychoanalysis. Programs were established, and several seminars were held during the spring and fall months. Invited speakers came (e.g., Roy Schafer) and the membership grew to more than 60 members.

Meanwhile, however, true to the psychoanalytic model everywhere, rivalry and infighting developed, particularly around the training committee. The training chair, Stanley Gochman, in his attempt to provide leadership in the development of a program and the naming of a faculty and dean, felt pressured. Seeking help from the organization as a whole, he was supported in the development of a conservative program based on the existing medical institutes, including selecting training analysts who were already trained in that system. Arguments centered around not only who would teach, but what would be taught and, indeed, what constitutes psychoanalysis. One faction believed that the group already contained training resources of its own, and this group won the election of 1981, with Rochelle Kainer becoming president.

At this time, 17 members, disturbed by the intensely politicized atmosphere and personal competitiveness, formed the Potomac Psychoanalytic Society, with Irving Raifman as President. Hilda Weissman was Recording Secretary to both groups, and continued so through the year. Others also were slow to make a complete break, but by the end of that year, there were two separate groups. These 17 sought a collegial, cohesive membership of senior people with no axe to grind and no ambition other than to provide each member with an atmosphere for learning, reflecting, and growing in understanding of psychoanalytic principles, philosophy, and techniques. The group, besides Sack, Raifman, Weissman, also included May Leisinger, Reuben Horlick, Gertrude Cooper, Sam Levinson, Donna Kozuch, Marilyn Keilson, Sammie Jones, Natalie Goodman, and others. The Potomac Psychoanalytic Society was designated a local chapter of Division 39 in 1986. The earlier group asked for chapter membership later, and still later split again because of further disharmony among its members.

During Irving Raifman's 4 year stint as President of the Chapter, organizational meetings were held monthly, bylaws of the chapter were written, and the framework of an institute was developed and created. The bylaws restricted membership to those individuals acceptable to the entire membership. The Society grew ever so slowly with members leaving town or becoming involved in other issues and being replaced by the same number of people acceptable to all. Because the Division later indicated that membership in a chapter could not be restrictive, the bylaws were amended to include all interested psychologists who were members of the Division. The framework of an institute is based on the development of need, and usually occurs when younger members join a chapter. A training program would be separate and apart from the Society, and is to develop based on the following criteria:

That the student completes his analysis with "no strings attached," other than he, or she, be able to function without countertransference issues interfering with treatment; that they attain a level of maturity acceptable to their peers and supervisors; and their analysis not be in any way controlled by the institute. In addition, there is no specification on the number of hours of analysis only that it be successfully completed; no specification is placed on the number of control hours of analysis, again only that it be successfully completed; that courses require no specific length of time, or numbers. And that a host of courses are available as guidelines for the students' selection; and it is not expected that a student attain the level of maturity and skills in less than the usual 4 years of study. An analyst is identifiable as an analyst when he or she feels confident in the role, and when viewed as capable and knowledgeable by their peers and supervisors.

As of this writing, there have been no candidates selected for training. The group membership in its present form does not see the need to ask for such status, nor does it seek to work for such a title. However, there have been two courses of study open to the membership other than the monthly meetings and presentations, namely, an ongoing study group and a seminar.

In the past, the Potomac Chapter also conducted a biweekly seminar that was devoted to case presentations, and which was led by yet another training analyst in the Washington area. This seminar ran for 2 years and will resume upon demand. Following Raifman's four successive terms of office, Samuel Levinson served as president for 2 years, Hilda Weissman for 1 year, and May Leisinger is the current president.

The Southeast Florida Association for Psychoanalytic Psychology: A Retrospective and Prospective

Antonio R. Virsida

BACKGROUND

The initiative for the establishment of the Southeast Florida Association for Psychoanalytic Psychology (SEFAPP) arose out of motives similar to those which had led to the establishment of the Division of Psychoanalysis. Psychoanalysis in Southeast Florida, notably Miami, Hollywood, Ft. Lauderdale, Boca Raton, and West Palm Beach as the major population centers, developed along slightly different paths when compared to most other areas of the country. Except for cities like New York and Los Angeles, local chapters of the Division of Psychoanalysis have preceded the development of training institutes. In Southeast Florida, a university-based and psychologist-operated psychoanalytic training institute preceded the establishment of the local chapter. Nova University's Postdoctoral Institute for Psychoanalysis and Psychotherapy (PDI) in Ft. Lauderdale, Florida, was at the time of its inauguration, in 1983, the only psychologist-operated psychoanalytic institute in the Southeastern United States. Launched by (former APA President) Max Siegel and Harold Lindner, Nova's PDI accepted its first class of eight candidates in 1983 and began a certificate granting training program in 1984 under the direction of Harold Lindner. Because there were approximately 20 trained psychoanalysts in Southeast Florida, and because both Siegel and Lindner were newcomers and relatively unfamiliar with the mental health community of Southeast Florida, Nova University's PDI looked toward New York for faculty members and affiliation with established training organizations.

Miami had a tradition of psychoanalytic study, training, and treatment at least since the mid-1950s. Although the Florida Psychoanalytic Society, a group under the auspices of the APsaA's Baltimore-Washington Institute for Psychoanalysis, enriched the local community, psychologists in Southeast Florida who were interested in psychoanalytic training faced obstacles similar to psychologists in other parts of the country.

Within this context, SEFAPP was launched by a disparate, but similarly minded group of psychologists including Christopher Corrie, Milton Eber, Robert C. Lane, Harold Lindner, Carl Newman, Bady Quintar and Antonio Virsida. Milton Eber and Harold Lindner were catalysts in the formation of SEFAPP, and Christopher Corrie and Robert Lane brought a wealth of knowledge and experience to the local organizing effort. Lane served SEFAPP in an ex-officio capacity.

A NEW ORGANIZATION

Milton Eber was appointed pro-tem President, Carl Newman served as pro-tem Treasurer, and Antonio Virsida served as pro-tem Secretary. The remaining charter members served as Board Members. All of the original SEFAPP Organizational Committee members were on the faculty of Nova University's PDI and, except for Bady Quintar, were members of Section I.

As early as the third board meeting in March 1988, we recognized the importance of recruiting members and of establishing organizational structures through drafting and ratifying bylaws. Also, in March 1988, we held our inaugural scientific meeting, which featured a presentation by Robert C. Lane and was attended by over 20 persons. Most of the attendees were candidates and faculty members from Nova University's PDI.

The next meeting content was primarily organized by discussions of external contacts and the lines of organizational authority within the context of the development of a Newsletter. The question of the role of the Board or Board Members as final arbiter and editor of the newsletter was discussed. We unanimously agreed that the "editor-in-chief [would] be a senior person in psychoanalysis." At this point, we also agreed to invite three psychologists, all Nova University PDI candidates, to become Board Members. Two of the three, Dorita Marina and Richard Westberry, accepted the invitation. This resulted in two changes; Nova's PDI and "junior persons in psychoanalysis" were further represented on the SEFAPP Board. At the meeting, Milton Eber suggested and the Board agreed to invite Daniel Stern to present his work on infant development to our membership and the mental health community. We thought it politically wise to invite two well-known Miamians to discuss Dr. Stern's work.

Three months after our initial scientific meeting, SEFAPP had a total of 18 members of which 10 were in Division 39. The Scientific Meeting was well attended and received. A consensus was reached that SEFAPP would invite our members to serve as presenters and discussants.

By October 1988, our membership had risen to 37. Most of our attention was given over to planning our scientific program and our Newsletter. The bylaws draft was again tabled until the next meeting. By February 1989, following conflict regarding membership standards, we completed a final draft of bylaws. The conflict was between those who wanted at least two categories of membership, based on the possession of a license to practice in Florida, and those who desired one membership category, to include persons who were interested in psychoanalysis, as well as licensed practitioners. The former membership definition carried, causing distress to those who viewed SEFAPP as an interest organization. Our attentions were then focused on the publication of a Newsletter and our scientific programs.

With the inaugural issue of SEFAPP's Newsletter soon to be published, a heated debate ensued about what details would be published regarding the lawsuit settlement. The Board voted against publishing a full report of the settlement, opting instead for a brief statement that the Institute for Psychoanalytic Training and Research (IPTAR) was the first non-APsaA training institute in the United States to be granted Provisional Status by the IPA. The controversy organized around whether a fuller report of the lawsuit settlement would be offensive to psychiatrist/psychoanalysts. One group thought that a fuller report would reflect us to be gloating, whereas the other group considered the settlement to be a milestone of multiple meanings, worthy of sensitive but full reporting. It was as if we were uncertain about our role as victor and whether we had the sensitivity and power to be authorities.

As judged by the quality of its scientific meetings, SEFAPP seemed to be thriving. Owing to Milton Eber's familiarity with a range of psychoanalysts, we held stimulating scientific meetings. Presentations by Robert Lane, Daniel Stern, Doris Silverman, Leslie Lothstein, Jay Greenberg, and Jed Sekoff were funded from a small treasury derived from membership dues, Board members donations and a Section IV grant. These excellent presentations were fairly well attended and very well received by our membership. Our membership grew to more than 40 and included psychologists, social workers, and master-level mental health professionals. Although we were excited and pleased about our apparent success, conflicts intensified as we approached the nomination and election of officers and Board Members. SEFAPP had been operating without ratified bylaws which, in essence, spelled out the nomination and election procedures.

REORGANIZATION

Some procedural questions were raised by the Board and Section IV was called on for assistance. Following Section IV's recommendations—that SEFAPP's first and second orders of business were, respectively, the ratification of bylaws and the nomination and election of Board members and officers by the general membership—there was a reorganization of the structure of SEFAPP.

A scientific and general business meeting was held on December 9, 1990. Over 20 persons attended a presentation by Fredric J. Levine, of Philadelphia. Nine of those attendees volunteered to serve on an expanded Organizational Committee. By March 1990, the bylaws were ratified and a scientific meeting was attended by over 30 persons. By April 1990, the nominations and elections were completed and Volume 2, Number 1 of SEFAPP's revised Newsletter *Psyche and Sol*, was published and distributed. Since then SEFAPP's membership had grown to more than 90 and scientific meetings have been attended by increasingly large numbers of members and non-members. The Education Committee initiated a Symposium/Brunch Series providing an informal forum for members presentation of papers and works in progress, as well as an opportunity for social exchange. Two study groups have formed, while two more are in the process of development. SEFAPP's proposal to Division 39's Committee on International Relations for funding of an educational exchange program with the Buenos Aires Psychoanalytic Society was approved. The SEFAPP Board is currently planning for our inaugural centerpiece, an annual half- or all-day conference that will feature internationally prominent psychoanalysts and discussants.

SEFAPP's Board and officers are representative of the community of professionals interested in psychoanalysis and includes senior psychoanalysts and former Board members. SEFAPP's reorganized Board values diversity and evolution, while maintaining a commitment to high standards of psychoanalytic discourse at various levels. The shift of emphasis from identity and standards to diversity and discourse is consistent with the changes that took place in the Division of Psychoanalysis.

DISCUSSION

Although there are similarities in the evolution and development of SEFAPP and Division 39, perhaps other local chapters as well, the absence of uniformity of experience and identity among Southeast Florida psychologist/psychoanalysts had an important influence on the organization and its functioning. Retrospectively, identity issues were stirred at each of our Board and scientific meetings. SEFAPP's original Board members had pursued their training interests in psychoanalysis along different paths and traditions. Three were trained in independent institutes created for the training of non-medical analysts, one studied privately, one trained in England, and another secured self-oriented psychoanalytic training as part of his training and experience as a psychologist. Such variation in experience and orientation and its possible influences affected our efforts to establish a local chapter in Southeast Florida. The conditions of local professional isolation and deprivation of recognition either threatened or touched all of us. We were for the most part transplants from other geographic areas, loyal to our prior experiences, and had difficulties in appreciating the requirements of the new context. We proceeded in a sequence from tenuous affiliation and conflict to redefinition and reorganization.

In conclusion, the preparation and writing of this chronicle leads to the hopeful sense that, although we repeated some of the mistakes of the past, we also have grown sufficiently to integrate, learn, and benefit from our differences.

The Southern California Chapter

Robert M. Aguado

Like in most communities in the United States, psychoanalysis in Southern California was held hostage, under exclusive medical domain. The two Los Angeles medical institutes, their graduates, and their societies limited the educational practice of psychoanalysis to MDs, with rare inclusion of an outstanding psychologist under waiver, and limited to research. Psychologists especially chaffed under this oppressive domination of the area Freud called psychology!

In the early 1970s, a group of psychologists and social workers came together to form their own institute in Los Angeles. Most apprenticed themselves by gaining a psychoanalytic education in a self-styled program with analysts who were bravely willing to analyze, supervise, and participate in clinical seminars and study groups. A few had obtained certification as psychoanalysts through institute training elsewhere. Along with an analyst not affiliated with APsaA, this group, under Ernest Lawrence's leadership, formed the Los Angeles Institute for Psychoanalytic Studies and began their first class of candidates.

Later, the Los Angeles Institute for Psychoanalytic Studies reached out further into community activity and began offering some courses for mental-health practitioners. Soon, an advanced group of psychoanalytically oriented practitioners formed the Los Angeles Society for Psychoanalytic Studies for collegial interaction, to study and to keep abreast of developments in psychoanalysis. For some, this became a springboard for beginning formal psychoanalytic training as candidates at the Los Angeles Institute for Psychoanalytic Studies.

The close relationship between the Institute and the then Society (study group) continued for some years. Faculty from the Institute served as presidents of the Society, presented papers and supervised programs. Several of the senior candidates also began to serve as presidents.

The Los Angeles Institute for Psychoanalytic Studies decided that their own activities within the Institute proper were becoming too extensive, and they were approaching graduating candidates within a formal society structure. The writer was asked to take over as President of the Study Group. The Los Angeles Institute for Psychoanalytic Studies separated itself from its formal tie to the Los Angeles Society for Psychoanalytic Studies.

The Study Group continued quite actively with this leadership. We mostly presented papers and had prominent analysts from the community who were usually quite willing to participate in programs to this group of interested mental-health professionals. Many of us were advanced clinicians with much training and experience in psychoanalytic work, but without certification as psychoanalysts (i.e., institute graduated).

We mostly met in my home. With valuable and important collaborative help and contributions, the programs were excellent and mostly in an intimate and collegial atmosphere. So, through the early 1980s, we met, studied and assisted each other in our own psychoanalytic work, adding a few people congenial to our efforts.

Efforts of our burgeoning Society were reported to the Division 39 Newsletter. It was with great pleasure that George Goldman and Bob Lane contacted me regarding the emergence of a Section within the Division to service and assist in the formation of Local Chapters. Representatives from about 15 groups around the country (outside of the heavily concentrated Greater New York area) met at the William Alanson White Institute in New York in December, 1984. Through the leadership of Murray Meisels, George Goldman, Bob Lane and Charles Spezzano, Section IV, Local Chapters, was formed.

With this enthusiasm and mutual support, the writer was highly motivated. Upon returning, he immediately convened a small leadership group of the Society to form a Local Chapter in Los Angeles. A meeting was announced for this purpose to all Division 39 members in greater Los Angeles (from Ventura to San Diego). A small group attended and many others indicated their support, although unable to attend. Our Society members also attended, and supported the formation of a Chapter. That group elected temporary officers and basic committees were formed (membership, bylaws, finance, dues, etc.). The officers also nominated a Board of Directors from interested individual psychoanalytic practitioners and representatives from significant organizations (i.e., professional–social work, nursing, psychiatry) as well as the psychoanalytically oriented training centers. This integrated psychoanalytic practitioners into one umbrella organization.

Several obstacles were encountered along the way similar to that in the development of other chapters. In our case, one of our original officers did not fulfill that temporary position, and instituted a writing campaign against the

Chapter. He sent voluminous briefs to the Section IV Senate and to the Board of Directors of Division 39, who were upset by these lengthy reports of our alleged misdeeds. In addition to this difficulty, our former parent group objected to the establishment of *any* Chapter in Los Angeles. They maintained that they legitimately represented psychological psychoanalysis in Los Angeles, and that a Chapter would dilute the efforts for psychoanalysis. The Division 39 Board, after reviewing all the facts, unanimously supported our position, at their Board meeting in August, 1986, and we then became officially the Southern California Chapter of Division 39.

Our membership has increased from the original 23 members in our organizing group to over 350 mental health professionals, with regular monthly scientific meetings, a group consultation program and individual study groups. We serve as an umbrella group for mental health professionals in our community, doing psychoanalytic work, as well as for representatives of established groups and agencies engaged in psychoanalytic practice and education. Representatives of the latter are members of our Board of Directors.

Division 39 is a productive force in our psychoanalytic community. The Chapter is currently assisting in the establishment of a psychoanalytic institute drawn from the membership of the Chapter. The Academy for Psychoanalysis is being formed with the aim to promote psychoanalytic education and practice from a more democratic and open process of education structured around a basic core curriculum, which then goes on to meet the individual candidate's own needs and interests. As in Michigan and Massachusetts, special attention will be paid to the advanced clinician and the problem of equivalency in an open Academy that encompasses training both within and outside the Academy. This has been accomplished in my affiliation as co-chair of the Department of Psychoanalysis at the California Graduate Institute under its president, Marvin Koven.

A Brief History
of the Vermont Chapter

Mark Adair

In 1979, there were two psychologist-psychoanalysts in Vermont. One of them was Rudolph Moz, then of Montpelier. Moz completed his psychoanalytic training in the 1960s, and came to Vermont in 1970. The other was Mark Adair, who trained in the 1970s, and settled in Montpelier in 1979. In 1983, Moz and Adair began weekly case discussions. With rumors abroad of a national local chapter movement, Moz suggested that this group of two elevate itself into a Vermont local chapter. Preparations were begun. Soon thereafter, Robert Barasch joined the weekly meetings. Barasch, a clinical psychologist, was one of the first psychologists to be licensed by the state of Vermont.

These three prepared to launch a Vermont Chapter whenever the national structure was established, but were dealt a blow when Rudolph Moz left Montpelier to relocate in Seattle. The group could now claim only one official Division 39 member—Mark Adair—and it had drawn perilously close to extinction. The new group of two redoubled its recruitment efforts, and by 1985 the Vermont Chapter had swollen to five members: one full, four associates. At this time Adair learned that the national structure was in place, and applications for charters were being taken. He applied for membership on behalf of the group, and the application was accepted.

With membership still so small, the group remained basically unorganized for 2 more years. In 1987, Carole Betts, a Canadian analyst and member of the IPA, joined the Vermont chapter. After some discussion, the group began in the Spring of 1987 to plan a scientific meeting and introductory seminars on psychoanalytic theory and technique. Despite many obstacles and setbacks, and with no outside assistance, VAPS (The Vermont Association for Psychoanalytic Studies) has put together five successful scientific meetings, and numerous seminars. The group has nearly 50 members, who live or practice in six states and Canada. After 6 years, the founder of the group, Rudolph Moz, returned to Vermont.

A History of Washington Psychologists
for the Study of Psychoanalysis

Nancy R. Goodman
Patricia Freiberg

WPSP is headed into its tenth year and continues on a steady growth path. What started as a small group of colleagues meeting in each other's homes has developed into a large interdisciplinary and complex organization. It has gone through one name change and has it's twelfth president this year. Its membership has increased from 20 people to the current 150 and is still attracting new members, recently voting to include a student status. With expansion has also come a continual process of defining and redefining of our identity as an organization friendly and encouraging to all viewpoints within psychoanalytic thought and practice. WPSP has proved to be sturdy and able to sustain conflict and tension when they have arisen. One major issue, the organization's role in training, has periodically surfaced producing outright conflict and at times splitting. An outstanding feature of the organization has been the establishment of a variety of educational arenas for membership and the community at large. We have seen steady growth in the amount and quality of types of professional offerings as well as in collaboration with other local chapters and involvement with national and indeed international psychoanalytic concerns. In this chapter, we take you through the maturing of the organization and also highlight some of the main issues which have risen over the years.

The birth of the organization took place in 1980, when Sallyann Amdur Sack called together an initial meeting of colleagues interested in psychoanalysis to develop a local chapter of Division 39. The initial impetus occurred shortly after Division 39 was organized. Sallyann Sack had been a candidate in the Baltimore-Washington Psychoanalytic Institute and had been refused a waiver unless willing to give up her private practice. Having read an article about Division 39 written by Murray Meisels, Sack decided to write Meisels and tell him of her experience. He wrote back that such experiences were common and were one reason for the formation of Division 39.

From its founding, training has been a major issue attracting membership and at some times causing splits. It was clear from the outset that psychologists wanted and needed a place to discuss their clinical and theoretical interests in psychoanalysis and psychoanalytic psychotherapy. Out of the energy of giving birth to a new organization, two major events occurred: conflict and cohesion. From the outset, members joined the group with clear ideas of what they wanted and needed. A very early effort was made to establish a training institute. Very quickly though, it became evident that there was no agreement nor compromise around what that institute would teach. The fundamental definition of, "what is psychoanalysis?" was impossible to resolve and differences of opinions between members defined factions more than a commonality of purpose. Out of that, the organization's first split occurred with some members developing a separate local chapter, the Potomac Psychoanalytic Society. Most importantly, the divisiveness then led to a coming together of ideas that provided a basis for the philosophy which has formed a solid base for WPSP becoming the largest interest group of psychoanalytically oriented clinicians in the Washington, DC, area. The remaining members of the original group agreed that the purpose of WPSP was to create a lively interest group for mental-health professionals, as well as professionals in related fields, who wished to share and explore ideas and information about psychoanalytic theory and practice. The organization embraced divergent schools of psychoanalytic thought, including, but not limited to, drive theory, object relations, self-psychology, and ego psychology. This central philosophy has become translated into a variety of functions of the group.

In the first few years of the organization, monthly meetings took place with two agendae. The first part of the meetings were spent on business aspects of the group. After that, a member presented a paper or led a discussion group. In addition, study groups were formed around topics of interest to members. All members were welcome to attend any of the study groups or meetings. Out of those years developed an atmosphere of respect for one another's ideas, a genuine sharing of thought, and an intense interest in learning. A visitor walking into a living room meeting would have felt the comraderie and salon type feeling. There was always good food, and lots of interaction. Lively debate occurred reinforcing the overall attitude that WPSP was a place to discuss all schools of psychoanalysis without needing to align with any one. That attitude still prevails.

With growth, the functions have expanded and the meeting places had to be reconsidered. By 1987, WPSP had to change its meeting place out of members' living rooms to a large room of a church. Current membership consists of about 50% Full members and 50% Associate members. Full members are psychologists who belong to Division 39 whereas Associate members are both psychologists and representatives of other disciplines. Concurrent with growth, there have been administrative and format changes. In the beginning, Board meetings took place half an hour before regular monthly meetings often taking issues immediately to the membership for consideration and voting. The combination of increased membership and more intense involvement in national issues such as Division 39, resulted in a change in the administration. Because it became too cumbersome to discuss everything in a larger group and because more time was needed for the growing number of issues, the Board was expanded and meetings held on a separate night. Board meetings are open to all members and most decisions are now made within the Board meetings. When it is necessary to take issues to the membership, it is now done quite formally with mailed ballots. Bylaws are continually revised.

As WPSP matured, the members decided to bring in outside speakers for a few evening lectures and/or workshops. Dinner meetings were held for the general membership starting in 1982, and became open to the community at large starting in 1985. As membership continued to increase, desire to communicate basic information along with summaries of presentations led to the publication of a monthly Newsletter. Subsequently an archives committee was formed to both keep copies of presentations and to have a way to disseminate copies to those interested. The Newsletter is now an essential vehicle of communication informing people of all activities both within the organization and within the larger psychoanalytic community.

The issue of training arose again around 1986 when a group of members who were already involved in teaching and training wished to have their group become a training arm of WPSP. That idea was rejected by the Board mainly because of concerns over issues of cohesion. Once again WPSP decided to keep its main philosophy and definition in line with being an umbrella organization open to all psychoanalytic viewpoints and being a general interest group for the professional community. Subsequent to this decision, the group which has been interested in training became the third local chapter in the DC area. For WPSP, the issue of training has been a complicated one which has consistently led to reinforcing the philosophy of the organization as a meeting ground for diversity and a desire to not become defined exclusively with any one viewpoint within the lively field of psychoanalysis. It may well be, that this part of our history is related in part to our presence in Washington, DC, where diverse training opportunities exist.

The organization continues to manifest its vitality. In 1989, WPSP sponsored a Freudian Legacy Conference, drawing from the general professional community and meeting in a hotel downtown. The Executive Board has, over the years, grown in the scope of its functioning. This past year, it had a day-long retreat to discuss the direction of the organization and future events. The Newsletter, while still a monthly offering, has been expanded. In addition, a periodical was introduced last year that summarizes papers and highlights the intellectual life of the organization. Most exciting, the membership is looking forward to hosting two Russian psychologists in 1990–1991. They will discuss with us the renewed interest in psychoanalysis in the Soviet Union, as well as participate in a mutual sharing of ideas. Not only has our interest expanded internationally, but WPSP is also more active and interested in the national issues of Division 39. More members are attending and becoming involved on national committees.

Over the past decade the organization has remained consistent in defining itself as a general psychoanalytic organization. It has remained open to the various schools of thought within psychoanalysis and continues to attract a growing membership who feel welcomed and at home. In the interest of remaining a broad-based organization, development of a training branch has not occurred. Because WPSP is located in a city that offers a multitude of training opportunities, many members do choose to avail themselves of training. In addition, members continue to be excited about pursuing a variety of theoretical and clinical interests and to expand the learning opportunities available within WPSP. We are clearly on the map in the Washington area community as the largest gathering of professionals interested in psychoanalysis. Professionals who define themselves as psychoanalytically oriented and want lively intellectual and social interaction with colleagues find these needs fulfilled through participation in WPSP.

The Presidents of WPSP have been: Sallyann Amdur Sack (President pro tem), 1980–1981; Sallyann Amdur Sack, 1981–1982; Rochelle G. K. Kainer, 1982–1983; Susannah J. Gourevitch, 1983–1984; Fonya Helm (formerly DeLong), 1984–1985; Thomas R. Kraft, 1985–1986; Shelley Rockwell, 1986–1987; Mildred W. Goldstone, 1987–1988; Harriet I. Basseches, 1988–1989; JoAnn Reiss, 1989–1990; Rona Eisner, 1990–1991; Denise Fort, 1991–1992; Mary Ann Dubner, 1992–1993; and Tessa Cochran, 1993–1994.

ACKNOWLEDGMENTS

We wish to thank the past and present presidents for their sharing of information and insight concerning the growth and development of WPSP.

A Brief History of the Washington Society of Psychoanalytic Psychology

Rochelle G. K. Kainer

The narrative of the history of the Washington Society of Psychoanalytic Psychology (WSPP) is best understood in the context of the whole local chapters movement in the District of Columbia area because their origins were intertwined. WSPP became an official chapter of Division 39 in 1988, but has been in existence since 1981 when it became clear that issues of training and formal education might topple the founding Washington Psychologists for the Study of Psychoanalysis (WPSP), our home base group which intended to be an interest group. In those pre-lawsuit days (against the APsaA), except for a few who had previous ties to Division 39, there was much less local interest in Section IV, with more interest in obtaining training, and going about it either through the medical institutes which were limitedly open to psychologists or by affiliating with a New York (Freudian) institute which was governed by psychologists. The effect of the lawsuit had definitely heightened awareness of the psychologists role in psychoanalysis and seems to have given a sense of permission to those who were previously hesitant to take their place in psychoanalysis separate from a medical authority.

Those involved with WSPP were primarily interested in a non-institute model of psychoanalytic education, now referred to (see proceedings of the Clark Conference: *Tradition and Innovation in Psychoanalytic Education*) as the Open Model. We were characterized as rugged individualists (ibid, p. 6). That probably was so, but one hardly thought about that as we went about our business of educating ourselves and others. Those initially involved with this phase of our development were Susannah Gourevitch, Rochelle Kainer, Rosemary Segalla, Monica Callahan, Barbara Wood, and Tom Kraft, with Gourevitch and Kainer the most active with the Section.

Our educational aims were administered through the WSPP arm: the Association for Psychoanalytic Study (ASP). It was a highly structured, noncredentialling 4-year program, with two, year-long courses each year. It ran in that form from 1981 to 1987. Then Section IV, which began to formally recognize local chapters in 1985, reversed its thinking on multiple local chapters.

The ideal became the single regional chapter, wherever possible, as formulated by the Division. With this shift and with so much individual overlap of WSPP and WPSP people, it was suggested that the former be under the umbrella of the latter. There was some uneasiness with that, and during a series of Board meetings of both organizations, the proposal was rejected. At that time, there was still little local interest in the Division. By the time the issue of formalization came up in the Local Chapters Senate, several crucial changes had occurred. There was a loss of institutional memory as new people replaced the old in WPSP and some uncertainty as to how it would function (i.e., as an interest group or in some training role). In addition, interest in Division 39 among the new group became stronger. All this (plus organizational naivete) had the unfortunate effect of strain between the two organizations in the early formal phases of WSPP.

However, as time has gone on, and through the efforts of many, the two organizations have reclaimed their original differing identities and co-exist profitably, with many Division 39 members and those that share a similar interest in psychoanalysis holding joint membership. In addition, the two groups also serve separate memberships, meeting specific needs which are not duplicated by the other group, such as courses (WSPP) and monthly meetings (WPSP). The first formal election of WSPP officers, with Rosemary Segalla, as President was held in 1989, succeeding a pro-tem board with R.G. Kainer as President pro-tem. Millie Goldstone, President-Elect, will take office in September of 1991. Elections are bi-yearly. WSPP has actively participated in the Federation meetings as a natural extension of interest in the local chapters movement.

The activities of WSPP have continued around the giving of formal courses, the most extensive at this writing is a three semester program on the theoretical and clinical issues in object relations and self psychology. Free standing courses are also being offered. The signature event has been the Fall lecture following the theme of psychoanalysis applied to the arts and humanities. We have also held a two day psychopharmacology seminar and have begun a Clinical Dialogue Saturday morning series that will include such topics as self psychology as applied to couples and groups, sadomasochism, the anti-libidinal ego, and addictions. With its members special interest in creativity, the formation of an expanded Newsletter, *Analytic Reflections*, is in preparation. It will contain analytic reviews of books and films, short psychological fiction, and guest columns. Thus, it probably can be said that our history indicates many people profiting from the resolution of what may be the inevitable conflicts of human desires and human wills.

The Western Massachusetts
and Albany Association
for Psychoanalytic Psychology

Paul Lippmann

Although there has been a rich psychoanalytic tradition in this largely rural part of the country, the many psychotherapists who practice here (in the Berkshires of Western Massachusetts—from Bennington, Vermont and Williamstown through Pittsfield and Stockbridge to Northwest Connecticut; in the Pioneer Valley to the East—from Keane, New Hampshire through Amherst and Northampton to Springfield; and in the Albany area to the west) have had little or no opportunity for collective professional development involving psychoanalytic thinking, practice, and training.

While our countryside has long been home to a significant literary and artistic tradition emphasizing themes of psychological depth and complexity (e.g., Hawthorne, Melville, Dickinson, etc.), psychoanalysis came to these parts in a significant way, beginning in 1948, when the Austen Riggs Center in Stockbridge welcomed an extraordinary group of creative psychoanalytic thinkers and clinicians (many moving here from Menningers). These included Robert Knight, Erik Erikson, David Rapaport, Merton Gill, Margaret Brenman, Roy Schafer, David Shapiro, Joseph Chassell, Edgerton Howard—a heady mixture of clinical psychologists and psychiatrists. Their pioneering work in theoretical and clinical psychoanalysis, however, did not extend much to the growing professional community's need for psychoanalytic discussion outside the confines of Austen Riggs.

As the population of psychotherapists working in clinics, in university psychology departments, in counseling centers, in psychiatric facilities and in private practice continued to grow, early efforts at organizing were largely unsuccessful. Perhaps the tradition of independent individualism characteristic of Western New Englanders played a role in maintaining a certain separateness and autonomy among us. Perhaps our rural nature worked against the kind of organizational efforts more characteristic of metropolitan urban settings. In any event, the early development of Division 39 and its hospitality to local organizations gave new impetus to the possibilities of our beginning to form a group devoted to psychoanalytic thinking in a broad sense.

In the early stages of the development of WMAAPP, Stephen Klein and Ester Shapiro from MAPP in Boston, Robin Siegal and John Wapner from Albany, and Frances Lippmann, Paul Lippmann and David Lotto from the Berkshires were instrumental, following an initial organizational meeting in 1986, in guiding our group over the next two years from a subsection of MAPP to independent status as a local chapter of Division 39. While most members are psychologists, we have been open, from the beginning, to participation by any interested professional.

Activities that have begun to address our need for psychoanalytic discussion have included courses and seminars as students and teachers are available (e.g., case seminars, introductory phases in psychoanalytic psychotherapy, dream interpretation, object relations theory, etc.), ongoing groups and workshops on ideas in progress, and both large and small professional meetings at which a mix of local, national and international figures in psychoanalysis have presented their ideas (e.g., Morris Eagle, Roy Schafer, Andrew Morrison, Adam Phillips, Harold Boris, Margaret Brenman). Our interests are widespread and have included meetings on the relationship between family therapy and psychoanalysis, on different paths to psychoanalytic practice, on psychoanalytic treatment of severely disturbed persons, on Ferenczi's impact on psychoanalysis, on the war against depth psychology as seen locally in the burgeoning impact of HMOs, and so on. To now, we have successfully maintained an open and pluralistic approach, embracing the rich diversity of psychoanalytic discussion.

In addition to the early members mentioned above, the following have been significantly involved in organizational and teaching activities: Jonathan Aronoff (current President), Harold Raush (our first President), Edward Emery, Eleanor Skinner, Joan Burkhard, Ted Ellenhorn, Tricia Everett, Norma Johnson, Harold Jarmon, and Gerard Fromm. We are a group with diverse orientations: classical and modern Freudian, interpersonal, object relational, self psychological, Jungian and others. We are a group where professional category is less relevant than interest in matters psychoanalytic. While depth psychology comes increasingly under attack from the general market orientation and the surge toward simplistic solutions in the surrounding culture, from the specific machinations of the HMOs, from departments of psychology and psychiatry that emphasize short term and organic-chemical solutions, it is increasingly important to remain connected to a pluralistic psychoanalytic psychology that emphasized the richness for practice and research of individual life study in depth.

There are several hundred professionals on our mailing list and about 80 members. We grow slowly, and attempt to maintain the warm friendliness and open cooperative spirit of our beginnings.

V

Allied Organizations

It is typical of organizations to form allied, arms-length associations to perform certain functions. For example, because of APA's policy that only it may accredit, local chapters have developed allied institutes to train and accredit in psychoanalysis. Those newfound institutes have now aggregated to form a Federation, which is discussed later. Similarly, the Foundation was formed to raise nontaxable funds, and GAPPP was developed to prosecute the lawsuit.

The Psychoanalytic Lawsuit: Expanding Opportunities for Psychoanalytic Training and Practice

Arnold Z. Schneider
Helen Desmond

> *Psychoanalysis is not a particular branch of medicine. I do not see how anyone can refuse to recognize this. Psychoanalysis is part of psychology—not even a medical psychology in the old sense of the term . . . but simply of psychology.*
> —Freud (1927, pp. 392–393)

Freud's words about the place of psychoanalysis, long denied and refuted by APsaA, have finally been realized. After five decades of medical/psychiatric hegemony over the training and practice of psychoanalysis in the United States, access to clinical training for clinical psychologists has been won. What is now known as, "The Psychoanalytic Lawsuit" was a Federal Anti-Trust Class Action lawsuit brought about by four psychologist plaintiffs against the APsaA, the New York Psychoanalytic Institute, the Columbia University Center for Psychoanalytic Training and Research, and the IPA. This chapter chronicles the historical roots, sequential development, and current resolution of this venture from the point of view of two of the plaintiffs.

Prologue

From its beginning in the United States and contrary to international practice, psychoanalysis was dominated by the medical establishment. The founding of APsaA came on the heels of the Flexner Report, which directed attention to raising the standards of medical education in this country and controlling the numerous medical diploma mills in existence at that time. Within this context,

APsaA (then primarily located in New York City) justified excluding nonphysicians from psychoanalytic training by arguing, "that the laws of New York State forbade it" (Oberndorf, 1953, p. 182) and established itself as the protector of the public from charlatans.

The early 1900s, when psychoanalysis was introduced, was a time of tremendous change in the world order. Civilization experienced the discovery of X-rays, the confirmation of radioactivity (antecedent to the concept of components of the nucleus of the atom), quantum physics, the science of genetics, and remarkable numbers of disturbing new movements in literature, music, and art reflecting the challenges of adapting to this new world. In the words of Clark: "Opposition to psychoanalysis was . . . more determined and less compromising than the conservative forces that fought rear-guard actions in science and art and literature" (Clark, 1980, p. 180).

Throughout its history, achieving legitimacy has been a dominant concern of the psychoanalytic community. In Europe, Freud, chafing at his failure to achieve academic recognition, welcomed nonmedical practitioners. In the United States the early practitioners of psychoanalysis sought acceptance and legitimacy by placing themselves under the banner of the medical establishment. In so doing, they emphasized psychoanalysis as a method of treatment and neglected its importance as a general psychology. Consequently, many European trained analysts and potential non-medical contributors were ostracized (Jacoby, 1986)—in effect limiting psychoanalysis' scholarly tradition while elevating its practice function. Ironically, in the long-term, psychoanalysis in the United States had come to be seen as overselling itself, and has lost credibility in the very eyes of those it was attempting to woo (Kirsner, 1990).

The exclusionary training practices conducted by APsaA clearly reflected its preoccupation with psychoanalysis as a practice—an emphasis very different from Freud's and one that the plaintiffs claimed was motivated in large part by economic concerns. Although economic damage was the necessary condition for legal means to redress this situation, from the outset the plaintiffs considered the more important issue to be the reversal of the process of stultification in psychoanalysis in the United States. Resuscitation of this important general psychology and method of treatment is the challenge now before both APsaA and non-APsaA affiliated researchers, theoreticians, and practitioners of psychoanalysis.

PRECURSORS TO THE LAWSUIT

Freud's (1926) defense of Theodor Reik and of so-called "lay analysis" (an unfortunate and antiquated term, erroneously suggestive of differences between analyses with medical and nonmedical analysts) and the 1927 symposium on lay analysis sponsored by the IPA outlined the various sides of the debate on nonmedical training, but did nothing to alter the restrictive situation in the United States. Actually, matters were shortly to worsen. With the shadow of Hitler looming over Europe, many European analysts fled Europe for America, swelling the ranks of analysts in the United States and engendering fears of economic competition alongside concerns for preservation of standards. That one third to one half of the immigrant analysts were not physicians exacerbated these fears while also threatening the medical hegemony of U.S. psychoanalysis.

By the late 1930s, APsaA constituted approximately two thirds of the IPA membership, placing it in a position of almost unquestioned political authority. In 1938, APsaA came to the last pre-war IPA Congress with two demands: an "exclusive franchise" on training in psychoanalysis in the United States and "total internal autonomy" regarding the establishment and monitoring of standards for training (Wallerstein as quoted by Shane, 1988). Thus was established what came to be known as the "1938 rule." Invoking "the 1938 rule," APsaA formally declared that there would be no training of nonphysicians in psychoanalysis. Later, during the course of the lawsuit, APsaA and IPA claimed this rule could only be changed by submitting a bylaws change to the voting membership of the IPA.

The issue of nonmedical training never fully vanished from APsaA's politics. In 1957, the Committee on Training for Research [later named Committee on Research and Special Training (CORST)] was formed. Thus, provisions were made for a very few research psychologists to obtain a research waiver and to undergo full psychoanalytic training. A condition of this training was that the candidate sign an oath (which was more often ignored than not) not to practice clinical psychoanalysis for other than research purposes.

Meanwhile, pressure within psychology for access to training in psychoanalysis continued to grow. A small number of non-medical institutes were formed, predominantly in the New York area and later in Los Angeles. Some psychologists on their own sought out personal analyses, supervision and/or participation in ad hoc study groups. APsaA frowned upon such self-directed training and kept a tight rein on its members. Some members of APsaA found their professional status jeopardized as it became known that they were teaching or supervising outside the auspices of APsaA. These domestic conditions, coupled with the prohibition against United States psychologists seeking training abroad in IPA institutes, meant that only a trickle of qualified, creative psychologists were allowed to participate fully in the development of psychoanalysis in the United States.

In the early 1970s, APsaA was confronted with numerous growing realities: a decreased candidate pool and a lowering quality of medical candidates (Minutes of the Ninth Meeting of the Committee on Prerequisites for Training, May 7, 1980; Meeting of the Educational Committee of the New York Psychoanalytic Institute, May 6, 1975); decreasing numbers of analysands (e.g., Campbell et al., 1982); the re-medicalization of psychiatry (Report of the Committee on

University and Medical Education to the Executive Council, December 20, 1984); and the recognition of the "stultification" and "malaise" of psychoanalysis in the United States (Minutes of the Second Meeting of the Committee on Prerequisites on Training, May 7, 1976). The question of non-medical training arose again—this time perhaps as a necessary measure for the survival of psychoanalysis in the United States. APsaA embarked on a decade of committees and discussions devoted to examine the question of non-medical training.

In May 1975, APsaA organized a Committee on Prerequisites for Training, chaired by Homer Curtis. Meeting twice yearly until its termination in December, 1981, this committee reported on December 4, 1977:

> It is clear to us that psychological aspects and experience embedded in the role of human caretakers are more important than the strictly medical or biological learning. (Report to BOPS).

And concluded in its final report:

> We have come to the conclusion that a modest expansion of our eligibility requirements to include doctors of clinical psychology allows us access to an additional source of highly qualified applicants without changing the essentially medical nature of our organization . . . to be able to take the cream of this crop (doctoral level clinical psychologists and doctors of mental health) and train them in our institutes would be a service to our organization, the community, and psychoanalysis. (Committee on Prerequisites Reports, December, 1981)

Spawned by the favorable reports from the Committee on Prerequisites, APsaA appointed Kenneth Calder to chair the "Ad-hoc Committee on Feasibility of Non-medical Training," which met first in May 1978. In its report to BOPS on December 16, 1981, while agreeing that it was feasible to train non-physicians, it deferred from offering a recommendation, merely listing favorable and unfavorable outcomes of nonmedical training:

PROS:
1. Deserving lay analysts will have available better training in the practice of psychoanalysis.
2. Hence, some patients will receive better analysis.
3. Classes in psychoanalytic institutes will be larger.
4. Classes may be improved by the addition of outstanding clinical psychologists.
5. A broader base for psychoanalysis can have several beneficial affects including the preservation of quality psychoanalysis during times of stress for the field of psychoanalysis.

6. Non-physicians may enhance psychoanalytic classes as a result of their greater familiarity with experimental and scientific models.

CONS:

1. Non-physicians as practitioners of psychoanalysis may be economic competitors with physician practitioners.
2. Physician analysts may lose favor with the American Psychiatric Association, the American Medical Association and science, in general, as a result of training of non-physicians.
3. Potential physician candidates may be driven away from the field if it is available to non-physicians.
4. The long range impact on the American Psychoanalytic Association might be loss of control of the association by physicians.
5. Analytic classes might be less good through the impact of non-physicians.
6. Non-physicians may lack the sense of responsibility for their patients common with physicians. In other words, medical training may have a particularly advantageous impact on trainees. (Report of the Committee of Feasibility for Non-medical Training to the Board of Professional Standards, December 16, 1981)

Lengthy discussion ensued at the BOPS meeting in December, 1981 (minutes of the meeting of BOPS, December 16, 1981), at which both the Prerequisites and the Feasibility Committees presented their reports. Attempts to bring forward a motion to approve what Robert Michaels described as an innovative program for non-medical training were thwarted and the motion was finally watered down to a statement "to affirm its approval of the goals of training clinical psychologists." One member of the Committee recognized that "what overhangs the discussion is a major political problem."

Unwilling or unable to respond constructively to the Committee on Prerequisites' conclusions, APsaA formed another committee—the Committee on Desirability of Non-Medical Training, chaired by Richard Isay. Acknowledging that doctoral level clinical psychologists met the prerequisites for psychoanalytic training and that it was feasible to train them, BOPS charged this new committee to determine whether it was in APsaA's best interest to admit non-physicians. This committee was unable to reach a consensus, merely generating another list of pros and cons.

Another committee, The Ad Hoc Committee on Non-Medical Training, chaired by Van Spruiell, formed in 1983, was charged with the task of developing a procedure by which nonmedical training might be implemented. The optimism that was generated among psychologists interested in training as a result of the Prerequisites Committee Report and of the formation of this new committee seemed to be justified, and was echoed by APsaA President Morton

Reiser. In his appointment letter to Van Spruiell he wrote: "There is no need to underline the importance of this issue which is *now ready for definitive action*" (emphasis added).

The Committee conceived of three models for training (with two models added by BOPS Fellows). The Committee, however, concluded that it could not agree on a clear cut direction. At the Executive Council Meeting in May, 1984, the vote, "not to take any action on this issue" was passed 32 to 7. The Committee's request to be discharged from its responsibilities was granted. In reading the Minutes of the Executive Council, BOPS, and the Committee of Members, it is clear that APsaA had arrived at a state of paralysis on this issue. The forces in support of non-medical training, and there appear to have been many, were neutralized by those who feared change—change in the market place and change in the medical identity of APsaA.

Realistic fears that standards would be eroded had been laid aside by the reports from the Committee on Prerequisites. A substantive issue regarding the decision not to support non-medical training was blatantly expressed during the April 1983 meeting:

> The members of (APsaA) enjoy a special position in our eyes and in the eyes of the profession and the lay public as MD-psychoanalyst and the real issue is whether or not this would be lost by opening full clinical and psychoanalytic training to non-medical applicants (minutes of BOPS, April 23, 1983, page 27).

Other statements in recorded Minutes that were obtained during depositions make it very clear that those in authority were concerned that the loss of affiliation with the medical establishment would translate into a loss of income. Again, considerations of the development or stagnation of the study of psychoanalysis and psychoanalytic theory fade into the background in the face of economic concerns.

A related development was an address by George Pollock, then President of the American Psychiatric Association, to the Presidents of Affiliate Societies at a December, 1983, meeting. He began his comments by focusing on APsaA's 10-year discussion on nonmedical training. He is reported to have announced that the American Psychiatric Association had been watching and reflected on, "how much the membership of the American Psychiatric Association were concerned with what happened in (APsaA)" (Minutes of the President's Meeting, December, 1983). He further suggested a joint meeting between APsaA and the American Psychiatric Association to discuss the proposals for nonmedical training, before APsaA voted on the issue. APsaA's own Newsletter [1984, *18* (1)] reported that "some councilors and fellows had difficulty feeling reassured that there was no threat or perjorative tone in this request for information and consultation, despite statements to the contrary by many others."

After 10 years of discussion and despite favorable reports from committees about the prerequisites for, feasibility of, and desirability for non-medical training, the issue was placed on the back burner during the May 1984, meeting of APsaA. The headline of their Fall 1984, Newsletter [*18* (3)] read: "Issue Appears Dead For Now; Board Recommendation to Poll Members is Defeated in Council (p. 1)." The new President of APsaA, Edward Joseph, confirmed the demise of the issue. In the APsaA Newsletter [*18* (3), 1984], Papernik's report stated:

> The new President is relieved that the recent polarization of the membership over the issue of non-medical training is, for the time being, no longer in the forefront. Having determined at the recent annual meeting that we have done all that we can for now, our institutional energy can now be diverted into other channels. (p. 6)

Concurrent with the extended debate over the training of nonmedical candidates in APsaA's own institutes was a second debate. APsaA conceptualized any training—teaching, supervision, and analysis for the purpose of training—other than under the auspices of the affiliate institutes of APsaA as unethical, illegal, and wildcat (see Plaintiff's Complaint). They referred this issue of unauthorized training for discussion to their Committee on Ethical Standards and are known to have taken disciplinary actions against members, including expulsions from membership. Yet, some medical psychoanalysts had the courage of their conviction and, often surreptitiously, provided training both to the few nonmedical institutes and to individuals who were engaged in self-directed training.

Again, APsaA engaged in numerous discussions over this issue, judging this practice as having grave, negative consequences, ostensibly for the public and for the preservation of standards, and attempting to find ways to control what APsaA was aware of as a growing amount of unauthorized training. In December 1981, the Executive Council unanimously approved the resolution, "that all psychoanalytic training by members of the American Psychoanalytic Association be conducted only through authorized training institutes and programs of the American."

In 1983, the Committee on Ethics of APsaA prepared an explicit statement forbidding participation in unauthorized training. Reporting on the new version of the code of ethics, Arthur Root emphasized that:

> This code states explicitly that members shall not participate in unauthorized training—that is, no individual may conduct the training of anyone outside an authorized institute including training analysis, teaching courses and supervision. (Minutes of the Board of Trustees, New York Psychoanalytic Institute, November 17, 1983, p. 5)

One month earlier, Arthur Root also is reported to have stated: "We are obliged to remind members of their ethical criteria and then to take disciplinary

action" (Minutes of the Education Committee, New York Psychoanalytic Institute, October 4, 1983, p. 5). Similarly, while denying the existence of prohibi-
tions in the bylaws preventing members from participating in training outside
of APsaA Institutes, Shelly Orgel admitted: "However, it is common knowledge
that it has been discouraged and cautioned about at various times. 'We deplore
it' is written somewhere" (Minutes, Committee on Institutes, December 17,
1984, p. 10).

In fact, the Minutes of the Executive Council (December 16, 1976) reflect
the consequences of unauthorized training:

> . . . In spite of several letters, including a registered one, to the Detroit society,
> Dr. Gaskill had had no response to the request that the society desist from un-
> authorized training. This matter will be referred to a committee which *will pro-*
> *ceed in the steps toward disaffiliation.* (pp. 33–34, italics added)

Also, under legal examination during his deposition, Shelly Orgel, [APsaA's designated witness regarding "policies or statements concerning the teaching of psychoanalysis by members of APsaA outside of the institutes affiliated with
(APsaA)]

> . . . ultimately was forced to admit that the American had adopted a series of posi-
> tions and statements "that were intended to, or in fact, did discourage members
> from participating in such unauthorized training" at non-accredited institutes.
> (Memorandum in Support of Plaintiffs motion for Class Certification, page 49; Or-
> gel, Depo Tr. 78-79)

Under the pressure of several threatened lawsuits (Florida, Seattle, Los Angeles, and Baltimore, none of which were realized) APsaA began to become
sensitized to the legal implications of their actions and assumed a more cautious
stance: "Our lawyers have advised us to go slow on this and not make a matter
of bylaws or censure of our members." (Minutes of the Committee on Institutes, December 17, 1984). In consultation with their attorneys, APsaA was
alerted to their potential liability under the restraint of trade laws. Some seemed
to have experienced themselves as existing above Federal law. The Minutes
indicate that Edward Joseph, then President-Elect of APsaA, found this legal
position incomprehensible. He again reiterated that, "training was a function
of the American Psychoanalytic Association delegated to the Board of Professional Standards and implemented under the supervision of the Board." The
Board concluded that, "The attorneys for the association do not fully understand this principle and the principles under which the Board operates . . . the
attorneys would need further education on this point" (Minutes, BOPS, April
27, 1983, p. 22).

However, apparently it was deemed prudent to change the language of Section 12 of APsaA's Principles of Ethics, which pertains to training issues. As

reported in *The American Psychoanalyst* [*18* (3), 1984], the section now distinguished "between the training for the clinical practice of psychoanalysis, per se, and training as psychotherapy." The section further reemphasized:

> Training in practice of psychoanalysis should be offered only when there is careful selection of participants and evaluation of the training and the progress of those enrolled in it; one should not attempt "solo" training. Finally no psychoanalyst may claim that training is in any way connected with the American unless that training is authorized by The Board of Professional Standards. (pp. 10–11)

Highlighting their growing awareness of the legal ramifications of their positions with regard to training, their Newsletter reported:

> A final change involved the deletion of the word "illegal" as a designation of the activities which now requests simply that "unethical behavior be reported." (p. 11)

Thus, although the language was changed, the status of unauthorized training as unethical and the de facto practice of restraint persisted. It was not until 1987, after the lawsuit's viability was more than a reality to APsaA, that its President, Richard Simons, wrote to all members of APsaA and conceded that they had in fact actively communicated ". . . that training outside of institutes affiliated with the Association is not in the public interest and, consequently, that it would violate established principles for our members to engage in such training" (p. 1). In the Memorandum in Support of Plaintiffs' Motion for Class Certification, Stromberg astutely observed:

> However, to avoid any possible "confusion," the President *stressed* that any member who does teach outside the American, in "programs that observe high quality standards" would "not be subject to any disciplinary or ethical proceedings on that account . . . . " As Shakespeare observed in *Hamlet*: we have reason to mistrust a person who "protests too much" (p. 50, italics added).

Before ending this section, it is important to point out that psychologists' attempts to communicate and negotiate with IPA and APsaA on these matters began well before the lawsuit was filed. For example, shortly after the birth of Division 39, Reuben Fine, then President of the Division, fruitlessly corresponded with, and met with, IPA representatives in an attempt to establish an affiliation. Discussions with APsaA also had been ongoing from 1981 until their breakdown in 1984. On October 12, 1984, Bryant Welch, Nathan Stockhamer, and Janet Spence (then President of APA) arranged a meeting attended by APsaA officers Edward Joseph, Homer Curtis, and Richard Simons. The meeting was an attempt to forestall the need for legal action because the nonmedical training issue had been declared dead by APsaA. APsaA's obdurate stance during and after that meeting made it abundantly clear that there was no likelihood that the matter would be settled cooperatively. At that meeting the psychologists were told that the training matter was a pocketbook issue for APsaA's membership (Welch Memorandum to Members of the American, November 26, 1984). Only after these and the history of other futile efforts did the lawsuit take form.

LEGAL ASPECTS OF THE LAWSUIT

The lawsuit was a civil action brought by four plaintiffs, Bryant Welch, Toni Bernay, Arnold Schneider, and Helen Desmond, on their own behalf, and on the behalf of, and as representatives of a class of psychologists. The complaint was filed on March 1, 1985, in the United States District Court for the South District of New York. The complaint declared that the defendants, the APsaA, the New York Psychoanalytic Institute, the Columbia University Center for Psychoanalytic Training and Research, and the IPA

> . . . . have restrained and monopolized interstate and international trade and commerce in the training of psychoanalysts and in the delivery of psychoanalytic services to the public . . . the restraints of trade and monopoly established and maintained by defendants lack any reasonable basis since, as defendants have conceded in publications and statements, psychoanalytic training and practice do not require or depend upon medical training. (pp. 1–2)

The court action was based on alleged violations of the Sherman Act. The Sherman Act was established to eliminate unfair trade practices, which deprived the public of the many values inherent in a competitive free enterprise system. For example, under the laws it is illegal to deny competitors access to resources or facilities (for example, training institutes) without which one cannot compete in a particular field. Similarly, imposing rules which interfere with a free flow of resources necessary to compete in that field (such as teachers) is also a restraint of trade. Monopolies and attempts to monopolize are per se illegal.

In defining the nature of the injury and damages, the Complaint indicated that

> . . . . defendants have conspired to and have adopted standards and practices which (a) unreasonably exclude non-MDs such as plaintiff doctoral degree psychologists from psychoanalytic education and training at American affiliated institutes; (b) unreasonably discriminate against, or impose anti-competitive burdens upon, doctoral psychologists who wish to pursue psychoanalytic training at American affiliated institutes; (c) unreasonably preclude and deter psychoanalysts from teaching non-MDs such as doctoral psychologists at institutes other than American affiliated institutes; (d) coerce psychoanalytic institutes in other parts of the world to deny admission to non-MDs from the United States even though those institutes admit non-MDs from elsewhere; and (e) thereby unreasonably restrict access to psychoanalytic practice for plaintiffs and the class they represent. (pp. 7–8)

The anti-competitive nature of the non-medical issue was clearly apparent in the numerous documents garnered through the discovery process and through the depositions. However, Robert Wallerstein succinctly stated the issues during the 1980 APsaA meeting in the panel report on *Beyond Lay Analysis*:

> As a science, we aim to enrich the quality of our participants and want to be sure not to screen out any who might enrich our dialogue. As a profession, we have to be cautious about the people we present to the public as psychoanalysts, and here the issue of the caliber and qualifications of other institutes must be considered. As a trade, like other trades, we traditionally try to restrict competition, limit membership, and train no more practitioners than the market will support. So, from a scientific point of view, we want to increase the number of participants, as professionals, we want to be careful, and from a trade position we want to lower the number of participants. (Wallerstein, 1981, p. 715)

Despite the extensive amount of reported and published data, the defendants denied the allegations and maintained that an MD degree was a necessary prerequisite (in opposition to their own accepted committee reports) for psychoanalytic training. Calling on the First Amendment, they claimed that their restrictions were a matter of academic freedom. They asked the Judge for Summary Judgement of the case (i.e., denial of the right to have the Court hear the case). On April 4, 1986, the Court denied the defendants' motion to dismiss the suit, noting, "there seems to be more than a bit of commercial motive behind the defendants' practices." In essence, the judges opinion ruled in the plaintiffs' favor on every point. Still, the burden of proof rested on our shoulders.

Now that the case was accepted as containing sufficient merit to be heard, our next step was to certify the class, an important step in establishing that the defendants' actions have a wide-spread effect on the public; that it would be terribly impractical for the Court and for individuals for separate motions to be filed; and that the questions of law and fact were common among members of the class.

At the Status Conference of April 22, 1986, the plaintiffs' attorney, Clifford Stromberg, won a significant tactical victory. The previous summer, the Court, in accord with its usual procedure, had ruled that discovery should be conducted on the class action issues initially. Then, only after the class had been established would discovery on the merits of the case begin. This would have provided the defendants with the opportunity to harass the plaintiffs and expose weaknesses in their case without being subject to like action toward them until the class had been legally established. After considerable procedural wrangling and over the defendants' strenuous objections, Stromberg persuaded the Judge to order consolidated discovery in which both the class issues and the issues of the merits of the case would be examined simultaneously.

The proposed class was defined as follows:

1) Possess a Doctoral Degree in Psychology; 2) are licensed or certified as psychologists; 3) have been engaged in the practice of psychotherapy; 4) have demonstrated their commitment to the psychoanalytic discipline by some of the means which were available to them, such as being a member of the Division of Psychoanalysis of the American Psychological Association, seeking to apply to an institution offering training in psychoanalysis, undertaking a personal analysis, or pursuing other opportunities for psychoanalysis training; and 5) applied for and were denied or had been deterred from even applying for, full psychoanalytic training at an institute affiliated with the American. (Memorandum in Support of Plaintiffs' Motion for Class Certification, p. 16)

The defendants argued that "the boundaries of the proposed class are far too vague and imprecise to allow for any meaningful determination of who is in and who is out." The plaintiffs response memorandum argued that there were "common issues as to conspiracy, antitrust violation, and harm to competition." It included 240 declarations by psychologists who stated how they had been denied or deterred from training.

Once these documents were filed the next step would have been for the judge to rule on the motion for class certification. However, as is quite common in the natural history of class action suits, there were renewed negotiations. Attorneys for the plaintiffs and the defendants hammered out the draft of a settlement proposal. While all parties concerned were frequently consulted during this process, only the attorneys met to work out the wording of the proposal. The Board of Division 39 was consulted during this process and it was only after the Board recommended to the plaintiffs that the proposed settlement be accepted that the plaintiffs did so. Even after both the defendants and the plaintiffs had agreed to the basic terms of the settlement, countless additional hours of negotiations were necessary before the wording of the various documents required for the filing of the settlement could be worked out (Desmond, 1988).

The legal action and the decisions behind its development and direction were highly technical and would require an attorney to elucidate succinctly and clearly. During the course of the lawsuit, however, we as plaintiffs learned that there were limits to what we could expect to garner from such a suit. In short, we learned about litigation as the art of the possible. We learned about the legal realities of points of law which, for technical reasons, can bar points of truth from being admitted as evidence. Delaying tactics, motions and counter-motions were all part of the legal process. We learned a new meaning for the word discovery—a lengthy, expensive and time-consuming process during which subpoenaed records were reviewed and plaintiffs, supporters of the suit, and defendants were deposed, that is, grilled for endless hours in search of evidence. Published comments or even those overheard were open to questions. Who said what and why at certain meetings were closely examined.

The rules of the legal game so greatly differed from those of the psychotherapist's relationship that the deposition experience became disorienting—

necessitating a paranoid-like hyperalertness and resulting in post traumatic-like sequellae. In a typical gambit, one defendant's attorney seduced the unsuspecting plaintiff into a sense of complacency, pleasantly chit-chatting and seemingly involving himself in jovial reparte; then, with no warning launched a pointed interrogation. It was only the plaintiffs' attorney's presence of mind and the non-verbal receptivity that had developed between client and attorney over the many hours of preparation that helped to save the day. It certainly did not take much time, or distance, to appreciate, respect, and at times desperately cling onto the experience, knowledge, guidance, and self-assurance of our attorneys, especially Cliff Stromberg.

In fact, the course of the suit progressed exceedingly well, with victories achieved at each step on the way, pointing to our ultimate success. The low point, or perhaps the below-the-belt punch, that we experienced occurred during Bryant Welch's deposition (November 9, 1987) when the attorneys for APsaA and for the New York Psychoanalytic Institute threatened to subpoena records of the plaintiffs' analyses to determine their analyzability. Their attorneys stated:

> The lawsuit is based on the assumption that the plaintiffs are or were analyzable. That by virtue of filing the lawsuit, the plaintiffs, therefore, have "put their mental condition into dispute" and have waived their rights to confidentiality and privacy. And that the defendants reserve their rights to gain access to the information divulged during the personal psychoanalyses of the plaintiffs, such information to be used in the legal proceedings to determine whether the plaintiffs are "analyzable" or for other purposes. (Welch deposition)

The plaintiffs, attorneys, and the Board of Directors of Division 39 were incredulous and appalled that such a threat could even be considered—that APsaA would permit its lawyers to attempt to breach the integrity of psychoanalytic confidentiality! The Division 39 Board of Directors condemned this threat and called on the New York Psychoanalytic Institute and APsaA to renounce and reject their attorneys' threat, and for the world psychoanalytic community to condemn their policy. Not long after this information was conveyed to members of APsaA and IPA, the attorneys' threats were rationalized and, ultimately, dropped.

Clearly, in response to the lawsuit, historic changes were taking place, even before the settlement agreement was reached. In December 1985, only 9 months after the lawsuit was filed, APsaA's Board of Professional Standards unanimously endorsed a plan by which they would proceed with nonmedical clinical training. The March 1986, report on the general membership's vote to approve such training indicated a 68% vote in favor of the recommendation. Thus, the clinical waiver process was initiated.

While APsaA staunchly denied that this revolutionary change was motivated in response to the lawsuit, the reality was evident. Even APsaA's own Newsletter began their report about the acceptance of the waiver process with the comment: "In a somewhat unanticipated change from the uncertain and divided attitude expressed in San Diego last spring . . ." [American Psychoanalytic Association Newsletter, *18* (3), 1985, page 1]. This sudden change, from burying the issue of non-medical training in May, 1984, to endorsing the clinical waiver process in December 1985, was possibly APsaA's attempt to persuade the Court that legal action was not justified. They hoped to bring the lawsuit to a quick end while denying any culpability. Further, had the lawsuit been dropped at that time, no assurance would have been provided that these changes would continue. The plaintiffs were aware, that without a legal resolution this change could quickly be rescinded or altered. In fact, as late as May 5, 1987, at a meeting of BOPS, Shelly Orgel, "reminded the Board that it is possible to stop implementation of the Gaskill proposal *at any time the Board chooses*" (Report to Members, L.A. Psychoanalytic Society and Institute, May 27, 1987, p. 2, italics added).

A second historic change was completed in July, 1987, when the IPA approved a bylaws change, proposed by the APsaA, altering the American Regional Association status—that is, "the 1938 rule." The bylaws change allowed non-APsaA-affiliated institutes to apply for membership in the IPA and for their members to be granted membership status in the IPA.

Through 1987 and into 1988, the process of discovery continued and, while committed to pursue this lawsuit to its completion, we also continued to be open to out of court settlement possibilities. One good faith attempt by the plaintiffs in May, 1986, failed when APsaA apparently attempted to use it to subvert and divide psychologists' support (discussed later). Finally, however, agreement was reached and, on April 17, 1989, the settlement agreement was approved by the court.

Generally, the terms of the agreement included:

1. psychologists and other qualified non-medical clinicians were eligible to train in American Psychoanalytic Association Institutes;
2. members of the American Psychoanalytic Association were permitted to teach in non-American affiliated institutes;
3. membership in the IPA was opened to all qualified psychologists and nonmedical institutes;
4. the defendants were ordered to pay $650,000 to the plaintiff class for costs and legal fees.

Although no quotas were set for admission to training in APsaA Institutes, the settlement guaranteed that the rate of admission for non-medical applicants would be "at least at a level, and with a geographical distribution, consistent with the current process . . ." The settlement then enumerates the actual numbers of applicants who applied (38) and who were accepted (32) under the CNMCT (Committee for Non-Medical Clinical Training) Program during the first year. These 32 applicants composed 28% of trainees that year. An additional 10% of the total trainees had been approved under CORST. In this way, the settlement essentially secures approximately 38% of national training spaces for nonmedical people outside of the New York area.

Important clarifications of the formal settlement agreement were necessary prior to the plaintiffs agreeing to sign. Thus, in an August 18, 1988, letter from the attorneys of APsaA, the procedures for the CNMCT process were spelled out. An August 16, 1988, letter from IPA attorneys defined the concept of "functional equivalence" whereby "an individual who has 700 hours of personal analysis on a three times per week basis will not automatically be granted or denied admission to the IPA. . . ." In that letter, IPA also committed itself to respect theoretical diversity.

Separate agreements were reached with the New York Psychoanalytic Institute and the Columbia, ensuring the freedom of their members to provide training to qualified clinicians and institutes outside of APsaA. With a large number of non-APsaA institutes in the New York vicinity, the plaintiffs, in consultation with the Division 39 Board, did not consider it imperative that these two institutes be required to provide training to psychologists. The plaintiffs considered this agreement to be supportive of the Division's ultimate wishes to develop and encourage psychoanalytic training institutes organized by psychologists. We also felt such an agreement would put greater pressure on APsaA institutes in other areas of the country to train psychologists.

Whereas the settlement achieved most of the goals originally sought by the plaintiffs, the final outcome of the agreement was limited by certain legal factors. The pivotal legal issues in this suit were based on anticompetitive and monopolistic arguments. Contrary to many people's beliefs (e.g., see Stolorow letter, *Psychologist/Psychoanalyst, 9* [1], 1989), the suit was not based on antidiscrimination arguments. One consequence was that the class could not expect perfect parity. Although we were highly cognizant of affirmative action issues, these simply were not feasible outcomes for this lawsuit. For the time being, because of the constraints of the law, we had to settle with the recognition that what we did achieve were, "reasonable opportunities for economic competition" (Welch *Psychologist/Psychoanalyst, 9* [1], 1989). The give and take nature of this process was summarized by Judge Mukasey's statement as he approved the Settlement Agreement: "Being aware that litigation is the art of the possible, I will approve the agreement."

DISSENTING VOICES WITHIN PSYCHOLOGY

Although the support provided by Division 39 for the lawsuit was overwhelmingly positive through the years, it was not unanimous. Questions were raised initially that greater access to APsaA Institutes would constitute a threat to the hopes and plans of developing psychologist institutes and to the enrollment of quality psychologists in non-medical institutes currently in existence. The unlikely possibility of developing psychologist institutes in many areas of the country, the importance of freeing APsaA members to teach at existing and developing institutes, and the benefits of membership in the IPA were among the considerations that helped to unify the Division's support.

Occasional questions about the validity of the suit were raised. For example, Helen Gediman (*Psychologist/Psychoanalyst, 6* [4], 1985–1986) questioned the lawsuit's allegations that APsaA teachers were actually restrained from teaching at non-APsaA institutes (she appeared to be in support of the remainder of the suit). She referred to the 1983 revision of APsaA's Principles of Ethics. Bryant Welch's clarifying response, also published in the *Psychologist/ Psychoanalyst* (*7* [2], 1986), helped to resolve that question. In his response, Welch warned of the need to "look at the *substance* of the American Psychoanalytic Association's behavior rather than simply the form of its current ethical principles" (p. 4). He also alerted the readership to avoid interpreting APsaA's behavior as a function of misunderstanding rather than facing their actual intent to discourage their membership from training psychologists.

A more significant threat to the unanimity of support arose in 1987. Zenia Fliegel, in possession of what was supposed to have been a confidential settlement negotiation document, filed a request with Fred Pine, then President of Division 39. She wrote:

> It is our understanding that the suit has been eminently successful in attaining its main objectives. The American Psychoanalytic Association proposes to relinquish its old pact with the International which gave it veto power over admissions from the United States; it also proposes to cease all attempts to discourage or limit the participation of its own members in the training of non-medical analysts. These were the primary concerns in the Division's initial (sic) support of the suit . . .
>
>   We respectfully request that the Board make every effort to persuade the plaintiffs to settle the suit, with appropriate safeguards, on the basis of the concessions already offered by the defendants. Failing that, we would urge the Board, with regret, to officially and publicly withdraw its support of continued litigation. (Letter distributed to Division 39 Board, March 7, 1987)

However, at this point in time, the proposed changes were not yet legally binding and easily could have been ignored or changed once the lawsuit was dropped.

Fliegel also objected to what she erroneously claimed to be "counterproductive demands contained in the plaintiffs' proposed settlement." In fact, the document to which she referred was a confidential document. The APsaA itself had "preconditioned all settlement discussions on an agreement of complete confidentiality" which we as plaintiffs abided by in hopes of furthering the process (Welch letter, February 23, 1987).

The history of the document is as follows: At the initiative of Robert Wallerstein, President of IPA, a negotiation meeting was assembled on May 31, 1986.
It was, in fact, requested on the heels of Stromberg's tactical victory at the
April 22, 1986, Class Action Status Conference. Each defendant was represented
by its officers and attorneys. Unlike the tenor of an earlier meeting on March
9, 1986, the tenor now was congenial. The IPA's stance, in particular, was decidedly conciliatory. The discussion was filled with promising ideas and proposals,
many of which were suggested by IPA representatives. At the end of the afternoon, despite the plaintiffs' stated request to resume meeting after a dinner
break, the defendants refused. The meeting was terminated before there were
any mutually agreed upon proposals. Rather, the defendants looked to the plaintiffs' attorney, in consultation with IPA's attorney, to formalize what had transpired. This summary would then be used as a "single text" point of departure
at a later meeting.

The four plaintiffs met in Washington, DC, after the May 31 meeting. Some
of us had not met personally prior to this time. In addition to getting acquaint-
ed, we needed to identify our current goals before meeting the next day with
our attorneys. The negotiations of the May 31 meeting were discussed. We
had a dual concern. We wished to draw as much as possible upon the suggestions offered by the defendants, especially by IPA. At the same time,
because the document we were to submit, in effect, would be the starting point
of negotiations, to begin with our bottom line in effect would be to give away
the store.

The next day, the four plaintiffs and Nathan Stockhamer met with our attorneys. Again, we had a dual agenda. Many of us had not met personally with
our attorneys. In addition to our getting to know each other, we had to clarify
our goals—now as a legal team.

Following completion of the document by our attorneys, it was disseminated
to the defendants. The only response we received from the defendants occurred
the following October. It was a vague and unenforceable settlement proposal
from APsaA, unresponsive to the issues discussed at the May 31 meeting. The
detailed elements focused on requirements protecting APsaA from any future
lawsuits by any other mental-health professionals on related matters—even for
future wrongdoings!

The plaintiffs considered that this document was not sufficient to allow the
negotiation process to move forward. However, while the plaintiffs held
APsaA's documents in confidence, somehow it ended up in the hands of Zenia
Fliegel. As Welch stated in his February 23, 1987, letter:

> . . . Ironically, most of these ideas to which Dr. Fliegel objects were actually origi-
> nated by the defendants . . . It was also understood by all present that further
> discussions were to be held with these stated propositions to be points of depar-
> ture for discussion. (p. 2)

And, in a different forum, Wallerstein stated:

> . . . My own conviction is that there is ample negotiating room between the two proposals and that the difficult, detailed negotiations are still ahead of us—but that we do agree in principle on a settlement based *"on terms as favorable as possible to the plaintiff class, consistent with the defendants' interests"* knowing that the various defendant parties have partially overlapping, but partially diverging convictions about the best conditions for psychoanalytic training . . . [*IPA Newsletter* (1987) *19* (1), p. 2, italics added].

Fliegel's motivation for her objections is not clear to the writers. To be sure, she did not contact the plaintiffs or their attorney to seek clarification, and some viewed her response as "premature," "alarmist," and "misleading" (Schafer, Frankiel, and Kaplan letter distributed at March 7, 1987, meeting), or as focused on discrediting the plaintiffs and the virtue of the lawsuit. Nevertheless, her letter was signed by 26 psychologists, many of whom were quite distinguished, and indicated considerable dissatisfaction with the lawsuit process to date (especially the secrecy).

The consequence of this set of circumstances was a special meeting of Division 39 Board of Directors on March 7, 1987, at which time there was full disclosure of these events as well as a full disclosure of all documents. (See reports of meeting in *Psychologist/Psychoanalyst 8* [1 and 2] 1987; *The Round Robin, 3* [1], 1987.) The meeting concluded with the Board, the plaintiffs, and members of GAPPP agreeing to take steps to insure broader communication and openness between GAPPP and the Division membership. GAPPP also invited the Board to serve in an oversight and advisory capacity. Also at this meeting, the Board unanimously reasserted its continued support of the lawsuit and approved a special $10,000 contribution in addition to its earlier pledges. Thus, a major danger to the lawsuit was overcome, and actually brought about stronger-than-ever collaboration between Division 39, the plaintiffs, and GAPPP.

"IT AIN'T OVER 'TILL IT'S OVER"

As plaintiffs and members of GAPPP, we listened to many sources of wisdom, not the least of which was Yogi Berra. During the months before and after the settlement was approved by the Court, problems began to appear. The first two of the four plaintiffs to apply under the CNMCT process were rejected the first time around. At the very time the final settlement points were being negotiated by the attorneys, the second plaintiff's application was turned down. Among other things, the denial of the waiver was based upon the rumor that this plaintiff had supposedly said she "would never under any circumstances return to analysis" (personal communications to Helen Desmond). In fact, this plaintiff had never precluded the possibility of further analysis for herself and had written her former training analyst informing him of her wish to resume analysis with him should such be appropriate in the future. This incident brought to the fore the necessity of including some protection for the plaintiffs.

Thus the Settlement included provisions to protect each plaintiff, Psychologist Class member, or any individual who assisted with the lawsuit from "retaliatory actions." The Settlement further stipulated that APsaA, "shall process the waiver applications promptly, fairly, and in accordance with established standards." Also, ". . . . in recognition of the special circumstances presented by being a named plaintiff," the Settlement provided additional safeguards by establishing a notification and monitoring mechanism to insure early identification and resolution of problems with the waiver process (Settlement Agreement, 4A and 4B).

After the Settlement was signed, we heard complaints about its implementation. We heard of lengthy delays of candidates' applications, of overly burdensome demands and of blatant examples in which applicants were rejected or deferred for specious reasons. Some APsaA institutes themselves objected to unwarranted second guessing by the CNMCT as their application for waivers in support of psychologists were rejected. Institutes were also straining under the demands of the waiver process that required voluminous documentation. Many institutes were reported to feel sufficiently intimidated by the waiver process that they added further demands on psychologists' applications, deterring many from applying. Several APsaA institutes objected vehemently to the CNMCT process and, for a period, an insurrectionist atmosphere took hold within APsaA with threats of disaffiliation and secession.

IPA, too, after rapidly accepting three institutes for provisional membership— the Freudian Institute in New York, the Institute for Psychoanalytic Training and Research in New York, and the Psychoanalytic Center of California in Los Angeles, suddenly halted its progress. Although the Settlement stipulated that IPA "seek affiliation of all qualified psychoanalytic groups in the United States not affiliated with (APsaA)" the conduct of site visits began to suggest they were seeking to exclude or limit membership. Procedures were vague and fluctuating and some Institutes' cooperation with one set of demands led only to another and then another set of new demands.

A major controversy arose around the concept of functional equivalence. IPA had agreed in the settlement that because the history of psychoanalytic groups in the United States resulted in different training procedures than for groups originally affiliated with IPA, they were prepared to accept individuals if, "overall they have functioned in a way that is equivalent to individuals who have been trained according to IPA standards" (side letter to the settlement, August 16, 1988). However, despite IPA's explicit statement indicating that analysts whose personal and supervised analyses were conducted three times a week, "will not automatically be granted or denied admission to the IPA," many of their later statements and actions contradicted the agreement.

As a result of this accumulating list of APsaA's and IPA's deficiencies in compliance with the Settlement Agreement, the GAPPP Board of Directors, at its semi-annual meeting in April, 1990, voted unanimously to establish a Commission on Settlement Enforcement. The Commission, Co-Directed by Arnold Schneider and Helen Desmond, was designed to fulfill a watch dog function regarding compliance and to serve as a central clearinghouse for information regarding settlement issues. By the end of its fourth month of existence, the Commission filed a comprehensive and extensively documented report with Clifford Stromberg, GAPPP's attorney, outlining major areas of APsaA and IPA non-compliance with the Settlement Agreement. At the time of this writing, communication between the respective attorneys has begun in order to rectify these problems outside of the courtroom.

The Commission's activity has already proven its value. One of the institutes applying for membership in the IPA, the Los Angeles Institute and Society for Psychoanalytic Studies, had experienced several years of frustrating and apparently obstructionistic treatment at the hands of IPA. Site visits were delayed and when they occurred were cursory, feedback was nonexistent or highly contradictory, and the existence of reports on site visits were denied by some IPA representatives only to be acknowledged by others. At the time that the Commission was established, a fourth promised site visit to the Los Angeles Institute and Society was almost one year overdue. Further, following Joseph Sandler's ascendancy to the IPA presidency, there were indications of a rapprochement between APsaA and IPA. Coincidentially, the nature of the site visits began to change from a collegial, helpful enterprise to an adversarial process (*American Psychoanalyst, 20, 23* [2 and 3], 1989). After the Commission's report was filed, our attorney addressed IPA's attorneys with our complaints. He underlined our determination to see this process through—even if it required a return to Court. Within weeks, the long promised site visit to LAIPS was rapidly assembled.

These and many other settlement issues are continuing to be monitored under the watchful gaze of the Commission. The Commission's consolidation of incoming and outgoing information has proved invaluable in developing a clear view of the areas of compliance and non-compliance with the lawsuit settlement and will be a major vehicle to assure the consistent and fair implementation of the settlement.

OUTCOME AND BENEFITS OF THE LAWSUIT

The lawsuit, from its inception through this day, has had numerous direct and incidental results, many of which are far from clear and may take years to evaluate as to their merit. Most objectively, it opened the doors to psychoanalytic training for numerous psychologists (and other mental-health professionals) that would surely have remained closed. Since the establishment of the clinical waiver process in 1986, 68 PhD and PsyD psychologists have been admitted to APsaA institutes for clinical training, compared to 142 candidates (many of whom were not psychologists) who were admitted under the research waiver over the prior thirty years. Since breaking down the barriers for IPA membership in the United States in 1987, three psychologist institutes have been accepted for provisional membership, with several more well on their way to joining that international organization. The change in APsaA's policy permitting its members to teach, supervise and analyze candidates outside of APsaA affiliated institutes has provided psychologists interested in organizing new institutes access to a greater array of resources. Unfortunately, for some members of APsaA, the assurance of legal protection from retaliation for such participation was necessary before they would participate.

However, these objectively definable benefits are only the tip of the proverbial iceberg. From the onset of the lawsuit, and at least during the duration of the lawsuit, a remarkable change occurred within the Division itself. A sense of unity of purpose linked the Division Board; the purposes were clear and just and the goals were almost always unanimously supported. The obdurate stance of APsaA and IPA only strengthened the resolve and unanimity of the Board. The victory of the settlement agreement for psychology and psychoanalysis increased the sense of self-esteem and feeling of first-class citizenship that had been developing since the birth of Division 39, and which had been given a boost by the years of legal activity. The articles written for the *Psychologist-Psychoanalyst* Newsletter through the years clearly reflect the changing spirit within the Division. As Irving Reifman communicated in his article in the *Psychologist-Psychoanalyst* (*8* [6] 1988, p. 7), now that we had broken the barriers of APsaA, we would be able to go beyond their doors and build our own homes—"indeed we have matured." Perhaps the lawsuit was a form of initiation rite, part of a developmental process expanding our own creativity, resourcefulness, and independence. We can play with formulations, but the future will hold the answers and evaluate our successes.

The lawsuit brought change not only to the Division, but also to APsaA. There are more students in classes[1] and, whereas we have yet to receive their current evaluation of the new group of candidates, their seeming interest to eliminate the Gaskill-Davis process and allow their institutes greater autonomy in admitting their own students attests to their recognition that psychologists can contribute positively to their training programs. Beyond this benefit, the lawsuit appears to have forced APsaA to confront their own internal problems more directly. Our coverage and success has empowered members within APsaA to assume greater control over their own destiny. Problems regarding disenfran-

---

[1]Editor's note. At the expense of attendance at some psychologist institutes.

chised graduates of APsaA's institutes and the degree of autonomy of local institutes, ever-present background sources of discontent within, are forcing APsaA to review its organizational functioning.

The lawsuit was also another blow to psychiatry's attempt to assert itself as the sole or superior purveyor of diagnostic and therapeutic services. With the open recognition by APsaA of the equality of psychologists to conduct psychoanalyses, we have established ourselves to ourselves, to the public, and to legislative/legal bodies as competent independent practitioners of diagnostic and psychotherapeutic services.

Of greatest importance is the potential that the results of this lawsuit can have on the future development of psychoanalytic thought. Arnold Cooper (1987,1990), hardly a friend of psychology, has written of the stultification of psychoanalysis in APsaA. This stultification can be attributed to the repressive atmosphere within APsaA, one symptom of which had been the years of restraint of psychologists from training and from contributing to the development of mainstream American psychoanalysis. With the breakdown of these repressive barriers and with a new spirit of collaboration comes the potential of a new era of psychoanalytic inquiry and creativity, theory building, research, and practice—all interdependent elements if psychoanalysis is to reach its potential. Thus, we may soon be able to resume the course initially envisioned by Freud, charted anew and guided by the influx of bright, creative, and committed psychologists trained also as psychoanalysts.

EPILOGUE

Our psychoanalytic training and experience teaches us well that our actions are multidetermined and that our motivations range from the altruistic to the narcissistic. The leaders of APsaA and IPA, the plaintiffs, and the leaders of GAPPP share in these basic human dynamics. It would have been far better to analyze our respective dynamics and trust in our conviction that insight could lead to change. However, years of attempts to establish an alliance to engage in shared exploration had failed. Our only recourse was the higher authority of the Court.

For the four plaintiffs and the leadership of GAPPP, the years of preparation and implementation of the lawsuit were filled with excitement and fear, triumph and disappointment, pride and disillusionment, and comradery and hostility. Analysis and reanalysis of actions and motivations around the lawsuit were daily activities. Its effects on personal, family, and professional lives were varied and profound. Insight into the workings of the legal system and into the functioning of groups and organizations were plentiful, though often painful. The meaning of truth is far different when sought by an attorney in a deposition than by an analyst or an analysand. Admired, respected, and identified with teachers, authors, and transference objects can lose their halos when closely viewed outside of the classroom, or consulting room. Lawsuits, like analyses, strip away the outer protective armor and decorative garments, often exposing less than flattering substances, substances which one may have preferred not to have seen in the first place.

What of the lawsuit itself? After the dust clears, it is our belief, albeit colored by strong wishes, that it will be the science and art of psychoanalysis that will have benefited. The wider pool of analytic candidates, the disassembly of the parochial, authoritarian restraining walls of the past and, hopefully, the collaborative competition between APsaA and non-APsaA institutes can provide the ingredients and impetus that psychoanalysis needs to move forward. We must be ever wary of our nemesis, the repetition compulsion, and make every effort to remain aware of its insidious and incessant presence and pressure.

This chapter comes to an end with full recognition that it merely precedes the next. Whereas the spotlight shone brilliantly on our legal efforts during this 5-year period, it should and must move on to illuminate a period in which its focus will be the ongoing work of psychoanalytic inquiry.

Final note: Since completing this chapter, APsaA has voted overwhelmingly to eliminate the waiver process for full clinical psychoanalytic training for clinical psychologists holding a PhD or PsyD, and for the Doctor of Mental Health and Doctor of Social Work degrees. The bylaw amendment was approved during the summer of 1991 by a margin of 771 to 146.

REFERENCES

Campbell, L., Lymberis, M., Campbell, B., Donovon, W., & deDordoba, P. (1988). The Cape Survey: Psychoanalytic training from the trainee's view. *Journal of the Council for the Advancement of Psychoanalytic Education, 2*(2), 10–21.

Clark, R. (1980). *Freud: The man and the cause.* New York: Random House.

Cooper, A. (1987). The changing culture of psychoanalysis. *Journal of the American Academy of Psychoanalysis, 15,* 283–291.

Cooper, A. (1990). The future of psychoanalysis: Challenges and opportunities. *Psychoanalytic Quarterly, 59,* 177–195.

Desmond, H. (1988). The final days. *The Round Robin, 4*(3), 3–6.

Freud, S. (1926). The question of lay analysis. *Standard Edition, 2.*

Freud, S. (1927). Postscript to the question of lay analysis. *Standard Edition, 20,* 251–258.

Jacoby, R. (1986). *The repression of psychoanalysis.* Chicago: University of Chicago Press.

Kirsner, D. (1990). Is there a future for American psychoanalysis? *Psychoanalytic Review, 77*(2), 175–200.

Oberndorf, C. (1953). *A history of psychoanalysis in America.* New York: Harper & Row.

Shane, E. (1988). Robert S. Wallerstein: Researcher, educator and organizer (Interview). *The American Psychoanalytic Association Newsletter, 22*(3), 1ff.

Wallerstein, R. (Chair). (1981). Beyond lay analysis: Pathways to a psychoanalytic career. *Journal of the American Psychoanalytic Association, 29,* 701–715.

A History of the American Board of Psychoanalysis in Psychology

Robert C. Lane

Following the acceptance of a diplomate in psychoanalysis by ABPP on March 4–5, 1983, Anna Antonovsky proposed a liaison committee to the Board of the Division. This committee consisted of: the chair of the education and training committee (Martin Mayman), the chair of the qualifications committee (Nathan Stockhamer), four members from Section I (Anna Antonovsky, Leopold Caligor, Kenneth S. Issacs, and Donald M. Kaplan), and three appointees by the president (Bertram J. Cohler, Bernard N. Kalinkowitz, and Robert C. Lane), with the President, George D. Goldman, and President-Elect, Ernest S. Lawrence as ex-officio members. The first meeting of the liaison committee was held on October 9, 1983. By this time, adding George Goldman, Ernest Lawrence, and Helen Block Lewis, made a total of 12 members on the committee.

At this first meeting, the Committee discussed criteria for admission to the examination for the Diplomate in Psychoanalysis, the nature of the examination and who would be the examiners. Criteria recommended were: graduation from an institute or its equivalent. The latter referred to receiving one's training and experience through noninstitutional, individualized, alternative routes keeping in mind the available training at the time. The applicant would be available to sit for the examination 4 years after the completion of a course of study. During that time the applicant shall have engaged actively in the practice of psychoanalysis concurrently treating a minimum of two psychoanalytic cases. The Committee accepted the course of study defined as the standards adopted by the Board of Directors of Division 39 in Los Angeles during the APA Convention in August, 1981. These standards were reported to the Divisional membership in the Newsletter and formed the basis of the Division's application to ABPP for diplomating. Bernard Kalinkowitz took exception to the frequency requirement of "three or more times a week," a precursor of what was to come.

The Committee made the following recommendations that were never implemented:

Those who completed training between January 1, 1975, and December 31, 1985, be grandfathered for eligibility to take the examination, the widest latitude being used to judge equivalency.

Those who completed training prior to January 1, 1966, be grandfathered into the diplomate without examination. They will have to demonstrate that they have been engaged in the practice of psychoanalysis.

Those who complete their psychoanalytic training after January 1, 1986, have to meet the standards adopted by the Division's Board of Directors and these shall be the ABPsaP standards.

The committee discussed the ways in which the examination could be designed, the efficacy of a written examination, the best way to give the examination, work samples, and so on. It was recommended that examiners have 5 or more years as training and supervising analysts, and that they attend an ABPP training session. Representation on the ABPP Regional Boards and the main Board was recommended.

These recommendations were to be presented to the Board of the Division on October 29, 1983, financial issues were to be discussed and the membership informed of all work in progress.

With such a productive initial meeting, one might have projected rapid happenings, but such was not to be. It was decided to form the American Board of Psychoanalysis in Psychology (ABPsaP), and the organizational meeting of this Board took place May 12, 1986, in a conference call, or some 2 years and 7 months after our acceptance, with only three members and the lawyer participating. What happened in the interim in which no meetings were held is not clear. Nathan Stockhamer was appointed Acting President; Kenneth Isaacs, Secretary; and Ernest Lawrence, Treasurer and Chairperson of the Board of Directors.

As early as June 1986, a letter was received from Donald S. Milman, Director of the Adelphi Postdoctoral Program in Psychotherapy, questioning the criteria for admission stating it was exclusionary, and declaring his concern that Adelphi graduates would not be admitted into the examination. He avowed that the acceptance of Section I's standards by ABPsaP would impinge on Adelphi's academic freedom. He further stated, "It is presumptuous, constrictive and non-creative to allow any narrow set of numbers to designate a professional." He felt it was his responsibility to make sure that, "our rights and privileges as a training institute are not violated." He also demanded to know where each member of the Board of Directors stood on the frequency and numbers issues.

The official August 24, 1986, ABPsaP meeting at the APA Convention in

Washington was canceled and rescheduled for September 21, 1986. A number of us did meet at the August meeting. In September, the ABPsaP bylaws were ratified, Lawrence was elected Chairman of the Board, and Stockhamer, Isaacs, and Cohler respectively President, Secretary, and Treasurer. There was clear dissention within the ABPsaP Board, which by this time had increased its membership to 15, adding Fred Pine and Roy Schafer, and filling the 15th member with the election of Ava Siegler. The examination, standards and philosophy, qualifications review, and grandparenting committees were formed, and Board membership was staggered into 2-, 3-, and 4-year terms.

In a letter dated September 29, 1986, Kalinkowitz resigned stating that the expression, "casting as wide a net as possible" only pertained to "grandparenting for the examination," and once that takes place the old frequency issues will arise once again. We received a letter dated October 29, 1986, from Donald Milman stating that Paul King, President of the Board of ABPP, indicated to him that unless there is consensus among psychologist-psychoanalysts in regard to ABPsaP, ABPP would not be supportive of diplomating in the area of psychoanalysis. To Milman, Kalinkowitz's resignation indicated no such consensus existed.

At the November 2, 1986, meeting, it was decided to send a letter to protesting Division 39 members, asking them to send us letters specifying what they suggest as post-grandparenting standards. Kalinkowitz's letter of resignation was discussed and the Board unanimously agreed to ask him to reconsider his resignation and offered a strong wish that he rejoin us. The examination was discussed, and Goldman and Lane, Co-Chairpersons, were to train with ABPP on November 15 to learn the format of their examination.

To complete our application to ABPP, they requested we respond to their twelve point specialty form. Each Board member was given a section with a deadline for completion of December 15, 1986. Letters were sent to both Kalinkowitz and Milman stating there were two steps in the diplomating process: (a) an assessment of the education and training background for admission to the examination, and (b) the question of excellence as demonstrated by the exam itself. We needed information and input from people regarding education and training so we can move toward consensus within our very broad constituency. In other words, we requested information on what the core education and training requirements should be and what members would like to see occur in the post-grandparenting phase.

A letter dated November 17, 1986 was received from Milman offering Adelphi's multiple admission criteria, requesting a heterogenous set of approaches rather than a monolithic pursuit, and stating a diploma from their rigorous program should be enough to meet all criteria. Irving Steingart wrote to the committee stating that a number of diplomate exams could be utilized for different psychoanalytic theoretical approaches.

In a letter from Helen Block Lewis dated November 24, 1986, she resigned stating, "I see no visible indication that the present Board is about to abandon its fixation on the equation between the intensity of depth of psychoanalytic experience and frequency of visits per week." Another central issue for her was that Murray Meisels was not added to the Board despite an agreement to do so at an informal August, 1986, meeting. Also, on November 24th, the Board received a lengthy letter from Kalinkowitz outlining NYU's quality control system.

Important events on March 8, April 8, and August 31, 1987 included Ruth Lesser being elected to the Board (to replace Kalinkowitz), the standards and philosophy committee introducing possible criteria for the Interpersonalists (written by Donald Kaplan), for Self-Psychology written by Roy Schafer and for Classicists written by Fred Pine following Steingart's suggestion. Other committees discussed their progress and gave reports. The January 9, 1988, meeting was canceled, and the meeting at the APA convention in August 1988 was unofficial. At this meeting, attended by Caligor, Goldman, Isaacs, Lane, Mayman, Stockhamer, and Kalinkowitz and Milman, several points were agreed upon: (a) any graduate from a bona fide program for training in psychoanalysis would be accepted into the examination pending their meeting ABPP requirements, and neither time limits nor restraints would be placed on any of the requirements for admission, and (b) with reference to requirements concerning post-analytic training experience, it was agreed that applicants had to be engaged in psychoanalytic work. On the question, how long after graduation one would have to wait to be admitted to the exam, there was little agreement, with 3, 4, and 5 years suggested. The quality of the experience during this interim was stressed. Applicants had to be doing analytic work, and they would have to submit a work sample of a case write-up showing knowledge of the analytic process. It was agreed because ABPsaP doesn't accredit training programs, we would ask the APA's Education and Training Committee to provide for accreditation of postdoctoral education as soon as possible.

At the November 6, 1988, meeting, Goldman, Lane, Lesser, and Siegler were reappointed to the Board, and a nomination committee was appointed to fill vacant seats. Dissention had again reared its head and led to the resignations of Kaplan, Pine, and Schafer. Although there had been agreement among the members who attended the unofficial meeting in August, numbers once again arose with some members insisting on strong standards, and there was an impasse. Members felt they were not bound by the August meeting as it was not official. This was particularly distressing as the Division was to grant $2,500 to the ABPsaP Board, was very supportive, and we had made a commitment to the Board to try and resolve our problems. Meanwhile the Examinations Committee continued its work, adding Ruth Ochroch as a consultant and speaking with Bernard Leibman, head of the Northeast Section of ABPP. He advised that we cover all five areas that other ABPP groups do, including professional involvement, competency, intervention techniques, assessment skills and ethics, and gave us specific step-by-step information on how to begin. Goldman and Lane spent a day going through the NE examination.

On December 4, 1988, Nathan Stockhamer wrote to Nicholas Palo of ABPP requesting to revive our affiliation stating differences regarding consensus were being resolved. A letter dated December 29, 1988, was received requesting we submit our completed application for identification of new specialities in psychology, and that our letter had been forwarded to Alan Webb. Lane suggested we ask James Barron, Editor of our Newsletter, to organize the 12 parts of the specialty form for us, which he completed some time later.

On January 12, 1989, the Examination Committee submitted its position paper. The Examination Committee requested the applicant's full application from the Admissions Committee, stressed analytic activity since receiving one's Certificate in Psychoanalysis or its equivalence during a 5-year post-graduate period, proposed a three tier examinations process, a four member examination's committee and outlined a four hour examination. The sample case write-up was to be on a case seen three times a week for a minimum of 2 years, and not previously presented. A letter from Kalinkowitz and Milman stated the three times weekly violated the spirit of the agreement established at the August meeting. There had been a misunderstanding, and the position paper was rewritten just stating that the case be a psychoanalytic case. A March 11, 1989, letter from Stockhamer outlined the events as they had happened including the Examination Committee's belief that the statement regarding the sample case had been satisfactory to Milman. Martin Mayman resigned due to illness. Alan Cooper, Milton J. Horowitz, Dorothy E. Holmes, and Milton Eber replaced the members of the Board who had resigned (Lewis, Kaplan, Pine, and Schafer).

On September 14, 1991 (revised November 10, 1991), Bertram Cohler issued a summary of ABPsaP's position. The Cohler report pointed out that psychologists show a diversity of views regarding the definition of the psychoanalytic process, what constitutes a psychoanalytic intervention, frequency of sessions, length of treatment and even the nature of psychoanalytic process. However in planning for recognition of advanced competence by ABPP, provisions must be made for a wide variation in psychoanalytic education. At the outset, there must be many routes into the examination.

Agreement has now been achieved in the following areas:

• The acceptance of the Kalinkowitz and the Qualification and Standards Committee's definition of what constitutes psychoanalysis.

• That all candidates for the Diplomate must meet ABPP standards, submit their CV's, transcripts, letters of recommendation, and payment of a $500 examination fee.

• That all candidates submit evidence of their psychoanalytic education, supervision, coursework, and analysis (equivalency if not a graduate of an institute), identify their theoretical orientation and training so they can be examined in that particular area.

• That the case example be a psychoanalytic case, that frequency of sessions not be emphasized, and content of interpretation, transference-countertransference manifestations, the nature of the analytic relationship shall be left to the examining committee which shall be in the candidate's self-identified theoretical orientation.

• Diplomating by ABPsaP will be by examination, there will be no grand-fathering. Examiners will be selected by three regional committees (East Coast, Mid-West, and West Coast).

• The examining committee will consist of four examiners, with at least two in the candidate's theoretical orientation, and a third in a closely connected orientation. The fourth shall represent the ABPsaP Board, chair the examination committee, and fill out the necessary ABPP forms. Candidates will be examined on their theoretical and technical knowledge of their theoretical orientation, a review of one of their cases, and understanding of someone else's case from process notes submitted to them.

• Applicants can appeal to the ABPsaP Board in relation to the composition of the examining team.

Since the Cohler report, there was a conference call on November 10, 1991. The Examination's Committee (Goldman and Lane, Co-chairs, Antonovsky and Caligor members, with Ruth Ochroch, consultant) has circulated its position paper twice and included all suggestions into its present form.

The Foundation for Psychoanalytic Education and Research

Oliver J. B. Kerner
Murray Meisels

The idea to establish a foundation arose in the early 1980s out of the manifest concern of the Division governance to further psychoanalytic training. This concern engendered considerable discussion and a series of committee reports, all of which focused on how to best provide the membership with opportunities for a formal psychoanalytic education above and beyond the programs located either in New York City or Los Angeles. Among the various proposals suggested to address the problem of free access was a dual track one: The first track in time led to a Section of Local Chapters; the second track was specific in its call for a national educational program. The foundation was to become the financial mechanism designed to fund such a nationwide educational program.

In discussions and debates over just how such a national program could be developed, it was rapidly discovered that the Division as part of APA could not offer an educational program that certified individuals. The APA Bylaws rule out certification. However, the idea of a not-for-profit foundation separate from the Division was considered a viable solution.

The Foundation became a reality in 1984 and was incorporated in Illinois. The structure of the Board of Directors was set up in such a way as to insure that a certain percentage of the directors would always be individuals active in the governance of the Division.

The original funding for the Foundation came from sizeable grants from the Division and Section I. This financial support was crucial in meeting the the Foundation's initial heavy legal and organizational costs. Early on the Foundation officers and Board embarked on a series of meetings designed to explore those ways which would best lead to additional funds. It became clear that without such monies the probability of providing grants to groups around the country remained a goal but not a reality. Despite best efforts it soon became clear that such various funding sources as corporate and familial foundations, as well as government agencies, had little or no interest in psychoanalytic education. A nationwide survey was most discouraging revealing only five organizations dedicated to mental health throughout the United States. Their prime interest was in prevention and/or amelioration but not in providing funds for the creation of psychoanalytic educational opportunities.

During this period the lawsuit against APsaA et al. had become a reality; this meant that all solicitations either from individual members, or from the Division itself, had to take a backseat to the financial demands of the lawsuit enterprise. Once the legal issues were resolved by the settlement, Foundation officers mounted a new fund-raising campaign designed to reach the total membership of the Division. A mail solicitation was prepared to honor several well-known psychologist-psychoanalysts. Each recipient was given a choice and their donation was duly noted. This fund-raising campaign raised between $1,000 and $2,000. It also stimulated an additional anonymous gift of $5,000. These monies have helped a great deal not only in meeting certain administrative costs but have made possible a series of modest grants to local chapters, new institutes, and regional study groups. At present the Foundation is husbanding its resources and plans to continue to offer small grants. The problem of adequate funding remains at this point.

A Brief Historical Perspective on the International Federation for Psychoanalytic Education

James W. Barron

Sponsored by Division 39, the initial meeting of those interested in exploring the desirability and feasibility of establishing a federation of psychoanalytic training programs took place in Washington, DC on May 5, 1990. The proposal to develop a Federation was the idea of Murray Meisels, who presented it to the Board of Division 39, which strongly supported the idea and funded the initial meeting with a grant for $10,000. Murray Meisels had initially envisioned that the Federation would be a home for the new institutes that were offshoots of local chapters, for existing institutes in New York and Los Angeles that had no national association, and as a common front for all psychoanalytic organizations.

The May 5, 1990 Meeting

The conference drew 68 individuals representing various psychoanalytic training programs and national mental health organizations. In the morning session participants briefly described their organizations and their interest in what a federation might provide. They suggested the following primary functions of the proposed federation:

- Provision of an overall organizational home for various mental health disciplines and programs that are engaged in psychoanalytic training and education.
- Encouragement of constructive dialogue and engagement among psycho-

analytic training programs from different geographical regions and with different theoretical/ideological perspectives.
- Fostering communication and sharing of resources.
- Functioning as an advocate for psychoanalysis in the way it is portrayed in the media and in public policy/legislative forums.

Participants raised the following questions and concerns:

- What should the balance of power be between the proposed federation and its constituents?
- Would the federation infringe on the autonomy of local training programs?
- What would be the relationship of the federation to Division 39? Would the two organizations have overlapping functions? Would they compete?
- What would be the relationship of the federation to the IPA? Would they overlap or complete?

In the afternoon session, there was considerable controversy about the best way to proceed. The primary conflict revolved around the question: How structured an organization should we become and at what pace? Should we form a steering committee to develop bylaws and a proposed slate of officers? Should we first attempt to define the functions and goals of the federation more fully? The consensus that emerged was that:

- It was premature and divisive to think of building any kind of centralized organization with membership criteria and accrediting functions.
- At this early stage, the organization should be loosely conceived and should evolve organically according to the needs of the participants.
- A planning committee, co-chaired by Jim Barron and Karen Rosica, would develop a follow-up conference focused primarily on substantive educational and training issues, and secondarily on organizational function and structure.

That follow-up conference took place on November 3–4, 1990 at Harvard University. Once again nearly 70 professionals from various health disciplines, theoretical orientations, and geographical regions in the United States and Canada, as well as the Soviet Union, were in attendance. A sample of panel presentations on the first day of the conference included: On Being Director of a Psychoanalytic Training Program; Common Cause: Visions of a Psychoanalytic Federation; The Evaluation Process in Psychoanalytic Training; and Teaching Diversity in Psychoanalytic Theory and Work: A Biographical Approach.

On the following morning, there were two large discussion groups. One focused on the overall purposes of the federation, with discussion coalesced around three questions: Is there a substantial need for a federation? What shape should the organization take at this early stage? How does the federation differ from other national psychoanalytic organizations? The group felt it was premature for the proposed federation to consider taking on accrediting functions, that it should focus it efforts on being an inclusive home and a resource center for interested individuals and training programs. Jim Barron and Karol Marshall agreed to Co-Chair a Committee on Organizational Purpose and Structure and provide a report of their findings and recommendations at the November, 1991, meeting.

The other morning discussion group discussed accreditation issues. Questions were raised such as: Should the federation serve as an alternative to APsaA? As such, could it accredit institutes whose programs do not fit the prescribed model or whose members for various reasons do not wish to affiliate with APsaA or with IPA? As you can imagine, discussion of these issues was lively. Stan Marlan agreed to chair a committee to investigate issues of accreditation, and report back at the November, 1991 meeting.

The November, 1991, Meeting

Our main task was to conceptualize a federation which would add genuine value to its constituents and to the larger community. Members of The Committee on Organizational Purpose and Structure suggested that the raison d'etre of the federation would be to enrich psychoanalysis by pursuing the following broad goals: Supporting the educational and training endeavors of analysts from different disciplines, geographical regions, and theoretical perspectives; not leveling, or obscuring differences among us in a kind of mindless anything goes eclecticism, and not trying to legislate uniformity, but rather sharply delineating those differences in constructive dialogue and learning from them; articulating the theory, practice, and applications of psychoanalysis to the larger community and working to overcome popular distortions, misconceptions, and anti-analytic bias; and fostering teaching and research in psychoanalysis in undergraduate and graduate programs.

Other ideas emphasized by Committee members were: (a) establishing a federation that would be dedicated to enhancing quality in a meaningful way while being respectful of autonomy and diversity; (b) establishing a consultive task force of psychoanalysts who, when invited by the local institute or training program, would visit the local institute or training program, observe, participate, engage in a dialogue with faculty and candidates, and provide feedback for the use of the local program, not for the use of the federation to judge or accredit; (c) establishing membership criteria which would include organizations and individuals, that is, formal training programs and institute as well as individuals who have graduated from those programs, and informal study groups; (d) encouraging "truth in packaging," that is, helping various programs to decide their modus operandi in detail (all those parameters we usually fight about such as number of sessions per week, number of hours of supervision, number of cases required for graduation, use or non-use of the couch, etc.); (e) not attempting to legislate the proper configuration but disseminating information about the range of configurations and operating environments; (f) discouraging individuals and programs, eventually by clearly written bylaws, from using membership in the federation as a marketing tool, thereby eliminating promotion and marketing as major reasons for training programs to join the federation, and at the same time freeing the federation of liability and the accompanying legal responsibility of having to monitor the member programs.

Committee members were cognizant of the need to achieve a workable balance between the power of the proposed federation and the power of the constituent members so as not to infringe unduly upon the autonomy of local training/educational institutes and programs. In addition, although the federation would be a unique organizational structure, it would be open to cooperation and collaboration with other existing psychoanalytic organizations with ongoing interests in training and education.

RECOMMENDATIONS

1. That the organization include psychoanalysts and others interested in psychoanalytic thought and scholarship from various disciplines and countries, and that it be named the International Federation for Psychoanalytic Education.

2. That the structure of the Federation include different sections, for example, a section of training programs and institutes; a section of individuals who have graduated from those programs; a section of less formally organized programs such as study groups; and a section of others with an interest in psychoanalysis such as philosophers of science, anthropologists, writers, and researchers. The basic principle should be that the Federation provide flexibility for various interest groups to form within its overall organizational structure and that those sections be free to establish their own membership criteria.

3. That while there is a deep concern with the ongoing complex issues surrounding accreditation, the Federation not seek at the present time to become an accrediting body.

4. That the Federation sponsor an annual fall scientific meeting focused on issues of education and training, understood to be part of a life-long professional development process; that a program committee be established to plan and implement the annual meeting, and to decide on location, theme, invited speakers, and so on; that, as it continues to evolve, the Federation sponsor a scientific meeting at feasible intervals (perhaps every 2 or 3 years) in different countries as an outgrowth of its commitment to the international psychoanalytic

community, particularly to those elements of the community that have been excluded by other forums such as the IPA.

5. That the Federation develop a variety of task forces such as: a group of psychoanalysts who, at the request of local training programs, would provide collegial consultation and feedback to enhance the quality of those educational programs; a group to address the teaching of psychoanalytic theory in undergraduate and graduate education; a group to work toward enhancing public understanding of psychoanalytic theory and practice.

6. That the Federation publish a newsletter informing members of its activities; that the newsletter include substantive articles regarding training/educational issues, such as various methods of evaluating candidates in training, various ways of thinking about and organizing curricula, providing supervision, and so on; that the Federation establish other ways of sharing information and resources, such as data banks regarding admissions and progressions criteria so that members can be aware of the range of approached.

7. That once we have agreement on the guiding principles of the Federation, we move to establish a broad-based steering committee to develop bylaws to implement those principles.

Motions presented to and passed unanimously by those present at the organizational meeting on November 3, 1991:

1. To accept the report and recommendations of the Committee on goals, purposes, membership as submitted on November 3, 1991 and as amended at this meeting.

2. To authorize the Co-Chairs to appoint a steering committee to work out bylaws, to prepare a slate of officers, to plan next year's conference.

3. To mail to interested persons and institutes, together with the report of this meeting, an application for membership in the International Federation for Psychoanalytic Education that involves (a) payment of dues and (b) rights to ratify bylaws and elect officers.

Thus was born the International Federation for Psychoanalytic Education.

VI

The Future

A useful way to deal with the future is by extrapolating from present trends. It could thus be expected that two or three new local chapters will form every year, a new section will develop every 2 years, and Division membership will increase at an annual rate of 200. Ten years hence, if these trends continue, Division 39 would have about 50 local chapters, 12 sections, and 5,500 members, and local chapters would have an additional 3,000 non-Division members, for a total of 8,500 colleagues. In addition, more institutes would develop as local chapters evolve. Bertram Karon provides a scintillating discussion of future possibilities.

The Future of Psychoanalysis

Bertram P. Karon

Psychoanalytic ideas so excited G. Stanley Hall, the founder of APA, that in 1909 he invited Sigmund Freud, Sandor Ferenczi, Carl Jung, and Ernest Jones to Clark University to present personally in the United States their understanding of psychoanalysis. According to Boring (1950), the historian of Experimental Psychology: "A score of distinguished psychologists were the other guests—James, Titchener, Cattell, and Boas among them" (p. 711). American psychology and psychoanalysis were momentarily united, but the union did not last. For political, economic, and psychodynamic reasons the two fields that belonged together were artificially separated. Only in 1979 was the Division of Psychoanalysis of APA founded, and within 12 short years we have grown to 3,500 members, not counting students, with no sign of leveling off. Even more important, it is a Division seething with intellectual and clinical ferment. Insight, intellectual rigor, and clinical competence are highly valued, and conformity is not.

THE POLITICAL FUTURE

The winning of the GAPPP lawsuit, opening up the institutes of APsaA to psychologists, and IPA to institutes not affiliated with APsaA, has been a remarkable step forward. Of course, George Allison, President of APsaA, has argued in a personal communication that the lawsuit only accelerated changes that would have occurred in any event. That well may be, and there certainly are many members of that organization, and an even higher proportion of the members of IPA, who have welcomed these changes. When the first three institutes from the United States unaffiliated with the APsaA were voted into IPA, they were greeted with a standing ovation.

But the changes had been bitterly fought in court by APsaA, and as could be predicted, the opposition did not stop after the settlement. Special conditions were placed on psychologist candidates in many institutes that added unnecessary years to the process. After the first institutes were admitted to IPA, changes were wrought in the procedures which were intended to slow down the processing of applicant institutes. IPA psychoanalysts appointed to key positions professed ignorance of the conditions of the legal agreement, and had to be reminded by being sent copies of their own lawyers' letters which were part of the settlement. It was necessary to appoint a watchdog committee, consisting of Arnold Schneider and Helen Desmond, to monitor good faith compliance and call attention to lack of good faith when it became too blatant. It was necessary to send letters from our lawyers to remind both APsaA and IPA of the legal situation. Luckily, the Division had voted to place its contribution to the GAPPP lawsuit in escrow, rather than being refunded. (Part of the settlement was that APsaA had to reimburse GAPPP for its legal expenses.) The watchdog committee had access to the settlement fund, so that they are not helpless to deal with illegal actions, and both APsaA and IPA were reminded of that fact. I was told by some representatives of APsaA that our decision to place the settlement fund in escrow was too aggressive and provocative, that we should have rendered ourselves helpless and depended on their good will. (The size of the settlement was due to the conscious strategy of APsaA: inasmuch as they were unlikely to win a trial, their strategy was to prolong the suit and run up the costs, because psychologists would be likely to run out of money before physicians did, and there is no legal redress if you cannot hire lawyers.)

Nonetheless, the changes have occurred, and are going forward. So far, however, only one additional unaffiliated institute has been accepted into IPA after the first three, and the process was slowed down and made unusually difficult. On the other hand, many of the individual restrictions for psychologist candidates in APsaA have been remedied. Strangely enough, the lawsuit is probably the best thing that has happened to APsaA and IPA in many years, because it has brought an influx of bright energetic young psychologists into those organizations, and into what had been the mainstream of psychoanalysis. If those organizations continue to represent the mainstream of psychoanalysis 20 years from now, it will be because of this new energetic source of contributors, although the mainstream of psychoanalysis 20 years from now is at least as likely to be our Division.

Within our Division there was some initial opposition to the lawsuit, on the basis of a belief held by some that unaffiliated institutes might not be able to survive, because the bright candidates might choose to go to institutes affiliated with APsaA if they were open. Obviously, institutes that are part of IPA but not of APsaA, will have no such problem, except for medical candidates, and it can be predicted that a higher percentage of even medical candidates will choose these institutes as time goes by. This opposition within our Division disappeared on the basis that minor problems for some institutes were not as important as the general furthering of psychoanalysis and psychoanalytic training.

It is my view that if unaffiliated institutes cannot compete in excellence with APsaA's institutes, then they do not deserve to survive. The fact is that the independent institutes are doing very well, because they do compete in excellence. Independent institutes must offer something of value that the APsaA's institutes do not, unless there is no APsaA institute in their area. Obviously, fair treatment of nonmedical candidates has been an attraction, which APsaA can and undoubtedly will remove. However, theories not traditionally associated with APsaA may still not be taught at many institutes, despite the fact that these ideas have influenced bright clinicians in any contemporary psychoanalytic community. For example, at the present time there are no interpersonal institutes in APsaA, and a student who wishes such training must seek it in an unaffiliated institute. The ideas of the British middle school are rarely presented in detail in any institute connected with APsaA. Bright candidates often are aware of the importance of these intellectual currents and wish to study with mentors who are knowledgeable. Many of the strong independent institutes afford exposure within a single institute to training analysts sophisticated within different intellectual traditions in psychoanalysis, whereas many of the institutes of APsaA are perceived as requiring orthodoxy or adherence to one point of view without exposure to others. They are often perceived as discouraging intellectual curiosity or clinical innovation. (Obviously, this is not true of all APsaA institutes.)

Any institute, affiliated or unaffiliated, will be judged by any sensible candidate on the basis of the quality of its faculty. You cannot teach what you do not know. If an institute has bright, creative, clinically competent faculty, it will attract good students as long as there is some way for the students to learn about the quality of the faculty.

Of course, psychoanalysis within medicine is in trouble. Over the past 20 years there has been a move to remedicalize psychiatry. In part, this was a hope to make it more popular with residents, or to deal with the antagonism of other physicians. Primarily, however, it was an attempt to deal with the financial problems of medical schools. Medical schools, as well as other parts of universities, have been in a financial crunch due to the cutbacks in federal and state support. One way of coping with these cutbacks is to hire faculty with research grants, where the overhead payments are very good for the budget. (The recent scandals at Stanford and other schools illustrate how important such funding has been as a revenue source for things unconnected with research.) But the federal government spends 10 times as much on biological and chemical research in psychiatry as it does on psychological factors, and the drug companies spend many times more than the government, and understandably they are only interested in potentially product-related research. Any moderately adequate drug-related research gets funded. Insofar as a Department of Psychiatry hires and retains faculty primarily on the basis of grant money, they will end up with a biological faculty who teach what they know.

It has always required less training and has always yielded higher income to be a biological psychiatrist; consequently, there have always been more bio-logical psychiatrists than psychoanalytic and psychotherapeutic psychiatrists (Hol-lingshead & Redlich, 1958). Traditionally, there have been two major streams of students in psychiatry. Included in the biological psychiatrists were the medi-ocre students. After the first year, medical schools traditionally have been reluc-tant to waste the investment in the students, and therefore reluctant to flunk them out. Often, the brighter students were encouraged to become surgeons, and some of the not too bright were encouraged to become psychiatrists. This has been one of the reasons psychiatrists have had to struggle for respect from their colleagues in medicine. There was a second stream of bright medical stu-dents who became interested in psychoanalysis, and who went into psychiatry because of their interests, despite being prodded by their instructors toward surgery or to internal medicine.

It is this second stream that has been specifically discouraged by the kind of psychiatry students are being taught in medical school. If you are interested in pharmacotherapy, there are many specialties in which the uses of phar-macotherapy are much more interesting and more powerful. Further, whereas psychoanalysis was always less lucrative than general psychiatry, and psychiatry less lucrative than general practice or the other specialties, the differentials have become so great that today one is asked in all seriousness by psychiatrists and medical students, "Can you earn a decent living as a psychoanalyst?" The an-swer depends on one's view of a decent living. Certainly, it is not likely that one will earn the $200,000 per year minimum that characterizes some specialities.

Whatever happens in medicine, there will be an increase in psychoanalysts from the professions of social work and nurse-practitioners. But the chief profes-sion of individuals who become psychoanalysts in the next 20 years will be psy-chologists.

At the present time APsaA numbers slightly over 3,000 members and the American Academy of Psychoanalysis numbers slightly over 800 members. This makes the Division of Psychoanalysis, with over 3,433 members, the largest psychoanalytic organization in the United States. Of course, all of our members are not psychoanalysts; but many are. Many others are interested in psychoanal-ysis as the basis for clinical work that is psychoanalytic, but not psychoanalysis in the narrow sense, or are interested in psychoanalysis as a generative set of scientific ideas. Many of these psychologists will eventually become psy-choanalysts, even in the narrow sense, or they may never become analysts but contribute more to our field than many who do.

Our only problems with APsaA have had to do with their defending the political and economic interests of medicine against those of patients and of psychologists, and against the scientific development and spread of the theory. Insofar as APsaA had furthered the scientific or clinical advancement of psychoanalysis, they have been constructive; insofar as they have limited the advancement of psychoanalysis in order to further the power or economic interests of physicians, they have been destructive. These battles should decrease, although we must expect them to resurface from time to time.

So far, we have discussed political battles with medicine. There are also political battles within psychology. We have seen the state psychological associations going from a position dictated by academic experimental psychologists, in which the state associations opposed the practice of psychology and in particular the practice of psychotherapy, to the point where they now primarily represent practitioners. This has been a benign change, because practitioners are more likely to pay careful attention to psychoanalysis, but there are some problems.

Some state organizations indentify with the medical model and oppose the rights of social workers to practice. In general, such short-sighted views will not prevail, especially because APA nationally supports the availability of competent psychotherapy and not its artificial limitation, and therefore supports social workers and nurse practitioners. As psychoanalysts, we very much welcome the training of social workers in psychoanalysis. Consequently, we will be involved in these pernicious local conflicts. (Indeed, not only are we very much in favor of the training of social workers in psychoanalysis and psychoanalytic therapy, and of qualified social workers practicing, but we have similar feelings about nurse practitioners and psychiatrists.) Although state psychological organizations will end up taking constructive positions on the practice of psychoanalysis, in some states there will be serious internal battles before this is achieved.

It should be noted that the organization of psychiatrist-psychoanalysts still tries to limit training and practice. Because social workers were not part of the lawsuit and do not have a watchdog committee with legal and financial resources to compel fair-play, even though the GAPPP settlement included social workers, APsaA has circumvented their own agreement by only training social workers with a D.S.W., a degree usually reserved for University faculty, but not most social work practitioners, where the traditional degree is an M.S.W. Consequently, most bright social workers will get their psychoanalytic training at institutes not connected with APsaA.

Nationally, APA at one time opposed the training of psychologists as psychotherapists, and the practice of psychotherapy by psychologists. The regional psychological associations tend to be similar to APA in orientation. Thus, the Midwestern Psychological Association printed on the program of every meeting in large letters, "The Midwestern Psychological Association is dedicated to the advancement of Psychology as a science, but not as a profession."

Originally the Division of Clinical Psychology (Division 12) of APA intentionally did not include psychotherapy as part of its definition of a clinical psychologist, and many of us would not join a division of clinical psychology that did not include psychotherapy. Psychologists Interested in the Advancement of Psychotherapy had to be organized outside of APA to meet the interests of psychotherapeutic psychologists. When it grew by leaps and bounds, it was introduced into APA by asking those of us who belonged to both PIAP and APA to join Division 12, where it was established as a Section. Eventually, such status did not meet the needs of its members, most of whom felt that psychotherapy was their most important function, and the Division of Psychotherapy (Div. 29) was established over the objections of Division 12. In 1979, it became clear that the Division of Psychotherapy did not meet the needs of those of us who were interested in what we felt was the most important, most central, and most interesting body of theory and clinical technique in psychotherapy. The Division of Psychoanalysis was formed over the objections of Division 29, who wanted it as a section. The Division has grown ever since.

Meanwhile, APA itself had included more practitioners. When the academic-experimental psychologists became aware that they no longer had a voting majority in APA and could no longer use that organization to stifle the development of clinical psychology, they panicked. They assumed APA would try to do to them what they had historically done to clinicians—limit their activities and limit the access of students and the public to them, and stifle their training. That clinicians had no desire to eliminate traditional academic experimental psychology was not perceived; projection held the day. The American Psychological Society (APS) was formed to "save" the academic-experimental psychologists from the non-danger.

However, despite APS, most academic-experimentalists belong to APA. Although a majority of the members of APA are now practitioners, 60% of the elected, appointed, and employed psychologists who are part of the APA structure are academic-experimental, and this subgroup still has a disproportionate effect on the policies and activities of APA. This will probably be tolerated indefinitely, because there is a wish not to drive these psychologists away. However, the perceived antagonism should diminish with time, because so much of it is based on projection.

Within APA, however, the Practice Directorate was founded, funded by a special assessment on practitioners and dedicated to dealing with practice issues. This has turned out to be an extraordinarily sensible move, and the Practice Directorate, under the guidance of Bryant Welch, one of the original defendants in the GAPPP lawsuit, has won some major victories already—the most important being the inclusion of psychologists and social workers in Medicare, the Capp versus Rank hospital privileges case in California, and the deferral of the reduction of Champus benefits. As of now, psychoanalysis and psychoanalytic psychology have a practical friend, who can and does organize effectively to deal with political (in the broad sense) and legal issues of importance, and is ready with advice on what needs to be done to solve practical problems. The Practice Directorate does not raise money for candidates, but it does effectively get accurate information to elected and appointed officials; and gets accurate information to psychologists, including psychoanalysts, about how to solve practical problems. It enters legal cases when appropriate. Under its aegis, the representatives of each state psychological association (three to five psychologists) talk to each of their Senators and Representatives, or their staff, once a year about relevant issues. At this time psychologists have a reputation of providing accurate information.

Some kind of National Health Insurance system will eventually be put in place in the United States, and the Practice Directorate, which has already organized the representatives of state psychological associations to provide accurate information relevant to this issue to their Senators and Representatives, probably will be effective in getting psychotherapy included, and in getting some support for psychoanalytic treatment. Of course, a great deal of the effectiveness of the Practice Directorate is due to the unusually capable and decent man who heads it, Bryant Welch. When he retires from that position, the next head will also need to be an effective individual who knows how to get things done in the courts, the legislatures, and the administration, and who understands what psychoanalysis and psychoanalytic therapy are about, in order for us to continue to make progress.

At the University level, the political problems among psychologists have been and remain intense. Academic experimental psychologists have usually opposed the hiring of psychologists with a psychoanalytic viewpoint. Partly this is based on the fear that if students have a choice, few would choose to study with traditional academic psychologists. Academic requirements and requirements for graduate school are rigged so as to discourage knowledge about psychotherapy and psychoanalysis. It is still the case that applicants to most graduate schools in clinical psychology are well advised to say their primary interest is in doing research with a clinical background.

However, the opposition among many academic psychologists has not stopped students, undergraduate and graduate, from becoming increasingly interested in psychoanalysis. It can be predicted that as more psychologists become psychoanalytically sophisticated, more students will become intrigued, and eventually academic departments may be swayed by the interests of the students. The growing interest in psychoanalysis in academic fields other than psychology—political science, sociology, anthropology, history, literary and artistic criticism—will keep the pressure on to present psychoanalysis within psychology.

In short, in academia, as in other arenas of political conflict, a prolonged, perhaps never-ending struggle will occur, but psychoanalysis will endure and prosper, despite dire predictions and efforts to stifle it.

THE SCIENTIFIC FUTURE

Undoubtedly there will continue to be diverse schools of psychoanalytic thought. But there will be three major changes brought about by the role of psychology in psychoanalysis. The first is that the different schools will talk to each other more. The attitude of most physicians to a theory is more like that of an engineer than a scientist—the theory is accepted as true, and the ingenuity of the physician is in the application of the theory to the conditions of a specific case. Psychologists, like most scientists, are more apt to consider a theory a point of departure.

The second major change is that there will be more appropriate decisions about theoretical matters on the basis of research. Case history material will take its rightful place as a major source of scientific information. Psychologists and psychologist-psychoanalysts will increasingly use case histories to refine and advance our theories and body of data, without the self-consciousness that has held them back in the past, because they had been intimidated by the arbitrary views of science taught in many graduate schools. But relevant systematic research will also be more consistently carried out and used to make theoretically relevant inferences.

The third major change is that experimental psychologists will develop more relevant research and seek out clarification of the overlap of our fields. There are practically no behaviorists among experimental psychologists today. Their own research has convinced them of the need to study cognition, the need to understand conscious cognitions, even in the laboratory. This has led them to postulate and investigate unconscious processes.

History, political science, sociology, anthropology, biography, and literary criticism will continue to turn to psychoanalytic theories as the only body of psychology that enlightens these fields and helps them clarify the human condition.

It would be presumptuous to try to guess in which directions psychoanalytic theory itself is likely to develop. Based on current trends we would expect further development in our understanding of object-relations and a greater incorporation of the views of the British "middle" school (Fairbairn, Guntrip, Winnicott, and their students). We would expect a continued development of self-psychology, but we would also expect strong developments within traditional ego-psychology, interpersonal theory, and Kleinian theory. Even Lacanian theory is beginning to appear on the American scene. The psychoanalytic theory of affects will undergo major revisions in the next 10 years. Krystal's (1988) work on affect regression, trauma, and the inability to feel is important, but the most important insights so far are to be found in Tomkins (1962, 1963, 1991, in press) *Affects, Imagery, and Consciousness*. It will be years before the implications of this work are assimilated, and the work of many others in this area will follow. Of course, the revisions in our understanding of female development will continue. This is an area of intense work by many competent theoreticians. Of those with whom I am familiar, the most useful so far have been Janine Chassaguet-Smirgel, Irene Fast, Carol Gilligan, Judith Kestenberg, Helen Block Lewis, Joyce McDougall, Jean Baker Miller, but it is an area which understandably has a large number of brilliant contributors.

THE CLINICAL FUTURE

The death of psychoanalysis as a clinical enterprise is always predicted, and this prediction never comes true. For the truth is that people do wish to get help through understanding themselves, that the help is real and palpable, and consequently psychoanalysis as treatment will never disappear. Moreover, we will learn more about psychoanalytic therapy, as opposed to psychoanalysis per se, as the number of clinical psychologists increase, and as there are more competent people asking what sensible thing can I do when reality does not permit undertaking psychoanalysis?

Psychoanalysts themselves have in many instances been responsible for destroying psychoanalysis as treatment. During the time when psychoanalysis was fashionable in medicine, many psychiatrists who were opposed to psychoanalysis became psychoanalysts, because it was the thing to do, but then acted in a way to discourage or discredit psychoanalysis, which they did not like. Further, such psychoanalysts readily accepted limitations on psychoanalysis, not as problems, but as excuses for practicing simpler, more lucrative, but less helpful treatments. Thus, in the 1950s, I took a postdoctoral fellowship at what I was told was the most psychoanalytic hospital in Philadelphia. All the psychiatric residents were in training to be psychoanalysts, and most of the staff psychiatrists were psychoanalysts. I was startled to learn that all the in-patients and 50 out-patients were given ECT every Monday, Wednesday, and Friday. When I asked how this could be, I was told that "It depends on what you mean by psychoanalysis." "We mean by psychoanalysis the treatment of the classical syndromes four of five times a week on a couch, if they can afford it. What do you do if they have something else wrong with them, or if they cannot afford it? Either you don't treat them or you shock them. We shock them. We think it's kinder."

This double-think was typical of the good private psychiatric hospital in the 1950s, according to Hollingshead and Redlich's (1958) classic study. The brochures stressed psychoanalysis and psychoanalytic therapy, but the hospitals derived the bulk of their income from the shock box.

Whereas, in the United States even then, there were far more biological than psychotherapeutic psychiatrists, it was nonetheless more prestigious to be a psychoanalyst. In Philadelphia I was introduced to the professional anomaly of psychiatrists, who were psychoanalysts for the prestige, but who ran shock practices for the income.

When the process of admission of new institutes to the IPA slowed down, it was startling to discover that it was the Co-Chair of the IPA Committee (Cooper, 1990) that reviewed applications who had written that the training of social workers and psychologists at these new institutes would mean that psychoanalysis would be more available; and, while that might be good for patients, it would lead to a decrease in fees and status for psychoanalysts. Further, he added that psychologist-psychoanalysts and social worker-psychoanalysts would include more women than men and that this too would lead to a decrease in fees and status.

Of course, no one who truly valued psychoanalysis would accept the view that making psychoanalysis more available to patients was a bad thing, or even reducing fees, if it made psychoanalysis more available. Such anti-psychoanalytic psychoanalysts have done as much harm as any external enemy.

The chief current threats, which can be expected to continue, to the practice of psychoanalysis and psychoanalytic therapy come from the medication (not "medical") model, from pseudo-biology, from the resurgence of ECT, from managed care, and from the unavailability of training.

The medication model, pushed by drug companies, is that anything can be treated with medication. When medications are found not to live up to their advertising, new medications replace them, until it becomes well known that they too do not live up to their advertising. Side affects are denied until a new medication is marketed (whose side affects in turn are denied). In order to help sales, the effectiveness of psychotherapy and psychoanalysis is denied. Studies are funded, such as those on schizophrenia, where psychiatrists without relevant psychotherapeutic training (referred to as "fully trained psychiatrists" or as "experienced psychotherapists") were found not to be more helpful than medication, and the findings widely distributed. (Interestingly, the only American studies with control groups that found psychotherapy more helpful than medication for schizophrenics used psychologists or both psychologists and psychiatrists as therapists.)

Despite this, with time it can be predicted that the public and the mental-health professions will learn that the side effects of anti-psychotic medication (or major tranquilizers) include brain damage, not only tardive dyskinesia in 30% of patients maintained on high dosage for more than 10 years, but subtler brain damage, like the evidence for tardive psychosis upon abrupt withdrawal, and increased dopamine receptors, even among rats given anti-psychotic medication. Both the public and the professions of psychology and psychiatry will become increasingly aware that the so-called evidence for brain abnormalities in schizophrenia are actually evidence for the brain-damaging effects of the medications. Thus, the MRI and CAT-scan findings are impressive, but autopsy studies of those same brain areas were negative until the "anti-psychotics" were in wide use (Breggin, 1990). The study of identical twins discordant for schizophrenia (Suddath, Christinson, Torrey, Casanova, & Weinberger, 1990) found diffuse brain damage correlated .50 with drug dosage, but this correlation was reported in their summary and in the media (Goleman, 1990) as non-existent because it only reached the .06 level of statistical significance.

Similarly, the evidence will become better known that anti-depressants are neither as effective nor as harmless as their advertising suggests. Moreover, patients are likely to discover that the anti-anxiety medications habituate (lose their effect) within eighteen months. For excellent reviews of all the empirical studies published so far comparing psychotherapy with medication for schizophrenia, depression, anxiety disorders, and attention deficit disorders, see Fisher and Greenberg (1989). The current state of the evidence is very different from the drug company advertisements, both to the public and to physicians, and very different from what is taught at most biologically oriented departments of psychiatry. The only inadequate chapter in that book is the one on ECT which is reminiscent of the "findings" on lobotomy, when it was popular. For the state of the evidence concerning ECT, the reader is referred to Breggin (1979) and Morgan (1991).

Of course, it is more lucrative to have a medication practice than to do psychotherapy. These are problems for psychiatry now, but there is a growing movement for psychologists to get prescription privileges. If this is successful, these will be problems for psychologists as well.

Pseudo-biology, which is closely related to the "medication" model, consists of presenting nonempirical biological theories as "facts," or poorly designed studies. This leads to pseudo-rigor, bolstering lucrative treatments that do not require understanding the patient, such as medication or ECT.

Thus, the technique of finding the gene for anything, whether or not it exists, is now well-known. For any finite number of individuals, some of whom have a disorder, if you run one gene after another until you get a match and stop, you can "prove" the biological basis of anything (as has been done for manic-depressive psychosis and for alcoholism); because there are 250,000 genes on the human chromosomes, a match by chance is guaranteed. The findings, of course, do not cross-validate, but they are published without cross-validation and cited as real; or nonreplications, when a different gene is found by the same procedure in a different sample, are cited as if they were cross-validations. In the long run, however, we can expect the truth to come out, as it did for the manic-depressive gene (Schmech, 1989).

Just as the data universally accepted as definitive on the inheritance of intelligence was found to have been faked, the adoption studies in schizophrenia widely cited to be rigorous, turn out to be extraordinarily flawed (e.g., see Lewontin, Rose, & Kamin, 1984; Lidz & Blatt, 1978).

The most rigorous available adoption data are the Finnish adoption study (Tienari, 1991) which found that the best predictor of schizophrenia was disturbed communication between the parents, and then to a lesser degree the interaction of genetic background (normal vs. schizophrenic biological mother) and parent–child conflict, and then to an even lesser degree of genetic background and lack of empathy. Although children of schizophrenic biological parents are more vulnerable to schizophrenia than children of normal biological parents, in both cases children only grow up to be schizophrenic if the rearing environment is disturbing in the way that Wynne and Singer have described. (Even this study included adoptions as late as 4 years, so it probably overestimates the role of genetics.)

As the dangers of medications become better known, and the flaws in what may well be characterized as the ideology of "biological determinism," as opposed to real physiological work, get better known, more and more patients will seek out psychoanalytic therapy for schizophrenia and manic-depressive disorders as well as for the lesser disorders.

The come-back of ECT is a symptom of a professionally bankrupt, if financially well-to-do, biological psychiatry, which believed the claims of the drug companies for anti-depressants. When the anti-depressants did not really work that well, biological psychiatrists returned to ECT because they were never trained in psychotherapy, and had nothing else they could do. In San Francisco in 1991, there were hearings on a local ordinance to ban ECT. Despite the testimony of its advocates, the ban was passed. (Unfortunately, the ban is symbolic, and has no force unless state law is also changed.) Among the testimony given by advocates was the amazing pronouncement that the procedures they used 2 years ago did produce brain damage and permanent amnesias, but the improved procedures they were using this year do not. Of course, the safety of each ECT procedure has always been announced with equal certainty as long as it was used. But the public and professionals are increasingly going to relearn that this is a dangerous procedure. Unfortunately, it will diminish, but remain for a long time, because it is still the most lucrative procedure in psychiatry. In the words of one psychiatrist, "The only way you can earn a decent living in psychiatry is with a shock practice. But people in my area seem peculiarly unwilling to allow themselves to be shocked."

Managed care, and the Health Maintenance Organizations, represent a threat, because they promise to provide help for the mental health needs of their subscribers, but in fact these promises are mostly fraudulent. The patients are told that they have 20 sessions per year, but even this inadequate care is not provided. The therapists are told to get rid of them in six. In the words of a physician who believes in the HMO model:

"There are problems either way. I think we have a better chance to provide decent care this way. I am under constant pressure in my own service to see so many patients per hour, which makes no sense, because some patients can be treated adequately in minutes and others cannot. But I fight the pressures on my own service, and I usually win. But mental-health services are a disgrace. You have told me you can do meaningful crisis intervention in six sessions. If they called it 'crisis intervention,' that would be all right. But they don't. The salesmen wouldn't like it. They tell the patients 'Psychotherapy won't help you,' when what they mean is 'Six sessions won't help you.' They tell the patient 'You have had psychotherapy and it didn't help you,' when what they mean is 'You had six sessions and it didn't help.' Sooner or later I am going to be in trouble, but I have decided that the only ethical thing for me to do is to tell my patients that they (or their spouse or child) have a condition which can be helped, but we are not equipped to provide it. If they can afford it, there are competent professionals in the community who can provide this help, and I will be happy to make a referral if they would like.''

When the HMO's proliferated in Michigan, private practitioners were worried. What happened was exactly what the writer predicted: Private practices dropped off dramatically, and within a year returned to normal, as patients discovered that six sessions for everything is often not helpful, and that the kind of therapist who is comfortable providing six sessions for everything usually has very little help of any sort to provide. Unfortunately, the poor get left out, unless they are over 65.

As a result of the campaign led by Bryant Welch and the Practice Directorate, anyone over 65 is entitled to psychotherapy under Medicare with a 50% co-pay. There is no cap on the number of sessions, so that psychoanalysis is covered, but there is a cap on the fee per session and the time must actually be spent, reasonable provisions. Sixty-five is not that old any more. Most psychoanalysts have discovered that Freud's dictum that patients over 40 were not analysable was mistaken; most of us have worked successfully with patients in their forties and fifties and sixties. Bernard F. Reiss has described working with people into their nineties.

However, the American health-care delivery system is in crisis and will change. It is the most expensive in the world, but it is not the most effective, judged by such reasonable standards as life expectancy. The HMO's, which originally were sold on the basis that they would save money by emphasizing prevention and discouraging unnecessary procedures, particularly surgeries, instead saved money by discouraging service, including preventive services. Thus, for example, the United States this year has had a measles epidemic, because HMO's have not been vaccinating, more traditional health insurance policies have discouraged vaccination by not covering it, and federal and state public health services have been cut back.

Consequently, there will be drastic changes in the American health care delivery system in the next 10 years. It is not clear what form that will take, but some form of National Health Insurance is likely, and coverage for psychotherapy is likely to be included, given the activity of the APA Practice Directorate. Despite the evidence that even long-term psychotherapy pays for itself in the reduction of other medical costs (Siegel, Hoffman, Ensroth, Karon, & Woodward, 1979) and that Germany included psychoanalysis in its National Health system without being fiscally irresponsible (Thoma & Kachele, 1987), it is unlikely that full psychoanalysis will be included (although that would certainly be desirable and could be similar to the Medicare provision). Undoubtedly, psychoanalytic therapy will be included, and the costs of full psychoanalysis would thus at least be partially subsidized for those who are motivated enough to seek it out.

Psychoanalytic training is already more available now than at any time in history. Institutes of APsaA are now open to psychologists throughout the country. High quality institutes unaffiliated with APsaA, almost all of which are staffed by members of our Division, are also widely available, and new institutes are being developed. Nonetheless, as Murray Meisels had recently pointed out, of 50 metropolitan areas of over a million people in the United States, 25 have no psychoanalytic training institute of any sort. Undoubtedly, the Division with its 26 local chapters will continue to help spread psychoanalysis, and help to create new local chapters and new institutes in the unserved parts of the country.

Other groups of currently neglected patients, such as psychotic patients, criminal populations, psychosomatic patients, learning disabilities, substance abusers, and so fourth, may be rediscovered as the limitations become clear of currently fashionable "treatments" which either do not work or only partially work. Brilliant beginnings which have not been continued, like the work of the Fraiberg group on "failure to thrive" infants, may be taken up again.

Meanwhile, psychologists with psychoanalytic training will be more available on college faculties and even in medical schools despite the political pressures to eliminate them. As young people come in contact with even a single instructor who exposes them to psychoanalytic thinking, new generations of professionals who want to learn more about psychoanalysis will replace us, and the field will go forward. Inevitably, the limitations of behavioral treatments and of medications will be learned by professionals as well as by the public at large. Today, and for a long time to come, the typical patient seeking psychoanalysis and psychoanalytic therapy has had three to five previous treatments, some of which were neither helpful nor ethical. Patients who really want help will continue to seek out psychoanalysis, while therapists who want to be helpful will seek out training as it becomes available.

IN SHORT

In Freud's (1938) words:

> I started my professional activity as a neurologist trying to bring relief to my neurotic patients. Under the influence of an older colleague and by my own efforts, I discovered some important new facts about the unconscious and the psychic life, the role of instinctual urges, and so on. Out of these findings grew a new science, psychoanalysis, a part of psychology, as the new method of treatment of the neuroses. I had to pay heavily for this bit of good luck. People did not believe in my

facts and thought my theories unsavory. Resistance was strong and unrelenting. In the end, I succeeded in acquiring pupils and bringing up an international psychoanalytic association. But the struggle is not yet over.

We, in the Division of Psychoanalysis, have developed a national psychoanalytic association of psychologists. It is the largest and the most important organization in psychoanalysis, scientifically and professionally, in the United States. But the struggle is not yet, nor ever likely to be, over.

REFERENCES

Boring, E. G. (1950). *A history of experimental psychology*. New York: Appleton-Century-Croft.

Breggin, P. R. (1979). *Electroshock: Its brain-disabling effects*. New York: Springer.

Breggin, P. R. (1990). Brain damage, dementia, and persistent cognitive dysfunction associated with neuroleptic drugs: Evidence, etiology, implication. *The Journal of Mind and Behavior, 11*, 425–464.

Cooper, A.M. (1990). The future of psychoanalysis: challenges and opportunities. *The Psychoanalytic Quarterly, 59*, 177–196.

Fisher, S., & Greenberg, R. P. (Eds.). (1989). *The limits of biological treatments for psychological distress: Comparisons with psychotherapy and placebo*. Hillsdale, NJ: Lawrence Erlbaum Associates.

Freud, S. (1938). The voice of Sigmund Freud. Introduced by Marie Coleman-Nelson. Original from the collection of Dr. A. F. R. Lawrence. Tape recording distributed by the *Psychoanalytic Review*.

Goleman, G. (1990, March 22). Brain structure differences linked to schizophrenia in study of twins. *The New York Times*, p. B15.

Hollingshead, A. B., & Redlich, F. C. (1958). *Social class and mental illness*. New York: Wiley.

Krystal, H. (1988). *Integration and self-healing: Affect, trauma, alexithymia: Psychoanalytic reformulations*. Hillsdale, NJ: The Analytic Press.

Lewontin, R. C., Rose, S., & Kamin, L. J. (1984). *Not in our genes: Biology, ideology, and human nature*. New York: Panntheon.

Lidz, T., & Blatt, S. (1978). Critique of the Danish-American studies of the biological and adoptive relatives of adoptees who became schizophrenic. *American Journal of Psychiatry, 140*, 426–435.

Morgan, R. F. (Ed.). (1991). *Electroshock: The case against*. Toronto, Ontario: IPI Publishing.

Schmeck, H. M. (1989, November 7). Scientists now doubt they found faulty gene linked to mental illness. *The New York Times*, p. Y 18.

Siegel, S. N., Hoffman, L., Ensroth, J., Karon, B. P., & Woodward, R. D. (1979). *Michigan Psychiatric Society Update, 1*(1), 1–4.

Suddath, R. L., Christinson, G. W., Torrey, E. F., Casanova, M. F., & Weinberger, D. R. (1990). Anatomic abnormalities in the brains of monozygotic twins discordant for schizophrenia. *The New England Journal of Medicine, 322*, 789–794.

Thoma, H., & Kachele, H. (1987). *Psychoanalytic practice*. Berlin: Springer-Varlag.

Tienari, P. (1991, August). *Interaction between genetic variability and rearing environment*. Paper delivered at the Xth International Symposium for Psychotherapy of Schizophrenia, Stockholm, Sweden.

Tomkins, S. S. (1962, 1963, 1991, in press). *Affects, imagery, and consciousness* (Vols. I, II, III, IV). New York: Springer.

Author Index

A

American Psychoanalyst, The, 321, 332
American Psychoanalytic Association
  Board of Professional Standards, 317, 318
  Committee of Feasibility for Non-medical
    Training, 317
  Committee on Prerequisites for Training,
    315, 316
  Committee on University and Medical Edu-
    cation, 316
  Newsletter, 318, 319, 326
American Psychological Association
  Division of Psychoanalysis, Executive
    Board, 87, 90
  Division of Psychoanalysis, Publications
    Committee, 65
  Division of Psychoanalysis, Research Com-
    mittee, 207

B

Blatt, S., 361, *365*
Boring, E. G., 351, *365*
Breggin, P. R., 360–361, *365*

C

Caligor, L., 144, *149*
Campbell, B., 315, *335*
Campbell, L., 315, *335*
Casanova, M. F., 360, *365*
Christinson, G. W., 360, *365*
Clark, R., 314, *335*
Claster, B., 184
Cohler, B. J., 5, *10*, 64, *69*, 340
*COMSIPP Structure, Function and Vision
    Document*, 146, *149*
Cooper, A. M., 334, *335*, 360, *365*
Cummings, N. A., 43, *54*

D

deDordoba, P., 315, *335*
Derner, G. F., 88, 167
Desmond, H., 324, *335*
Dilling, C., 184
Donovon, W., 315, *335*

E, F

Eichorn, D. H., 63, *69*
Ensroth, J., 363, *365*

Subject Index

A

American Board of Professional Psychology (ABPP), 8–9, 341
American Board of Psychoanalysis in Psychology (ABPsaP), 8–9, 336–341, *see also* Accreditation, Qualifications in Psychoanalysis
  areas of agreement, 340–341
  Section I v. Section V positions, 17
  Section V position, 202
  survey study, 53–54
  conflict about qualifications, 337–341
Accreditation, 203–205, *see also* ABPsaP, Qualifications in Psychoanalysis
APA
  as model, 165
  attitude to psychoanalysis, 96, 354–357
  convention program, 84–87
APA Council, 3–4, 156–159
  liaison to, 162–163
Appalachian Psychoanalytic Society, 217–219
APsaA, *see also* Lawsuit
  as model, 99, 165
  history of, 124
  isolation from other disciplines, 126
  exclusion of psychologists, 13–14, 95–97, 256–257, 284–285, 297, 313–314, 352
  its effects on psychologists' identity, 95–97, 125, 314
  role of Division of redressing, 121–122
  research consortium, 208–209
  the future, 351–355
Austin Society for Psychoanalytic Psychology, 220–221
Awards committee, 135–137

B, C

Baltimore Society for Psychoanalytic Studies, 222–223
Central offices, 4
Chicago Association for Psychoanalytic Psychology, 224–226
  history, 224–225
  institute, 111–112, 214, 225
Chicago Open Chapter for the Study of Psychoanalysis, 227–230
  purposes of, 228–229
Cincinnati Society for Psychoanalytic Psychology, 231–234
Clark Conference, 108–109, 121–126, 128

369

Printed in the United States
by Baker & Taylor Publisher Services